The
RIGHT
TO BE HUMAN

To Geri

W9-BBJ-357

Saludos —
and best wishes —
Edward
Hoffman

Other Books by Edward Hoffman

The Man Who Dreamed of Tomorrow: The Life and Thought of Wilhelm Reich
The Way of Splendor: Jewish Mysticism and Modern Psychology
Sparks of Light: Counseling in the Hasidic Tradition
The Heavenly Ladder: The Jewish Guide to Inner Growth

Future Visions: The Unpublished Papers of Abraham Maslow

The Drive for Self: Alfred Adler and the Founding of Individual Psychology

Visions of Innocence: Spiritual and Inspirational Experiences of Childhood

The RIGHT TO BE HUMAN

A Biography of *ABRAHAM MASLOW*

EDWARD HOFFMAN, Ph.D.

Reprinted by FOUR WORLD PRESS, 1997
POST OFFICE BOX 695
Commack, New York 11725
Phone: (516) 864–1912   Fax: (516) 864–7429

Library of Congress Cataloging in Publication Data

Hoffman, Edward
  The right to be human.

  Bibliography.
  Includes index.
  1. Maslow, Abraham H. (Abraham Harold)
  2. Psychologists—United States—Biography. I. Title.
  BF109.M33H63   1988   150'.92'4 [B]   87-33518
  ISBN 0-87477-461-6

Copyright © 1988 by Edward Hoffman

All rights reserved. No part of this work may be reproduced or transmitted in any form or by any means, electronic or mechanical, including photocopying and recording, or by any information storage or retrieval system, except as may be expressly permitted by the 1976 Copyright Act or in writing by the publisher.
Requests for such permissions should be addressed to:

Four Worlds Press
Post Office Box 695
Commack, New York 11725
Phone: (516) 864–1912   Fax: (516) 864–7429
Design by Deborah Daly

Manufactured in the United States of America
10 9 8 7 6 5 4 3 2 1

First Edition

To Laurel

Contents

CONTENTS

ix

Acknowledgments

Over the last five years, the immense and challenging task of constructing Abraham Maslow's biography would scarcely have been possible without the help of many people. These men and women, some quite advanced in years, have been generous with their time and advice beyond any biographer's expectations.

Bertha Maslow and her two daughters, Ann Kaplan and Dr. Ellen Maslow, provided much personal material and their special perspective on Maslow's family life, which was so important to him. In particular, Bertha Maslow's guidance, hospitality, and encouragement have been invaluable. Harold Maslow, closest in age to his famous brother, and Will Maslow, his cousin and closest teenage companion, were also important confidants.

Abraham Maslow's friends, colleagues, and students were a lively source of information about the man they loved and admired. Through their warm and heartfelt recollections, something of his spirit has come to touch me personally. Through hundreds of conversations with those who knew him well, I have been fortunate to gain a clear and consistent picture of what Maslow was like as a person, not merely as a prolific writer, compelling teacher, and influential thinker.

I wish to thank:

His friends and colleagues in psychology, counseling, business management, publishing, and related social science fields, including Dr. Heinz Ansbacher, Dr. Warren Bennis, Dr. James Bugental, Dr. Rogelio Diaz-Guerrero, Dr. James Fadiman, Dr. A. D. Fisher, Dr. Viktor E. Frankl, Betty Friedan, Henry Geiger, Dr. Margaret Gorman, Dr. Thomas Greening, Dr. Stanislav Grof, Richard Grossman, Dr. Gerald Haigh, Clara Mears Harlow, Dr. Willis Harman, T George Harris, Dr. Mary Henle, Dr. Jean Houston, Andy Kay and his family at the Kaypro Corporation, Dr. Stanley Krippner, Dr. Timothy Leary, George Leonard, Elisabeth Settlage Liberman, Dr. Rollo May, Felix Morrow, Dr. Lois B. Murphy, Michael Murphy, Dr. Jane Richardson, Dr. Carl Rogers, Dr. Nevitt Sanford, Dr. B. F. Skinner, Dr. Robert Tannenbaum, Dr. Miles Vich, Dr. Walter Weisskopf, Dr. Michael Wertheimer, Colin Wilson, and Lord Dr. Solly Zuckerman.

Those with whom he was close at the Saga Corporation at the end of his life, including William Crockett, William Laughlin, James and Marylyn Morrell, Kay Pontius, and Earl C. Royse.

Those who knew him as a colleague during Brandeis University's founding and developing years in the 1950s and 1960s, including Dr. Saul Cohen, Dr. Lewis Coser, Dr. James Klee, Dr. Max Lerner, Dr. Frank Manuel, Dr. Ricardo Morant, Dr. Ulrich Neisser, Dr. Abram L. Sachar, and Leonard Zion.

Those doctoral students who studied closely with him at Brandeis, including Dr. Joel Aronoff, Dr. Joseph Bossom, Dr. Donald B. Giddon, Dr. Bonnie J. Kaplan, Dr. Richard Lowry, Dr. Norbert Mintz, Dr. Ann C. Richards, Dr. Deborah Tanzer, Dr. Arthur Warmoth, and Dr. Gunther Weil.

Other students at Brandeis, including Steven Andreas, Patricia Barbanell, Robert Bobley, Dr. Janet David, Dr. Jeffrey Golland, Dr. Lawrence Gross, Abbie Hoffman, Neil

Kauffman, Lois Lindauer, Judith Roberts, Diane Roskies, Ellen Sher, Dr. Avrom Weinberg, and Lois Zajic.

Those who were close to him during his Brooklyn College years of the 1930s and 1940s, including former colleagues Dr. Edward Girden, Dr. Daniel Katz, Dr. David Raab, and Dr. Seymour Wapner. (Dr. Solomon Asch, unfortunately, was too ill to offer assistance.)

Several of his former students at Brooklyn College, including Sydelle Bloom, Lucille H. Cooper, Naomi Dressner, Beatric Fink, Estelle Gilson, Al Green, Pearl Green, Shirley Love, and Robert Rothstein.

Those who knew Maslow during his Madison, Wisconsin, students days in the 1920s and 1930s, including Dr. Walter Grether, Dr. Lucien Hanks, Jr., Dr. Richard W. Husband, Dr. Alice Ambrose Lazerowitz, Dr. Emanuel Piore, Dr. Ross Stagner, and Dr. Eliseo Vivas.

In offering me the hospitality of their homes during the interviews, Dr. Joel Aronoff, Henry Geiger, Dr. Lucien Hanks, Jr., Dr. Timothy Leary, Dr. Frank Manuel, Dr. Rollo May, Michael Murphy, Dr. Jane Richardson, Dr. B. F. Skinner, Dr. Ross Stagner, Dr. Robert Tannenbaum, and Dr. Walter Weisskopf showed me particular kindness, for which I am grateful.

I also wish to thank Dr. Rogelio Diaz-Guerrero, Dr. Lucien Hanks, Jr., Dr. Max Lerner, Dr. W. Edward Mann, Bertha Maslow, Will Maslow, James and Marylyn Morrell, Dr. Jane Richardson, Dr. Ross Stagner, and Dr. Michael Wertheimer for reading and commenting upon portions of the manuscript.

Much appreciation is expressed toward the History of American Psychology Archives at the University of Akron. Dr. John Popplestone and Dr. Marion White McPherson—Director and Associate Director respectively—and Mr. John V. Miller, Jr., Director of the University of Akron Archival Services, helped make my trips to the voluminous Maslow Archives there as productive, efficient, and pleasant as possible.

The following individuals and their staffs also provided considerable archival direction and assistance:

Dr. Jonathan F. Fanton, President of the New School for Social Research

Dr. Evelyn E. Handler, President of Brandeis University

Dr. Bernard W. Harelston, President of City College of the City University of New York

Dr. Robert L. Hess, President of Brooklyn College

Dr. Bill Lacy, President of Cooper Union for the Advancement of Science and Art

Dr. Irving Shain, Chancellor of the University of Wisconsin at Madison

David Sills of the Social Science Research Council

David Trager, Dean of Brooklyn Law School

The following individuals also provided archival assistance: Dr. Eugene Graziano of the University of California at Santa Barbara; James H. Huston, chief of the Manuscripts Division of the Library of Congress; Colin Jones of New York University Press; Saul Mallis and Elizabeth White of the Brooklyn Public Library; and M. J. Rossant of the Twentieth Century Fund.

Research suggestions and help were also provided by Deborah Breed of the Association for Humanistic Psychology, Steve Chapin, Mary Constance, Jane Howard, Dr. Stanley Krippner, John Krop, Dr. Guy Manaster, Dr. Judith Modell, K. Dean Stanton, and Dr. Paul E. Stepansky. Regina Damiano, Harvey Gitlin, and Nathalie Lilavois served most capably as research assistants.

Gratitude is likewise extended to my publisher Jeremy P. Tarcher and editor Janice Gallagher for their editorial judgment and sustained commitment to publishing a full account of Maslow's life and career.

I wish to offer special thanks to Aaron Hostyk and Dr. W. Edward Mann for their many conceptual contributions to my efforts. My parents and brother, as well as Gertrude Brainin and Dorothy Smith, were a constant font of enthusiasm during my research and writing.

Above all, I would like to thank two individuals for their boundless patience and encouragement. My son Jeremy, often playing beside me as I sat before my computer, or insisting that I take a break, helped me stay balanced and cheerful. My wife, Laurel, more than any other person, gave me the intellectual and emotional support to complete this project and fulfill my own goals for it.

Preface

A braham Maslow, who spearheaded humanistic psychology, was a visionary who inspired many people during his lifetime. As a bold psychological thinker, he was a genius; his ideas have exerted a tremendous and still-growing influence throughout the social sciences, the business community, and the wider culture. Aside from the sheer originality and brilliance of Maslow's creative work, he attracted many adherents through the force of his warm, magnetic personality. In his vibrant presence, ideas and hopes that had seemed romantically utopian became possible.

Although we never met, I have always regarded Abraham Maslow as a teacher and mentor. As an undergraduate at Cornell University in the late 1960s, I discovered in his writings an intellectual excitement that helped motivate me to major in psychology. In contrast to much else I was reading, Maslow's work had an immediacy and vitality. His vision of humanistic science, particularly psychology, as a powerful force for truth and world betterment was enticing. At the time, there were many voices clamoring for change. For me, Maslow's was unique in the way he addressed us: not with a formal, preconceived agenda, but with an insistence that we strive to realize our potentials. I can still recall "bull sessions" lasting far into the night as friends and classmates grappled with the challenging questions that Maslow had raised: What is self-fulfillment really about? What values make for a worthwhile life? And to whom can we look for models of "self-actualizing" men and women?

I learned of Maslow's sudden death in 1970 several months after it occurred. He had been at the peak of his acclaim at the time, and the news came as a shock to me. But Maslow continued to seem so alive through his work during my doctoral studies at the University of Michigan that I scarcely felt aware he was gone. My fellow graduate students and I continued to expound his principles in published articles about educational innovation, care for the disabled, and other prominent concerns in our field. As a consultant to schools and mental-health programs in Ann Arbor, I sought to shape into reality his conviction that we have intrinsic needs for creativity and self-expression.

For more than a decade after Maslow's death, I waited, like many others, for a full-length biography to appear. In the 1970s, several informative accounts were issued that highlighted new aspects of Maslow's immense and growing influence, in fields as diverse as existential psychology, business management, and organizational development. But no major contribution to our understanding of the man and his ideas was forthcoming. In 1982 I decided to embark on this biographical project.

Initially, my goal was simply to tell the story of Maslow's life and career in American psychology: to trace his early interests and training, his mentors and influences, and his seminal achievements in the science of human personality and motivation. He had not lived long enough to write an autobiography, and his impact was certainly powerful enough to warrant a comprehensive look. This objective seemed broad enough to encompass the scope of Maslow's full biography. But now, five years after I began this challenging project, my objectives have widened.

Abraham Maslow remains a hero to me—one whose intellectual courage and idealism were infused with humanity. In working on *The Right to Be Human*, I feel that I have made a lasting friend whose life is even more fascinating than I had originally suspected. He knew virtually every important psychological-social thinker of our time. His career bridged the beginnings of modern American social science and contemporary trends. In some ways, therefore, I have found myself writing a history of twentieth-century psychoanalysis, anthropology, education, managerial theory, and, of course, psychology. Through Maslow's eyes, I have become acquainted in a new way with the work of many of the most well-known figures in these fields. Indeed, in the course of my research, I have had the opportunity to correspond with and meet some of Maslow's famous living contemporaries. Additionally, I have acquired two other purposes in writing this book: To correct the distortions of Maslow's theories that resulted from their popularization, and to expose some of the intriguing work that Maslow left unfinished.

As is true for many great thinkers before him, Maslow's ideas have been badly distorted in their inevitable popularizations and retellings. But few intellectual figures in modern times have been so misinterpreted by both their admirers and detractors. For instance, Maslow's evocative notion about self-actualization as the goal of individual life has often been twisted to the point of near-unrecognizability from its original context and meaning. At the time of his premature death, he was becoming increasingly alarmed over the way in which his carefully developed humanistic pronouncements were misused by self-proclaimed supporters to justify obvious self-indulgence and hedonism. On the other side, cultural critics have repeatedly misrepresented Maslow's life and outlook. Almost to the point of absurdity, this gentle scientist-philosopher has been attacked as an enemy of reason and community, a panderer to narcissism. I hope to set the record straight with respect to Maslow; to correct as thoroughly as possible the many distortions that continue to surround his legacy.

My final objective is simultaneously simpler and more ambitious. Maslow was by nature an intuitive rather than a systematic thinker; new ideas came to him everywhere and at all hours, often dismaying his family. At the time of his death, he was immersed in not one or two, but literally dozens of unfinished psychology and social science projects. Much of this work was interdisciplinary, integrating his unique approach with political theory, business management, organizational development, criminology, and education. Some of these projects he hoped to complete within the year; others he viewed as decades long in scope. After a near-fatal heart attack in 1967, Maslow regarded these efforts as seeds he was planting, perhaps to reach fruition in his grandchildren's and great-grandchildren's time. He referred to such writings as his treasured gift to these unborn children—his and ours.

It is my intent, therefore, to throw light on Maslow's fascinating unfinished projects, which I have found to be relevant to his most exciting work. Perhaps, through this exposition, some of these seeds will find new soil in which to take hold.

If I have managed to accomplish these objectives in some small way, my purpose in writing this book will have been fulfilled.

CHAPTER ONE

A Brooklyn Boyhood

> *I was a terribly unhappy boy . . . My family was a miserable family and my mother was a horrible creature . . . I grew up in libraries and among books, without friends. With my childhood, it's a wonder I'm not psychotic.*
> —*A.M.*

*A*t the turn of the twentieth century, one of the largest social migrations in history was in full swing. Throughout Eastern Europe, millions of impoverished Jews were abandoning centuries of settlement and coming to the United States for economic and political freedom. Feudalism had survived in the old country until well into the late nineteenth century. Pogroms continued in the face of indifference, if not tacit encouragement, by the czar and his court. No matter how little they knew about the new land that awaited them, many Jewish immigrants felt life was bound to improve.

Among them was Samuel Maslow. At the age of fourteen, he left his parents' home in Kiev, a Russian city with a large Jewish population. Somewhat against the wishes of his patriarchal family, and with no money, he crossed the sea on his own. In part he was rebelling against his domineering father, who had, for instance, thwarted his son's youthful desire to play the violin.

When Samuel arrived on the shores of the promised land, according to later family tradition, he spoke only Russian and Yiddish and knew virtually nothing about the United States. All he had was a note pinned to his lapel with instructions for his care, to be read by the relative taking him in. Samuel spent a couple of years in Philadelphia, learning the new language and performing odd jobs before relocating to live with other relatives in New York City.

There he entered the cooperage business and soon married his first cousin Rose. Neither Samuel nor Rose boasted any distinguished scholars or figures of wealth among their ancestors. Rose's family was more religiously observant than her husband's.

On April 1, 1908, their first child was born in Manhattan. In keeping with Jewish custom, they called him Abraham after a deceased relative. At intervals of about two years, Rose gave birth to three more sons and three daughters. One girl, Edith, died in infancy. Abe, as family members called him, grew up as big brother to (in order of birth) Harold (born Hympe), Paul (born Solly) Ruth, Sylvia, and Lewis.

Abraham Maslow's earliest memories, dating back to his preschool years, were about his mother, and they were not pleasant. Although rarely observant of Jewish religious ritual, she was a superstitious woman who often disciplined the boy for minor misbehaviors by threatening him with God's relentless punishment. Decades later, he recalled such admonitions:

> I tested these various things out that she said and did research at the age of four and five . . . Various notions about things—that if you do such and such, God will strike you down. Well, I did them and he didn't strike me down . . . I remember one: If I climbed through the window, I wouldn't grow. So I climbed through the window and then checked my growth . . . And so it went, on down the line.

From such youthful forays into the world of scientific exploration, the young Maslow developed an intense mistrust of religion and a proud atheism. Highlighting his mother's rather unintentional influence in this regard, he commented, "To me, as a child . . . [superstition and religion], it was all the same. And I learned from her, certainly, to despise everything about it."

Although Maslow probably did not appreciate the irony until many years later, his youthful atheism hardly mattered to the anti-Semitic youngsters with whom he came into frequent contact in his urban world. As an adult, he often referred both privately and publicly to the pervasive and intense anti-Semitism he experienced during his formative years and its profound effect upon his early outlook. He also referred vaguely to anti-Semitic experiences later on, from the 1920s through the 1940s.

classroom and give me a book to read, a first- or second-grade reader, perhaps. And then I would sit for an hour or so until the regular morning class began at eight.

I did this in spite of the fact that there was an older boy "laying" for me. Whenever he caught me, he would kick and punch me, usually for some reason I do not remember. I think it was because I was one of the first Jews in the school.

Although Maslow's parents were not intellectually oriented, they both valued education. His father especially emphasized its importance in life: Reflecting the young Maslow's favored status within Jewish culture as the oldest son, relatives also encouraged him to be the young scholar.

No doubt, too, his scholastic interest provided emotional stability in an otherwise troubling childhood. As the first-born, he found the arrival of a new sibling every few years to be a hard adjustment. The death of his baby sister Edith was particularly upsetting to him. During Maslow's early years, his fragile self-esteem was also affected by his family's frequent moves; the situation made it doubly difficult for the shy youngster to form and maintain friendships.

In part, Maslow's shyness was associated with a deep-seated feeling that he was both different and strange. While many of his peers came from similar, upwardly mobile Jewish immigrant families, he encountered few youngsters who shared his intellectual bent. Through his elementary school years, until he met his cousin Will Maslow at about the age of ten, he felt himself to be so far apart because of his precociousness that he thought of himself as "a freak with two heads."

He also was acutely self-conscious about his appearance. He went through most of his childhood and early adolescence with an aching sense of shame concerning his scrawny physique and big nose. When the fires of puberty began to smolder within him, he regretted that he lacked the kind of appearance that might attract a girl. His fantasies were of mighty body-building, becoming an Adonis with a transformed torso and an equally transformed social life. "I was a very ugly child and youngster . . . I felt peculiar. This was really in my blood, a very profound feeling that somehow I was wrong. Never any feelings that I was superior that I can remember. Just one big aching inferiority complex."

Matters did not improve when his father, a rather insensitive though not malicious man, asked rhetorically at a large family gathering, "Isn't Abe the ugliest kid you've ever seen?" Such thoughtless remarks affected the boy's self-image so much that for a time he sought out empty cars when riding the subway, "to spare others the sight" of him, as though he were horribly disfigured.

Maslow's isolation from peers was compounded by a sense of alienation from his parents. His childhood relationship with his father was emotionally distant, but one that was far from rare among many Jewish immigrant families of the era. Each workday, Samuel left their Brooklyn home early in the morning to commute to his barrel-repair business on Greenwich Street in lower Manhattan. He didn't return until close to his son's bedtime, usually after socializing for a while with male friends. On weekends, Samuel occasionally took Abraham out for a baked apple or similar treat at a nearby restaurant. Other than that, he was not very involved in his oldest son's day-to-day life. Working all day to support Rose and their steadily increasing brood, Samuel had little desire and even less energy for emotional intimacy with his son.

There also was a darker reason why Samuel was not often home: his marriage had soured. He stayed out of the house as much as possible to avoid exposing the children to stormy parental battles. Sometimes Samuel took extended "business trips," returning only when his longing to see his children became intense. In those days, especially among Jewish families, even spouses who detested one another often felt obligated to stay together "for the children's sake." Thus it was not until their oldest son was away at college that Samuel and Rose finally divorced.

As a young adult, Maslow was therefore rather bitter about his father's having been largely an absentee figure. In a characteristic diary entry he penned at around the age of twenty-four, he reflected, "My childhood and boyhood were miserably unhappy. In retrospect, it seemed so dark and sad a period that I wonder how I accepted it so unquestioningly. I can find no single glimpse of happiness in all my memories . . . My father misunderstood me, thought me an idiot and a fool. Probably, too, he was disappointed in me."

His relationship with his father did become closer in later

years. Not long after Samuel's divorce from Rose in the early 1930s, he came to live with Abraham and Abraham's wife, Bertha, in an extended-family arrangement in Brooklyn. Samuel had lost his business and savings as a result of the Depression. In this situation, he and his oldest son got along well together, and a true reconciliation seems to have taken place before Samuel's remarriage and death some years later. For the rest of Abraham Maslow's life, he had kind words to speak of his father, typically remembering him as "a very nice fellow, we were friends until he died."

His relationship with his mother was a different matter entirely. He grew to maturity with an unrelieved hatred for her and never achieved the slightest reconciliation. He even refused to attend her funeral. He characterized Rose Maslow as a cruel, ignorant, and hostile figure, one so unloving as to nearly induce madness in her children. In all of Maslow's references to his mother—some uttered publicly while she was still alive—there is not one that expresses any warmth or affection. In this respect, Maslow differs from several major psychological theorists of our age such as Sigmund Freud and Carl Jung, who were much more devoted to their mothers than to their fathers and who have been referred to by some modern critics as "mama's boys."

Maslow's own comments and the recollections of his closest family members and friends suggest several reasons for his antipathy toward his mother. He never ceased to remember with contempt his mother's religious superstition, her threatening him with divine retribution for the slightest childhood infractions. Yet, in a backhanded way, Maslow came to value this upbringing and regarded it as having helped, through negative example, to spur him toward a love of scientific exploration.

Much more damning, Maslow came to feel, was the miserliness with which Rose ran her large household. He recalled bitterly that she kept a bolted lock on the refrigerator, although her husband was making a good living. Only when she was in the mood to serve food would she remove the lock and permit her children to take something to eat. Whenever the young Maslow had a friend over to the house, she was especially careful to keep the refrigerator bolted.

In a more general way, Maslow as an adult remembered

her as an extremely unloving and rejecting mother. He also felt that she had hurled far more hostility at him than toward any of his siblings. Occasionally he recalled with rancor how Rose always served the choicest parts of the boiled chicken or the cream from bottled milk, to the younger children, never to him. Though Maslow was never a practicing Jew, it is intriguing to note the strong, characteristically Jewish cultural association of food and love in such complaints.

Whenever he voiced his opinion in family conversations, Rose inevitably belittled or disparaged him. Her favorite retort, one that he found intolerable as a youngster, was, "Abe, you don't know what's good!"

On occasion, Maslow shared with his own children several specific memories of his mother that to him exemplified her personality. One afternoon, he had returned from a favorite activity, hunting for old 78-RPM records among Manhattan's second-hand shops. He was excited to have found several he had been seeking. He laid out the 78s on the living room floor and proudly inspected his growing collection. Rose entered and warned him to pick up the records immediately. Absorbed in his newfound treasures, he absentmindedly ignored her and left the room for a few minutes. When he returned, his mother was standing over the records with a look of fury. "What did I tell you?" she screamed. Then, as he looked on helplessly, Rose proceeded to grind her heels into every record until they lay shattered. With a satisfied expression, she left the room.

Another episode points to an even greater streak of cruelty in his mother. As a youngster, he was walking alone one day, when he discovered two abandoned baby kittens on the street. He decided to take them home and care for them. Quietly he carried them into the house and down into the basement. That evening, Rose came home and heard the kittens' meows. She descended to the basement and found her son feeding the kittens from a dish of milk. Doubly enraged that he had brought stray cats into her house and then used her dishes to feed them, she seized the kittens. Before his horrified eyes, Rose smashed each one's head against the basement wall until it was dead.

If such incidents were typical of his childhood, it is no wonder that Maslow harbored hatred for his mother and described her as literally "schizophrenogenic" (schizophrenia-inducing). He felt that only the kindness and warmth of his uncle Sam Schilosky, Rose's brother, had kept him from falling into madness as a child, especially right after Harold was born. He even blamed the fatal illness of baby Edith on his mother's neglect. Yet, neither Abraham nor any of his siblings developed marked emotional problems. Nor did the younger Maslows generally share their brother's remembrance of Rose as a cruel and horrible figure. In fact, as Maslow rose to international prominence in the field of psychology, his occasional public statements about her caused several of his siblings considerable anguish.

Nevertheless, Maslow never softened his attitude toward Rose, despite several years of psychoanalysis in later life. He never forgave her or even tried objectively to understand her as a victim of her own upbringing or as a victim of her unhappy marriage. After leaving home as a teenager, he saw Rose only a few times during the rest of her life. In late middle-age, with obvious venom, he wrote:

> What I had reacted to and totally hated and rejected was not only her physical appearance, but also her values and world view, her stinginess, her total selfishness, her lack of love for anyone else in the world—even her own husband and children—her narcissism, her Negro prejudice, her exploitation of anyone, her assumption that anyone was wrong who disagreed with her, her lack of friends, her sloppiness and dirtiness, her lack of family feeling for her own parents and siblings, her primitive animal-like care for herself and her body alone.

> I've always wondered where my utopianism, ethical stress, humanism, stress on kindness, love, friendship, and all the rest came from. I knew certainly of the direct consequences of having no mother-love. But the whole thrust of my life-philosophy and all my research and theorizing also has its roots in a hatred for and revulsion against everything she stood for.

Strong words from a man who was admired by so many for his warmth and kindness.

Although Abraham Maslow recalled his childhood as a

bleak time, he developed one close friend, his cousin Will Maslow. In about 1917, when Abraham's family moved into their home at 961 Dumont Avenue in the Brownsville section of Brooklyn, Will lived nearby. It must have come as a wonderful lift to Abraham finally to find an emotionally and intellectually compatible peer. Some two years later, the family moved again, this time to the more affluent middle-class area of Flatbush. Fortunately, Will's family also moved nearby, and Abraham began to sustain his first real friendship. Still a loner by temperament, he nevertheless joined Will and other peers in athletic games around the neighborhood. Punchball (played with a small, hard rubber ball) was a favored street sport in Brooklyn. Because their Flatbush house, at 577 East Fifth Street, adjoined a tennis court, the Maslow youngsters soon became avid tennis players as well.

In the spring of 1921, Maslow went through his final bout with his parents' Judaism. Although Rose and Samuel were not very religiously inclined, they felt obligated by Jewish tradition and family pressure to hold a bar mitzvah ceremony for Abraham. In Judaism, each male reaching the age of thirteen is required to read a biblical passage in Hebrew before other congregrants in the synagogue. Historically, this coming-of-age ritual has carried great significance for Jewish families, and as first-generation Americans, the Maslows undoubtedly felt some attachment to it, especially in regard to Abraham; the eldest son's role is one of great status in Jewish culture.

Having come to associate Judaism with bearded and alien old-world Orthodox immigrants, the boy went through his bar mitzvah preparation under severe duress. By his early teens, he viewed Orthodox Judaism, along with other religions, as intellectually nonsensical. His mother's superstitious threats and admonitions signified to him what religion was really about. He regarded religious observance as something performed only by the most naive or by utter hypocrites. As Maslow recalled much later, "It wasn't until I went to college that I found honestly religious people, who were decent and who were clearly neither hypocrites nor feebleminded."

Maslow had been exposed to no formal Jewish education during his childhood. Almost inevitably then, he was bound to experience the bar mitzvah ritual as empty, particularly when required to memorize words he did not understand. To a bright, questioning thirteen-year-old like Maslow, this aspect of the ceremony was especially painful. But even more so was the speech he was expected to give praising his parents for their selfless devotion to him. To publicly mouth words that contradicted his strongest emotions was more than he could bear. In describing what formal religion had meant to him in his early years, Maslow recollected:

> I was taught by rote certain Hebrew passages. I wasn't interested in Hebrew, so I didn't care to learn the language at all. I was just trudging through this task, which was imposed upon me, and then I was supposed to make a speech . . . They just picked them out of books that were sold in stationery stores, and they always started, "My dear mother and father," and I had to make this speech, and it was just terrible.

> And then, in the middle of the speech, as I started talking about the blessing of my dear mother—you were supposed to turn to your mother and say, "My dear mother, to whom I owe my life, and to whom I owe my upbringing," and "to whom I owe this, that, and the other thing," and "How I love you for it"—I burst into tears and fled, just ran away, because the whole thing was so hypocritical I couldn't stand it.

Ironically, young Maslow's disgust for the whole affair was misinterpreted by its chief witness. As her oldest son bolted in tears from the synagogue podium, Rose Maslow triumphantly turned to the assembled relatives and announced, "You see! He loves me so much he can't even express the words!" She thought, or perhaps wanted the others to think, that he had been overcome by feelings of devotion.

CHAPTER TWO

Struggles of the Mind

> *Humanistic concerns were a very large part of the reason that I went into psychology from philosophy. I became impatient with philosophy, at all the talking that didn't get anyplace.*
>
> *I remember as a youngster, right through the first years of college . . . schools, lectures, any lecture in the city, and I was there . . . I was always awed by the people on the [lecture] platform, but they were so far distant that I don't think it ever occurred to me that I could be like them, to be one of those gods! I didn't even think of it, until the middle years of college.*
>
> —A.M.

*I*n January 1922, Maslow entered Boys High School. Generally ranked as the top high school in Brooklyn, it attracted boys from all over the bustling borough, those most motivated and intent on advancing to college. Despite the humble economic origins of its students, Boys High over the coming years boasted thousands of successful graduates in commerce, the arts, and the professions. Novelist Irwin Shaw, one of its famous alumni, later quipped, "It taught me all I needed to know to get out of Brooklyn."

As its name suggests, no girls attended. Boys High was located in the Bedford-Stuyvesant section of Brooklyn, a lower-middle-class neighborhood several miles from Flatbush. Maslow traveled there daily by trolley, meeting his cousin Will, who often bicycled to school when weather permitted. The two cousins, both tall and with rugged features, soon grew inseparable; they were dubbed "the Gold Dust Twins" in their senior yearbook.

Physically confident and outgoing, even brash, Will was an important influence in helping his cousin overcome much of his shyness and isolation. Aside from their classes together, the Maslow cousins collaborated in part-time jobs during holidays and summer vacations. One of their most lucrative ventures, initiated by Will, involved delivering flowers for a shop in one of Manhattan's most elite neighborhoods. While Will needed such jobs because of his family's financial straits, Abe was able to adopt a far more cavalier attitude toward work. His father was doing well in business and encouraged his oldest son to devote full attention to school.

Ethnically, the majority of students at Boys High were first-generation American Jews, born to unskilled or semi-skilled European immigrant parents. Most of the families lacked the middle-class accoutrements that the Maslows had acquired, but they shared the common expectation that their sons would grow up to use their heads and not their hands to make a living. These parents prized education as the key to a better life for their children and stressed academic achievement as the means to personal and social improvement.

Surrounded by bright peers inculcated with this outlook, young Maslow found Boys High to be a stimulating place. He served as an officer in various academic clubs and became editor of the Latin magazine. He also edited *Principia*, the school physics paper, for a year. During his teens, Maslow was also somewhat athletically inclined. He was gangly in those days, weighing only about 130 pounds although nearly six feet tall, and often envied the prowess of more muscular classmates. In his twenties, he reminisced, "In general, I tried to compensate for what I felt was a great [physical] lack by forcing my development in the direction of athletic achievements . . . once almost subscribing to one of those courses advertised in the physical culture magazines. I had been interested in athletics, playing on some teams, hanging on to the outskirts of others."

In those years Maslow was an avid tennis player, and whenever weather permitted, he joined Will and friends at the tennis court. He participated, too, in middle-distance running, softball, handball, and punchball. He served as nonplaying captain of the Boys High baseball team.

In a diary entry dated April 22, 1924, Maslow reviewed the events of Easter vacation during his junior year of high school. The account offers a revealing look at his concerns:

> I feel lousy, rotten, bad, sick, nauseated, tired. I've had five days' vacation and in those five days I haven't accomplished a thing except perhaps Friday, when I went down to New York [Manhattan] and worked in a driving rain until 4 o'clock when I felt so miserable, I was so soaked that I quit, and Willy, feeling the same way, joined me. Saturday I saw [my friend] Manuel, an extremely exciting game, but we lost 6 to 5, and this would hardly make me happier. Sunday I went to the Prospect [theater], saw a miserable show and went home, feeling still more dejected.

> Monday and today I killed time, didn't do a thing although I intended to go to the "Y" [YMHA or Young Men's Hebrew Association]. But Pop gave me a talk on his money problems, showed me how hard-pressed he really was, and I decided to quit the "Y" and save the money. This talk made me feel still more gloomy. Today I spent a still lousier day. I started to go the movies, changed my mind, loafed some more, and had a catch [tossed a ball around].

By his high school years, Maslow was already an omnivorous reader. He enjoyed science, especially physics, and in 1923 or 1924 wrote an article for the school's *Principia* predicting the possible use of atomic power for submarines and ships. In the library, he had earlier stumbled upon Niels Bohr's *ABC of Atoms* and had been very excited by it.

He also read a great deal of fiction. His favorite books included the various series about Tom Swift and Frank Merriwell, and those written by Horatio Alger. In his junior year, Maslow experienced a true intellectual awakening. His physics teacher, Sebastian Littauer, recommended to the class that if they really wanted to read something absorbing, Upton Sinclair's books were a must. That casual suggestion catalyzed Maslow's slumbering societal and moral interests. In a diary note dated January 31, 1932, about eight years after the event, he recollected:

I remember, I think, how I really started off on the intellectual life. It was at Boys High and Mr. Sebastian Littauer did it by bringing up Upton Sinclair's *Mammonart* [an exposé of the art business] to the physics lab. He read aloud to Willy and me a part about Dostoyevsky and prostitutes. I think that surprised and shocked me a little, for I was awfully repressed then; a teacher talking about such things was a very unusual thing . . . I don't remember why exactly, but Willy and I got *Mammonart* out [of the library] and read it. Perhaps it was because the mention of the prostitutes attracted me, or Littauer's saying what a good book it was . . . That started me off. I read everything Sinclair had ever written. Otherwise, I was still reading adventure and baseball or college stories.

Through Upton Sinclair's muckraking novels, Maslow became a democratic socialist in political outlook and idealistically committed for the rest of his life to working for a better world. More than forty years later, Maslow wrote to Sinclair in the mid-1960s to express gratitude for the latter's inspiring influence upon him.

Soon after Maslow encountered Sinclair's writings, he discovered that his father's bookkeeper subscribed to *The Nation*, the prominent democratic-left periodical of the day. There were always copies in his father's business office, and Maslow became an avid reader. Eugene Debs, Norman Thomas, and other American socialist leaders became his heroes. There was also a series of "socialist classics" available for twenty-five cents each, including those embracing utopian visions, and Maslow eagerly devoured the entire series. Charles Dickens's *Hard Times*, which vividly depicted the horrors of nineteenth-century English working-class life, also made a strong impression on him.

Complementing Maslow's extracurricular readings were his assignments in history classes, perhaps his favorite subject at Boys High. As he studied American history his junior year, Thomas Jefferson and Abraham Lincoln became his heroes. Decades later, they continued to serve as prime exemplars for Maslow when he began developing his theory of self-actualizing individuals. Like many others born to immigrant parents who had suffered through pogroms and persecution, Maslow had great respect for America's revolutionary founders and their dream. Although he was impatient with the deficiencies of the United States, Maslow, in keeping with the democratic outlook of Eugene Debs and Norman Thomas, believed by his late teens that significant change in America was necessary to maintain and further the nation's original ideals. Years later, he also regarded his early socialist outlook as having been a secular parallel to the age-old prophetic thundering within the Jewish tradition for law and social justice.

During Maslow's high school years, he met his cousin Bertha Goodman. She had come to New York City from Russia in March 1922, at the age of thirteen, and was a year younger than Abe. Her parents, Pearl and Solomon, had come to the United States nearly a decade earlier, planning to get settled before bringing her over. When World War I erupted, international travel became dangerous and exceedingly difficult. Bertha thus grew up with relatives in Russia, separated from her parents for the rest of her childhood. She now lived with her parents in a comfortable, predominantly middle-class neighborhood in the Bronx, about an hour's subway ride from Flatbush.

Through letters and conversations, Abe had heard much about this cousin. He adored Aunt Pearl, Bertha's mother, and regarded her as a warm, good-humored person, always making do with her family's meager financial resources. She had an artistic flair, too, that he liked very much. Her husband was in the upholstery business. Almost immediately upon Bertha's entry into the Goodman household, Maslow found himself attracted to her beauty. Because she barely spoke English, he offered himself as tutor. From then on, Abe visited with Bertha and her family almost weekly. She was the only girl his age with whom he even chatted socially during his teens.

Despite Maslow's intellectual ability and love of reading, he remained shy and retiring, especially toward girls. In the winter of 1925, the time had come for him and his fellow seniors to apply to colleges. The top school of their choice was prestigious Cornell University in upstate New York, the only Ivy League institution that accepted Jews in other than token numbers. To have any chance to enroll there, most Boys High youngsters needed to obtain a full scholarship. This meant taking Cornell's special scholarship examination. Will was hoping to get accepted by Cornell and urged his cousin to take the test too. Maslow adamantly refused. It seemed an impossible dream. As he recalled many decades later, "It was just inconceivable and I didn't even take it seriously in consciousness."

His reluctance to apply to Cornell may have been because his grades at Boys High were not outstanding. He was ranked only in the second quarter of his graduating class of 625 members. With mediocre grades that included 69 in Economics, 72 in Chemistry, and 75 in both freshman English and a two year sequence in Biology, he may have felt discouraged by Cornell's selection process. But Boys High had a statewide reputation for excellence, and with his broad range of extracurricular achievements, Abe certainly stood a chance of being admitted, Will thought. His own grades were only slightly better.

Several months passed. As Abe expected, he was accepted into the public City College of New York, along with just about every other Boys High student with adequate grades. Then one day Will excitedly announced the news to his cousin: Twelve Boys High classmates had won Cornell scholarships, and Will was among them. Initially thrilled with Will's success, Abe soon became gloomy when he realized that his best friend was leaving and he would be lonely once more.

Before starting City College in September, Maslow took his final teenage job at a summer resort hotel in the Catskill Mountains. The vacation area, about a two-hour drive north of New York City, affectionately came to be known later as the Borscht Belt. It catered almost exclusively to New York City's Jews, temporarily escaping sweltering tenements and row houses each summer for a bit of fresh air, together with bountiful portions of hotel food and inexpensive entertainment. The rural region was flourishing in the twenties, with dozens of hotels and bungalow colonies. Many of the most famous Hollywood comedians got their start here, including Jack Benny, George Burns, and Groucho Marx. But as Maslow discovered that summer, the Catskills were no paradise for lower-echelon service workers. Writing nearly forty years later about enlightened versus authoritarian forms of management, Maslow vividly recalled his youthful experience as an unskilled laborer under the "old-school" managerial style:

> I signed up for a summer job at a resort hotel as a waiter
> . . . and then paid my way up to the hotel and was made a
> busboy instead at much lower wages and, as it turned out,

without any tips at all. I was simply swindled in this situation.
I didn't have the money to go back, and anyway it was too
late to get another job for the summer. The boss promised he
would make me a waiter very soon, and I took his word for
it . . . [But after] about two weeks, it . . . became clear that
the man was simply swindling us all and trying to snatch an
extra dollar or two out of the situation.

Finally, for the July Fourth holiday, there were three or four
hundred guests in the hotel, and we were asked to stay
up for most of the night before, preparing some fancy dessert
which looked pretty but which took a huge amount of time.
The staff all got together and agreed to do this without com-
plaint; but then after we had set the first course of dinner on
the Fourth, the whole staff walked out and quit the job.

This was, of course, a great sacrifice financially to the workers
because it was already too late to get good jobs and possibly
too late to get any job, and yet the hatred and desire to
retaliate was so great that the satisfaction of doing so remains
with me to this day . . . This is what I mean by really bad
[working] conditions and what I mean by [labor-manage-
ment] civil war.

After a summer job like that, college life must have looked
appealing. Maslow found himself enjoying most of his coursework at City College, a sprawling concrete campus in northern
Manhattan. While taking a full academic load, he worked part-
time as a watchman at the First Italian Frame Company. He
regarded the job as ideal, for it gave him time every evening
to read, write, and think in blissful solitude. The clamor and
petty tensions of living with his parents and five younger siblings were sometimes so distracting that he began to romanticize about living in penal solitary confinement among his
books and papers. In an undated diary entry from that fall,
Maslow shows clear indication at the age of seventeen of already planning a scholarly career in the humanities. (He had
not yet discovered the field of psychology.)

In this entry, Maslow also expresses a strong sense of his
intellectual power and superiority, despite his mediocre high
school grades. This attitude is coupled with an intense desire,
perhaps born of some deeper insecurity, to be accepted by the

finest scholars. These twin aspects remained ingrained in Maslow's personality throughout his life.

I am a student at the College of the City of New York. My career through high school was distinguished and now in college promises to be brilliant. I have been given to hope that I might make some progress in philosophy, my chosen favorite. My writing has been commended warmly by my English professor. I flatter myself that my college education has not been wasted on me. Already I have found keen delight in warm discussion with scholars of the highest order, whose esteem I think I have won or shortly will win.

My studies of literature of the world have roused and developed in me a keen, burning sense of beauty. So a later development, I have found growing within me an ardent, longing love for music. My critical sense is growing rapidly.

Wonderful vistas stretch before me, for I can see my mind gradually evolving into a clear-sighted, deeply analyzing instrument. It can grasp more readily thoughts which before made me almost weak with exasperation as I tried in vain to tie them together and bring them out into view. I am soberer, sure in my thinking. I have possibility. There is latent power within me.

During the last year, I have played with the thought that I might perhaps get a fellowship in philosophy and study at it for some years. I should also study logic and mathematics, both calculated to clear the mists from my brain, to allow it to work more smoothly.

Maslow had one academic nemesis that first semester at City College—trigonometry. It was a required course for all bachelor of science students, and he "loathed, despised, and hated" it. In a characterological pattern typical of Maslow's approach to activities he disliked, he simply stopped attending the class. At the end of the term, he fell back on his past study habit of feverishly cramming the night before the final exam. This method had served him all through Boys High.

He did pass the trigonometry test, but the instructor failed him in the course anyway, because of his frequent absences.

"All my begging and wheedling and whining and trickery and fast talk, it didn't do any good," Maslow recollected with grudging admiration. "He just failed me."

Because of that failing grade and several C's in required courses, including art, chemistry, and Spanish, Maslow was placed on academic probation for his second semester. His performance steadily improved, and by summer semester it was clear that English and the social sciences were his strengths.

Intellectually, Maslow took pride in a fiercely rationalist outlook, with contempt for anything that smacked of the slightest religious sentiment. To him, religion or spirituality of any sort was synonymous with the superstitious narrow-mindedness he had associated with his mother since boyhood. In a diary entry dated July 31, 1926, Maslow caustically responded to his philosophy professor's comments praising the New England transcendentalist movement's leading philosopher, Ralph Waldo Emerson:

> A man formulates a theory. It is made by himself. He knows that if he believes it, his life will be made more tranquil. He reasons thus: "It's a pity I can't believe it. I see it's unfounded and baseless. If I did not see the fallacies in it, and thought that it was a true doctrine, I would lead a happier life. If I could only believe in it."

> So he does. He believes with a blind faith. It takes the aspects of religion to me, for religion is nothing but a blind, unreasoning faith.

During his sophomore year, Maslow fell under the spell of music. In retrospect, he regarded as a catalyst the advanced music appreciation course that he took in the fall of 1926. Although Maslow had strong esthetic leanings, being drawn to poetry, too, he had confidently begun to view himself as a tough-minded rationalist in all matters. He felt genuinely troubled by his immense attraction to the tender graces of music. For several months, Maslow struggled with the need to defend and even justify, to himself, this unexpected predilection. In an undated diary entry he insisted:

> *Music, let it be known, is an end in itself* and *not a means to an end!* I hear 200 voices and 100 instruments

screaming to the open heavens the joy that was Beethoven. I hear Debussy reproduce for us an exquisite mood of delicious warm languor. I hear a Mozart minuet and the whole dainty, precious era is conjured up before my mind.

Need I then excuse myself for thrilling joy, my living ecstasy by saying that I listen only to forget about the rest of life? No! It should rouse us to the essential goodness of life, the worthwhileness of existence, and enable us the more easily to bear the pains and pettiness that also make up our lives. It should make life more easy . . . Is not ten minutes of Debussy expiation and more for a week of subway?

In another diary notation that year, Maslow again tried to justify philosophically his attraction for something as sensual as music. Interestingly, this entry seems to foreshadow the influential stance he took more than thirty years later in the 1950s and 1960s as a leader of humanistic psychology—that we are all motivated by transcendent values that lie beyond purely rational knowing:

Nature presents to us various incentives and inducements for living. These we call the ends of life. Without them, we would have no reason to continue our existence. Various such are love, parenthood, intellectual mastery, art, and sundry others rather few in number. These ends in life are fundamental and we cannot explain them. We can only accept them.

What they are, where they come from, who gave them to us—these are questions we cannot answer.

It is in this spirit of unquestioning acceptance that I listen to music, for me the highest of the arts. It is to me one of the reasons for living. One of the most important, even in comparison with love, the most important of all ends of life.

I need not explain, therefore, why I love music. It is enough to say in answer to the question "what music means to me" that I see the fundamental, primary, basic place . . . music fills in our lives. I say, music to me is one of the reasons for living, one of the most important gifts nature has bestowed upon us in our effort to induce us to carry on [the] race. As nature is beyond reason, just so is music beyond reason, and therefore it is beyond the province of mankind to apply logical rules to it.

During 1925 and 1926, Maslow's idealistic interest in socialism continued to grow. His Brooklyn home was only a short subway ride from Manhattan, where some of America's leading public forums for intellectual debate were held. He eagerly attended popular weekly public lectures at Cooper Union College. Speakers included renowned figures in the humanities and social sciences, such as Reinhold Niebuhr and Bertrand Russell. Maslow also attended talks and classes at the Labor Temple and the Rand School, both centers for socialist thought, where teachers included Will Durant and Norman Thomas. Maslow's heroes were writers and social intellectuals who espoused a thoroughgoing condemnation of philistinism and economic inefficiency. Influenced by thinkers like Thomas, Maslow wrote in one fiery diary entry of the mid-1920s:

> How stupid at bottom is a system of economic society that will exhort its more fortunate members thus, "Waste. Waste! It is your sacred duty to waste! Food—clothes—labor! Waste as much as you can! You are beholden to society to squander, ruin, misuse, scatter, and destroy!"

We have a story in point. President Coolidge, an economical man, decided to use his hat for two seasons instead of throwing it away at the end of the first year's wear. The ensuing publicity brought his intention to the ears of the hat manufacturers associations all over the country. At once came the indignant cry that the President was setting a bad example to the country and that the hat business would suffer consequently. Because if more people began economizing on hats, the profits of the hat men would decrease. They would be forced to use less labor and there would be more added to the army of unemployed.

The result was that the President retracted and announced publicly that he was intending to buy a new hat. This was given wide publicity.

Thus it goes. The moneyed profligate, seeking to justify himself for his reckless dissipation of money, has good reason ready to hand.

Maslow's trenchant declarations notwithstanding, his socialist bent was almost purely an intellectual's posture and not an activist's. He was sincere in his convictions at the time. But unlike his cousin Will, who actively campaigned for Norman Thomas and got to know him and other Socialist Party leaders well, Maslow was temperamentally too much the loner to participate in, much less enjoy, the noisy debates, backroom caucuses, and door-to-door campaigning that characterized 1920s party politics.

On September 28, 1926, Maslow began legal studies at the evening program of Brooklyn Law School. Located in what was euphemistically known as "downtown Brooklyn," the institution was not academically prestigious, but its admission policy permitted him to enroll as a part-time student while still working toward his undergraduate degree at City College during the day. Brooklyn Law School mainly attracted students of Maslow's background, hardworking sons of New York City's recent immigrants. Local politicians interested in judgeships and similar patronage positions also filled its classes. Indeed, this was the school's chief local reputation for many years.

Maslow enrolled on his father's insistence that he become a lawyer. Samuel Maslow had dreamed in his youth of entering the profession himself and probably hoped to satisfy this ambition vicariously through his bright son. He reasoned that Abe's analytic mind and excellent verbal skills could be put to good use in legal work. "My son, the philosopher" might constitute a good introduction for his eighteen-year-old at a family festivity, but Samuel was too much the self-made businessman to prize the financially uncertain life of a scholar for Abe.

To permit time for legal studies, Maslow took only two full-credit courses at City College, English and music appreciation. From the outset, Maslow disliked the course content at Brooklyn Law School. He found the introductory course material dry and boring, but he probably had expected that. More dismaying was the near total absence of moralistic considerations in the class discussions of legal cases, which "seemed to deal only with evil men, and with the sins of mankind."

On the evening of November 29, Maslow's class was discussing the topic of spite fences. The concept offended his idealistic sensibility of how people should behave toward one another. He walked out of the class, leaving his books behind. He came home and announced, to his parents' surprise, that he was quitting law school. His disappointed father asked, "Well, then, what do you want to study?" The answer: "Everything."

Samuel Maslow could not fathom such a reply, but he resignedly allowed Abe to transfer to Cornell. The move would multiply expenses for the household, but Samuel reasoned that under cousin Will's influence at Cornell, Abe might discover what he wanted to do with his life.

In the winter of 1927, Maslow transferred to Cornell University in Ithaca, New York. He had found little intellectual excitement in the austere, student-as-subway-commuter milieu of City College. He hoped that Cornell might offer greater academic stimulation.

In leaving New York City he also sought to distance himself emotionally from his cousin Bertha, with whom he was falling in love. "I wanted to flee from Bertha because we were so young, and I couldn't get close to her anyhow, and it [the relationship] was half-blissful, half-painful." His parents had begun to discourage the incipient romance. He thought that the increased geographical distance would lessen his attraction to her.

Another reason for Maslow's transfer, of course, was Will, who was enjoying Cornell immensely. Because Abe had not applied for a scholarship, he was unable to afford the hefty tuition at Cornell's privately endowed College of Arts and Sciences. As an alternative, he applied to its state-supported College of Agriculture. By entering Cornell through this "back door," with nearly free tuition, he could join Will and enroll in some liberal arts courses for no extra fee.

Maslow's move from Brooklyn to rural Ithaca marked a milestone. Aside from brief summer jobs in the Catskills, he had never really left his parents' supervision. Now he was on his own for the first time. Given the antagonism Maslow felt toward his mother and his emotional distance from his father, this move was a welcome release from family pressures. Nestled in the scenic hills of the Finger Lakes, Cornell was also a far more attractive and appealing place than City College. "It was very beautiful, it was my first time away from home, from the sidewalks of New York," Maslow fondly reminisced in later life. "I happened to have friends—through Will I had friends— and I had some of this romantic college life which I had seen in the movies, and I felt like a college man."

The two cousins lived together in a small rooming house close to campus. At 319 College Avenue, the three-story building lay across the street from the Red and White Grocery in an area populated mostly by students and known as Collegetown. It was a quiet, tree-lined section of shops and wooden-frame houses converted to apartments and furnished rooms. Because nearly half of Cornell's post-freshmen lived in fraternity and sorority houses, Collegetown had the reputation of housing the lesser-status "independents"—bohemians and those neither interested in nor acceptable to the Greek letter societies. About a fifteen-minute hilly walk to campus, Collegetown and the building where Maslow lived have changed little over the decades.

The cousins became friendly with the other students in the building and shared a communal bathroom with them. There was a warm camaraderie among the group; they often talked about their classes and interests.

Maslow was outgoing and friendly in this group. While a conscientious student, he was by no means an obsessive one or a grind. The matter of finance, though, weighed heavily upon his shoulders. Tuition at the School of Agriculture was minimal, but living expenses in Collegetown were far more than they would have been had he remained at home. Like Will, he partly supported himself by working as a waiter at a fraternity. The job was easy and provided free meals and a small salary. However, surrounded by the fraternity men on whom he waited, Maslow felt acutely self-conscious of his origins and somewhat demeaned at having to serve those whom he regarded as his intellectual inferiors. Many years later, he recalled with some rancor, "In the entire time I worked as a waiter, I don't think anyone talked to me even once . . . I felt completely isolated outside of my own little community of outcasts and outsiders."

Part of Maslow's sense of personal isolation at Cornell

stemmed from the climate of anti-Semitism that flourished there. Fraternities and sororities excluded Jews and other minority groups in less-than-subtle terms. It was equally well known that many Ithaca landlords refused to rent to Jewish students. The Cornell *Sun*, the official student newspaper, routinely barred Jews from staff positions.

Despite Maslow's financial diligence, his father considered him careless with money. The subject was a sore point between them. One day, when Samuel drove up for a visit with Will and Abe, he launched into his usual sharp disapproval of the way his son was managing finances. Suddenly, Abe seized a handful of coins from his pocket and hurled them in fury out the window. He cried, "Why does everyone always talk about money!" Will and Samuel, shocked, looked at each other wordlessly. Then the father went down to the street to pick up the coins.

During his single semester at Cornell, Abe Maslow's grades were neither outstanding nor dismal—B's in psychology, economics, and physics, and C's in geology and meteorology, with a D in required ROTC drill. Despite the school's Ivy League reputation, he found none of his courses intellectually inspiring. Even in elementary psychology, his expectations were badly crushed. As he later recalled, the subject matter was "awful and bloodless and had nothing to do with people, so I shuddered and turned away from it."

The professor of the psychology course was the renowned Edward B. Titchener. One of the founders of American psychology, and a contemporary of Sigmund Freud and William James, Titchener was a rather pompous Oxford-trained academician. He lectured to his audience of sophomores while wearing full academic robes, which he once said gave him "the right to be dogmatic." His coterie of graduate assistants sat in the front row and his array of laboratory apparatus sat imposingly on the lectern.

Titchener's structuralist school of thought had once been dominant in American psychology. He and William James had engaged in acrimonious debates during the 1890s. But structuralism had gradually fallen by the academic wayside. By the time Maslow took Titchener's course in 1927, the professor had become aloof and alienated, more interested in his collection of ancient coins than in keeping abreast of the latest developments in the field that had spurned him. Most of Titchener's colleagues by the mid-1920s sadly regarded him as a bitter, antiquated thinker who was still fighting a scientific war long since forgotten by everyone else. Titchener scarcely let his students know that anything other than structuralism existed in American psychology. It is hardly surprising that Maslow found so little to interest him in the field he would later choose as his lifework.

In retrospect, Titchener's approach to psychology could not have been further removed from Maslow's impassioned social goals. Maslow found "nothing to do with people" in structuralism precisely because there was nothing applied in it to find. Titchener stressed that psychology is solely the empirical study of consciousness—specifically, our experience of sensation, images, and feelings. The single method he accepted was "scientific introspection," employing carefully trained assistants to introspect in the laboratory setting and to report aloud what they perceived when various colored wheels were rotated or various tones were sounded. Even more dogmatically, Titchener defined certain introspections as correct and others as in error, with his opinion carrying the final authority. He also contemptuously dismissed the rapidly growing and useful branches of the field, such as educational, abnormal, and industrial psychology, as beneath "true" or "pure" science.

One aspect of Titchener's course that Maslow found intriguing, however, was the discussion of extrasensory perception, or ESP. Returning from class one day, he excitedly related to Will what had just been covered in his ordinarily boring psychology course. As they talked, Abe wondered whether ESP really existed, and if so, whether he possessed any ability. Will proposed that they conduct their own experiment. At the rooming house that night, Will and the other students proceeded to hide an object and then ask Abe to enter the room and guess what they had hidden. He guessed correctly the first time . . . and the second, and the third. He correctly guessed every single object. By the time the experiment was over, Abe was so excited that he could hardly wait to tell Titchener the next day. In the morning, Will took Abe aside and told him that the group had played a trick on him. They had agreed prior to the experiment to tell Abe that any guess he made was correct. As Will had suspected, his cousin took the joke well.

Generally, though, Maslow was repulsed by what psychology, as represented by Titchener, seemed to be about. Maslow later commented that he had temporarily lost all taste for the field as a result of this course. Nor did he experience much intellectual ardor in any of his other courses at Cornell.

Maslow's semester at Cornell was not only academically disappointing, but he found that he missed Bertha a great deal. On occasion he even lit candles before her photograph at night. Still shy with women his own age, he did not date at all at Cornell. The unfavorable sex ratio on campus—more than three-fourths of the students were male—and his Jewish background limited his dating opportunities.

In Maslow's self-appraisal of his experience at Cornell, only one thing about the school made a lasting impression on him—its honor system of test administration. Nearly forty years later, while addressing the issue of how much freedom employees should be granted in the workplace, he mused:

> I am reminded of the way the honor system worked when I was an undergraduate student at Cornell University . . . It was really amazing that about 95 percent (or more) of the student population, I would estimate, were very honored, very pleased by this system, and it worked perfectly for them. But there was always that 1 or 2 or 3 percent for whom it didn't work, who took advantage of the whole business, to copy, to lie, to cheat on examinations, and so on.

This experience, coming relatively early in his life, helped shape Maslow's view that no system of psychology, education, or business management can be comprehensive without taking into account those whom he called the "crooks and bastards" of the world.

Maslow returned in June 1927 to his parents' Flatbush house in a low mood. Yet, as he proceeded to reenroll at City College, he was by no means despondent. His months with Will, away from his parents and siblings, had matured him, and the scenic splendor of Cornell and its environs had exposed him to a world different from Brooklyn's concrete pavements.

Now a lanky nineteen-year-old who had experienced Ivy League life, Maslow found himself more self-confident and certain of his own opinions.

He was enormously attracted to Bertha and was determined to be with her. But he was still painfully shy with women and unable to declare his feelings. For several weeks, Maslow frequently visited Bertha and her family at their home. Although he had always been affectionate toward Aunt Pearl and the other relatives, it was obvious to them that his lingering visits had only one objective: to spend as much time as possible with Bertha. Still, he was too bashful even to invite her out for a casual date.

One day, Maslow was visiting as usual. In a quiet moment, he sat down hesitantly beside Bertha. They exchanged warm glances. As the silence grew, she gazed at him demurely and moved a bit closer. Timid and yet wanting desperately to touch her, Maslow sat there, hesitating. Bertha's sister Anna, older and more experienced in affairs of the heart, intervened in this slow-motion romance. Shoving him toward Bertha by the scruff of his neck, she exclaimed, "For the love of Pete, kiss her, will ya!" Startled, and almost intimidated by Anna's shove, Maslow did so. Bertha "didn't protest or fight back," he recalled. "She kissed back and then life began."

Maslow always regarded that first romantic kiss as one of the greatest moments of his life, a true peak-experience. It had a tremendous effect on his self-image, for now he felt worthy of adult, sexual love and companionship. "I was accepted by a female. I was just deliriously happy with her."

In September, Maslow resumed his education at City College. Having completed most of his required courses, he was free to choose the subjects that really excited him: the humanities and social sciences. Ironically, the course that had the most powerful impact on Maslow was one he did not even finish: philosophy of civilization. Its professor assigned William Graham Sumner's book *Folkways*, a work that Maslow came to regard as "a Mount Everest" that influenced his entire career. As he later recalled, "This is exactly what our professor warned us about on the first lecture of the semester. 'If you read this book you can never be the same again. You can never be an innocent.' He was right."

Sumner had been a founder of American sociology and a

fierce exponent of the nineteenth-century intellectual movement known as Social Darwinism. Teaching at Yale University
until his death in 1910, he wrote *Folkways* as a side project to
a far more ambitious work entitled *The Science of Society*,
published posthumously in a four-volume series.

Folkways, issued in 1906, brought immense popularity
and fame to its author. It was composed of almost seven hundred pages of rich ethnographic detail, culled from the writings and reports of anthropologists, explorers, missionaries,
and travelers. Although *Folkways* eventually passed into intellectual obsolescence, when Maslow read it in the 1920s it was
still the definitive work on cultural variability, introducing
concepts such as folkways, mores, and ethnocentrism into
scientific and even popular language.

Sumner wrote the book partly to clarify his notion that
humans have held tremendously variable beliefs and customs
over the course of world history and civilization. Each culture's
members tend to view its own mores as correct, proper, or
even divinely commanded, and to dismiss differing perspectives as wrong, crazy, or evil. To dramatize his thesis, he se-
lected practices abhorrent to modern sensibility, such as infan-
ticide and child sacrifice, incest, cannibalism, slavery, blood
revenge, and witchcraft, each of which was deemed normal
and indeed moral by its own culture.

Although Sumner rarely makes the point explicit, he af-
firms for the reader that only the light of reason today keeps
us from embracing the brutal, bloodthirsty folkways of our
not-too-distant past. He is unsparing in his explication of how
organized religion in particular has served to advance some of
the world's worst atrocities, and devotes a full page to "Torture
in Civil and Ecclesiastical Trials," commenting, "In the course
of its work, the Inquisition had introduced torture into the
administration of Christian justice and into the mores."

But what specifically *changes* such mores, so that torture,
for example, is no longer officially acceptable in the Western
legal system? From what source do our civil liberties come?
Here, Sumner pressed the argument associated with the Social
Darwinist outlook: A few superior individuals in every generation affect the entire culture. These are the leaders and the
enlightened ones—in our own time, the scientists and thinkers. As for the others, Sumner contemptuously called them the
"masses." Of these, he wrote:

> Every civilized society has to carry below the sections of the masses a dead weight of ignorance, poverty, crime, and disease. Every such society has, in the great, central section of the masses, a great body which . . . lives by routine and tradition. It is not brutal, but is shallow, narrow-minded, and prejudiced . . . It can sometimes be moved by appeals to its fixed-ideas and prejudices. It is affected in its mores from the classes above it.

Filled with vivid accounts of taboos and popular manias, group hallucinations and mass delusions, and the cruel persecutions they have fostered throughout history, *Folkways* is not a book to bolster one's faith in humanity. In his trenchant descriptions of "savages," "magic," and the like, Sumner did not need to force his conclusions upon the reader. Without rationality and science, we are little better than dogs fighting for scraps on a garbage heap, he suggested. Civilizations have come and gone; so can ours if we unthinkingly allow past mores to dominate us.

Folkways is a powerful work, and it is not hard to see why it inflamed Maslow so much. One evening that fall, on his job at the First Italian Frame Company, he began to read Sumner's book. The message struck Maslow with the force of revelation: Sumner was not simply describing the archaic past, but Maslow's own life as well. For he too had suffered from superstitious narrow-mindedness, exemplified by his mother and the boys who had thrown rocks at him. Perhaps, Maslow reasoned, he might devote himself to fighting such irrationality and employing his intellect for creating a better world. He vowed to make such a task his life's mission.

> I had a great feeling of dedication and oblation. This is what I wanted to be and to do. I sort of swore that I was going to [do it]. Something like the religious ceremonies of vowing and of offering oneself on the altar. And then I wanted to do it totally . . . This was a total dedication.

During the 1927–1928 school year, Maslow and Bertha spent a good deal of time together. She was the first and remained the only woman he ever dated. Living about an hour's subway ride away in the Bronx, she would often meet him midway in Manhattan, particularly around City College and the New York Forty-second Street Library, Maslow's favorite haunts. They frequented plays and concerts on weekends. Avid music lover Maslow secured a job at the refreshment stand in Carnegie Hall where, twice a week, he could listen for free to the New York Philharmonic under Walter Damrosch's baton.

Despite Maslow's passionate love for Bertha, almost everyone he knew opposed the courtship. His only real friend, Will, was away at Cornell and unaware of how serious the romance had become. Samuel and Rose especially disapproved of their collegiate son's dating an immigrant girl still struggling through high school. In their vernacular, Bertha was a "greenhorn," an unsophisticated newcomer to the United States and a social step down for their first born. Weren't there any girls in college for him to date? they would harangue him. Why did he have to pick his cousin? Though they themselves were first cousins, Samuel and Rose raised the specter of hereditary defects if the romance led to marriage.

Over their objections, he continued to go out with Bertha. He even researched the medical literature about the offspring of first cousins, and triumphantly informed his parents that the risks were no greater than normal if both parents were healthy. In fact, Maslow argued, if the parents were of superior genetic makeup, their children would actually benefit. But such appeals to reason made little difference to Samuel and Rose or, to a lesser extent, to Bertha's parents.

In the spring of 1928, Maslow decided to transfer to the University of Wisconsin. Such a long-distance move, he felt, might temporarily cool off his relationship with Bertha. After all, neither was yet twenty-one. The move would also remove him once more from parental pressures and dominance. Maslow's other motive for this decision was more intellectual. He had heard a lot about the educational innovation and liberal atmosphere at the University of Wisconsin and believed it would be a good place to continue his studies in philosophy. Its catalogue listed three faculty members with whom Maslow especially hoped to study: Hans Dreisch in biology, Kurt Koffka in psychology, and Alexander Meiklejohn in philosophy. Finally, it was a state university; tuition would be affordable, even for an out-of-stater.

That summer, Maslow talked about his career plans with

one of his former philosophy professors at City College, John P. Turner. The latter recommended several psychology books. Only one made any impression on Maslow, but it hit with the force of a bombshell: *The Psychologies of 1925,* edited by Carl Murchison of Clark University, a set of essays by the leading psychologists of the day. What particularly inspired Maslow were the three by John B. Watson, founder of American behaviorism. For the rest of his life, Maslow regarded this discovery of behaviorist psychology as a turning point, the specific determinant of his choice of psychology as a career. He never forgot this moment of intellectual exultation, which came as he sat in a reading room of the Forty-second Street Library:

> The thing that really turned me on was Watson's chapter
> . . . In the highest excitement, I suddenly saw unrolling be-
> fore me into the future the possibility of *a science of psychol-*
> *ogy,* a program of work which promised real progress, real
> advance, real solutions of real problems. All that was neces-
> sary was devotion and hard work.

When Bertha met him outside the library, Maslow was nearly euphoric with the realization that he had discovered what he wished to do with his life. Watson's vision was intoxicating to him. "In high excitement and exhilaration, [I] danced down Fifth Avenue, jumping and shouting and gesturing, trying to explain to [Bertha] what it meant," he recalled.

In retrospect, it may seem odd that Maslow, renowned in his mature years as a founder of existential and humanistic psychology, was so enamored with early behaviorism. These movements arose in the 1950s and 1960s specifically to voice a differing outlook on human nature and existence. But in the context of the times, Watson's behaviorism had much to offer an idealistic and scientifically minded person like Maslow.

For one thing, Watson provided a clear alternative to the moral vacuum of Titchener's scientific approach. Behaviorism had originated in animal work, specifically, Ivan Pavlov's experiments in Russia conditioning dogs to salivate to artificial stimuli like bells. In 1919, Watson had apparently proved that identical techniques could be applied to humans. Turning his attention to what lay beyond his laboratory windows, he wanted psychology to be committed to social improvement. In his three essays in *The Psychologies of 1925*, Watson identified racial prejudice, ethnic snobbery, and the use of physical punishment in child-rearing and education as representative targets for behaviorist change. All of these practices, he insisted, arose from superstitious or irrational beliefs; the dispassionate hand of science and its tool of conditioning would sweep away such erroneous ideas. Citing Sumner approvingly, Watson commented, "Civilization has to some extent stripped from man these superfluous reactions to objects and situations, but many still persist, especially in the realm of religion."

This outlook appealed strongly to Maslow, who shared Watson's faith in rationality as the means to a better society. Maslow found particularly enticing Watson's optimistic belief in the nearly total malleability of human nature. Aside from the accidental juxtaposition of birth and social class, Watson believed, we are all born equal and alike in our possibilities. It is only our environment, what shapes us, that makes us different from one another. Change the environment and you can change human nature, Watson argued. In a famous statement, advanced in the material Maslow read that day, Watson declared:

> Give me a dozen healthy infants, well-formed, and my own specified world to bring them up in and I'll guarantee to take any one at random and train him to become any type of specialist I might select—a doctor, lawyer, artist, merchant-chief, and, yes, even into beggar-man and thief, regardless of his talents, penchants, tendencies, abilities, vocations and race of his ancestors.

Such a philosophy meshed perfectly with Maslow's progressive stance. In essence, Watson's behaviorism seemed to stand for everything that Maslow at age twenty most strongly believed in: reason, social improvement, and the elimination of irrationality and superstition through the pure spirit of science. With a sense of excitement, he prepared to leave Brooklyn's familiar streets for the unknown Midwest. "I was confident that here was a real road to travel, solving one problem after another and changing the world," he recollected. "That was it. I was off to Wisconsin to change the world."

CHAPTER THREE

The Making of a Psychologist

> *I wanted to be a good psychologist, and I did
> all the things that an eager, ambitious young
> man would do—joined everything and so on.
> But I think that was really secondary to mak-
> ing a contribution. Contribution is the real
> word here. If I hadn't felt that I could make
> a contribution, I would have left the field. [To
> become] a big shot made no difference. I took
> courses which I hated. I took every damned
> thing, whether I liked it or not. The only
> question was: Would it make me a better
> psychologist?*
>
> —A.M.

*I*n September 1928, Maslow arrived in Madison, Wisconsin, to continue his college education. This was his first venture more than a few hours' drive from New York, and the wide-open spaces of the Midwest presented new vistas. But he was hardly the only New Yorker or Easterner at the university. Under Wisconsin Governor Robert La Follette's progressive influence at the turn of the century, the school had achieved a far-reaching reputation for scholastic excellence and academic freedom with a liberal campus atmosphere. Maslow was one of several hundred New York students there.

He obtained a private, furnished apartment in a rooming house near campus, in an arrangement similar to what he had with Will at Cornell. Though Maslow was now living alone, he had an easy opportunity to meet others and quickly became friendly with a young man named Emanuel "Manny" Piore, a fellow New Yorker. The two had been nodding acquaintances back East, but here their mutual background caused their rooming-house friendship to blossom. Piore was a physics major (he later became research director of IBM) and rather contemptuous of Maslow's infatuation for the fledgling field of psychology.

Without becoming personally antagonistic, they often debated long into the night the merits of their respective disciplines. Years later, Maslow looked back on these conversations as the impetus for his forceful writings on psychology's legitimacy as a science and its relation to the larger scientific community. In the midst of their sometimes heated discussions, Maslow probably recognized more than a kernel of truth in Piore's criticism. In those days, psychology was struggling to escape its academic association with philosophy and to achieve a separate identity as a hard science like biology and medicine. In some respects, this struggle continues.

On his own in a locale far more rural than Brooklyn, Maslow found much in Wisconsin that was new to him. For example, he recalled, "I took hot water for granted until I went to Wisconsin at age twenty and learned that it didn't just flow out of a tap. It cost money and had to be paid for. This was a surprise, I remember."

Maslow was especially innocent with regard to his professors. His expectations about their intellectual brilliance had been unrealistic. As he recalled, "I was looking for Socrates and Plato." Although he was initially disappointed not to find such thinkers on the Madison campus, Maslow still tended to regard his teachers with awe, as otherworldly figures. He never forgot his experience of disbelief on discovering his illustrious philosophy professor relieving himself in the adjoining urinal in a campus men's room. "What did I think at the time," Maslow humorously reminisced, "that professors didn't have bladders or kidneys?"

As the Wisconsin autumn turned chilly, Maslow found himself thinking of Bertha constantly. He could not bear to live apart from her any longer; he considered marriage. His parents still opposed the idea, and he could not change the reality that he and Bertha were first cousins. Moreover, as a full-time student he lacked the means to support a family. Confessing his dilemma to friends and professors, he received a uniform reply: "Don't be foolish to commit yourself . . . you're too young . . . you can't even support yourself yet, so how can you support a family?" No one encouraged him to marry. Perhaps afraid of the answer, he did not solicit his cousin Will's opinion.

Nevertheless, just as Maslow had made up his mind to quit law school despite his father's objection, he followed his heart and sent Bertha a telegram announcing they would marry in New York over his Christmas recess. He felt so sure about his decision that he did not even bother to ask Bertha for her consent. But she was equally in love and immediately agreed. On December 31, 1928, the two cousins were wed in an intimate ceremony before members of their immediate families. Out of his meager savings at Cornell, Will bought them a set of matching pajamas.

Upon the resumption of school at Madison, the newlyweds settled in a comfortable apartment near campus. Although Bertha had not yet earned her adult's degree at Walton High School in the Bronx, she was accepted into the University of Wisconsin as a special student. With generous help from their parents, who now accepted the marriage with hopeful expectation, they were together at last.

Academically, Maslow had experienced a shock upon registering for his first term in September. The three professors with whom he had most desired to study—Dreisch, Koffka, and Meiklejohn—were gone. They had been visiting professors, and the university catalogue had not indicated this clearly, much to Maslow's dismay. However, still excited by the vision that Watson's writings had awakened in him, Maslow took a full load of psychology and philosophy courses.

From the outset, Maslow was delighted to encounter a stimulating intellectual atmosphere at Wisconsin. There was a homey, small-town midwestern friendliness on campus that Maslow liked very much. His professors were interested in chatting with him and listening to his ideas, an experience that he found intoxicating and very different from what he had found in New York. City College had been an urban commuter school where faculty and students alike dispersed at the end of each class, making leisurely intellectual debate unlikely. As for Cornell, the competitiveness and snobbery that upset Maslow there were central to its private, elite Ivy League status.

Wisconsin's psychology department was small and convivial at this time. It numbered four full-time faculty members and graduated about three Ph.D.'s each year. At a weekly departmental seminar, faculty and students discussed the latest research in a warm, face-to-face manner. Even before Bertha joined him in the winter of 1929, Maslow found that several of his professors took him under their wing. He became especially close to Eliseo Vivas in philosophy and William H. Sheldon, his psychology adviser. Later, Ernest Marchand in American literature and Norman Cameron, Harry Harlow, and Richard W. Husband in psychology treated him as a promising scholar. Of Marchand, Maslow recalled, "He fed us, took us home, and . . . treated me like an adult, like an equal." Sheldon, who later became famous for his theory linking body type and personality, even taught Maslow how to buy a suit. Maslow joined others for camping trips to Idaho and Wyoming. The ambience was very different from the concrete impersonality of City College, and as Maslow fondly reminisced, "There was dinner and parties and driving together to conventions and meetings. I was in a sense taken into the intellectual community."

Having suffered through years of emotional isolation as a consequence of his scholarly bent, Maslow flourished in the atmosphere at Madison. His record shows uniform excellence in coursework beginning in his first term there, and he was named to the National Honor Society for academic achievement. Between the fall of 1928 and the spring of 1930, when he received his B.A., Maslow completed nearly every class necessary for the advanced degree in psychology, so that he could spend his "blessed graduate years without any required courses, just doing research and studying and reading."

Marriage gave Maslow heightened emotional security and, for the first time, he felt truly welcomed into the social world of other bright students. His best friends among his fellow psychology students included Rod Menzies and Paul Settlage (both of whom died early in life), as well as Lucien Hank, Jr., and Ross Stagner, who have gone on to distinguished academic careers. The Maslows did most of their socializing with other young married couples; the salaries of graduate assistants, especially after the onset of the Depression, made casual visiting the only entertainment they could afford. Years later, Maslow documented some of his student partying during Prohibition days:

I drank dago a couple of times and felt very daring and adventurous. I never bought or drank any hard liquor because of the danger of wood alcohol, etc. We *did* swipe pure alcohol from the chemistry labs. I remember [a friend] Sam bringing some to a party, and then it was mixed with flavorings that weren't dangerous. And we made our own beer.

Maslow's psychology training at Wisconsin was decidedly experimentalist-behaviorist. Seized by the inspiring image of human progress through the steady march of science, Maslow was pleased with this academic emphasis. Most of his undergraduate studies, aside from philosophy courses that he initially chose, were geared toward such subjects as anatomy, physiology, and animal behavior. He spent a good deal of time in laboratories and learned to perform animal dissections with considerable dexterity. To help round out his scientific training, he elected courses in chemistry, zoology, and physics.

Such an approach to psychology was then dominant in American academia and remained so for many years. As Maslow later recalled, "All my professors were researchers and some of them—Clark Hull, Norman Cameron, and William H. Sheldon—were almost evangelistic in their excitement about the behaviorist promise." Maslow especially enjoyed Hull's lectures in experimental and behavioral psychology. But not his laboratory class. Hull (who left Wisconsin in 1929 for a teaching post at Yale and emerged in the 1930s as the foremost American behavioral theorist) discouraged Maslow's interest in doing research with Sheldon. Perhaps Hull viewed Sheldon as insufficiently behaviorist; in any event, Maslow heeded the advice, and later worked with Harry Harlow instead.

Under Professor Richard W. Husband, Maslow took Modern Viewpoints in Psychology, another stimulating course. It covered the history of psychology—structuralism, functionalism, Gestalt, psychoanalysis, and other theoretical issues. According to Husband, Maslow took to this subject avidly, "as he was always semiphilosophical" in orientation.

One psychology course Maslow disliked was statistics, which he regarded as trivial and unnecessary. Dating back to his failing trigonometry at City College, mathematics had been his nemesis. However, he came to recognize the importance of statistics in experimental research when, in the fall of

1931, he and his friend Stagner took a first-year medical course
in physiology, taught by W. J. Meek. In the laboratory sessions,
the two aspiring psychologists repeatedly chided Meek about
his failure to frame framing medical research questions in statistical terms. In another, rather undemanding course in educational psychology, the two friends decided to team up to
enliven things: One would "innocently" raise a highly abstruse
question, while the other would launch into a ponderous response. Then, before their somewhat baffled professor and
peers, they would reverse roles.

To those who associate Maslow's name solely with the
humanistic writing that marked his later career, it may seem
surprising that he was initially impressed with laboratory experimentalism as the path to psychological knowledge. But it
would be a serious mistake to dismiss his early training as
irrelevant to his seminal studies of the hierarchy of needs,
self-actualization, and peak-experiences. Maslow repeatedly
rejected this interpretation of his lifework: "It may sound peculiar in view of [my humanistic psychology work], but I still
feel the same love and admiration for objectivistic research. I
have not repudiated it nor will I attack it as such. All that
happened is that I was forced to realize its limitation, its failure
to generate a true and useful image of man."

Although a committed psychology major at the University
of Wisconsin, Maslow retained a fierce love of philosophy. He
typically excelled in such courses; however, he had a particular
aversion to German philosopher Georg Hegel. When asked to
present a paper on Hegel's work, Maslow found himself unable
to get past the first page and simply avoided coming to class.
Among the philosophers he most respected, Spinoza remained
an intellectual hero for the rest of Maslow's life.

In contrast, Maslow viewed more contemporary deists
like William James with considerable contempt, and sarcastically dismissed James's *Will to Believe* as "the last despairing
rationalization of a previous believer in God." In a 1928 undergraduate paper, Maslow caustically argued:

> Our earth does not seem to be made for us, as a home
> is made for a man by an architect. If there were such an
> architect or designer, he made a sloppy job of it and should
> not be trusted in the future. This planet resembles, so far

as its fitness for our needs goes, a dilapidated hovel rather than the mansion we earthly creatures have decided we deserve.

In another, perhaps more revealing, philosophy paper, Maslow curtly dismissed the work of Ralph Waldo Emerson, patrician of the New England transcendental school, for his embrace of spiritual sentiments. Such a rejection was certainly consistent with Maslow's intense humanistic rationalism and was a view held by many thinkers of the time, such as those associated with New York's Ethical Culture Society. But Maslow proceeded to make a fascinating confession. Apart from its somewhat sophomoric tone, it stands as one of his few self-disclosures concerning an encounter with transcendent experience. It also foreshadows the position he would come to adopt nearly thirty years later upon venturing into the heady waters of mysticism. In this course paper, Maslow contended that "otherworldly" episodes require no metaphysical shift or belief in a divine order. Rather, mystical experience, however ecstatic, can be explained wholly within the province of human nature and its hidden potential:

> As for [Emerson's] proof of the existence of the Over-Soul by the mystic experience, I have but this to say. I have myself once had the mystic experience . . . [in which] I experienced a blind groping for something, an overwhelming sense of unsatisfied desire, a helplessness which was so intense that it left me almost weeping. And never did I ascribe this to any Over-Soul or any other such concept. It is cowardice [to do so] . . . At the moment of the mystic experience, we see wonderful possibilities and inscrutable depths in mankind . . . Why not ascribe [the wonder of the experience] to man himself? Instead of deducing from the mystic experience the essential helplessness and smallness of man . . . can we not round out a larger, more wonderful conception of the greatness of the human species and wonderful vistas of progress just faintly glimpsed against the future?

Over the course of his years at Wisconsin, Maslow submitted several papers to the *Journal of Philosophy,* but none was accepted for publication. These included an essay in

1929 on the need for scientists to more precisely define technical words such as *consciousness* that also have multiple popular meanings. Another, written in 1931, he entitled "The Science of Psychology." It represented a rebuttal—in part to the argument of physics major Emanuel Piore—that psychology is not a true science. As might be expected, Maslow affirmed that "psychology differs from the physical sciences quantitatively and not qualitatively . . . it partakes of all the characteristics which mark the other sciences." Much later in his career, Maslow came to articulate a far more original perspective on this issue, by emphatically declaring that the study of humans cannot be undertaken in the same value-free way that scientists study chemical reactions or distant galaxies.

During this period, Maslow discovered anthropology. Since reading Sumner's *Folkways,* he had been attracted to the notion of cross-cultural differences but had done no further reading on the subject. At Wisconsin, his direct influence in this realm was Bertha's professor Ralph Linton, who was quite friendly with students. After some sixteen years as a field and museum anthropologist, Linton had entered academic life in 1928 as associate professor of anthropology at the University of Wisconsin; the following year he was promoted to full professor. Linton had not yet written his magnum opus, *The Study of Man,* which would later bring him international acclaim at his post as chairman of anthropology at Columbia University, where the highly respected department included Ruth Benedict and Margaret Mead. But at Madison, he was already an extremely stimulating lecturer and teacher and had the unusual ability to interest casual students like Maslow in professional anthropology. Maslow wrote:

> About 1932 . . . I first read [Bronislaw] Malinowski, Mead, Benedict, and Linton. For me, this was all a tremendous revelation and I went around lecturing at the psychology classes of various instructors about this new dispensation for psychology. I was convinced that psychology had been ethnocentric. I decided for myself to be a part-time anthropologist because that was *sine qua non* for being a good psychologist. Otherwise, you were simply a naive local. And I remember lecturing everybody else about it, too.

Maslow embraced anthropology's cross-cultural outlook so ambitiously that he prepared a paper to present before the Wisconsin Academy of the Arts and Sciences in March 1932. His topic was "The Necessity of a Social Philosophy of Mental Hygiene and Psychoanalysis." Typically for Maslow, he developed acute stage fright before his presentation and fled from the gathering. Original and well reasoned, Maslow's paper was essentially a critique of the mental hygiene and psychoanalytic movements of the day for their unexamined cultural biases and their inability to question Western culture and its role in contributing to specific forms of emotional distress:

> Psychoanalysis . . . acts on the assumption that the individual is always wrong and proceeds to do its best to adjust him to the environment, neglecting usually the possible necessity of adjusting the environment to the individual. The plain truth of the matter is that twisting and warping a human being is far easier than changing the social structure, and takes less courage besides.

Maslow went on to offer the example of a man with a strong sex drive: "In our society, he is bound to get into trouble . . . if his drives overcome his inhibitions. Few people realize, though, that these same drives would be a great social asset in another society . . ." In short, Maslow was condemning the burgeoning therapeutic movement for its cultural shortsightedness.

In Germany that same year, Wilhelm Reich, Freud's former protégé, was launching a similar intellectual attack on the hidden biases of psychoanalysis. Reich, however, was a confirmed Marxist activist who was most opposed to the social and political conservatism that seemed inherent in Freud's pessimistic view of human progress.

Another unpublished 1932 paper by Maslow also reveals the direction of his cross-cultural critique. Although he did not discover Reich's work until much later in life, he espoused the strongly Reichian view that governments have no right to pass laws governing sexual behavior between consenting adults. To believe otherwise, Maslow insisted, is to embrace values like the sanctity of monogamy that have no demonstrable scientific validity but merely reflect cultural folkways. Throughout the early 1930s, Maslow held strongly to cultural relativism: the belief that it is scientifically impossible to judge or to evaluate another culture's values from our own cultural perspective. Later, Maslow would veer sharply from this position.

During this exciting period of intellectual growth, Maslow was obligated to embark on the more mundane task of choosing a topic for his master's thesis. It was here that he began to recognize the limitations of the ardent experimentalist-behaviorist outlook of his professors. Initially, in 1930, Maslow decided to do his thesis on esthetics; specifically, on the psychology of music appreciation. His professors vetoed this topic as too "muddled" for investigation. Next, Maslow offered to study the meaningfulness of words in affecting verbal learning, but this topic was also deemed too "soft-minded." Finally, Professor Hulsey Cason assigned him research in a somewhat related area: learning, retention, and reproduction of verbal material. To Maslow's uninitiated parents and siblings back in Brooklyn, the term *reproduction* conjured up wild images of sexual behavior, but his work was far less provocative than they imagined.

Maslow's master's thesis is interesting only as an illustration of what mainstream academic psychologists of the time considered good research. In brief, he presented college students (enrolled in introductory psychology) with lists of three-letter words like *run,* nine to a card, on 100 cards. His goal was to determine the effects of various experimental conditions with respect to the students' recall of the words that were flashed before them.

Half the students were exposed to each card for ten seconds (called the *learning* phase of the experiment), then to a blank card for five seconds (the *retention* phase), and then given fifteen seconds in which to recite the nine words they had just read (the *reproduction* phase). Each sequence of learning, retention, and reproduction constituted one *trial.* A rest period followed. The other half were likewise exposed to each word card for ten seconds, but were shown the blank card for fifteen seconds and then given just five seconds to verbally reproduce the words. Maslow rang a bell in half of each of the three experimental phases to determine how the stimulus affected the students' recall. Finally, Maslow varied the rest period, from five to forty seconds, between presentations of complete trials. His results suggested that variable learning conditions produced worse recall than did consistent conditions. He also found that the ringing of the bell tended to interfere with the learning process; it was especially distracting during the initial presentation phase of the cards.

Maslow regarded the research as embarrassingly trivial, but he completed his thesis in the summer of 1931 and was awarded his master's degree in psychology in October. Afterward, he was so ashamed of the thesis that he removed it from the psychology library and tore out its catalogue listing. Ironically, Professor Cason admired the research enough to urge Maslow to submit it for publication. Much to Maslow's surprise, his thesis was published as two articles in 1934.

During Maslow's years at Wisconsin, he served as teaching assistant to Sheldon and later to Husband, who taught general psychology, consisting of two lectures a week to some five hundred students. The large class broke up into sections of twenty-five each twice a week. Husband recalls that Maslow "did a great job and inspired many students to take further courses in psychology." His friend Stagner likewise recollects that Maslow—tall, with rugged features and an infectious sense of humor—was especially admired by female students. Harry Harlow similarly remembered Maslow as one of the most popular teaching fellows in the department:

> [Maslow] made extremely adequate contact with his undergraduate students, particularly if they were female, bright, and beautiful. These platonic contacts enabled him to experiment along research lines that . . . were thirty years ahead of the time . . . He spent a great deal of time carrying out what might be regarded as semianalytic sessions with the students. At least it didn't turn the students against psychology, for one of the brightest and prettiest of students married an eminent psychologist subsequently.

During the Depression, Madison was a hotbed of left-wing radicalism. Several of Maslow's friends flirted with radical politics and, to his admiration, Stagner and his coworkers almost captured city hall when backing others for socialist candidates in 1933. Even Bertha, who was not politically oriented, attended socialist party meetings for a while and enjoyed the shared idealism and friendships she found there. For decades the state of Wisconsin had been home to a populist movement of farmers, manual laborers, and native intellectuals. Milwaukee had long been famous for its socialist mayor and other public officials. Nevertheless, Maslow was not politically active. His cultural critique of American life was strictly an intellectual's, not an activist's.

In one respect, however, he was drawn into the socialist spirit of the times. He and Bertha joined in a cooperative living arrangement with several students in a "rotting old house" on Adams Street near campus. They shared meals and chores and got along well together. But even then, Maslow stood somewhat apart with his political moderation. Responding to a casual conversation about the evils of capitalism, he startled his more radical friends one day by heatedly asserting, "Well, you know, there are some good capitalists!" Perhaps he was thinking of his father at the time.

In 1931, campus radicalism touched Maslow directly when the Wisconsin legislature announced plans to abolish salaries for state university teaching assistants in a money-saving effort. Several student organizers, including Stagner, got up petition drives and scheduled meetings with university administrators. Maslow signed the petition but became no more involved than that. Student activism was successful in persuading the university to negotiate a formula by which teaching salaries were cut based on seniority and level of position.

Although Maslow was generally happy at Wisconsin, he sometimes felt emotionally alone and unappreciated among his mentors and peers. When seized by such moods, which occurred sporadically throughout his life, he would resort to introspection in his diary. In the following passage written around the fall of 1930, Maslow examined his career options. He had apparently not yet begun the primate research he would soon find so exciting:

> I have decided formally that I am not the research or experimenter type. I am rather a dilettante type. My desire

for knowledge spreads itself all over the intellectual and refuses to bore in at one particular spot.

I don't know what to do about my career. Teaching would be all right, I suppose, but I would always be rebellious at the lack of intellectual freedom. The possible alternatives that have suggested themselves to me were medicine or business. Either is freer than academic life if not quite so congenial. But then I wouldn't have time for study and reading, and I can't do without that.

After musing about his future, Maslow reflected at length upon his Jewish background. With the prospect of finishing graduate studies, he was faced with the painful reality of seeking a college teaching position as a Jew in the midst of the anti-Semitism that flourished in Depression-era academia.

Maslow already had been urged by friends and faculty alike to consider changing his name from Abraham to something less ethnic, like Axelrod. Maslow's brothers had anglicized their equally Jewish-sounding names. Even though Maslow may not have known it at the time, his professor Harry Harlow had changed his name from Harry Israel some years back for professional reasons. Harlow was not Jewish but had recognized that the old Iowa farm-name would be no career asset.

The influx of New Yorkers onto the Madison campus had triggered some anti-Semitism there, most of it subtle. Maslow was acutely sensitive to such displays of prejudice, apparently more so than most of his Jewish peers. In fact, he refused to join the university's alumni association after graduation because of the anti-Semitism he had encountered among students and faculty. In a revealing diary entry from his student days, he commented:

They are all so cautious. No one of them minds me because I am a Jew. At the same time, if any of them had the hiring of me they would none of them take me on, so sensitive are they to the folkways around here, to just the general feeling in the air about Jews. No one would object if I were taken on, but still they would never do it, so fearful are they of doing anything wrong.

If I weren't a Jew, of course I would easily get a job. As it is, I am almost sure not to. What shall I do? Hang on the hope that I will run across some brave man who is willing to hire a good man even if he is a Jew?

The Jewish problem? I had almost made up my mind to dodge it. To change my name—to be a "white Jew," a "good Jew." But then I read Ludwig Lewisohn's *Island Within* . . . he changed my mind for me. I wouldn't dream of it now. If I'm a Jew, I'm a Jew, and I'll stuff it down your throat if you don't like it.

Even at the age of twenty-two, Maslow was not a man to let prejudice stop him from reaching his goal. In his two years at Wisconsin, he had grown tremendously in intellectual prowess and was committed to becoming a masterful psychologist and thereby changing the world. His determination was intense.

CHAPTER FOUR

Monkey Man

*My primate research is the foundation upon
which everything rests.*

*My work with monkeys, I am sure, is
more "true," more "accurate," in a sense,
more objectively true than it would have been
if I had disliked monkeys. The fact was that
I was fascinated with them. I became fond of
my individual monkeys in a way that was not
possible with my rats.*

—A.M.

*Abe never forgot his debt to monkeys, or per-
haps we should say their debt to him.*

—Harry Harlow

*M*aslow had found much that was stimulat-
ing in his initial psychology training at Wisconsin, but he had
not yet developed any area of specialization upon completing
his master's degree requirements. In planning his doctoral
work, he therefore felt somewhat frustrated. None of his
professors had really excited him with their own research interests, nor had he found anything to ignite his intellectual
enthusiasm. Maslow regarded his only empirical research, his
master's thesis, as an embarrassment. But when he registered
for Harry Harlow's research practicum in the winter of 1931,
matters changed dramatically.

Harlow's name has long been linked with his landmark
accomplishments in studying the higher capacities—social behavior and learning—in primates. For more than forty years,
he pioneered in research into peer development and mother-
infant bonding ("learning to love") in monkeys. Millions probably still recall the depiction of this research in their introduc-

tory psychology textbooks: photos of winsome-looking baby chimpanzees clasping their mothers in loving embrace or staring with vacant, forlorn eyes when forcibly separated from them. Harlow's work is also definitive in proving that monkeys have an innate curiosity to explore their environment.

When he arrived in Madison in the fall of 1930, Harlow was a boyish-looking recent Ph.D. from Stanford University, age twenty-four. On his first day as an assistant professor he kept being mistaken for a lost freshman as he tried to find his way around Wisconsin's sprawling campus. He was just recovering from this ordeal when he reached his office, to find Abraham Maslow sitting at his desk. Maslow said, "Hello, do you know where Dr. Harlow is?" The latter stared at him for a moment, then replied, "Yes."

A native of Iowa, Harlow had done his doctoral dissertation on social facilitation of feeding behavior in rats, a topic he had found trivial and boring. His appointment at Wisconsin called for him to teach introductory psychology and to direct the animal laboratory. He worked hard on his teaching and became popular among students for his sharp wit. He quickly discovered that the second part of his assignment was going to be a challenge. When he asked to be shown the animal laboratory, he was told, "We tore it down last summer."

Harlow's first research interest at Madison was in the cortical localization of higher intellectual functions in humans. Specifically, he asked, where in the brain is "thinking" done? Stanford University had given him a solid background in physiology and neuroanatomy, and monkeys seemed appropriate research animals because of their evident cognitive capacity. Since the Vilas Park Zoo in Madison had an adequate collection of primates, Harlow could begin his work. But before he could map monkeys' brain regions, he needed to develop a standardized set of tests to measure their visual-perceptual and learning abilities. After that he planned to sever certain specific brain areas to see how that affected performance on various tests. Ironically, Harlow would soon become much more interested in the learning process of monkeys than he ever would in the makeup of their central nervous systems.

Maslow became Harlow's research assistant and, eventually, his first doctoral student. The initial task hardly seems likely to have aroused Maslow's interest; Harlow put him to work doing "a million boring delayed-reaction" experiments with monkeys. These were exercises in intelligence testing of primates. The experimenter would present a bit of food to a caged, hungry monkey. Then the experimenter would visibly place the food beneath one of two cups. After a specified number of seconds elapsed, the monkey would be encouraged to find the food under the correct cup. The purpose of the experiment was to determine how the monkey's success rate varied with the amount of time delay, as well as with its species, age, and other factors.

To Maslow's surprise he began to enjoy this research. For one thing, Harlow, only three years Maslow's senior and single at the time, was more like a peer than a supervisor. He was a "very brilliant man . . . I had dinner at his home, and so on. And we had chats and we could talk about things." Maslow particularly enjoyed the professor's vivid wit, illustrated by Harlow's reminiscence of their early research with an animal named Jiggs,

> . . . the nicest and sweetest orangoutan that had ever lived at any zoo for fifteen years. We gave him two oak blocks, one with a square hole and one with a round hole, and a square plunger and a round plunger. He learned to put the round plunger in the round hole and the square plunger in the square hole, but he never learned to put the square plunger in the round hole. He worked incessantly on this unsolvable problem for six weeks and died of perforated ulcers, but at least he died demonstrating a level of intellectual curiosity greater than that of many University of Wisconsin students.

Maslow found Harlow an appealing research colleague. The monkeys appealed to him as well. Like Harlow, he found them intriguing to watch and emotionally engaging. "The fact is that I was fascinated with them. I became fond of my individual monkeys in a way that was not possible with my rats."

A photograph from the *Wisconsin State Journal*, dated July 19, 1931, shows Maslow and assistant Harry Yudin standing before a monkey cage at Madison's Vilas Park Zoo. The alliterative headline proclaims, "Primates Pick Proper Pea." The caption reads, "Abraham Maslow, assistant in the psychology department at the University of Wisconsin, putting 'Pat,' a West African mandrill, through one of the delayed reaction tests by which Professor Harry F. Harlow is determining whether monkeys have image patterns like human beings." A lanky, youthful-looking, shirtsleeved Maslow stands with head slightly cocked, watching closely as Yudin arouses a monkey's interest with a morsel of food.

Harlow's team completed the research shortly thereafter. Published in the *Journal of Comparative Psychology* in 1932, it was entitled "Delayed Reaction Tests on Primates from the Lemur to the Orangoutan." Harlow generously added Maslow's name as junior author although he had done none of the writing. Harlow first reviewed previous scientific studies using the delayed-reaction test as a measure of human and primate intelligence, then described his specific procedures and results. In essence, the study suggested that there are clear cross-species differences among monkeys with regard to solving this task, as well as marked individual or intraspecies differences. There was additional evidence that if a monkey is unable to solve the problem immediately through insight, it typically keeps at it through trial-and-error learning until it eventually finds the answer.

The research was little more than a useful contribution to primate psychology, but Maslow was excited about the prospect of seeing his name on a published scientific paper. He traveled to New York City later that summer and initiated his own, smaller-scale replication of the study at the Bronx Park Zoo, near Bertha's parents' home. The results confirmed the earlier findings, and also hinted at the possibility that young monkeys lack the cognitive capacity of their elders with regard to this task. This time Maslow wrote the scientific article himself and returned Harlow's favor by adding the professor's name to its authorship. It was published in the *Journal of Comparative Psychology* in 1932.

By the fall of 1931, Maslow was pleased with the year's events. He had discovered his scientific calling, he believed, and anticipated fulfillment of his vision to contribute to knowledge, and ultimately world betterment, through science. More specifically, he decided that monkey research would be his chief area of professional interest.

Through sentimental eyes in later years, Maslow tended to look back with pure affection upon his "hard-nosed" experimental training under Harlow and others. In reality, he often felt frustrated by the lack of a broad intellectualism among psychology faculty and peers at Wisconsin. He loved philosophy, especially Spinoza and Socrates, and he was passionate about ideas; most of his colleagues seemed little concerned with such matters. In his early graduate study, Maslow was already drawn to theory and grand system-building in the old-style European tradition. He had secretly begun writing a definitive text to encompass all of existing psychology within one conceptual framework. Maslow clung to this dream until well into middle age; by the mid-1950s the psychology field had become so large and fragmented that he abandoned the task as impossible.

He also disliked the high-pressure, publish-or-perish professorial attitude at Wisconsin toward scientific discovery. Of course, this orientation to empirical research was, and has remained, dominant in virtually every major university and discipline throughout the country. Perhaps somewhat naively, then, Maslow complained in his diary:

> The emphasis here is all on getting ahead. Getting ahead is synonymous with doing one piffling experiment after another and publishing as a result one piffling paper after another . . . Two articles are good, four are twice as good. It's all very mathematical apparently. There is a direct relationship between number of articles published and your "goodness" as a psychologist.

Maslow went on to vent his contempt for what he considered the intellectual cowardice of his psychology professors and peers. In this regard, he never gave up this youthful and idealistic attitude. Throughout his life he condemned the timidity of most of his fellow academicians in the social sciences to venture beyond the safest currents of their disciplines. In this same diary entry, he commented:

> They all remind me of a bunch of businessmen or politicians with their noses to the wind, eager to know what is being done and what are the current folkways among American psychologists. It is fashionable now to despise Gestalt psychology. Accordingly, they all despise it. If it were the folkway to admire it, they could admire it. They experiment

only in problems that are being done at the time . . . They
seem to be a bunch of intellectual castrates . . . But God
dammit, I'll keep my own intellectual virility if it kills me. To
hell with their jobs.

With this attitude, and because of the chaotic nature of
Wisconsin's primate research facilities, Maslow considered
completing his doctoral work elsewhere. By the winter of
1932, he had to make his plans for the following academic year.
Maslow decided to study with Robert Yerkes of Yale University, the world's leading researcher in primate behavior. Maslow was never shy about making the acquaintance of those
dominant in a field that interested him, and Yerkes had established himself during the late 1920s as the top "monkey man"
in psychology. His massive book *The Great Apes,* published in
1928, had been acclaimed around the world as the definitive
text on primates.

At the time, Yerkes had just established a unique research
facility under Yale's auspices in Orange Park, Florida. He had
chosen the site because of its hospitable climate for monkeys.
The Anthropoid Experimental Station, as Yerkes called it, was
nestled among orange groves fifteen miles from Jacksonville.
It consisted of a laboratory with offices and experiment rooms,
a service building, and a quarters building with eight animal
rooms. Each winter, Yerkes and his family came down from
New Haven and lived there as he carried out his studies.

In a letter dated February 11, 1932, Maslow wrote Yerkes
that he was eager to study with him at Yale. "My plans for the
future are not completely definite," he added. "I am wavering
between the study of perception in primates (illusory perception, etc.) and the study of social behavior. I should like your
advice on this point."

Maslow listed as academic references his psychology
professors over the previous four years at Wisconsin—Hull,
Sheldon, Cameron, V. Allen Henmon, Husband, and, of
course, Harlow. Listing his courses in psychology and related
fields, Maslow then closed the letter with both directness and
deference: "To be quite frank, I am very, very anxious to study
and work with you. It was your book on the *Great Apes* that
first turned my thoughts to primate psychology, and to complete my academic career under your tutelage would be the
only satisfactory course for me now."

Yerkes, working at the experimental station in Florida, quickly responded to Maslow's letter: "I have just received your letter of February 11, with its indication of your desire to work in our laboratories and its personal information. We shall be glad to consider you for junior assistantship on stipend of $600, if such appointment would interest you."

Matters looked promising to Maslow until he received a disquieting letter from Yerkes, dated March 10. Yerkes reported that some of Maslow's application materials had been mistakenly forwarded to the Yale Graduate School Admissions Office, while others had been sent to Yerkes's office at New Haven, and still others had come to the experimental station in Orange Park. As a result, it was too late to gather the papers and consider Maslow for a doctoral fellowship to begin the next fall. Yerkes's letter had a cordial ring, and he suggested to Maslow, "Since you have so nearly completed the requirements for degree at Wisconsin, would it not be better to remain there for another year in order to complete thesis and obtain the degree, and thereafter, if it seemed wise, hope to come to us for a year or two on National Research Council, Social Science Research Council, or other fellowship or assistantship?"

Maslow must have been disappointed, but he responded with equal cordiality. "If my application for a fellowship is rejected," he wrote, "I shall finish up in one more year at Wisconsin and then come to work with you with your permission."

That same month, Maslow embarked on a new area of animal research, one that may appear to the casual observer an even more unlikely interest for Maslow than primate learning: food preference in animals. Yet, even at the end of his life, Maslow prized this work as contributing to an understanding of the innate "wisdom of the body" with respect to animal and, by implication, human existence. Between 1932 and 1935, he published four articles dealing with the applied and theoretical aspects of this topic, first with dogs, then with monkeys.

In summary, Maslow found that the higher an animal species on the phyletic scale, the more variable its food preferences. That is, individual pigeons had been shown to be more variable than individual white rats in what they choose to eat; primates are likewise more variable than pigeons; presumably, humans are the most variable of all. Maslow drew one important conclusion from this finding, as stated in his 1935 paper, "Appetites and Hungers in Animal Motivation":

> As we ascend the phyletic scale, the white rat as a subject for experiments in motivation would seem to be less suitable than the monkey, if we are interested in comparative, rather than animal, psychology. If the object in studying animals is to better understand man, the rat is not as suitable for purposes of comparison since . . . appetite apparently plays a less important role in them than it does in monkeys and humans.

Maslow's second major conclusion foreshadowed his later, highly influential theory of human motivation. Displaying the creative clarity with respect to theory that would be his hallmark, Maslow insisted that even an apparently simple physiological drive, such as an animal's hunger, encompasses qualities that transcend sheer physical survival. He pointed out that monkeys exhibit what he called appetite—that is, eating certain foods even when their hunger drive is sated. He had shown experimentally that monkeys will eagerly seek treats like peanuts and chocolates after refusing ordinary items of their diet when they are no longer hungry.

In humans, Maslow noted, this behavior is even more common:

> It is possible to tempt almost any person to eat further, even if he is already sated, provided that he be offered food that is especially tempting . . . Certainly, primary hunger is no longer present at the end of a heavy dinner; nevertheless, ice cream is gladly eaten where bread or soup or potatoes may be entirely refused.

Maslow's point was that hunger and appetite are different, and that researchers must take this dichotomy into account in designing future experiments with animals. Although he did not move beyond this discussion to reach a more general theory of motivation (this would come in the early 1940s), Maslow's understated position was clearly an empirically based rejection of the dominant behaviorist psychology of the time. He was affirming that animal behavior cannot be understood as motivated only by the need to gratify sheer drives for survival. And if the actions of monkeys and apes could not be explained in this way, neither could those of our own species.

During this period, Maslow also participated with Stagner and Harlow in a research problem involving dogs. Its purpose was to test a widely believed behaviorist view: that learning takes place within the animal's sensorimotor system. Their method was to paralyze dogs with curare, an anesthetic, then assess their learning while they were unable to move and were breathing by artificial respiration. Harlow was already done with the project, but his two tireless assistants continued the study, modified to their own purposes. It was one of Maslow's few laboratory experiments, as opposed to his naturalistic or observational work with animals.

During 1932–1933, Maslow's interest in Freudian psychology was awakened. The catalyst was Kimball Young, a social psychology professor at Wisconsin. Although Young was probably more disparaging than laudatory when he discussed Freud (who was at the apex of his long career in Vienna at the time), it was on his recommendation that Maslow read *The Interpretation of Dreams*, Freud's landmark work. Maslow experienced the book as a revelation. "The reason I was so impressed with [it] was that it fitted with my experience and nothing else did that had been offered me. Also, I could see in new ways things I hadn't seen before."

Maslow's discovery of Freudian theory soon led him to Alfred Adler's writings, which he also found exciting. Both thinkers offered convincing arguments about the basic motivation for human behavior. Freud insisted that unconscious sexual impulses underlie all of our actions. Adler emphasized our hidden striving for mastery and power. Which conceptual system was more accurate and which, as a psychologist, should Maslow adopt?

Between early 1932 and early 1933, Maslow kept mulling over the equally attractive but seemingly antagonistic theories of Freud and Adler. He had the vague wish to put them to the test, but how? Harlow, his research mentor, would not allow any psychology thesis that was not carried out with animal research. To extrapolate such notions as Freud's Oedipus theory to dogs, or Adler's concept of sibling rivalry to monkeys, seemed farfetched and hopeless.

As Maslow reviewed his observational notes on the Vilas Park Zoo monkeys one day, he experienced the "aha!" flash of creative discovery. He realized that he had been accumulating for months detailed data on both sexual and dominance behavior, and that there appeared to be a relationship between them.

In March 1933, Maslow followed Yerkes's suggestion and made a formal application to the National Research Council for a fellowship in biological sciences. He expected to finish his doctoral work at Madison within the year and planned to advance his psychology career with further study of primates. In a seven-page proposal to the National Research Council, Maslow described his ongoing doctoral dissertation, "the object of which is to discover exactly what quantifiable relations exist between the social and sexual behavior of monkeys." His research with monkeys, he contended, had begun to indicate that sexual behavior in primates—and presumably in humans as well—is strongly related to patterns of dominance. "I consider one of the chief merits of my work to be the way in which it suggests new approaches to many vexing problems of human sexual and social relations," Maslow wrote, "particularly those of the marriage state, which also involves a delicate balance of dominance and sexual status."

After affirming his interest in working with Yerkes for a year, Maslow outlined six areas of research that he intended to investigate, focusing on the general topic of dominance and submissiveness in monkeys. One was to study how very young animals come to acquire their dominance status; another called for investigation into the effect of the adult female's sexual cycle on her social life. Maslow's preliminary data had suggested that dominant female monkeys temporarily lose their dominance when they come into heat.

Maslow had high hopes for continuing his ground-breaking research at the prestigious facilities of Yale. He had every reason to believe that he would be found qualified for this work. Several months passed, and Maslow was politely informed by the National Research Council that his application had been rejected. On his personal carbon copy of the research proposal, Maslow wrote, "I was told some years later that I didn't get any grant or fellowships because of anti-Semitism."

In the summer of 1933, Maslow took respite from monkey work by going camping with Professor Richard W. Husband. Bertha had gone back to New York City for the summer, leaving Maslow alone for a few weeks. Husband, a bachelor at the time, was completing his first book, *Applied Psychology,* and believed they could use a break from the rigors of academia. The two young psychologists roughed it in Colorado, Idaho, South Dakota, Utah, and Wyoming. Husband remembers, "I paid all expenses, car, etcetera. He paid only for his own food, which we cooked on a gasoline stove for about sixty cents a day. I can honestly say that we ended that month much better friends. A camping trip, being together twenty-four hours a day, not in luxury surroundings, is a real test of two people. Abe was never a strong person, so . . . without calling attention to it, [I] did three-fourths of the heavy work."

The friendship extended to their mutual academic duties. Through Husband, Maslow got to know psychologist Gardner Murphy at Columbia University, who soon played an important mentoring role in Maslow's budding career.

Back in Madison, Husband decided one day to show a film on animal psychology to his general psychology class. Remembering that Maslow was doing his dissertation on social behavior in monkeys, Husband asked if he might borrow one of Maslow's films of monkeys to show the freshman students. Maslow nodded and motioned to a stack of reels. Husband grabbed one reel at random and hurried to class. He recalls:

> The film opened with two monkeys in a cage. In a few seconds, they became "man and wife" [mated]. So on, eight or ten such episodes. This was fifty years ago, you realize, and the mixed class was shocked. But I couldn't do anything but let the film finish and apologize weakly for not reviewing it before class. This was part of Abe's thesis research, which was on dominance in primates, including sexual dominance.

In the study of dominance and sexuality in monkeys, Maslow had entered an almost wholly unexplored realm. His professors at Madison knew little about the subject, a situation that suited the independent-minded Maslow just fine. In fact, only a few researchers around the world had investigated these intriguing aspects of primate behavior. One who had was

Solly Zuckerman, a young London biologist. In a striking example of how the scientific zeitgeist operates, just as Maslow was developing the link between sexual and dominant behavior in monkeys, Zuckerman, was putting to press his own observations on the importance of dominance in the monkey social order.

Published in 1932, Zuckerman's well-received book, *The Social Life of Monkeys and Apes,* represented the first scientific look at dominance behavior in these species. Maslow found it interesting but concluded that Zuckerman, reflecting a more biological training, had failed to go far enough in delineating the vital role that dominance plays in monkey social relations, especially sexual. Maslow was convinced that a great deal of monkey sexual behavior, such as the incessant heterosexual and homosexual mounting engaged in by both males and females, was actually an expression of dominance-subordination. He thought that to prove this hypothesis experimentally would constitute an exciting and far-reaching dissertation.

With minimal direct supervision from Harlow or anyone else in the department, Maslow carried out his doctoral research in two phases. The first comprised naturalistic observations of monkeys at the Vilas Park Zoo. From February 1932 through May 1933, Maslow spent hours each day unobtrusively taking notes on about thirty-five primates of various species. Their ages ranged from newborn to senility. His purpose was to define and record as accurately as possible every instance of dominance or sexual behavior. He found that dominance behavior in monkeys included preempting foods from others, bullying, mounting, and initiating fights. Subordinate behavior included cringing, passivity under aggression and mounting, and flight from aggression. The sexual behavior seemed endless. As Maslow later recalled, "The screwing went on all the time." It was manifested in a variety of heterosexual physical positions and also involved homosexual relations between both males and females.

Maslow conducted the second, experimental phase of his work between mid-1933 and early 1934. This was the heart of his doctoral research. He built a plywood observation chamber some six cubic feet in size. Then, he assigned twenty monkeys into various same-sex pairs with each matched as closely as possible in size and weight to its partner, because evidence showed that the larger the monkey, the more dominant.

After both monkeys in each pair were deprived of food all day, they were removed from their separate cages and placed together in the observation chamber, and food treats were thrown in. Either Maslow or his assistant carefully recorded their observations for the next twenty minutes. This length of time constituted one experimental trial. Then the monkeys were returned to their respective cages and fed complete meals.

Maslow and his assistant tested twelve monkey pairings, each averaging about twenty trials of observation. As he had anticipated, Maslow found dominance behavior between the two monkeys in each pair, such as over access to the food and sexual interaction. Although caged monkeys are probably more frustrated than those living in the wild, there is little reason to question the general design of Maslow's study. Subsequent naturalistic work at Wisconsin's Primate Laboratory has repeatedly confirmed his broad findings.

In three papers published in 1936, Maslow set forth his results and conclusions. The first two papers correspond closely to the two experimental phases of his doctoral work, while the third is a theoretical exposition on the link between sexual conduct and the dominance hierarchy in monkeys.

In essence, Maslow's initial hypothesis was substantially confirmed. Much of what appears to be sexually motivated contact among monkeys, especially their ceaseless mounting, is an expression of power reflecting each animal's status within the dominance hierarchy. The higher a monkey's dominance position, the more likely it is to mount its subordinates; the lower its position, the more likely it is to be mounted by others. Dominance was usually associated with size, but sometimes a smaller monkey would achieve high dominance through its demeanor. The most dominant monkey, the overlord, could be male or female. If the latter, Maslow observed, she might never be mounted at all because the males feared her. Maslow found noticeable differences in sexually motivated versus dominance-motivated mounting. He also noted that "sexual behavior is used as an aggressive weapon often, instead of bullying or fighting, and is to a large extent interchangeable with these latter power weapons."

From such observations, Maslow advanced an original theory of primate sexuality. He contended that within the monkey social order there exist two distinct but related forces that culminate in sexual relations among individuals: the hormonal urge to copulate, and the need to establish one's dominance with respect to overlords and subordinates. It seemed an inescapable conclusion that a monkey's dominance or power status determined its expression of sexuality, not the other way around. In short, Adler, not Freud, appeared to be more correct—at least by analogy to human life.

However, Maslow wisely refrained from drawing any analogies to human sexual relations. Believing that such comparisons were scientifically premature, he preferred to let others make their own judgments about the study's applicability to human situations. Yet, he excitedly planned to obtain data through further primate research that might enable him to look at human sexuality, such as marital relations, in a new light. He ended his theoretical paper by recommending that Adler's notions about sex and power be reassessed in view of the primate research.

Many decades later, Harlow, by then the leading primate investigator in the United States, commented that Maslow's doctoral work had stood as definitive in the field for approximately thirty years. His finding that dominance among monkeys is established by means of gaze in a rapid, mutual sizing-up, and rarely by resort to fighting, was an especially important contribution. "To say that he was ahead of his time is an understatement of magnificent magnitude."

Even during Maslow's intense experimental work with monkeys and dogs, he maintained a sharp interest in human personality research. From his primate observations and his close reading of Adler's writings, Maslow became especially intrigued about the nature of dominance in our own species. He believed he had discovered an extremely important though little recognized force in social relations. In a sense, his later studies of self-actualizing people can be traced back to this initial focus on the "strongest" individuals within the human social order. Maslow was most interested in the characteristics of dominant women. With his friend Lucien Hanks and others, he spent many stimulating hours attempting to define their qualities. Throughout Maslow's life, he was fascinated with and highly attracted to bright and articulate women.

In their efforts to identify dominant women, Hanks encouraged Maslow to look at style of dress as a statement of self-expression. Presumably, the more dominant the woman, the more eye-catching her clothing. To test their hypothesis, they ventured down to Madison's lakefront area to observe how dominant women (ones they knew from the university) presented themselves in bathing suits. Undoubtedly, there were many stalwart University of Wisconsin males eyeing the coeds on warm spring days, but Maslow and Hanks were probably the only ones doing so under the aegis of science.

During Maslow's peak years of animal research, he developed a keen interest in hypnosis as "a royal road to knowledge and a necessary kind of research." In the fall of 1933, he and his friend Rod Menzies conducted several experimental sessions with a female student identified in Maslow's handwritten records as "Adele." The sessions were rather mundane tests of her degree of hypnotizability. Nevertheless, Maslow felt obligated to be secretive about such work because of its taboo status in American academia. "There was a university rule that hypnosis was forbidden, on the ground, I gather, that it did not exist. But I was so certain that it did exist (because I was doing it), and I was so convinced of [its importance] that I did not mind lying or stealing or hiding." Until well into the 1970s, orthodox psychology dismissed hypnosis as the pseudoscience of stage magicians, charlatans, and faith healers. Only recently has hypnosis been deemed worthy of respectable therapeutic use and scientific investigation.

Maslow maintained a strong interest in hypnosis throughout the 1930s. Although he never embarked on formal research on this subject, he was one of the few academic psychologists in the United States to take it seriously in a scientific way. He corresponded on theoretical concerns with Milton Erickson, an isolated investigator then, who has come to acquire almost legendary posthumous status as the "father of modern hypnosis" and a near-wizard in its therapeutic application.

By the spring of 1934, Maslow had completed the requirements for his doctorate in psychology at the University of Wisconsin. Although exhilarated with his monkey results and plans for follow-up, Maslow had a more pressing concern: to find a pertinent job in the depths of the Depression. His friend Ross Stagner, who had received his doctorate in 1932 and had superb research credentials, had been able to obtain only a one-year postdoctoral fellowship and then had been unemployed for nearly a year. There was no money for new teaching or research jobs, and few people were leaving the jobs they had.

At the time, an "old-boy" network dominated academic hiring practices. Mainly through word of mouth, Professor A would hear of an impending opening in Professor B's department. The two would exchange letters, perhaps get together over drinks at a convention. Names would be dropped, then a suitable applicant from Professor A's graduate program would be approached informally and, if found acceptable, offered the position. As might be expected from this method of staffing, many psychology departments in the 1930s were suffering from academic inbreeding: a psychologist would eventually teach at the university where he had obtained his degree and later hire other graduates from the same ranks.

The University of Wisconsin's graduate psychology program had an excellent reputation, and Maslow had distinguished himself with journal publications and an original research thrust. He was also outgoing and friendly. But the "old-boy" network was a decided handicap to Maslow in the respect of his Jewish background. A few college departments at the time were willing to hire a Jew if he (even more rarely she) were exceptionally agreeable in every other aspect. But many, perhaps most, would under no circumstances consider a Jew for permanent appointment. They would sooner let a position go unfilled.

Maslow's professors again suggested that he change his first name to improve his career prospects, but he adamantly refused. Bertha, quite serious, threatened to divorce him if he did so. In Maslow's perception, they honestly tried their best to help him land a college teaching position, but he was turned down for about a dozen openings around the country.

Maslow's heart remained set on further work as an academic psychologist, but he and Bertha could not live on air. Seeing no other choice, he decided to enroll in medical school. On September 24, 1934, he was accepted into the University of Wisconsin's medical school in a two-year program, since he had already completed related coursework and obtained his doctorate in an allied discipline. He had no real interest in a career as a practicing physician but vaguely planned to combine the M.D. and Ph.D. degrees into a research position. Meanwhile, he continued to teach introductory psychology as a teaching fellow.

The year's turn of events was depressing for him. It was the first real failure he had experienced since coming to Wisconsin six years before, and his attitude toward medical training was mostly one of resignation. On the positive side, Maslow needed to register for only two required courses, both in anatomy, for he had already taken physiology and physiological chemistry.

He soon discovered that his heart was not in medical studies, which were far more demanding physically and emotionally, if not intellectually, than his psychological research. Throughout his life, it was characteristic of Maslow to quit anything that bored him or did not "feel right" for him, rather than to struggle on in self-conflict. Medical school was one example. Reminiscing in his diary decades later, he telegraphically recalled, "Violently disinterested year of medical school—no go, although attracted to parts of it. Had to leave medical school, partly because of huge amount of time required for anatomy course which bored me—all rote."

Maslow's medical school transcript shows that while he achieved a B in one anatomy course, he dropped the other without officially withdrawing and therefore failed. He did not bother to register for the winter semester beginning in February 1935.

One reason for Maslow's dissatisfaction with medical school was his reaction to patient care. As part of his training, he worked for several weeks at a clinic affiliated with the medical school. Sentimental and sensitive by temperament, Maslow found it difficult to dissociate himself from the pain and distress of his patients. One day, he was called upon to assist in giving a blood transfusion to a young girl who kept crying. Unable to withstand her anguish, he decided at that moment that being a physician was not for him.

Maslow's single term of medical training left him with a lasting concern about the health care system's attempts to banish or deny tender feelings and compassion in treating suffering individuals. The experience raised for him the even larger question of why the emotion of tenderness is taboo in our culture, rarely acknowledged, much less expressed.

Nearly thirty years after this experience, Maslow vividly described his medical training in an informal lecture in March 1965 entitled "The Taboo of Tenderness: The Disease of Valuelessness."

I was in medical school about thirty years ago, and things were different then. There was a depression. Life was real. Life was earnest. It was quite a different atmosphere, and it was only in the medical school that there were some efforts at desacrilization of the following sorts.

I didn't consciously realize it then, but in retrospect it seems clear to me that my professors were almost deliberately trying to harden us—to "blood us," as you say with training animals—to teach us to confront death and pain and disease in a cool, objective, unemotional manner. For physicians, that has some sense, even though I don't buy it altogether.

The first operation I ever saw—I remember it well—was almost paradigmatic in its efforts to desacrilize: that is, to remove the sense of awe, privacy, fear, and shyness before the sacred and the forbidden, and of humility before the tremendous, and the like.

A woman's cancerous breast was to be amputated with an electrical scalpel. It cuts by burning to prevent metastasis . . . Half the kids there got nauseous. The surgeon made carelessly cool and casual remarks about the pattern of his cutting, paying no attention to the [freshman] medical students rushing out in distress. Finally, he cut off the breast, tossing this object off through the air onto a marble counter where it landed with a plop.

I have remembered that plop for thirty years. It had changed from a sacred object into a lump of fat, garbage, to be tossed into a pail. There were, of course, no prayers, no rituals or ceremonies of any kind, as there most certainly would be in most preliterate societies . . . Here, this was handled in a purely technological fashion: the expert was emotionless, cool, calm, with even a slight tinge of swagger.

The atmosphere was about the same when I was introduced—or rather, *not* introduced—to the dead man I was to dissect. I had to find out for myself what his name was. Somehow, I felt that I had to. He had been a lumberman. He was killed in a fight. This was a young man, and I had to learn finally to treat him as everyone else did: not as a person, but as a cadaver. That is a different category.

So also for the dogs that I had to kill. I think they did this deliberately. We had to kill dogs needlessly in my physiology class. We used to practice surgery and experiments of various sorts. And again, this was to be cool as you killed these beautiful animals, when we had finished with our demonstrations or experiments.

The new medics themselves tried to make their deep feelings manageable and controllable, not only by suppressing their fears, their compassion, their tender feelings which were just below the surface, but even their tears. Plenty of times we felt like crying, as we identified with patients, with their diseases, with their awe before stark life and death.

Since they were young men, they did this in adolescent ways. For instance, getting photographed while eating a sandwich while being seated on a cadaver. That was standard protocol, a standard procedure. We nearly all did that. I didn't, but most medical students did that . . . casually pulling a human hand out of the briefcase at the restaurant table, or making standard jokes about the private recesses of the body.

Certainly, we had to physically examine girls. Well, that was easy, because there was a standard form for it. But it touched you when you had to make a rectal examination of a father— in effect, your father—or to make a vaginal examination of a mother—in effect, your mother or your grandmother—

which we had to learn to do and which simply could not be managed very well. This was somehow a sacred act, somehow sacred places.

If you've read Freud, you must know how profound the feelings are that are aroused by such a procedure. Yet everybody tried to make jokes about it. I don't remember anybody's admitting to any emotion of any kind about all of this ... The casualness, the unemotionality—all of them covering over their opposites—this was all thought to be necessary since tender emotions might interfere with the objectivity and the fearlessness of the physician. I'm not sure it was necessary.

Clearly, Maslow was not emotionally suited to medical training. His heart was still in experimental research. He had already committed six years to psychological training and had begun to distinguish himself in this work. But how was he to secure an appropriate position? If nothing came through, what would he do?

CHAPTER FIVE

Explorer of Sex
and Dominance

*I thought that working on sex was the easiest
way to help mankind. If I could discover a
way to improve the sexual life by even one
percent, then I could improve the whole
[human] species.*

—*A.M.*

After he dropped out of medical school,
Maslow's life fell to its lowest ebb in several years. He continued to teach classes as a psychology fellow at the University
of Wisconsin, but that had been intended only as a temporary
position to offer a modicum of income while he was studying
to become a physician. In the dead center of the Depression,
Maslow knew that jobs for experimental psychologists, particularly Jewish ones, were almost nonexistent. Such tensions
began to strain his relations with Bertha. Commenting in his
diary about their conflict, he noted, "We had no money at all
this year—worse than ever before."

In March 1935, Maslow was devoting nearly all his available hours to preparing a second major presentation based on
his doctoral findings. That coming fall, the American Psychological Association's annual convention would be held at the
University of Michigan in Ann Arbor, bringing together most
of the leading psychologists in the country. Maslow had submitted a successful proposal and was scheduled to participate
in a research symposium on animal psychology chaired by the
eminent Edward L. Thorndike of Columbia University.

The paper, "Dominance-drive as a Determiner of Social
Behavior in Infra-human Primates," was Maslow's most ambitious and potentially important work yet. He was amassing
evidence to argue that dominance-drive is a key determinant

of social behavior and organization not only among monkey species but also among other mammals and birds. In a sense, he was formulating a metatheory based on dominance-drive to account for much social behavior among higher animals. With the heightened visibility this important presentation might bring, he hoped to land a job.

Then, suddenly, Maslow received word from Edward L. Thorndike at Columbia University. He was so impressed with Maslow's research skill and his findings on primate dominance, although he disagreed with some of the specific interpretations, that he offered him a postdoctoral fellowship. The position would entail assisting Thorndike on his new research project, "Human Nature and the Social Order," at the Institute of Educational Research.

Maslow was elated about the prospect of an exciting research position in New York City, and he was grateful to Columbia psychologist Gardner Murphy for lobbying on his behalf. Maslow did not know it until years later, but Murphy had nearly jeopardized his own academic position by pressing for the hiring of a Jew. On April 23, Maslow wrote in his diary, "For the first time, my future looks hopeful—almost bright."

Maslow was gaining a measure of public acclaim for his monkey studies. On May 9, the *Milwaukee Sentinel* ran a front-page story on the intriguing research. In the newspaper photograph, Maslow gazes at a small monkey cradled in his arms. The caption reads, "A. H. Maslow, psychologist at the state university, is being hailed as the author of an 'epochal' piece of research work on the subject of social structure among monkeys. He is shown above in his laboratory with one of the subjects of his experiments."

In July, official word came about Maslow's new position in a letter signed by the dean of Teachers College: Maslow was appointed scientific assistant in the Division of Education at Thorndike's Institute of Educational Research. The position would last from August 1, 1935, through June 30, 1936. The salary was the munificent sum of $1650—or $150 a month.

In the economic straits of the Depression, this salary was quite a coup. At the time, New York City's schoolteachers were earning approximately $35 a week under far less luxurious working conditions. If their relationship worked out successfully, Thorndike told Maslow, a permanent teaching position at Sarah Lawrence College in nearby Bronxville might be in the offing. On July 31, just before leaving the Midwest after seven years, Maslow wrote in his diary: "How different things look! A fat fellowship at Columbia with good possibilities of a job after that. Respect from all the departments. Certain of the affection of my friends! Going to meet fine people next year! My paper is working out beautifully!"

Maslow and Bertha settled into a pleasant apartment off 110th Street in Manhattan near Columbia. He felt that Thorndike had rescued him from the Depression itself.

Soon after coming to work for Thorndike, Maslow underwent a battery of intellectual and scholastic-aptitude tests. Thorndike had pioneered such testing and still exerted great influence in the field. His colleagues at Teachers College, Irving Lorge and Ella Woodyard, administered to Maslow a variety of tests, including the CAVD that they had helped develop. (The test's initials referred to four sets of tasks: (verbal) completions, arithmetical problems, vocabulary, and directions.) As Maslow recollected, "They gave me tests until I was blue in the face, tested for weeks." When they finished testing, they told Maslow only that he had done well.

"Human Nature and the Social Order" was a five-year research project begun in 1933, funded by a $100,000 grant from the Carnegie Foundation, an impressive sum for social science study in those days. The project marked the culmination of Thorndike's long, prestigious career. The research involved a team effort to explore "the nature and control of the fundamental psychological forces operating in the world of work and welfare of man." It was based on Thorndike's conviction that modern psychology could provide public leaders with information valuable for effective and "scientific" policy-making in social affairs like education, welfare, and criminology.

Politically, Thorndike was a moderate who had faith in science's ability to solve the massive problems of the Depression in a rational, pure-minded way. He believed that a thorough understanding of such alleged social instincts as gregariousness, mothering behavior, and the hunting instinct in males, and even more vaguely defined traits like dominance and submissiveness, could form the basis for intelligent decisions to eliminate illiteracy, poverty, crime, and war. In the excitement of Franklin D. Roosevelt's New Deal, the concept of social planning, sometimes called social engineering, had its most fervent exponents.

Thorndike's grant authorized him to hire several research assistants. Maslow's assignment was "to determine the relative percentages of hereditary versus environmental influences concerning a variety of human social behaviors." After only a few weeks, Maslow grew bored and impatient and began to procrastinate in the data analyses for which he had been hired. Temperamentally, he was incapable of persisting in any activity that he disliked, and "Human Nature and the Social Order" simply did not make much sense to him; virtually all human endeavors seemed a mixture of both genetic and cultural factors.

But there was also a more emotional aspect to Maslow's recalcitrance: he was still very much involved with his own highly original research on primate dominance and sexuality. It is unlikely that in this early stage of his career Maslow would have enjoyed being assistant to anyone rather than director of his own research program.

The safest way to object to Thorndike's project appeared to be in scholarly terms. Giving much thought to the possible consequences, Maslow wrote his supervisor-benefactor a pointed rebuttal to the entire concept of "Human Nature and the Social Order."

Maslow's memorandum was entitled "A Statement on the Instinct Problem: Submitted to Dr. E. L. Thorndike." The brief paper sheds an interesting light on Maslow's intellectual stance at the time. He began by asserting, somewhat tenaciously, "I feel a summary statement of personal views to be necessary if my future papers on instinct are to be at all intelligible, since any statement . . . on innate human nature is so completely dependent on the viewpoint of its author." Then, a bit cavalierly, he added, "I feel this to be true [despite] the fact that my views with respect to this problem are in a state of flux."

Basing his argument on several broad areas of research, encompassing biology, psychology, and anthropology, Maslow insisted that the major issue for a project like "Human Nature and the Social Order" is not whether a human behavior like gregariousness originates in heredity or environment, but how easily the behavior can be modified. "If a certain connection between a stimulus and a response is very easily broken, it seems to me to make little difference whether or not it be genetically or environmentally determined."

Maslow proceeded to map out his own position with respect to the "nature vs. nurture" controversy that so intrigued Thorndike. "Human nature is not indefinitely malleable," Maslow declared. "Certain drives there are, and satisfied they will be in one way or another, regardless of the governmental, economic, and social taboos extant at the time."

The above phrasing perhaps owes more to Maslow's parental Yiddish inflection than to his academic scholarship, but his meaning was plain enough. He then affirmed the view he had first raised in his animal food-preference studies. Conceding that every species has certain innate motivations for behavior, Maslow insisted that the higher the species on the phylogenetic tree, the less important its species-wide drives or instincts; and, simultaneously, the more salient the *differences* in the impulses among individual members of the same species. He wrote:

> This is not to say that there are no original stimuli and responses to drives, but rather that these are modifiable to a high degree. They may be obscured, overlaid, or completely replaced by other stimuli and responses . . . In other words, a culture must deal with drives but it may do so in many ways; no one way is necessarily called for by original nature although the degree of necessity varies with drive. The hunger drive may be satisfied by many more objects than would be capable of satisfying the sex drive.

> This modifiability of stimulus and response to drive is apparently less true for animals than it is for humans . . . I have found an increasing variability in so simple a function as food preference from hens to rats to monkeys to men . . . The stimulus and responses to a drive grow more and more modifiable as we go up the evolutionary scale.

Maslow ended his paper with the remark, "This viewpoint differs from your 1913 statement [on instincts], chiefly in a change of emphasis and its . . . pragmatic character."

Maslow knew he was being arrogant in presenting this memorandum, which he later characterized as intellectually "snotty" in tone. A more timid subordinate might have deferentially asked for an appointment to discuss his job duties. But this was never Maslow's way. Moreover, he had already jeopardized his position by beginning unauthorized research on human sexuality and dominance. Without informing Thorndike, Maslow recalled, "I was [already] interviewing females in his office, and everybody was scandalized."

Thorndike summarily summoned him to his office. Maslow half expected to be fired, and he now realized that if he lost this position, in the depths of the Depression, he would be unlikely to find another.

But Thorndike was an unusual man. He revealed that the CAVD exam had shown Maslow to have an astounding IQ of 195; in the other tests Maslow had taken, he had made the second-highest score ever recorded. Thorndike promised a stunned Maslow he would support him for the rest of his life if he were unable to secure a permanent job. Then, he told Maslow frankly, "I dislike your work [on dominance and sexuality], I wish you wouldn't do it, but if I don't have faith in my intelligence tests, who will? And I'll assume that if I give you your head, it'll be the best for you and for me—and for the world."

With that remark, Thorndike put his office and desk at Maslow's disposal and told him to do whatever he pleased. He could come in once a month to pick up his paycheck. Having said that much, Thorndike then terminated the meeting.

Maslow initially found the news of his genius-level IQ disturbing. He had never considered himself quite so bright. Decades later, he recalled, "I went off dazed . . . walked [Manhattan's] streets for days trying to assimilate this . . . He made me feel important. Thereafter, if I retreated in the face of [intellectual] opposition, I'd [sometimes] wake up in the middle of the night and say, 'But dammit, I'm smarter than he is. Why should I feel that he's right and I wrong?' "

For the rest of Maslow's life, he regarded his IQ as a mark of triumph. At parties and social gatherings, he liked to spark conversation by casually inquiring about someone's IQ and then volunteering his own. He once asked his Brandeis colleague Max Lerner, the well-known political analyst, "Do you know what your IQ is?" "No, I don't think so," replied Lerner. "Don't worry," Maslow assured him, "it's probably almost as high as mine." Few in Maslow's circle of acquaintances did not hear about his IQ score. Perhaps an emotional insecurity born of his iconoclasm in psychology, especially as the voice for "tender-minded" or humanistic concerns, compelled him to mention his IQ as if defending his acumen.

With the intellectual freedom that Thorndike's remarkable arrangement offered, Maslow hoped to develop his career in experimental psychology with primates. In the fall, he wrote to the National Research Council reaffirming his desire to obtain a fellowship for further laboratory study of dominance and sexuality. On November 11 he received the curt reply, "Your application for a fellowship submitted in 1934 is still on file"; he was asked to reapply if he wished to be considered for the coming year. Maslow then entertained the notion of leaving Thorndike's Institute and obtaining a research position among local pediatric clinics or maternity hospital units, but Thorndike's fierce opposition forced him to abandon that idea. Having no alternative in sight, Maslow decided to go ahead with his interviews in the study of human sexuality and behavioral dominance.

Maslow's motive for such unconventional (by the standards of the time) psychological research, was largely a scientific interest in following up his ground-breaking work with monkeys. He believed that much human sexual activity was subordinate to the drive for dominance, and he wanted to test his hunch. He also had a more personal and humanitarian goal. As his unpublished papers from the early 1930s reveal, he was extremely critical of the taboo-laden outlook that dominated mainstream sexual mores in American society. For most youngsters and adults alike, he felt, sex was enshrouded in silence and secrecy, a situation that led to mass-scale anxieties, shame, and embarrassment. As he later recollected, "I thought that working on sex [by gathering data on sexual behavior] was the best way to help the world. If I could discover a way to improve the sexual life by even one percent then I could improve the whole species."

Before embarking on his sexological research in late 1935, Maslow reviewed the previous scientific work in the field. His enthusiasm was probably buoyed by the realization that he was entering largely unknown territory in psychology. Freud and Havelock Ellis had been the founders of modern sexual study, although their approaches had little in common. Freud had developed his ideas in the 1890s and early 1900s almost entirely from the case histories of a small sample of affluent Viennese women psychiatric patients. Unlike Freud, Ellis had been a timid man who could not bear to talk face-to-face about sex. Consequently, his work depended almost entirely on letters from well-educated Englishmen. Of the other researchers, like Wilhelm Stekel and Richard von Krafft-Ebing, who had led the way in studying sex over the previous half century, none was American.

It was not until 1915 that an American physician named J. M. Exner was courageous enough to question nearly one thousand male college students, through mailed surveys, about their sex lives. Exner asked only eight questions, too few to obtain a detailed picture of their sexual behavior, but his study marked the beginning of sexual research in the United States. The pace of such exploration was hardly intense; as of 1935, there had been little more than a dozen published sexological reports. Nearly all had relied upon written questionnaires, a notoriously poor way to get reliable data in this largely taboo realm.

The major exception, Maslow found, was a study by G. V. Hamilton published in 1929. Originally entitled *A Research in Marriage,* it later emerged as a popularization called *What's Wrong with Marriage?* Hamilton had employed face-to-face directed interviews with questions written on cards. He had interviewed 100 married men and an equal number of married women, all from New York City. Twenty-one percent were undergoing psychoanalysis—hardly a representative cross section of the American population, in either social class or mental health. Hamilton had been trained as a psychiatrist but his initial research background, like Maslow's, had involved the study of monkeys. Hamilton's work also had been courageous. As late as the early 1930s, at least two American psychology departments had fired researchers because the administrators were not yet ready to look objectively at sex.

Maslow began his interviews undaunted. He looked forward to the challenge of trailblazing such psychological terrain. Since he held no teaching position at Columbia, not even as a lowly section assistant, obtaining interviewees was no easy task. Initially, he relied on friends among the graduate students and then allowed word of mouth to take its course. Thus, most of Maslow's interviewees were middle-class, college-educated people in their twenties, married, white, and Protestant. He realized that such a sample was not statistically representative of the wider population but felt that in exploratory research, the issue was not significant. In a sense, he was right.

At first, Maslow conducted his interviews in a tentative manner. He hardly knew what to ask, other than to pose questions that might help him compare sex and dominance in humans with that of monkeys. To assess human sexuality, Maslow had only the few prior, largely flawed studies as his foundation; and to identify and measure human equivalents of dominant and subordinate monkey behavior, he had no previous work to draw upon. Gradually, Maslow began to focus his questions as he acquired a clearer picture of dominance behavior, such as posture and gait, in our own species.

At the same time, Maslow realized that a major obstacle in this research was his interview method. While he had been able to objectively measure the monkeys' sexual and social acts at the Bronx and Vilas Park zoos, he now had to rely mainly on the highly subjective self-reports of his human subjects for data. For this reason, he decided to pinpoint their *attitude* or emotional tendency to dominate—what he termed their dominance-feeling. This trait, which Maslow likened to self-confidence, would be far easier to determine in an interview than actual, everyday behavior.

This decision did not end Maslow's difficulties. He was still faced with the dilemma of how to determine accurately the subjects' sexual activity. Most of the women seemed honest and open, once they had chosen to reveal their personal lives to him; but the men were far more evasive and tended to lie, exaggerate, or distort their sexual experiences. After interviewing about fifteen men, Maslow decided to engage only women as subjects. His motive was not entirely scientific. As he much later confided, "I was still sort of young, and got a thrill of excitement interviewing the women."

With each interviewee, Maslow initially sought to establish good rapport. If she appeared overly anxious or suspicious, he terminated the interview. But if a mutual rapport seemed to develop, he offered a short explanation of the interview's general purpose. He warned the woman that many questions would be embarrassing, some extremely so, and that the procedure might be emotionally upsetting. He was not exaggerating. The items inquiring about dominance-feeling were mild enough; for example, "Do you ever like to feel smarter than a man you date? Do you feel superior to most women you know?" But the sexually oriented questions, would be considered intrusive, even by today's standards. These included, "What kinds of men do you find most sexually attractive? How often do you masturbate? What particular fantasies do you experience while masturbating? What are your physical preferences during lovemaking?"

After obtaining a broad picture of their personal tastes, habits, and lifestyles, Maslow slowly progressed to intimate questions about sexual attitudes, desires, fantasies, and experiences. Since he had found a significant relation between monkeys' copulatory postures and their dominance status, he also asked what sexual positions the woman preferred. With this innovative, semiclinical research technique, he typically spent close to fifteen hours over a period of days with each interviewee.

Not all were eager or willing to tell him about their most private side. As Maslow's research progressed through late 1935 and early 1936, he noticed a frustrating pattern. While women high or moderate in dominance-feeling were usually cooperative in submitting to the embarrassing interviews—some even volunteering after hearing about Maslow—almost none who seemed low in dominance-feeling volunteered or completed the interview. Low-dominance women frequently refused to continue with the interview despite hours of patient reassurance. Maslow sometimes pleaded with them to cooperate "for the good of science," usually to no avail.

To make his study worthwhile, Maslow knew he had to incorporate interviews with at least a few women low in dominance. To find willing participants became his top priority at Columbia's Teachers College. He developed a rough test of dominance-feeling (or self-confidence) that could be administered by paper and pencil to large numbers of people in just a few minutes. In this way, he could readily find the interviewees needed. Maslow called it the Social Personality Inventory for College Women. Its questions included, "Do you often feel that you get enough praise? When you meet people for the first time, do you usually feel they will not like you? Are you a good conversationalist?" He steadily refined it over the next few years.

While conducting his intriguing interviews, Maslow also carried out a more conventional investigation under Thorndike's supervision. The only effort at which the two worked together, it was a relatively minor study in both design and results, entitled "The Influence of Familiarization on Preference." Maslow submitted it for publication in the fall of 1936. In his introductory remarks, he wrote, "This experiment was made at the suggestion of Dr. E. L. Thorndike and under his direction. He is not responsible, however, for the form of this paper and its conclusions."

In essence, Maslow's goal was to investigate the effect of repetition on our liking for a specific object or task. Over a succession of days, he presented college women with seventeen different sets of simple stimuli and activities, such as looking at certain paintings, copying specified sentences, and reading certain foreign words. In conclusion, he found that some commonplace tasks seem to become more likable or agreeable because of sheer exposure, whereas others do not.

The research was notable in one respect: it was Maslow's first study since 1930 to involve humans rather than dogs or monkeys. Fifteen Barnard College students served as experimental subjects. The work with Thorndike also heightened Maslow's sensitivity to the importance of precision and attention to detail in scholarly or scientific endeavor. Many years later, he fondly recalled Thorndike's guidance:

> He urged me, made me, plan the whole thing out in advance, with a timetable worked out to the minute before I ever started. I realize now that if I had done it any other way, it just wouldn't have amounted to anything. He was right and I was wrong in the approach to that particular experiment.

Satisfied that he had taught Maslow something about experimental research, Thorndike did not assign him any further tasks. But the two got along well, and Thorndike frequently invited the Maslows to parties at his home. An old-fashioned man who wore slippers and an evening jacket around the house, Thorndike was not one to throw wild parties. Typical soirees consisted of playing with his guests all kinds of IQ-test-like word and arithmetic games. At the Institute of Educational Research, Thorndike watched over Maslow in what his protégé regarded as a fatherly fashion.

Thorndike believed that true scientific creativity is most likely to manifest itself when individuals have the time and opportunity to explore their own interests at their own pace. His preferred method of supervision, therefore, was to find promising young scholars and help them develop through an enlightened laissez-faire policy. Thus, while Thorndike could not bring himself to discuss with Maslow, even on an intellectual plane, the interviews on women's dominance and sexual behavior, he insisted on Maslow's right to chart his own course.

Coupled with this farsighted perspective in Thorndike's personality was a gentlemanly demeanor that Maslow found endearing. "He taught me much about kindness and nobility that he never put into writing," Maslow noted.

Maslow conducted one other empirical effort during his time at Teachers College. A minor collaboration with Walter Grether, who had been an undergraduate friend at the University of Wisconsin, it marked Maslow's last experimental work with animals. It was designed mainly by Maslow but carried out by Grether and an assistant at the new Primate Laboratory in Madison in the fall of 1935. The purpose of the limited study involving eleven monkeys was to examine "the solution of a noninstrumental problem [of learning] involving the synthesis of two separate situations." The findings affirmed that primates show significant individual differences in problem-solving abilities. In other words, some monkeys are smarter than others.

Meanwhile, Maslow continued his interviews on human sexuality and dominance. By January 1937, he had completed work with about one hundred women and fifteen men. That month, he submitted for publication the first of several papers on his emerging findings. "Dominance-feeling, Behavior, and Status" first defined and highlighted each of these three facets of human social behavior. Besides briefly outlining his results, Maslow discussed the practical scientific problem of accurately studying human dominance. Perhaps most interesting, he also speculated on how our degree of dominance-feeling affects our daily life, such as in work and marriage. Emphasizing the influence of social values in shaping male-female relations, he observed, "The very definite training that most women in our culture get in being 'ladylike' (nondominant) exerts its effect forever afterward."

Maslow ended his article by identifying several kinds of social behavior that appear common to both monkeys and humans. Although he stressed the influence of culture in affecting our social behavior, he wrote:

> It is interesting to note the indications of a few universal ways of expressing dominance and subordination. For instance, so far as our study has taken us, we have found no group in the world where kneeling, bowing, or prostrating oneself before another person is an expression of dominance. These and similar forms of behavior express *only* subordination in all those cases in which they have any social [or] personal meaning at all. The same tendency [exists] in monkeys (for the dominant animal to be above the subordinate), [suggesting] a deeper significance in this trend than would appear on the surface.

Maslow was hinting that human beings possess a certain biological core to our nature that cultural and historical forces can affect or modify but not override. Throughout the rest of his career, Maslow came to emphasize our innate emotional and spiritual capacities. First, however, he embraced the far more fashionable social science doctrine of cultural relativism.

During the next few years, Maslow published several studies based on his face-to-face interviews with women. The first was submitted in January 1938 and appeared in print the following year. "Dominance-feeling, Personality, and Social Behavior in Women" was aimed at establishing the importance of dominance-feeling in human personality functioning and relations. Maslow identified related traits including shyness, timidity, inhibition, modesty, and conventionality. For these and other aspects of social conduct, the women's particular degree of dominance-feeling strongly affected their daily lives.

High-dominance women tended to be more socially independent and self-confident and rarely embarrassed before others. Intriguing to Maslow, they also were more unconventional in their attitudes, including those relating to sexuality. They preferred unconventional people as friends, and disdainfully rejected popular stereotypes about how "ladies" should behave in the family setting or at the workplace. In contrast, low-dominance women were more shy, passive, inhibited, and conventional in their attitudes, sexual and otherwise.

In 1940, Maslow published information about his new test, the Social Personality Inventory, designed to objectively measure dominance-feeling (which he now called self-esteem) in college women. Printed and made commercially available by Stanford University two years later, the test became widely used in psychological research. Of the 140 women he had interviewed earlier, he was able to track down and test all but 18.

"Self-esteem (Dominance-feeling) and Sexuality in Women" represented Maslow's last published study on female personality. It appeared in 1942, nearly three years after he had completed his interviews and test work. It is unclear why he waited so long before presenting the results; it may be that his new job and added family responsibilities slowed him.

In this closely reasoned article, Maslow's research prowess is at its best. He utilized several ways to assess women's sexual attitudes and conduct, such as their degree of promiscuity. Although American social mores have certainly changed since the late 1930s, Maslow's observations appear fundamentally valid today. In fact, in the early 1960s, author Betty Friedan cited his sexological studies to help advance the feminist approach to psychology as distinct from the Freudian.

In brief, Maslow found that women experience and regard sexuality very differently depending on their dominance-feeling. Highly dominant women viewed sex more casually, as a pleasurable, physical experience in its own right. Married or single, they were more likely to acknowledge and act upon their sexual feelings, either through masturbation or adventurous lovemaking, in a variety of ways. High-dominance women were also more prone to homosexual and other forms of sexual experimentation, and more accepting of nudity. In contrast, middle-dominance women were rather conventional in their sexual attitudes and behavior. If married, they gladly expressed their sexuality through physical love for their husbands, but otherwise felt little interest in sexual matters. For low-dominance women, sexuality within marriage was seen as an unpleasant duty; if single, they considered sex in ethereal, romantic, "happy-ever-after" terms, while feeling revulsion for the reality of physical nudity and eroticism. To Maslow, therefore, "practically all the books on sexual and love technique make the stupid mistake of assuming that all women are alike in their love demands. Even more absurd, they speak as if the sexual act were merely a problem in mechanics, a purely physical act rather than an emotional one."

His data had important implications for marital happiness, Maslow contended. Ideally, husband and wife should be similar in their degree of dominance for their sexual relationship to be mutually satisfying. Otherwise, spouses will regard and experience this aspect of marriage very differently, and serious problems might arise.

Maslow also noted that the more dominant the woman, the greater her willingness, even eagerness, to reveal her sexual attitudes, desires, and experiences. Therefore, any sexological study based on volunteers "will always have a preponderance of high-dominance people and therefore will show a falsely high percentage of non-virginity, masturbation, promiscuity, homosexuality, etc., in the [wider] population." Even studies based on anonymous surveys appeared of dubious validity, "for it is probable that a far higher percentage of low-dominance individuals will not return their questionnaires." In the mid-1940s, Maslow and sexologist Alfred Kinsey, who relied almost wholly on volunteers' reports for his highly publicized data, would come to much antagonism over this issue (see chapter 9).

At the peak of Maslow's interest in the psychology of human sexuality, he contemplated several major research studies. One idea was to interview female prostitutes for their detailed accounts on this age-old but poorly understood aspect of social-sexual activity. Another plan was to investigate men's sexuality and its relation to traits of dominance-feeling and dominance-behavior. Maslow suspected that this relationship was just as true for men as for women: the more dominant the individual, the more sexually promiscuous. He noted that "sex [becomes] a kind of dominance or subordination behavior or at least a channel through which dominance-subordination may be expressed." Given the attention this topic has come to

arouse in the American political arena since revelations of the
Kennedy brothers' philandering behavior first surfaced, it is
likely that Maslow would have made a cogent, lasting contibu-
tion. However, he never began such ventures. Soon after the
United States entered World War II, he abandoned sexological
research for more global concerns; most notably, the nature of
human motivation and self-actualization.

At the same time, he experienced a personal revelation
that gave him a different perspective on his sexological research. He recalled much later:

> One day, it suddenly dawned on me that I knew as much
> about sex as any man living—in the intellectual sense. I knew
> everything that had been written, I had made discoveries
> with which I was pleased. Then I suddenly burst into laugh-
> ter. Here I was, the great sexologist, and I had never seen an
> erect penis except one, and that was from my own bird's-eye
> view. That humbled me considerably.

During the period that Maslow worked at Teachers College, Thorndike was under treatment for heart disease. His
physician had given him strict orders to avoid overexertion,
especially related to work. One rainy Sunday afternoon, Maslow came to the Institute for Educational Research to do some
research analysis. As he entered the deserted building, he was
startled to see Thorndike entering as well.

Sheepishly, the latter explained that he was there simply
to add columns of figures and to perform other arithmetical
calculations. He enjoyed such activity, he explained, and his
administrative tasks usually kept him from dealing with raw
data. Because the elevator did not operate on Sundays, Thorndike proceeded to mount the stairs. To Maslow, he wore the
look of a small boy caught eating forbidden cookies.

Thorndike sought to help his gifted assistant find a permanent position for 1937. An opening materialized at a nearby
college, and Thorndike confidently made the appropriate
overtures on Maslow's behalf. He was shocked and angered to
learn that because of Maslow's Jewish background, he would
under no circumstances be considered. Thorndike, a tolerant
man, should not have been surprised. His own employer, Columbia University, routinely barred all but a handful of "show-

case" Jewish professors from tenured faculty positions. Some departments, such as English, simply refused to hire any Jews. Fortunately, Maslow did not need to test the sincerity of Thorndike's promise to support him for the rest of his life if necessary. Through the help of Solomon Asch, later acclaimed for his studies of conformity, Maslow was hired by Brooklyn College. The job paid badly and offered only the lowly academic rank of tutor (below instructor), but it was a full-time, tenure-track position. As part of the municipal college system of New York City, Brooklyn College was then one of the few institutions around the country to hire Jews in any significant number. It was not prestigious, but it was at least in familiar territory. He and Bertha moved to a Brooklyn apartment for his new post, which would begin in February 1937.

Thorndike had not had much intellectual influence on Maslow during their year and a half together. Nevertheless, Maslow's position at the Institute for Educational Research marked a milestone in his developing career. As an advanced research assistant with no formal duties, he had time to explore many new areas of interest and to write more than a half-dozen professional papers for publication. Also, his connection with prestigious Columbia University gave him a basis for getting to know older, more established psychology colleagues. Perhaps, if he had met Thorndike at another time, Maslow might have been more collaborative in mood; but in 1935, he was just beginning to establish an independent professional identity and was eager to generate his own program of research and scholarly inquiry. Temperamentally, though, Maslow was incapable of remaining a subordinate to anyone for long. He had to feel that he was on his own in almost everything he did.

Maslow later commented that he had regretted the lack of a coherent social philosophy in Thorndike's well-meaning but ineffectual project, "Human Nature and the Social Order." But Thorndike's striking kindness ("I think that he was practically angelic") and its importance during those Depression years was the greatest reward Maslow experienced at the Institute for Educational Research.

CHAPTER SIX

At the Center of the Psychological Universe

> *[Returning to New York City] was like coming out of the dark into the light. It was like a farm boy coming to Athens. Many of the great European and American originators were available, even to a young student, and I have many of them to thank for their kindness and patience. No young man has ever been so fortunate in his teachers and friends as I.*
>
> —A.M.

*W*hen Maslow returned to New York City in the summer of 1935 after seven years in Wisconsin, he felt a tremendous sense of excitement. Even as a self-conscious teenager, he had skillfully capitalized on New York's unparalleled intellectual resources. With his research position with Thorndike at Columbia and a convenient apartment with Bertha on the Upper West Side, Maslow was eager to broaden his outlook. Although he prized his training in experimental psychology, he had found it intellectually narrow in a way; his midwestern professors had been parochial, sometimes even xenophobic, in disparaging his interest in such contemporary European thinkers as Freud, Alfred Adler, and the Gestalt psychologists. Back in New York, he was free to pursue his own interests unfettered by departmental demands.

During his absence, New York City had become more than ever a center of intellectual discourse. Since Hitler had come to power in Germany two years before, a steady migration of scholars, including leading social scientists and psychoanalysts, had taken place from Central Europe to the United States. By mid-1935, New York was home to a lively community of foreign-born social thinkers.

It was an historically unprecedented situation, and Maslow knew it. Almost immediately upon settling in, he zealously sought out many of these figures. Some were quite famous, like Adler; others, like Erich Fromm, were still obscure. But public notability was of little concern to Maslow. He possessed an intuitive sense of excellence in choosing teachers and mentors during the next few years.

Between 1935 and 1940, Maslow came to know and study with Adler, Fromm, and Karen Horney in the field of psychoanalysis, and Kurt Goldstein, Max Wertheimer, and Kurt Koffka in Gestalt psychology and neuropsychiatry. He also became close with dozens of other émigré social scientists and psychoanalysts. Each mentor treated him somewhat differently, but all exerted a profound effect on his developing career and system of thought. Maslow always looked back with nostalgic fondness, and gratitude, for this marvelous experience in what he aptly described "the center of the psychological universe":

> I never met Freud or Jung, but I did meet with Adler in his home, where he used to run Friday evening seminars, and I had many conversations with him . . . I think it's fair to say that I have had the best teachers, both formal and informal, of any person who ever lived, just because of the historical accident of being in New York City when the very cream of European intellect was migrating away from Hitler. New York City in those days was simply fantastic. There has been nothing like it since Athens. And I think I knew every one of them more or less well.

If New York in the mid-to-late 1930s was like Athens, then its Parthenon was probably the New School for Social Research. From Maslow's recollections, it seems he spent nearly as much time there as at home with Bertha. In the years that Maslow frequented the New School, it was a remarkable place, both for the quality of its faculty and for its atmosphere of intellectual community. It is ironic that the chief American center for many of Europe's greatest social thinkers was not some venerable, ivy-draped university like Harvard, Princeton, or Columbia, but this new and almost wholly unendowed school for adult education, lacking both research facilities and a graduate training program.

Founded in 1919, the New School was composed of a set of brownstone mansions in New York's Chelsea area, west of Broadway and south of Twenty-third Street. From the beginning, the New School intended to provide a haven for radical thinkers, and boasted such distinguished faculty as historian Charles Beard and sociologist Thorstein Veblen. Nearly all of its course offerings lay in public affairs, social science, and social work, and most of its students were college graduates seeking additional credits for job-related study. Despite its academic competence, the New School suffered major financial problems in these early years and was forced to curtail its activities drastically in 1922 until a massive reorganization could be effected.

That year, Alvin Johnson, a gifted and farsighted young academician, took over as director, having been a board member and journalist at *New Republic* magazine and a professor at several prestigious universities. Under his administrative hand, the New School began to grow, and by 1927 he decided to relocate to a building of its own. In January 1931, the New School opened its doors at 66 West Twelfth Street on the edge of Greenwich Village. The neighborhood's bookshops, artists' lofts and studios, and inexpensive restaurants and bars provided a bohemian background for the New School's innovative curriculum. The New School quickly established a reputation among sophisticated New Yorkers as the true intellectual center of the Village, far more so than New York University or Cooper Union, its academic neighbors.

By the spring of 1933, the New School was primarily an experimental institution devoted to adult education and modern art, with a full-time faculty of only four or five. It had been restored to financial solvency and had begun to achieve recognition for scholarly excellence in the social sciences, philosophy, and the arts. The school displayed in its lobby striking murals by Thomas Hart Benton and Jose Clemente Orozco.

That April, the Nazis expelled all Jewish and socialist scholars from their university positions in Germany, and Johnson saw an opportunity for the New School. Within six months, he raised enough money to bring a dozen, and later a score, of the most distinguished refugee scholars to the New School. To accommodate them, he established a self-governing research institute within the New School called the University in

Exile. Johnson thus transplanted a group of German social scientists to the United States and fulfilled his pledge of more than a decade before to build the New School into a major institution for social science thought.

Over the next ten years, the New School became one of the most extraordinary intellectual conclaves in the world. Social scientists, philosophers, and artists from throughout Europe and the Americas grappled with fundamental issues confronting the twentieth century. In contrast to most large American universities, which were quite cool in their welcome to the refugee scholars, the New School represented a veritable haven.

The original twelve refugees who had arrived in 1933 and 1934 were largely responsible for giving the University in Exile its unique character. Nearly all were German men (there was one woman among them) of secular Jewish backgrounds. They were empirically oriented rather than "pure" philosophers. Politically, they were strongly antifascist and left-of-center to varying degrees. The émigrés eventually merged with the New School to become the Graduate Faculty for Social and Political Science. The only psychologist among them was Max Wertheimer, who, with his friend Horace Kallen, helped form the New School's graduate program in philosophy and psychology.

Johnson wanted to ensure that his European faculty did not become an isolated foreign enclave. Therefore, he helped organize the General Seminar, an interdisciplinary weekly meeting in which all the New School's faculty participated. The General Seminar explored a single issue at a time, chosen by the whole faculty; for example, the nature of German and Italian fascism.

Spurred by the General Seminar's success, Johnson helped sponsor a scholarly journal called *Social Research*. The seminar also inspired several faculty members to organize a second regular meeting to focus on methodology of the social sciences. Led by Wertheimer from 1933 to 1943, this methodology seminar complemented the rather politically oriented General Seminar by exploring broader, more philosophical issues like the study of values and epistemology. The entire New School faculty attended Wertheimer's seminar, for they respected him as a creative teacher and brilliant scholar.

Of all the émigré mentors Maslow came to know in New York, he cherished Wertheimer (1880–1943) as his most inspiring teacher. Maslow revered him not only for his incisive intellect but for his warmth, kindness, and unassuming manner, a living example of a self-actualizing person. Because Maslow saw Wertheimer as a key influence upon his own career, it may be worthwhile to examine Wertheimer's life and work in some detail.

Born into a middle-class Jewish family in Prague, Wertheimer was initially interested in a legal career but soon turned to philosophy and psychology, which he studied in Prague, Berlin, and Würzburg. After receiving his doctorate in 1904, he did research at a number of European institutions, and in 1910 he joined the distinguished faculty of the University of Frankfurt. Its social philosophers included Karl Mannheim and Paul Tillich, and its Institute for Social Research boasted such major scholars as Theodore Adorno, Max Horkheimer, and later the young Erich Fromm. As a municipal school, the University of Frankfurt was not subject to centralized control and therefore offered a haven to Jewish scholars during the conservative counterattack against Weimar Germany's cosmopolitanism of the late 1920s.

At Frankfurt, Wertheimer was a congenial and eclectic scholar who wrote on topics ranging from ethics and logic to experimental psychology and the music and language of primitive cultures. His reputation came as the founder of Gestalt psychology. This important approach originated in 1912 with a famous experimental paper on the perception of apparent movement. From the fairly specific findings, Wertheimer, together with his colleagues Kurt Koffka and Wolfgang Köhler (who went on to achieve renown as the cofounders of Gestalt psychology) carried out a host of studies on human perception. Their results led Wertheimer to advance a new and powerful theory of human cognition. Because he emphasized the importance of gestalts or "wholes" in thinking and perceiving, he called the approach Gestalt psychology.

Wertheimer argued that people learn through insight—the "aha!" experience—and not through trial and error, as behaviorists like Pavlov and Watson insisted. What the "aha!" experience entails, Wertheimer contended, is our sudden perception of a gestalt—a whole, a pattern that makes sense. He and his colleagues devised many clever experiments to prove their theory of how we process images and sounds. Some of these, like the hag/pretty woman and vase/human face pictures, are still used to illustrate principles of perception. Another appealing demonstration involved the incomplete melody. Because we form auditory-perceptual gestalts, Wertheimer and his coworkers posited, most of us can readily recognize melodies by hearing only a few notes.

In 1917, Köhler performed his famous study with apes, showing that they, too, have the "aha!" experience in learning. His method was to place a bunch of bananas just beyond a caged ape's reach, and to put a stick on the ground beside it. After unsuccessfully trying to grab the bananas with its bare hands, the animal would suddenly seize the stick and knock down the bananas. This appealing experiment gave much impetus to the Gestalt notion that we learn through insight and not through countless tiny increments. Decades later, the behaviorist and Gestalt viewpoints both came to be absorbed by psychology for their valid contributions about learning.

By the mid-1920s, Wertheimer began to advance a philosophical outlook articulating the Gestalt axiom that the whole is almost always different from the sum of its parts. "There exist natural circumstances in which what happens in the total is not conditioned by the nature of the parts or their mode of combination, but on the contrary, what occurs in any part of this whole is determined by the inner structural laws of this entirety." As Wertheimer told a lecture audience, all of Gestalt psychology is embodied in this formulation.

At the same time, he proposed a new scientific method by which to understand human awareness and its experience of outer reality. He insisted that deductive logic cannot possibly be the only, or even the most important, tool for knowledge of the world. He offered the analogy of a listener to a symphony. No amount of rational analysis of individual parts—violin, bassoon, or drums—can reveal the design of a Beethoven symphony, yet hearing the whole makes the individual parts clear. Wertheimer further taught that trying to think in gestalts is the most effective style of learning, for it involves a process of inner "centering."

In 1933, shortly before Hitler's appointment as chancellor of Germany and the university purges in April, Wertheimer

heard a segment of one of Hitler's radio speeches. After listening closely for a few minutes, he and his wife decided to leave
Germany the next day. He did not wish to raise his young
children in a country where Hitler might be elected chancellor: he had understood Hitler's gestalt. The family moved to
Czechoslovakia, where Wertheimer was contacted several
months later by the New School's officials. That September, he
joined its faculty.

Until his death a decade later, Wertheimer taught all levels of psychology and philosophy at the New School, including
Basic Problems in Psychology, The Psychology of Music and
Art, Gestalt Psychology of Teaching and Learning, Logic and
Scientific Method, and On Better Thinking. He also gave a
number of seminars, including a provocative joint effort on
Power, Domination, and Freedom with Karen Horney. Partly,
because his English was rough, he used a piano to punctuate
his lectures.

From Maslow's first contact with him in 1935, Wertheimer proved to be a unique and inspiring teacher. He responded readily and warmly to Maslow's interest in his work,
and a close, father-son relationship developed. Unlike many of
his rather stiff Germanic colleagues, Wertheimer would get so
excited while lecturing that he sometimes leaped onto a desk
for emphasis. Outside the classroom, he was just as informal
and would think nothing of playing on the floor with his children while Maslow and other colleagues visited. He had a
wonderful wit and could laugh at himself or situations in a
good-natured way.

Maslow also considered Wertheimer a genius as a psychological thinker, so much so that he even attended his introductory psychology course for several years. Unlike Maslow's psychology professors at Wisconsin, Wertheimer exhibited a vast
knowledge of history, philosophy, and the arts in the best
European tradition. Wertheimer was especially stimulating in
his ability to relate philosophical questions—for example,
"Why don't people behave more ethically toward one another?"—to practical problems of modern psychology, such as
the nature of motivation and cognition.

Wertheimer introduced Maslow to the insights of Eastern
thought; his lecture on "Being and Doing" in 1942 exerted a
tremendous effect on Maslow's developing approach to per-

sonality. Wertheimer argued that Western psychology is much too preoccupied with goal-seeking behavior and needs to learn from Eastern thinkers about the "unmotivated" qualities of human experience such as playfulness, wonder, awe, esthetic enjoyment, and the mystical state. On another occasion, a Chinese woman presented a paper on Lao Tzu, the Taoist philosopher and mystic. Maslow then began to read books on Eastern philosophy, especially Taoism.

Wertheimer also offered guidance ·to Maslow on his research projects, such as the studies of dominance-feeling, emotional security, and sexuality. Wertheimer's emphasis on values and their role in human life came to occupy a key place in Maslow's own system of thought. In addition, Wertheimer helped awaken Maslow's interest in the psychology of art and music. In later years, Maslow conducted research and offered theoretical papers reflecting his involvement with this evocative and little-understood realm.

Few other American psychologists of the time were as affected by the Gestalt founder as Maslow was. For one thing, the New School began to train doctoral students only toward the end of Wertheimer's life. Since the school lacked laboratory facilities, he was unable to advance his intriguing ideas experimentally, and strong empiricism has always been the hallmark of American psychology. In addition, because Wertheimer's seminars attracted people from a host of disciplines, he covered a wide range of topics—perhaps too wide—including political issues like European fascism and the future of democracy.

Finally, Wertheimer was simply not a very systematic or prolific researcher. He never produced a serious treatise of Gestalt psychology, leaving that job to others. In fact, he wrote only one book, *On Productive Thinking*, and that was published posthumously in 1945. In Maslow's estimation, Wertheimer's stature as a discoverer of the human mind might have equaled Freud's had be been as forceful and productive an exponent of his own ideas.

He influenced Maslow through class lectures and countless informal conversations, not through his writings. In Maslow's articles during the 1930s and 1940s, he generally cited Wertheimer's unpublished New School lectures or private comments, so it is hard to determine just how Wertheimer helped shape Maslow's evolving work. However, Wertheimer did write several papers during this time that may offer clues as to why Maslow viewed him as a major influence.

"Some Problems in the Theory of Ethics," published in 1935, was a strong attack on the relativist outlook that dominated social science of the time. It was Wertheimer's belief that cultural relativism was a once helpful but now obsolete conceptual development in social science. He posited three relevant stages of thought: in the first, ethnology had mistakenly assumed modern European values like private property or sexual monogamy to be culturally universal; in the second, cultural diversity seemed to demand the embrace of absolute ethical relativism; in the current, third stage, the existence of universal though subtle ethical values was affirmed. Wertheimer recognized the difficulty of determining the nature of these values but insisted that science has both the responsibility and capacity to "clear up the field." This was almost precisely the outlook Maslow would come to espouse.

In this same intriguing article, Wertheimer briefly described the existence of what Maslow twenty-five years later would call peak-experiences. Wertheimer observed that there are moments in our lives when we feel awakened and suddenly become aware of our finest and most worthy qualities, as if they had been long forgotten or missing. He also voiced an optimism, shared by Maslow, that behind the exterior of most people lie decent, moral qualities that are often rarely expressed. "There seem to be layers in men," Wertheimer wrote, "and it is a question of fact what the inner layers of men really are."

In a parable-like essay entitled "A Story of Three Days," published in 1940, Wertheimer sketched out new territory for psychological exploration, ground that Maslow would seek to cover in coming years. Decrying the dominant emphasis on illness rather than health in the psychology field, Wertheimer commented, "Are there not tendencies in men and in children to be kind, to deal sincerely [and] justly with the other fellow? Are these nothing but internalized rules on the basis of compulsion and fear?" Poetically praising the ability of many youngsters to show compassion and altruism, Wertheimer insisted that an urgent task of social science is to study these tendencies and their development "in children, in men, in the dynamics of society."

At the New School in September 1938, Maslow achieved his dream of studying with another giant of Gestalt psychology, Kurt Koffka (1886–1941). Born in Germany and trained at the University of Berlin, Koffka had given up philosophy for the empiricism of experimental psychology, just as Maslow had a generation earlier. Koffka quickly gained a reputation as a precise and gifted researcher. Alongside the work of Wertheimer and Kohler, Koffka's innovative studies of human perception helped establish the new approach known as Gestalt psychology. In 1921, his book *Growth of the Mind* (translated into English three years later) catapulted him to international acclaim.

Koffka had emigrated to the United States in 1924, largely for professional, not political, reasons. He had not suffered through forced exile as had Wertheimer and many others. Initially a visiting professor at Cornell, Koffka taught briefly at the University of Wisconsin, then at Smith College in Massachussetts. There, he took a special nondepartmental research fellowship. The administration's plan was for him to hold the post for five years and then be snapped up by a prestigious university with a major graduate program. Some twelve years later Koffka was still teaching at Smith; no major offer had come his way. He had secured a regular chair in Smith's psychology department.

Maslow sat in on Koffka's course at the New School, where he substituted for Wertheimer, and found it inspiring. Three years before, Koffka had published his major book, *Principles of Gestalt Psychology,* based on decades of his experimental and theoretical research in Germany and the United States. It was the most definitive work to date on the Gestalt approach. Drawing on this material for his lectures, Koffka advanced a strong empirical outlook coupled with a systematic way of thinking that Maslow admired. Like Wertheimer, Koffka was a thinker whose far-reaching interests included philosophy, ethics, the psychology of art and music, and the scientific study of values. Koffka taught that the "value experience" is one of the most significant aspects of human existence and as such needs to be understood in depth by modern science. In his lectures at the New School, he further sensitized Maslow to the relevance of such issues for a truly comprehensive approach to the mind.

However, Maslow found to his dismay that few of his

American psychology colleagues were interested in attending
such foreigner-led classes. In later years, Maslow recollected
with bitterness how hard he had tried to lure others to these
thought-provoking seminars, and how less than a handful had
joined him, aside from émigré psychologists George Katona
and Martin Scheerer. "Wertheimer was probably the only
first-rate psychologist in the whole city," Maslow recalled in his
diary, "and the shits couldn't be coaxed to come."

In an illustrative episode that Maslow remembered with
rancor, he repeatedly invited one Brooklyn College colleague
to accompany him by subway down to the New School to hear
Wertheimer lecture. Finally, she agreed to attend, but then
did not show up. A few days later, Maslow learned to his disbelief that she had instead attended her own professor's second-
hand lecture on Wertheimer's theory of Gestalt psychology.

Another key figure with whom Maslow studied at the New
School was Karen Horney (1885–1952). Unlike most of her
foreign-born colleagues living in New York City, she was neither Jewish nor a refugee but had come to America for personal and professional reasons. Born in Germany, Horney was
the daughter of a Norwegian sea captain and a Dutch mother.
After marrying in 1909, she raised three daughters while pur-
suing a medical degree at the University of Berlin. She took
further psychiatric training in Berlin, where she was in-
structed by Franz Alexander and Hanns Sachs, two of Freud's
closest associates, during World War I. In 1919, Horney began
to practice as a psychoanalyst; at about the same time, she
joined the faculty of the Berlin Psychoanalytic Institute.

Over the next thirteen years, Horney emerged as perhaps
the first ardent feminist thinker and critic of Freud from
within the ranks of the psychoanalytic movement. As early as
1924, she bluntly criticized Freud's blatantly masculine biases
and shortly thereafter began developing an innovative, neopsychoanalytic theory of women's psychology. Through such
provocative articles as "The Flight from Womanhood" and
"Inhibited Womanhood," she acquired a growing reputation
both in Europe and abroad.

In 1932, Horney relocated to the United States to take a
senior staff position at the newly formed Chicago Institute for
Psychoanalysis. Its director was Alexander, her former

teacher-analyst in Berlin. She was not a Jew and therefore not in immediate political danger, but she recognized that the Nazis, on the verge of gaining power, were out to obliterate psychoanalysis and would not let her practice what they despised as "Jewish psychology." Just getting over a painful divorce, Horney was also eager for a change of scene. Unfortunately, she and Alexander did not get along well. In 1934 she relocated to New York City, where she opened a full-time psychoanalytic practice.

Unlike many of her fellow émigrés, Horney had the inclination and personal warmth to form friendships with a number of American social scientists. In the fall of 1935, soon after affiliating with the New York Psychoanalytic Institute, she received an invitation from the New School's dean, Dr. Clara Mayer, to present her ideas on feminine psychology and other topics in a series of public lectures. Horney eagerly accepted and entitled the first of her many courses, "Culture and Neurosis."

In this enthusiastically received course, Horney strongly emphasized the role of social forces—what was coming to be known as *culture*—in shaping women's so-called feminine approach to life. Sharply rejecting Freud's strict biological determinism, Horney argued that women tend to act timidly or passively because our culture shapes them to be that way, not because of their immutable physical makeup. Alongside her anthropology friends at Columbia University, including Ruth Benedict, Margaret Mead, and Ralph Linton, and later fellow psychiatrist Abram Kardiner, Horney further criticized Freud's unproven statements about normal versus deviant behavior, sexual or otherwise, in both men and women. The 1930s were the heyday of the outlook known as cultural relativism, promulgated by Mead and others, and Horney became one of its chief psychoanalytic exponents.

Based on these lectures at the New School, in 1937 Horney published her first book, *The Neurotic Personality of Our Time*. She not only advanced such ideas as those mentioned above but went on to insist that various cultures produce certain specific neuroses or types of emotional disturbance. She identified modern capitalism, especially its American form, as a breeding ground for a particular kind of neurosis centering around the inability to receive and give affection freely. By overemphasizing individual competitiveness and minimizing our needs for love and friendship, American culture was creating a widespread neurosis unknown in less industrialized or primitive cultures.

In 1939, Horney published her second book, *New Ways in Psychoanalysis*, which presented an overall critique of Freud's biological and pessimistic stance. Yet, while attacking orthodox Freudian theory in several respects—especially its lack of cross-cultural understanding, its sexual underpinnings, its derogatory view of women, and its overemphasis on "anatomy as destiny"—Horney supported many basic psychoanalytic notions. Rather than seeing herself as anti-Freudian, she expressed the hope that Freud's many brilliant insights could be incorporated into a more up-to-date and relevant system of thought.

In other works, Horney criticized the axiomatic Freudian notion of infantile sexuality as erroneous and a misinterpretation of children's healthy desires for physical reassurance. With such statements, Horney gradually incurred the enmity of New York's leading orthodox analysts. They began to view with increasing alarm her explicit rejection of fundamental Freudian tenets. Finally, in 1941, when she began to advocate self-analysis as a potentially useful technique, the dominant clique at the New York Psychoanalytic Institute disqualified her as a training analyst and instructor. She then founded her own psychoanalytic association and training institute with the help of a coterie of like-minded psychiatric colleagues and social scientist supporters.

Maslow came to know Horney while she lectured part-time at the New School. He attended some of her earliest presentations and made her acquaintance in the eager and outgoing style that characterized his manner with older figures whom he respected. Through his position as a postdoctoral research assistant to Thorndike, Maslow also became friendly with Horney's circle of anthropologists at Columbia, especially Benedict and Mead. Whenever Horney offered a course at the New School, several of which were interdisciplinary in focus, Maslow was there, avidly taking notes, asking thoughtful questions, and raising interesting issues from his background as an experimental psychologist.

In his research and theoretical papers through the late

1930s and early 1940s, Maslow frequently referred to Horney's book *The Neurotic Personality of Our Time*, often in the context of how America's particular cultural values hamper the development of strong self-esteem and emotional security. He found it especially useful in making sense of his interview findings concerning women's dominance-feeling, dominance-behavior, and sexuality.

Later, when Horney broke with the orthodox analysts and created her own association, Maslow became a regular visitor to her monthly scientific meetings. He also accepted invitations to lecture about his psychological work. Other presenters included Benedict, Fromm, and psychiatrist Harry Stack Sullivan. Maslow found such gatherings intellectually exciting and sometimes scintillating. Some indefinable spirit of enthusiasm animated the audience, which included psychiatrists, social researchers, analytic patients, and interested lay people.

In one famous meeting, Fromm was to be the speaker and Benedict to head the discussion. Without prior notice, Sullivan suddenly mounted the podium before the lecture. His first comment, "I am a schizophrenic," drew an audible gasp, then a round of applause, from the audience. Horney applauded especially loudly. When questioned later about this encouragement, she replied that she had admired Sullivan's courage in self-revelation, whether true or not.

Perhaps Horney's greatest impact on Maslow was her effort to synthesize psychoanalytic and cross-cultural insights in developing a theory of personality and therapeutic treatment. In this important stage in his career, he learned firsthand that it was possible to retain many fundamental Freudian notions while still searching for new paths to understand human nature and potential.

Erich Fromm (1900–1980) was another key European-born mentor during this formative period. More than any other psychoanalyst of his time, he succeeded in acquiring a large popular audience in America as a social critic. He also exerted considerable influence on his colleagues in psychiatry, psychology, and allied professions. When Maslow first met and studied informally with him, however, Fromm was an obscure psychoanalytic émigré.

Born in Germany to middle-class Jewish parents, Fromm

was descended from a long line of rabbis and, unlike most of his colleagues, was reared in accordance with strict religious orthodoxy. After studying intensively with both rabbinic mystics and socialists—including the kabbalah scholar Gershom Scholem, then a young man—Fromm planned to become a rabbi. At the universities of Frankfurt and Heidelberg, he was drawn beyond religion to philosophy, psychology, and sociology and did his dissertation on the religious orientation of modern Jews. Although he broke with Jewish observance in his late twenties, the Old Testament and Talmud remained for him a source of moral inspiration.

After obtaining his doctorate in sociology at the age of twenty-two from the University of Heidelberg, Fromm decided to become a psychoanalyst. At the time, in line with Freud's wishes, the training of lay (nonmedical) analysts was common practice. Fromm trained in psychoanalysis at the University of Munich in 1923–1924, and then at the Berlin Psychoanalytic Institute. There he met and married his first wife, Frieda. After completing their training, the two helped found and direct the Psychoanalytic Institute of Frankfurt.

Soon afterward, Fromm joined the faculty of the University of Frankfurt's Institute for Social Research. Under the leadership of Max Horkheimer, the Institute promoted an unorthodox Marxism. Although Fromm was not a political activist, he had come to believe that modern capitalism was directly responsible for many social and ultimately individual problems of the post–World War I era. He flirted with Trotskyism but thereafter maintained a lifelong commitment to democratic ideals. During this time, he energetically began searching for a synthesis between the Freudian and Marxist approaches to human existence—one of the first psychoanalysts, along with Wilhelm Reich, to do so.

When Hitler came to power, Fromm realized that his future in Germany was precarious. He accepted a visiting lectureship in 1933 at the Chicago Psychoanalytic Institute, where Horney was teaching, and came to the United States. In 1934, he decided to leave Germany permanently, become an American citizen, and settle in New York City. There he opened a successful private practice as a lay psychoanalyst while continuing to teach at the Institute for Social Research. By then, the institute had affiliated with Columbia University.

Fromm remained at this post until 1941, when he became a professor at Bennington College in Vermont.

During the mid-to-late 1930s, Fromm was not well known beyond his fellow refugee analysts and social scientists in the New York area. He and Horney became intimate friends and exerted a strong influence on each other's work. As some of their colleagues liked to joke, Horney learned political theory and sociology from Fromm, and he learned psychoanalysis from her. Under her initial prodding, he wrote his first book, *Escape from Freedom,* published in 1940. Creatively melding psychoanalysis and historical-social criticism to explain the alarming spread of fascism in the modern industrial world, this work elevated Fromm to international fame and a large and enthusiastic audience.

Around 1936, at the Institute for Social Research in Manhattan's Morningside Heights, Maslow met Fromm, a brilliant but reserved man of medium build who wore rimless spectacles. After hearing Fromm give a particularly provocative lecture one evening, Maslow introduced himself, and before long a friendly, collegial relationship developed.

Although they had quite different personalities, intellectually they suited each other well. Besides attending Fromm's lectures, Maslow occasionally joined him socially at his apartment on Central Park West. For the most part, Maslow at first behaved deferentially toward his somewhat older and more austere colleague. As soon as he began to challenge Fromm and act more like an intellectual equal, their relationship cooled. After Fromm left New York for Bennington, the two saw little of one another for many years except at formal conferences.

What had especially attracted Maslow was Fromm's passionate concern for social justice and world betterment. Perhaps more than any of the other émigré psychoanalysts, Fromm vigorously espoused a humanitarian outlook, and an insistence that the chains of mass neuroses could be broken forever by sweeping social and economic change. To the socialist-minded Maslow, Fromm was not just another German Marxist taking potshots during the Depression at the inequities of American capitalism. He articulated a persuasive and novel approach to psychology and human personality.

At the center of Fromm's thought in the 1930s lay the

notion of social character. Building on foundations laid by
Reich and the Berlin group of psychoanalysts, Fromm argued
that individual character types are molded by the social and
economic order in which we live. We cannot possibly claim to
be untouched by the larger social institutions around us; from
childhood onward, their underlying values affect us in countless subtle ways. It was Fromm's view, too, that modern capitalist society generates particular character types, such as the
hoarding personality and the authoritarian personality. Synthesizing Freudian and Marxist thought, Fromm asserted that
such disturbed character types could be effectively treated on
a mass scale only by radical changes in society.

In *Escape from Freedom*, Fromm more broadly argued
that the modern individual's struggle for freedom—that is, to
think for oneself and express oneself unhindered—is by necessity anxiety-producing and even frightening, for it involves a
confrontation with one's ultimate aloneness in the world. Such
anxiety keeps many people from engaging in the battle; instead, they seek a means of escape from freedom by blindly
following authoritarian religious or political leaders. These
powerful figures, of course, promise their followers security
and happiness in exchange for giving up independent, critical
thinking and judgment. Unfortunately, Fromm insisted, many
people in the twentieth century are only too glad to act on this
bargain.

To Maslow, this line of reasoning was compelling, and
through the 1940s he repeatedly cited Fromm's work in his
own developing writings about personality and political attitude. Fromm also believed in the validity of Horney's notion
of self-analysis and devoted some time each day to the practice, which he regarded as critical for personal growth. Maslow
likewise adopted self-analysis daily for his own emotional
development.

Perhaps the most important and certainly the most famous of Maslow's mentors was Alfred Adler (1870–1937).
Their close relationship was cut short by Adler's death, but it
left an indelible mark on Maslow's career. It would be no
exaggeration to characterize Maslow as one of the first American psychologists to recognize and build upon Adler's insight-
ful teachings.

Born in a Viennese suburb to a middle-class Jewish family,

Adler received his medical degree from the University of Vienna in 1895. He originally specialized in ophthalmology but changed to neurology and finally psychiatry after being inspired by Krafft-Ebing's lectures and Freud's writings. Adler published his first articles on the role of organic inferiority— often a congenital bodily defect—in personality formation. His stress was on the individual's attitude toward the defect rather than the defect itself; in cases of what he called overcompensation, people turn their handicap into a challenge for growth and prowess. Having suffered from rickets in childhood, he was familiar with this psychological condition.

In 1902, Adler joined Freud's nascent psychoanalytic movement and became a member of the Wednesday evening discussion group held at Freud's home. The two men were initially close and shared many similar ideas, but Adler steadily deemphasized Freud's sexually oriented theory of personality development and neurosis. By 1911, he broke decisively and permanently with Freud to disseminate his own system, which he called Individual Psychology. By this time, Adler taught that the child's struggle for power and competency, not bodily gratification, is the basis for personality. Instead of the Oedipus complex that Freud posited, Adler insisted that every child becomes involved in a battle for power in the family, for we all seek to overcome an infantile sense of inferiority in a world of larger and stronger adults.

Unlike Freud, Adler was politically outspoken. An ardent socialist, he believed that many social problems, like juvenile delinquency and crime, resulted from inequitable conditions that cause youngsters to develop pent-up feelings of inferiority. A reformist rather than a revolutionary, Adler called for altering methods of child-rearing and education to effect greater mental health in society.

During World War I, Adler served for four years in the Austrian army medical corps. Through such wartime duty, he advanced the notion of a basic human striving for social interest or good will toward others. In other words, he proposed that we are inherently social animals who enjoy companionship and engaging in helpful behavior. Although he came to stress social feeling as an important aspect of healthy child development and adult personality, he was never clear about whether this trait is inborn or must be learned. After the war, Adler and his colleagues established a network of child-guidance clinics in Berlin, Munich, and Vienna. For a time, Adler served as director of the Vienna State Institute of Pedagogy, but devoted most of his subsequent career in Vienna to private practice.

Beginning in 1926, Adler became a frequent visitor to the United States. To help publicize and fund his child-guidance clinics, he regularly undertook exhausting cross-country tours to lecture at medical schools, universities, child-guidance clinics, religious organizations, and parent-teacher associations. In the 1929–1930 academic year, Adler taught at Columbia University, and in 1932 became professor at Long Island College Hospital in New York. During this period he spent half the year in Vienna and the other half in the United States, where he felt intellectually lonely. One year after Hitler came to power in Germany, Austria's new Fascist government shut down the child-guidance clinics attached to state schools. Sensing ominous danger, Adler emigrated permanently to the United States in 1935, settling in New York City.

That same year, the twenty-seven-year-old Maslow, fresh out of Wisconsin, sought out Adler as a mentor. Since his days as a graduate student, Maslow had been interested in Adler's approach to human personality. In a way, Maslow's entire doctoral study of dominance and sexual behavior in monkeys had been a test—the only type his rigidly experimentalist professors at Madison would have permitted—of Adler's theory that the drive for power underlies much of our social actions. Planning a variety of follow-up studies with primates and humans, Maslow was more convinced than ever of the centrality of Adler's ideas, and eager for further inspiration.

In 1935 Adler was offering an open-house class on Friday evenings at the Gramercy Park Hotel where he occupied a suite. To meet and study with Adler in this informal setting seemed an ideal opportunity for Maslow. Much to his surprise, only a small number of attendees came regularly, and thus it became possible for him to get to know Adler personally. Maslow was impressed with Adler's erudition and brilliance, and frequently invited friends and colleagues to join him to hear Adler. Among them was psychologist Heinz Ansbacher, who became a major disseminator and interpreter of Adler's work for the English-speaking world.

Maslow also often met Adler for dinner. Adler initially did

most of the talking, expounding on his theories, reminiscing about his past accomplishments, and encouraging Maslow in a fatherly way. He was pleased with Maslow's monkey work as a confirmation of his own notions. Maslow was still in his twenties and undoubtedly felt somewhat intimidated by this famous colleague of Freud's, nearly forty years his senior.

On one memorable occasion, Maslow was dining with Adler at the Gramercy Park Hotel's restaurant and casually asked a question that implied Adler's former discipleship under Freud. Adler became very angry, his face flushing, and began to talk so loudly that heads turned in their direction. He insisted that he had *never* been a student, follower, or disciple of Freud but had always been an independent physician and researcher. The very notion that he had been Freud's disciple, he nearly shouted was a "lie and a swindle" concocted long ago, after their break, by Freud himself. Maslow, who had never heard Adler speak of Freud at all, was dumbfounded by this outburst.

For most of the eighteen months that Maslow associated with Adler, the two got along well. But—in a pattern that Maslow would later encounter with many of his other mentors—as soon as he began to act more like a colleague and equal rather than a disciple, Adler began to respond with growing irritation.

Their last meeting took place in early 1937. After a lecture and heated group discussion in Adler's suite, he thrust Maslow into a corner and, staring at him closely, asked, "Well, are you for me or against me?" Shocked and hurt by the implications of Adler's remark, Maslow decided not to return soon for another soiree. In May, he heard that Adler had died of a heart attack while on a lecture tour in Scotland. For many years, Maslow regretted their spat and wished that their stimulating relationship could have ended on a more inspiring note.

Although they knew each other personally for only a brief period, Adler's influence on Maslow was strong. He gave his younger colleague specific encouragement concerning the written reports of his Wisconsin primate research and his ongoing interviews exploring women's dominance and sexual behavior. Adler also turned Maslow's attention to the notion of social interest as a basic human trait. Throughout Maslow's career, he came to argue that altruism, compassion, love, and friendship are fundamental and ultimately inborn human tendencies, although they may be crushed by harmful early experience. Adler's emphasis on the importance of constitutional makeup in affecting personality development also played a key part in Maslow's subsequent thinking.

Above all, Adler influenced Maslow in his optimistic and progressive outlook. In stark contrast to Freud's gloom about the human condition, Adler fervently taught that social institutions can be reformed and revitalized for individual betterment. In this respect, a favorite activity of Adler's was to take children dismissed as intellectually backward as a result of low IQ scores and, by therapeutically building up their self-esteem, significantly improve their academic performance. Such an emphasis on environmental factors affecting mental functioning precisely fit Maslow's viewpoint at the time. In one unpublished paper, he even faulted Adler for not stressing cultural issues enough in his theory of human nature. Indeed, though never a disciple of Adler's—Maslow was always much too independent for that—he readily acknowledged the great intellectual debt he owed him.

The last of Maslow's refugee mentors was Kurt Goldstein (1878–1965). A seminal figure in modern neuropsychiatry, his name is often associated with the Gestalt approach. Like most of Maslow's intellectual guides in New York, Goldstein was born into a secular German-Jewish family. As a youngster he learned to play the cello, and retained a special love for cello music throughout his life. At Breslau University and Heidelberg, Goldstein initially pursued philosophy and literature but decided upon the study of medicine. He became interested in the origin of mental illness, which was then largely explored through the fields of neuroanatomy and neurophysiology. (Freud, for example, had done his early research on the neuroanatomy of the lamprey eel.) To his surprise, Goldstein found that he enjoyed working in the pathological laboratory. He began to investigate the puzzling relation between patients' psychotic symptoms, like hallucinations and bizarre behavior, and the postmortem findings of neuroanatomy.

In 1903, Goldstein received his medical degree from Breslau University, having done his dissertation on the neural structure of the human spinal cord. Over the ensuing years, he held positions in several German clinical and research settings. A prolific researcher, he produced dozens of papers on a broad range of neurologic and psychiatric topics, from alcoholism and schizophrenia to sensorimotor disorders. In 1906, Goldstein conducted innovative research on the nature of memory loss in several types of psychiatric and neural illnesses. Such work helped lay the foundation for effective assessment and therapeutic treatment.

At the Neurological Institute in Frankfurt, which Goldstein joined in 1914, he carried out his most important medical discoveries. The influx of wounded soldiers from the trenches of World War I brought an unprecedented opportunity to observe and treat brain injury in large numbers of previously healthy adults. Almost overnight, the Institute grew into a major clinical center for assessment and rehabilitation. With several gifted colleagues, including psychoanalyst Frieda Fromm-Reichmann (then married to Erich Fromm), Goldstein focused on how brain trauma affected thinking, judgment, and behavior. Through the research findings that resulted, Goldstein and his coworkers formulated wider principles about human mental functioning, providing pathological support for many basic ideas of Gestalt psychology.

In his nineteen years at the Neurological Institute, Goldstein's career steadily advanced. Eventually, he became its director and combined administrative duties with continuing involvement in research. Under his leadership, the institute became a major world center for the study and treatment of brain injury. With a humane and compassionate outlook, Goldstein transformed the soldiers' hospital into a familylike setting.

Later he developed an interest in psychotherapy from a neurological, as opposed to a psychoanalytic, perspective and helped to found the International Society for Psychotherapy. In 1930, Goldstein took a new post, perhaps the most prestigious of its kind in Germany: overseeing neurological research at a hospital unit created for this purpose and affiliated with the University of Berlin. At the age of fifty-two, he expected to maintain this fulfilling position for the rest of his career.

But Goldstein became a marked man as soon as Hitler came to power. In January 1933, the Nazis jailed him as a menace to the state; he was released on the condition that he leave the country immediately. Fortunately, the Rockefeller Foundation undertook to support him for a year in Holland. Living in an Amsterdam boarding house without his family, he devoted full time to his writing and completed what was to be his key work, *The Organism*. Written in German, the book was published in Holland in 1934. The English translation appeared in the United States five years later, entitled *The Organism: A Holistic Approach to Biology Derived from Pathological Data in Man.*

In this landmark treatise, Goldstein integrated decades of his applied and theoretical activity in neuropsychiatry. The book was hailed for its broad philosophical scope as well as its scientific relevance. Like his friend Albert Einstein, Goldstein always sought to place his scientific work within a larger philosophical and moral context.

In 1935, Goldstein left Europe to settle in the United States. He spoke little English and had little desire to start his professional life over again in middle age, but he had nowhere else to go. Arriving in New York City, he attempted to build a self-sustaining private practice in neurology and psychiatry. However, unlike Fromm, Horney, and many others of his German compatriots in exile, Goldstein was not a member of the psychoanalytic émigré community and found it difficult to establish himself in America. Over the next five years, he held only a series of temporary research positions in the New York area in an effort to reestablish his studies of human brain injury and its effective assessment and treatment. At times, he became sardonic and even bitter over the refusal of all major U.S. universities to hire him. Finally, in 1940, he secured his first real academic post, at Tufts Medical College near Boston.

It is not clear when Maslow first met Goldstein, but it seems likely to have occurred around 1940, perhaps through their mutual friend Wertheimer. Maslow's initial reference to Goldstein's work appeared in 1941; *Principles of Abnormal Psychology* cited Goldstein's book *The Organism*. Thereafter, in nearly every theoretical paper Maslow published, he mentioned one or another of Goldstein's writings and always his magnum opus.

They were not as close as Maslow had been to Horney and Wertheimer, perhaps partly because Maslow had two young daughters at home and much less time to socialize with colleagues. But throughout his later life he considered Goldstein, more than three decades his senior, to have exerted a vital influence on his own emerging approach to human nature. As chairman of Brandeis University's psychology department in the 1950s, Maslow expressed some of his gratitude by hiring Goldstein as a part-time faculty member.

Far more than for his specific research findings, Goldstein excited Maslow by his broad philosophical stance, one based on biology's solid ground. In *The Organism,* Goldstein had not merely presented a lucid summary of thirty years of neurological study; he had sought to draw as large a picture of human functioning as possible by extrapolating from information revealed in his empirical work with the brain-injured. Virtually no other theorist of the time was rooted this way in bodily (what Goldstein liked to call *organismic*) anatomy and functioning. Although as a psychologist Maslow was intensely interested in cultural and social issues, as a trained experimentalist he had never lost his respect for rigorous empirical research.

Maslow found most important Goldstein's idea that the only real way to understand human functioning is through a holistic emphasis—to see each person as an integrated biological entity and not as a collection of bodily organs, reflexes, and mental skills. Goldstein rejected the dominant psychiatric tendency to reduce people to "bags of symptoms," or convenient labels like "neurotic" or "psychotic." Every individual lives as a whole being, and the whole is always more than the sum of its parts, Goldstein insisted. For example, when a person suffers trauma to a major brain region, governing abstract reasoning or speech, his or her entire personality changes. In assessing, treating, and rehabilitating such patients, the goal should be to understand the person as a damaged but still unified biological entity struggling to maintain its existence.

Goldstein's concept of self-actualization—perhaps his most important formulation to influence Maslow—was related to this notion. In a vague, almost purely philosophical way, Goldstein offered the term to describe the innate desire or predilection of every organism, including the human being, to achieve its potential. For example, his research with brain-injured people showed that when one part of the brain is wounded, another part may take over its role, to maintain an optimal overall level of functioning.

In a like manner, Goldstein believed, we each have an inborn unconscious drive to fulfill our particular biological nature. Though rarely specific as to what this really entails, he gave as examples the intense, even painful, urge that an artist or musician experiences to create something new. Much to Goldstein's disapproval, Maslow later seized upon the term *self-actualization,* but changed its connotation, when he synthesized his own theory of human motivation and personality.

That intriguing development still lay several years ahead. Before Maslow reached that point in his professional activity, he had much to assimilate and experience.

CHAPTER SEVEN

Idylls with the Blackfoot Indians

> As things stood while I was studying anthropology in 1933–1937, cultures were unique, idiosyncratic. There was no scientific way of handling them, no generalizations that you could make.
>
> The first and foremost lesson that [I] learned from a field trip was that Indians are first of all people, individuals, human beings, and only secondarily Blackfoot Indians. By comparison with similarities, the differences, though undoubtedly there, seemed superficial.
>
> —A.M.

As Thorndike's research assistant at Columbia in 1935, Maslow had sought to develop his keen interest in anthropology. Still hoping to continue his primate research on dominance and sexuality, he found himself with the opportunity to study informally with some of the leading anthropologists in the country, and Maslow was never one to ignore a chance for intellectual growth. With his friendly, confident manner, he soon became a familiar figure to anthropology faculty and graduate students at Columbia. He became a virtual fixture at the departmental colloquia and got to know Margaret Mead and others there quite well. The format was for a guest speaker to offer a presentation on his or her fieldwork or theoretical interests. The audience, composed mainly of anthropologists, would then ask questions or raise issues in a lively and at times heated exchange.

Maslow found Columbia's anthropology department a stimulating place. In the fall of 1937, Ralph Linton, one of

Bertha's professors at Wisconsin, came to Columbia as a visiting professor. The next year, he was appointed head of its prestigious anthropology department. Though Linton was cordial, Maslow became especially close to one faculty member, Ruth Benedict. In many ways, he was intensely drawn to this quiet radiant woman. She appeared almost angelic to him, and with Max Wertheimer at the New School became for Maslow an exemplar of what he would come to call the self-actualizing person. He adored her wit, intellectual brilliance, and kindness.

In her late forties when Maslow met her, Benedict had entered anthropology rather late in life. Born of old American farming stock, she had grown up on a farm in Norwich, New York. Her father had died when she was two, leaving her mother to raise three children in a frugal manner. In 1923, after a decade of unfulfilling and childless married life, Benedict began doctoral work in anthropology at Columbia at the age of thirty-five. She was partially deaf from childhood, so fieldwork was never easy for her and she relied mainly on English-speaking informants for her interviews.

Under the tutelage of Franz Boas, Benedict found religious aspects of ethnology intrinsically interesting. She published her first article on "The Vision in Plains Culture," and her dissertation was on "The Concept of the Guardian Spirit in North America." She served as editor of the *Journal of American Folklore* beginning in 1923 and, in 1934, her landmark book *Patterns of Culture* was issued. Translated into five languages, it has probably been the single most widely read work of anthropology, helping millions of people to enlarge their understanding of the rich cultural diversity of human life.

When Maslow met her, Benedict aimed to enhance the cross-fertilization of the various social sciences: psychology, psychiatry, and anthropology. During the 1930s, Columbia was a hotbed of such activity. Anthropology books by Mead, Linton, and others in that circle are still read more than fifty years later for their insight and freshness of thought. Within the field of psychiatry, Abram Kardiner in New York City, with whom Maslow became close friends, was another important figure in this movement to bring cross-cultural research to bear on fundamental issues in the social sciences. As Mead recalled, "These years of [Benedict's] teaching activity were the years in which the word *culture* was becoming a familiar term in the social sciences, the years in which interrelationships between psychology and psychiatry and anthropology were developing."

It may seem surprising that Maslow, an experimental psychologist who had done most of his research on dogs and monkeys, was accepted so readily by Columbia's anthropologists. But by the mid-1930s, he had already begun to distinguish himself as one of the few psychologists in the United States knowledgeable about cross-cultural issues. Upon request from his friend Ross Stagner, then editing the anthology *The Psychology of Personality,* Maslow wrote a chapter on the anthropological perspective concerning human personality. By this time he had amassed a tremendous body of material on cross-cultural findings with respect to human behavior, especially abnormal or deviant. The book, published in 1937, established Maslow's expertise in this realm.

In the mid-1930s, Maslow embraced the notion of cultural relativism: every culture is unique, all values and mores are relative, and no culture therefore can judge as better its own values, much less seek to impose them upon another culture. Maslow soon came to reject this belief, but it was at the time widely espoused among anthropologists, and was associated, as well, with racial tolerance and progressive thinking. To most social scientists, the alternative seemed to be a return to the outmoded concept of the "white man's burden," which had given nineteenth-century Western colonialism its moral justification. The cultural relativist position also stressed that all religions ultimately embody an ethnocentric outlook, and Maslow certainly supported this notion.

In the chapter he wrote for Stagner, "Personality and Patterns of Culture" (an allusion to Benedict's book), Maslow wrote:

> The anthropologist can teach us many things, but one lesson that we *must* learn from him is that of *cultural relativity.* We must treat the individual first as a member of a particular cultural group, and only after this treat him as a member of the general human species. Any ethical judgments on behavior are a judgment of a cultural group.

It is justifiable, of course, to approve or disapprove of certain behavior, but no references can or should be made to universal or absolute criteria of goodness or badness of behavior for the simple reason that there are none.

In this chapter Maslow also affirmed the belief that science could furnish a new set of values—replacing those of the world's religions—to promote the well-being of all peoples. In this regard, while he denied the existence of universal criteria for *morality,* he argued that science had the potential to find universal criteria for human *health:*

> The biologist is able to say that a taboo on the most plentiful source of food is bad in terms of biological survival. The psychologist may say that cultural suppression of a fundamental human urge [Maslow had specified the sex drive in an earlier paper] will create more unhappiness and conflict than if there were no such repression. He may say that very widely differing social norms for various strata or classes within a single cultural group produce so much friction, maladjustment, and conflict that they should be wiped out. Scientists in all fields may one day cooperate in some such endeavor and tell us the best way to run our own culture in terms of more absolute scientific judgments.

In light of world events in the half century since Maslow wrote these words, it has become clear that scientists possess no special wisdom when it comes to dealing with value-laden social or even health-related issues. Especially in view of how German physicians and academicians readily cooperated with Hitler, Maslow's faith that scientists can supply us with the best answers to "run our culture" seems rather naive. But we must place Maslow's outlook in the context of the times, and in the 1930s science seemed a pure beacon to many intelligent people striving for a better world.

During their collegial friendship, Benedict urged Maslow to engage in real fieldwork and experience another culture directly. She insisted that until he did so, he could not really shed his own cultural biases. Though Maslow had done some informal fieldwork with Linton at the University of Wisconsin, he resisted Benedict's advice for quite some time. In early

1938 he finally assented. Benedict believed that the Northern Blackfoot Indian tribe in Alberta, Canada, would be a good place for Maslow to work.

Under her sponsorship, Maslow applied for a grant-in-aid from the Social Science Research Council for the summer of 1938, when he would be free from his teaching duties at Brooklyn College. He later recalled, "I did the Blackfoot fieldwork as much out of a sense of duty as wanting to. I was a little afraid of it, too." His proposal, which was accepted for funding, focused on the study of dominance and emotional security among members of the Blackfoot tribe by means of his newly developed attitude questionnaires. Benedict was supportive of Maslow's research plan, but chiefly wanted him to simply get "into the field."

Maslow had two fieldwork companions on the trip. Jane Richardson, a new doctoral graduate of Columbia's anthropology department, had been part of an anthropological team studying the Kiowa Indians of Oklahoma in 1935, and had done her thesis on these Plains Indians. Since then, she had been eager for another opportunity to do Indian fieldwork. Ruth Benedict felt she would be a knowledgeable companion for Maslow and sponsored her under a grant similar to his. Richardson knew Maslow from his days as Thorndike's assistant at Teachers College; she had provided him with nearly six hours of personal information for his studies of female dominance and sexuality. Her background as the daughter of a Berkeley, California, professor had intrigued him, and she willingly recounted her upbringing and values. When Maslow reached the part of his questionnaire that asked explicit sexual questions, however, Richardson politely terminated her participation.

The third member of the team was Lucien Hanks, Jr., a friend of Maslow's from their Madison days. Hanks was a newly appointed instructor at the University of Illinois at Urbana. While working toward his psychology doctorate at Columbia, Hanks, like Maslow, had become keenly interested in anthropology and gotten to know Benedict. Knowing of his friend's desire to do some summer fieldwork and aware that he owned a car they could all use, Maslow invited him to complete the team. Hanks had been planning anthropological exploration in South America. When his older brother died suddenly, Hanks promised his parents not to risk his own life by venturing into the jungle. The Blackfoot reserve in Canada seemed a far safer environment, and won his parents' approval.

For Maslow, the timing of the trip could not have been worse. His first child, Ann, had been born in January, and the new parents agreed that it would be wiser for Bertha to stay in Brooklyn with the baby. Hygienic conditions on the Indian reserve were known to be poor.

When Maslow and his two colleagues embarked on their fieldwork, there were four separate Blackfoot Indian reserves: the Southern Piegan of Montana, the Northern Piegan, the Blood Indians, and the Northern Blackfoot of Canada. The team visited the last, the most northern of the four. Approximately eight hundred Northern Blackfoot inhabited an area some forty miles long and five miles wide, between the Canadian Pacific Railroad and the Bow River. The reserve adjoined two white villages, Gleichen and Cluny, each numbering just a few hundred people. The Blackfoot members did most of their shopping in Gleichen. Sixty miles away lay the larger city of Calgary. The headquarters of the Blackfoot reserve lay near Gleichen, where the tribe's office, hospital, and social hall were located.

Economically, the Northern Blackfoot enjoyed a unique status. In about 1910, under intense pressure from the Canadian government, the tribe relinquished about half of its reserve land to the superintendent general of Indian affairs. As stipulated by the complicated agreement, the government official sold the land to white settlers, at a time when land prices were at their peak. As a result, the Department of Indian Affairs managed a sizeable fund to be used according to the discretion of the autonomous Blackfoot Tribal Council, subject to the government agent's veto. By 1938, after nearly thirty years of accrued interest, this fund was yielding roughly $120,000 per year to the Blackfoot. According to the initial terms of the agreement, the money could be used for virtually any constructive purpose to benefit the entire tribe, but not for cash payments to individuals.

When Maslow, Richardson, and Hanks set out to study the Blackfoot, the tribe's fund had made it the only self-supporting Indian tribe in Canada and was a source of economic and social security. From the fund came weekly rations of food for all, special rations for the old, and assistance for those starting to farm. The fund also helped to build new Indian cottages on the reserve and maintain the modern, efficient hospital built in 1923.

Separately, Maslow and Richardson traveled by train to Madison, Wisconsin, where Hanks was visiting his parents and recovering from surgery for an impacted wisdom tooth. He lent them his car and later joined them at Gleichen.

As far as the eye could see, the terrain consisted of a flat, rolling prairie that stretched to the distant ridge of the Rocky Mountains. The Blackfoot reserve itself was divided into farms, each with a three-room cottage. Three or four farms clustered together at the corners of plots and shared a single water pump. Most of the Indians raised wheat and oats, with only fair success. Over the past several years, a relentless drought had blown away most of the topsoil, and the land had a bleak appearance.

On their first day in Alberta, Maslow and his colleagues met the Canadian agent for the Blackfoot reserve, who told them the government had approved the project. However, approval by the Blackfoot Tribal Council was essential, too. If the chiefs vetoed the fieldwork, Maslow and his companions would have little reason to remain.

The meeting with the tribal council began stiffly, with the Canadian agent initiating formal introductions. Hanks recalls, "Some of the chiefs on the council had chiefly names [like Charging Bull]. Others did not."

The Blackfoot chiefs gazed silently at the three white strangers and waited for their presentation. No one said anything. None of the researchers had expected anything as formal as this, and for once in Maslow's life, he appeared to be at a loss for words. Finally, Richardson started to speak. As an anthropologist familiar with Plains Indian mores, she knew that women were not supposed to address the chiefs before the men present had opened their mouths. But for them to sit there dumbstruck would have been far worse, she reasoned.

Maslow then made his presentation. As humbly as he could, he explained that he was but a lowly, ignorant white man who knew nothing of Blackfoot ways. He wanted to beg the tribal council's forgiveness in advance, he declared, for any unwitting, foolish mistakes he might make in violating their customs and traditions. But, Maslow concluded, his intentions were good and he sincerely wished to learn about their magnificent people.

Maslow undoubtedly intended this self-effacing speech to disarm the Blackfoot chiefs. However, it represented another blunder. As Richardson remarked, "That wasn't the way to approach the chiefs at all. Do you think they wanted to hear they had someone *dumb* in their midst? No, they wanted someone with *standing.*"

In the end, the Blackfoot Tribal Council gave the go-ahead to the three fieldworkers, and they began to set up camp. Maslow and Hanks slept in one tent on the Indian reserve, Richardson in another. Conditions were primitive. There was not even an outhouse, merely gulleys. Both Richardson and Hanks had camping experience, so Maslow had the most difficulty in adjusting to the rustic lifestyle. On many evenings, Hanks recalls, the two of them would return famished to their tent and find that dogs and prairie dogs had eaten their food. Although Maslow and Hanks considered themselves sophisticated in their cultural awareness of American folkways, apparently their cross-cultural vision had its limits. Richardson remembers having to do all the cooking for the three—"because she was a woman," and because she could handle it better.

Once set up on the reserve, Richardson, Hanks, and Maslow generally went their separate ways during the day and joined one another after nightfall. Each morning they awakened early and, over breakfast, planned their schedules for the day, deciding who would be dropped off and picked up where and when, since they shared Hanks's car.

Following the formal method of anthropological research Richardson had learned from Franz Boas at Columbia, she sought out the tribal elders to obtain their recollections of Blackfoot life in more free-spirited times. The old ones liked to talk for hours about war deeds, or the sadly vanishing religion of the medicine bundles, sacred objects used in ritual ceremonies.

As a psychologist, Hanks attempted to study the social status of the Blackfoot's mentally ill members, and how the

Indians regarded and treated their insane. Initially, he found this task difficult, for the Blackfoot were reluctant to discuss the matter with a stranger. After a while, some of the Indians quietly began to take Hanks into their confidence. He learned that psychotic individuals—those who thought they were beavers, for instance—did exist on the reserve and were a source of shame and embarrassment to their families. Meanwhile, Maslow spent much of his time in the little town of Gleichen. His funded research plan was to study the nature of personality dominance and emotional security among the Indians by administering his questionnaires. Maslow found the younger Indians more receptive than the old-timers, who spoke little English and tended to be long-winded. Therefore, he frequented the pool hall to interview the young Blackfoot males.

Maslow also had dealings with the white storekeepers who ran the town's businesses, and here he experienced the first of several intense surprises that summer. His preconceived notions were off-base. Decades later, he recalled:

> I came into the reservation with the notion that the Indians are over there on a shelf, like a butterfly collection or something like that. And then slowly I shifted and changed my mind. Those Indians on the reservation were decent people; and the more I got to know the whites in the village, who were the worst bunch of creeps and bastards I've ever run across in my life, the more it got paradoxical. Which was the asylum? Who were the keepers and who the inmates? Everything got all mixed up.

Fortunately, Maslow had a very helpful Indian informant that summer with the colorful name Teddy Yellow Fly. He was about fifty years old. The son of a Chinese father and a Blackfoot mother, Teddy had grown up on the edge of the reserve; his father had run a store in town, after coming to the area as a railway worker. Teddy was the most educated and English-proficient member of the council of chiefs, having attended a Canadian agricultural college. A well-read man interested in learning, Teddy had startled Maslow and his colleagues on their first meeting by casually producing a copy of Bene-

dict's *Patterns of Culture* and commenting, "This is interesting."

Teddy Yellow Fly was especially revered among the
young, progressive-minded Indians on the reserve. He was
very much aware of Canadian governmental control and was
restless for more local autonomy. On at least one occasion, he
went to Ottawa (the Canadian capital) to represent his people
politically. Teddy was also quite wealthy by Blackfoot standards and was the only one in the tribe who owned a car. But
what most impressed Maslow about Teddy was his kindness
and generosity:

> People would come and say, "Teddy, how about the key
> to your car?" And he would pass over the key. As near as I
> could make out, owning the car for him meant paying for the
> gas, fixing the tires, coming out and rescuing people in the
> middle of the reservation who didn't know how to handle it,
> and so on.

> Obviously, the fact that he possessed the only car in the
> whole society was a point of pride, pleasure, and gratification
> rather than attracting to him envy, malice, and hostility. The
> others were glad he had the car and would have been glad
> if five people had had cars instead of just one.

In this way Maslow was exposed to the economic and
social values among the Blackfoot. He soon discovered that
despite the sizable tribal fund, the members still needed to
work to secure cash. Some sold cattle or horses, which were an
adequate source of income, but most made a meager living
from the sale of farm products on their individually owned
(more precisely, *leased*) farms. With few exceptions, the Indians were not as successful in farming as their white counterparts. Since farming brought in scant income, employment for
most Blackfoot men consisted of working in the coal mines on
the reserve, haying, doing manual roadwork, or other occasional jobs like trapping.

It was clear to Maslow that the Blackfoot Indians differed
among themselves in their amount of personal wealth. To determine accurately the relation between wealth and emotional
security, Maslow started to investigate who was wealthy by

Blackfoot standards. In seeking out such information, he experienced another surprise:

> When I asked the white secretary of the reserve who was the richest man, he mentioned a man none of the Indians had mentioned—that is, the man who had on the books the most stock, the most cattle and horses. When I came back to my Indian informants and asked them about Jimmy McHugh, about all his horses, they shrugged with contempt. "He keeps it," they said, and as a consequence, they hadn't even thought to regard him as wealthy.

> White-Headed Chief was "wealthy," even though he owned nothing. In what way did virtue pay? The men who were formally generous in this way were the most admired, most respected, and the most loved men in the tribe. These were the men who benefited the tribe, the men they could be proud of, who warmed their hearts.

As Maslow discovered, fundamental to the Blackfoot, and to Plains Indians in general, was a marked emphasis on generosity as the highest virtue. To most Blackfoot Indians, wealth was not important in terms of accumulating property and possessions: *giving it away* was what brought one the true status of prestige and security in the tribe. The wealthiest individual in Blackfoot eyes was the one who had given away the most to others—not merely in one big display of generosity, but in continuous demonstration. With Maslow's strong socialist sensibility, this superbly moral and altruistic approach to wealth among nearly illiterate Indians was astounding.

The most vivid manifestation of the Blackfoot attitude toward wealth and sharing was the annual Sun Dance ceremony, particularly the ritual known as the giveaway. It took place each year in late June. Maslow referred to it repeatedly in his later writings, and it was perhaps the most striking event of all that he witnessed about Blackfoot culture:

> In this ceremony, all the tepees of the society gathered in one huge circle. The rich men of the tribe (rich meaning those who have worked hard and accumulated a great deal)

would have accumulated mounds of blankets, food, bundles of various sorts, and sometimes very pathetic things—cases of Pepsi-Cola as I remember. As many possessions as a man could have accumulated during the previous year were piled up.

I am thinking of one man I saw. At one point in the ceremony, in the Plains Indian tradition, he strutted and, we would say, boasted; that is, told of his achievements. "You know that I have done so and so, you all know that I have done this and that, and you all know how smart I am, how good a stock man I am, how good a farmer, and how I have therefore accumulated great wealth."

And then, with a lordly gesture, a gesture of great pride but without being humiliating, he gave this pile of wealth to the widows, to the orphaned children, and to the blind and diseased. At the end of the Sun Dance ceremony, he was stripped of all his possessions, owning nothing but the clothes he stood in.

Another related aspect of Blackfoot life that Maslow found appealing: "Wealth was such a good index of intelligence, capacity, and hard work." The son of poor Jewish immigrants, Maslow strongly felt in the Depression years that one's economic well-being in America was determined more by capricious, outside forces than by one's abilities. The Blackfoot culture exemplified for him the "good economic order," in which a person's material success is the product of personal motivation.

Perhaps precisely because of the institutionalized and ritualized generosity built into Blackfoot culture, Maslow expected to find its members rather emotionally secure. Friendly and open in demeanor, he quickly won the cooperation of the Indians whom he sought out for his questionnaire; his offers of tobacco brought many willing participants, too. Initially, Maslow had high expectations for his carefully constructed test of personal dominance. But he soon discovered it to be so shot through with American cultural norms as to be worthless. "The test was ridiculously useless when used to measure secure people," Maslow later commented. "Many of the questions in this test were completely incomprehensible to the Blackfoot; others were merely funny."

For instance, one of Maslow's dominance questions was, "How do you regard a man who is blunt in his speech?" Since all Blackfoot spoke bluntly to one another, the question was useless. Another question asked, "How do you react to the shy, timid, and bashful kind of man?" This was likewise useless, because there were no such men among the Blackfoot. The question Maslow asked the women, "How do you feel about being a housewife and mother as a life-job?" was incomprehensible to them, since no other options existed. It would have made as much sense for an outsider to ask us, "How do you feel about living in three dimensions?"

But what was most unproductive about the dominance test, Maslow found, was simply that "it gave no index of the true dominance-feeling of the people taking [it]." Because of Blackfoot cultural values, they acted in ways that we might call dominant or assertive, just because all tribal members expected them to. In this sense, Maslow's questions might be likened to a hypothetical anthropologist who comes to our own culture and seeks to measure dominance or assertiveness by our likelihood of wearing clothes in public. Regardless of our personal brashness or timidity, we all exhibit this behavior since it is such a powerful cultural norm.

Maslow realized that he had to revise his entire theoretical approach to human dominance. He commented several months later, "I realized that my test of dominance was a test of dominance-in-an-insecure-society [that is, ours] and that it assumed the universal presence of a rather strong drive to power, which was not present in the Blackfoot."

However, Maslow found his second research tool—the test of security/insecurity—to be useful in relation to the Indians. It appeared to be valid across cultures. To Maslow's amazement, he found that the Blackfoot were so emotionally secure "that about eighty to ninety percent of the population must be rated about as high in ego-security as the most secure individuals in our [own] society, who comprise perhaps five to ten percent at most."

Maslow had rephrased or eliminated several questions because of their cultural bias, but he felt confident in concluding that the Indians' responses showed "in a fairly clear light the relative security of the people being tested." Therefore, he emerged from this phase of his cross-cultural personality research convinced that "an insecure person, no matter what his culture, will tend to show the same general characteristics of insecurity, such as eagerness for power and a feeling of uncertainty about the feelings of people around him."

As a thorough scientist, of course, Maslow was not content to base his conclusions merely on test questions. During many observations that corroborated his questionnaire results, he found the Blackfoot Indians to be quite emotionally secure in their day-to-day activities. In today's terminology, the tribal members seemed to suffer less from self-doubt and self-consciousness than do people in our more competitive and impersonal way of life. For instance, Maslow commented, "In the most solemn ceremonies of the Sun Dance, an actor made several mistakes which caused uproarious laughter among the onlookers. This did not in any way humiliate the individual, for he himself laughed and appeared to treat the incident as lightly as everyone else."

Maslow observed an even more memorable example of the Blackfoot's emotional security. One of the most respected men in the tribe was scheduled to make a speech of praise prior to the formal ceremony of bestowing tribal names upon Maslow, Hanks, and Richardson. (Maslow's was "Na Me Ta Pi Go An," which, roughly translated, meant "Chief of the Northern People.") The man had previously confessed that he had been a drunkard but was slowly losing the taste for liquor. However, Maslow observed:

> When he appeared for the speech, he was drunk and had to support himself as he stood on the platform. Before starting to speak, he told [me] that he was under the influence of alcohol, and then proceeded to chat about other things without embarrassment or humiliation. The speech was rather rambling and disjointed but nevertheless forceful. The applause at the end seemed to be about what it would have been had the speaker not been drunk.

> Only one person commented on the incident, a compensatory person who had been trying to curry favor with [me] and knew that the speaker was [my] closest friend in the

tribe. After the speech, the speaker asked how [it] had sounded [and I] honesty reported that it had been very impressive. The speaker seemed pleased and said, "It would have been even better if I weren't under the influence of alcohol."

To follow up his finding that the Blackfoot seemed more emotionally secure than adults in U.S. society, Maslow turned his attention to child-rearing practices on the reserve. This was an area of anthropological research in which his friend Margaret Mead had pioneered. Although he had no formal training in cross-cultural child study, he was a keen naturalistic observer, as well as a new father. As a result, Maslow found much that was fascinating in the way Blackfoot parents treated their children.

Generally, the Blackfoot Indians seemed very attached—almost inordinately so, by North American standards—to their children. They constantly provided youngsters with food treats and other displays of affection. Yet, curiously, misbehavior was rare among Blackfoot children and punishment infrequently needed. It was so unusual for a child to have to be told something twice that such children were given a special name meaning, literally translated, "hard ears."

For Maslow, the good conduct among Blackfoot children was the direct result of parental emphasis upon personal responsibility. Parents encouraged even their youngest children to do things for themselves and not to expect adults to be servile to their needs. Throughout his life, he remained a staunch advocate of the firm yet loving approach to child-rearing he had observed on the Blackfoot reserve. In an article nearly thirty years later, Maslow admiringly noted:

The Blackfoot Indians are strong characters, self-respecting men, and they were the bravest of warriors. They were tough characters . . . If you watched to see how they developed this, I think it was through greater respect for their children. I can give a couple of examples.

I can remember . . . a toddler trying to open a door to a cabin. He could not make it. This was a big, heavy door and he was shoving and shoving. Well, Americans would get up and open the door for him. The Blackfoot Indians sat for half an hour while that baby struggled with that door, until he was able to get it open himself. He had to grunt and sweat, and then everyone praised him because he was able to do it himself. I would say that the Blackfoot Indian respected the child more than the American observer [did].

Maslow offered another vivid example of how Blackfoot parents enhanced their children's maturity:

[There] was a little boy that I was very fond of. He was about seven or eight years old, and I found by looking very closely that he was a kind of rich kid, in a Blackfoot way. He had several horses and cattle in his name, and he owned a medicine bundle of particular value.

Someone, a grown-up, turned up who wanted to buy the medicine bundle, which was the most valuable thing that he had. I learned from his father that what little Teddy did when he [was] made this offer—remember he was only seven years old—was to go into the wilderness by himself to meditate.

He went away for about two or three days and nights, camping out, thinking for himself. He did not ask his father or mother for advice, and they didn't tell him anything. He came back and announced his decision. I can just see us doing that with a seven-year-old kid.

It is interesting to note that both these examples involve boys rather than girls; although Maslow may not have considered the notion, it is possible that what he perceived as the Blackfoot emphasis on developing childhood responsibility was mainly a method for socializing males.

Maslow also came to respect the depth of friendship among the Indians. The warm and close social relations, he believed, constituted another reason why Blackfoot Indians seemed more emotionally secure than people in our own society, despite our greater material wealth. Having always enjoyed being part of a large, extended family while growing up in Brooklyn, and later as an adult, Maslow could well relate to this aspect of Blackfoot life:

> Every person has many relatives and friends scattered over the reserve and on other Blackfoot reserves on whom he may call for help. Visiting between relatives and friends is frequent, and sleeping overnight at any relative's or friend's home is a usual procedure.

> The boys and girls of any age group are far more closely bound together than in our society. They do the same things, join societies at the same time, and are always together. One's age-mates are called *nitaka*, which means "my friend of my own age." The ties of this friendship pattern are closer than other patterns. Thus, every boy and girl will have ten or twelve people who are called *nitaka* and who are considered close friends.

> Of this group, one or sometimes two, and rarely three, are selected as especially close friends. These may be called *nitakomima*, "beloved friend." Such close friends may be likened to brothers but among the Northern Blackfoot are ordinarily far closer to each other than brothers in our own society. From the point of view of whites, such friendships appear almost idyllic. There is complete mutual trust, loyalty, and affection.

In other respects, too, Maslow found much to admire about the Blackfoot way of life. He was impressed with the absence of crime and violence (other than an occasional fistfight between young, intoxicated males), the widespread and effective use of humor to diffuse tensions among tribal members, and the lack of financial jealousy or greed.

Above all, Maslow permanently abandoned his notion of cultural relativity as a result of his contact with the Blackfoot. Thereafter, he rejected the concept as erroneous and an obstacle to understanding human nature. In a summary report to the Social Science Research Council several weeks after his fieldwork, he expressed this transformation in his outlook:

It would seem that every human being comes at birth into society not as a lump of clay to be molded by society, but rather as a structure which society may warp or suppress or build upon. My fundamental data supporting this feeling is that my Indians were first human beings and *secondly* Blackfoot Indians, and also that in their society I found almost the same range of personalities as I find in our society—with, however, very different modes in the distribution curves.

I am now struggling with a notion of a "fundamental" [or] "natural" personality structure.

Although Maslow found much that was appealing about Blackfoot culture, he became increasingly homesick as the summer progressed. He missed Bertha and especially the baby. He kept staring at Ann's photograph like an icon, and later recalled, "I missed her awfully, so kept looking at the picture and reacting as if to something or someone totally loved." He wrote to Bertha frequently, and whenever he received news from her about the family, he felt uplifted.

Maslow had another reason to feel lonely that summer. Partly through Maslow's encouragement, Hanks began to court Richardson, and before long, the two were falling in love. Both single and in their late twenties, the pair shared many interests. Maslow's presence each evening became an increasingly unwelcome intrusion into the budding romance, which would lead to lifelong marriage.

Having accomplished more than he had hoped in his fieldwork, Maslow left the other two shortly before summer's end and returned to New York City, where Berth and baby Ann awaited him.

CHAPTER EIGHT

Revelations at Brooklyn College

In my career as an experimentalist in the laboratory, I felt quite comfortable and capable with my heritage of scientific orthodoxy. But insofar as I was a psychotherapist, an analysand, a father, a teacher, and a student of personality—that is, insofar as I dealt with whole persons—"scientific psychology" gradually proved itself to be of little use.

In the 1930s, I became interested in certain psychological problems, and found that they could not be answered by the classic scientific structure of the time. I was raising legitimate questions and had to invent another approach to psychological problems in order to deal with them. This approach slowly became a general philosophy of psychology, or science in general, of religion, work, management, and now biology.

—A.M.

The newest addition to New York City's academic system, Brooklyn College had been founded in 1930. It was composed of five old rented buildings in downtown Brooklyn, a gritty area encompassing mostly municipal and office buildings, printing shops, and stationery stores. But shortly after Maslow joined the faculty, the founders' dream of a real campus for the school was realized. In the residential, relatively more serene area of Flatbush, not far from where Maslow had spent his teenage years, Brooklyn College officially opened its new doors on October 18, 1937.

A crowd estimated at seven thousand assembled that day

in front of the academic building to hear speeches from Mayor Fiorello La Guardia, Brooklyn Borough President Raymond V. Ingersoll, and President William Boylan of Brooklyn College. The finishing touches, such as landscaping and walks for the Georgian setting, were not yet in place, but the campus was a reality.

During Maslow's first days as a full-time psychology tutor, he discovered that the Brooklyn College student body was vastly different from that he had known at Columbia and Wisconsin. Both those schools were prestigious, with ample research funding and extensive housing facilities, and imbued with a sense of collegiate tradition. Their students came from a diversity of backgrounds, some representing the well-to-do elite of their regions. In contrast, their counterparts at Brooklyn College were much like Maslow and his former peers at City College in the mid-1920s, the sons and daughters of immigrants.

In more than half the homes of Brooklyn College students, English was not the only language spoken. Only a handful of the fathers held professional jobs; most were garment workers, salesmen, craftsmen, or owners of small shops. The mothers worked mainly in lower Manhattan's garment industry or held clerical jobs. More than eighty percent of these homes were Jewish, and Yiddish was often the preferred language of parental reading and discourse. Few of the families were highly religiously observant, but many were tied loosely to a synagogue or a Jewish fraternal organization and quite conscious of their foreign origins.

The students were socially as well as ethnically homogeneous. Reflecting their prior success in the Brooklyn public schools, they tended to be younger than the national average for first-year college students. Having skipped several grades, many were sixteen, some even fifteen, upon entering Brooklyn College. Most lived with their parents in small apartments and had little direct knowledge of the world beyond the city. To many, a trip to the Catskill Mountains two hours away was the only exposure to countryside and open skies. They possessed little social poise but were eager to learn, and Maslow soon developed a close rapport with them.

He must have been reminded of his younger self in their brash manner and tendency to rely on verbal prowess to get through most situations. From his own experience, he was familiar with the unromantic reality of commuting to college classes by subway and trolley. He knew, too, about lack of privacy at home and the resulting frustration. In a way, Maslow realized, his students had it rougher than he had: the Depression exerted far greater tension than he had known in the more buoyant Brooklyn of the 1920s. Close to a third of his students' fathers were unemployed. For most students, the choice was either a municipal college or none at all.

The Brooklyn College students were academically gifted; their average scores on standardized college-entrance tests were typically in the nationwide top six percent. They were ambitious and hard-working, with a strong sense of their own natural intelligence.

It is fortunate that Maslow found his students so congenial, for his teaching duties were demanding. The administration clearly considered faculty research and original scholarship as subordinate to the goal of educating undergraduates. Like virtually all other faculty members, Maslow was assigned to teach five sections of two or more courses per semester. The teaching load left little time or energy for creative scholarly activity. At a major research university like Columbia, in contrast, the typical teaching load was two classes, or a single seminar, per semester.

Initially, Maslow taught abnormal psychology, then added a course in 1940 that he dubbed The Normal Personality. This was an innovation; academic psychology, when it dealt at all with human emotions, had concentrated almost exclusively on aberration and illness. Perhaps most influenced by Max Wertheimer, Maslow began to develop an approach to understanding average or even ideal psychological functioning, in contrast to the Freudian emphasis on neuroses and more severe disturbances.

Promoted to psychology instructor after one year, Maslow waited eight more years for his next advancement—to assistant professor—despite his productivity. Such snail's-pace promotion was typical of administrative policy at Brooklyn College, which depended on New York City's yearly budget for funding.

Aside from the school's heavy emphasis on teaching, Maslow found the administrative set-up somewhat constraining. Its psychology faculty was small and made up only a subdiscipline within the philosophy department. Initially his fellow psychologists were Solomon Asch, Edward Girden, Gerald Lawlor, Charles Winslow, and Austin B. Wood; four had received their doctorates from Columbia. Not long afterward, Helen Block Lewis and Herman Witkin joined the psychology faculty. As an isolated minority within the philosophy department, Maslow and his colleagues felt hampered; any academic innovation had to be formally discussed and voted upon by the entire department, a cumbersome and politicized process. Even within the small coterie of his colleagues, Maslow encountered major splits along philosophical, psychological, and political-ideological lines. While he got along adequately with most of his fellow psychologists, his only close friend among them was Asch.

Maslow and his colleagues agreed on one thing—the need for their own department. To several of them, Wertheimer seemed the ideal choice to serve as head. He possessed an international reputation and was already living in New York, teaching at the New School for Social Research. Maslow, of course, nearly idolized Wertheimer and was eager for the hiring. In early 1939, Wertheimer was offered the respectable salary of $7500 per year to head the new department. Much to Maslow's disappointment, Wertheimer backed out, claiming prior commitments, and no chairman took over until Daniel Katz in 1943.

Maslow also taught evening classes to earn extra money. Though similar in background and motivation to their day counterparts, the evening students were several years older, predominantly men, and especially serious about their studies. They were also more fatigued, often having worked all day before coming to class. Maslow therefore tried to enliven his evening lectures. His favorite method was to open by saying, "Let me tell you about an interesting article I've been reading," and then proceed to relate it to the scheduled course topic, such as motivation or child development. Largely for financial reasons, he also taught summer school regularly.

By the early 1940s, Maslow was so admired by students that he was known as "the Frank Sinatra of Brooklyn College"—a reference to another immigrant's son who was making a name for himself in a somewhat different field. Warm and witty, always eager to elicit students' opinions, Maslow was much liked. As a lecturer, he had a relaxed and easygoing manner and encouraged students to ask questions and offer comments. Tall and slender, with a bushy moustache and smoking a pipe, Maslow was a memorable figure to his students. In the late 1930s he was barely thirty years of age; but to eighteen- and nineteen-year-olds living with their immigrant parents, he represented sophistication itself. Many of Maslow's female students seem to have developed romantic crushes on him. His courses invariably filled up early during registration; some students wept in frustration when informed they were too late to enroll.

Maslow was so much esteemed that he could affect his students in ways not typical for professors, especially in the municipal college setting. For instance, one day his new colleague Paul Settlage, a close friend from Madison, Wisconsin, came to Maslow with a serious problem. As a midwestern Protestant with a quiet, polite manner, Settlage confided that he was becoming increasingly anxious in trying to teach his course. He had never met students so talkative, boisterous, and unwittingly disruptive in class. Even in a friendly manner, he could not get the Brooklyn-reared students to allow him to lecture unhindered.

Maslow came to the rescue. He went to each of Settlage's classes and firmly told the students that, as a fellow Jew, he felt obligated to let them know they were unintentionally upsetting his colleague. Gently explaining that their brash manner was acceptable by Brooklyn's ethnic standards but not by those of outsiders like Settlage, Maslow advised them to show greater decorum. He demonstrated several examples of proper classroom etiquette. Afterward, Settlage found his students quiet and responsive.

Maslow was also innovative in his teaching methods. For several years, he invited interested students to his home to discuss psychological issues in a relaxed, convivial atmosphere. Maslow's home on Ocean Avenue was just a block or two from campus. Only the most interested, usually about ten or twelve per semester, attended the lively discussions. Maslow's purpose was not therapeutic but educational; he believed that the best way to make psychological theory come alive is to directly relate it to our own experiences in life. As intellectual backdrop, he often referred to contemporary theorists like Karen Horney, particularly her concepts about basic needs such as self-esteem and the nature of anxiety and neurosis. To provide structure for the weekly group discussions, he encouraged each student to write in advance something autobiographical, something about his or her dreams or sexual history, and be prepared to share such comments with the group.

To many participants, the openness of the discussions in Maslow's home was astounding. Many had never experienced such provocative conversation, with topics running the full gamut pertaining to human emotions. It was rare for them, even with parents or friends, to talk seriously about innermost values, goals, and aspirations. To be sitting in their professor's home and to be genuinely respected for their opinions on such matters was intoxicating. Sharing their ethnic and geographic origins, Maslow put them at ease but was always careful to maintain a certain professorial distance.

Sometimes students would bring up an immediate concern, such as their own academic future. On one occasion, the issue was raised of anti-Semitism in the graduate school admission process. What should they do, they asked Maslow, when faced with the space marked "Religion" on their graduate school applications? Maslow, himself no stranger to prejudice, pragmatically advised, "Write down that you're Unitarian. It's the closest thing to being Jewish."

Discussions often addressed the topic of sexuality. Most young men and women at Brooklyn College were virgins with little sexual experience. Living with their parents, they had limited opportunity for sexual activity. In their predominantly ethnic-Jewish homes, sex was virtually a taboo subject, and many found it difficult to broach the subject even with close friends. For the esteemed Professor Maslow to invite discussion about sex was a momentous experience for many, especially in light of the group's coed makeup. He encouraged them to be as candid as possible in relating their sexual attitudes and encounters. Honest self-disclosure, he believed, does much to remove our anxiety and awkwardness about sex. For this reason, Maslow required his students to write sexual autobiographies.

Maslow generally voiced a liberal and tolerant outlook toward sexuality. But as one who had married at twenty the only girl he had ever dated, he was no revolutionary. Drawing on anthropological studies, he liked to point out that worldwide human culture has demonstrated tremendous variability with regard to sexual mores and customs. What one culture calls perverse may be deemed perfectly normal by another. He affirmed to his students that we all experience sexual feelings, that they are natural and nothing to feel embarrassed about. Masturbation is a good, healthy way to relieve sexual tension, he emphasized. Disparaging the portrayal of sex in tawdry novels and suggestive Hollywood films, Maslow criticized their image of instant physical attraction leading to ecstatic lovemaking. In a warm, paternal manner, he would say, "The first time you experience sex, you'll be disappointed. It's not the way the novels portray it."

In Maslow's more private musings, he expressed a stronger critique of mainstream social mores about sexuality and the body. For example, in an unpublished paper in 1939, he wrote:

> I have the feeling that a spread of nudism would be a step in the direction of greater ease and equality for men and women, for many reasons. First of all, it would make them less strange to each other; there would be less sexual exploring merely for the sake of curiosity. It seems to me also that such love as would emerge would be more on the social and emotional side than on the purely physical side.

Throughout his life, he remained an advocate of nudism for those who wished greater casualness and friendship between the sexes, and he himself was comfortable with this practice, occasionally engaging in it himself.

Maslow believed that many other changes in our society's sexual attitudes were necessary to promote greater happiness. Besides stressing the importance of early education to eliminate or lessen children's anxieties about sex, he highlighted the importance of wider public policy shifts. "The removal of economic, social, and legal disequalities [between the sexes] is also a necessary step," he wrote. "In order for such a program to be ultimately effective, tremendous changes in the economic place of women would have to be made."

It would take nearly half a century in the United States before legislative and court decisions would begin to expand women's economic and vocational rights in the way Maslow envisioned. As for attitudinal shifts concerning sex education or nudity, his ideas are finding popular acceptance only slowly.

In one respect, Maslow might be regarded as traditional by today's standards. He advised that monogamy through marriage (either serial or lifelong) ultimately provides the most satisfying sex life, and that casual sex is rarely very exciting or fulfilling, despite what the popular media tell us. While Maslow acknowledged the legitimacy of premarital sex, he generally recommended that his students control their strongest impulses until they found the right person. To accept sexual desires as natural does not automatically mean we should act on them, Maslow cautioned; emotional maturity always involves self-restraint. For men and women with strong sexual desire, he suggested, masturbation offers a natural release.

To complement his lectures on human sexuality, Maslow for many years assigned as a textbook *The Happy Family* by David Levy and Ruth Munroe. Published in 1938, and reprinted frequently through the 1940s, this work offered a warm and optimistic view of sexuality, marriage, and child-rearing. Its authors, who became Maslow's close friends, articulated the liberal, "enlightened" outlook of the time. Levy and Munroe criticized the popular rosy stereotypes about these often problematic aspects of modern American life. Decrying the romantic, they-lived-happily-ever-after myths surrounding sexuality, marriage, and child-rearing, they insisted that only psychological realism, especially on the necessity for compromise, makes for healthy, happy relationships. They agreed with Maslow that in a world of human imperfection, marriage and stable family life offer the greatest opportunity for true fulfillment.

Perhaps more than any specific advice about sex, it was Maslow's general approach that affected his students. Unlike almost everyone they knew, parents or peers, he treated the subject in an open, matter-of-fact way, without smirking or embarrassment. Both in his home seminars and regular Brooklyn College classes, his remarks on sexuality mirrored his larger message to students: learn to look within, strive to develop your potential, and think for yourself. As one former student, now a retired attorney, recalled, "He always told us, 'Be all that you can in life. It's the best way to be happy.'"

In Maslow's first few years at Brooklyn College, teaching consumed much of his energy. His research productivity diminished considerably, but he was hardly intellectually idle. He began to devote increasing attention to understanding the nature of the "normal" human personality, especially the issue of motivation: What do we really want? And, perhaps more important, what do we really need for happiness and fulfillment in life?

The year 1938 was a crucial one for Maslow as his new psychological outlook emerged. One impetus was his summer fieldwork with the Blackfoot Indians (see chapter 7). Before that experience, he had clung to the notion of cultural relativism. Afterward, cultural relativity seemed more and more questionable, and he found himself returning, somewhat ironically, to the implications of his studies with monkeys: our biological makeup may be far more significant than cross-cultural studies had suggested. Perhaps, Maslow thought, previous fieldworkers had relied too much on personal and superficial impressions instead of more empirical forms of psychological assessment. During Christmas week 1938, he reported at the annual convention of the American Anthropological Association in New York City:

> It [now seems] more important for a psychologist to know what kind of personality man has than to know that he is a Blackfoot Indian. . . . If these comparisons turn out to be valid, it will be obviously impossible to hold to any extreme form of cultural relativity, which would think of the human as a mere lump of clay to be shaped by cultural pressures into any form whatever. Rather, we shall probably have to make room for some notion of fundamental or natural "tendency-to-have-a-certain-type-of-personality" with which each human comes into society—and which the society will have to take as a fundamental datum, perhaps to build upon, perhaps to repress, or warp, or reshape.

For much of the five decades since Maslow voiced his critique, the cultural relativist outlook remained a pillar of American social science. However, in recent years the approach known as sociobiology has gained intellectual respectability. It is led by thinkers like Harvard's Edward O. Wilson, who insist on the importance of coming to terms with our biological nature and its impact upon social relations and social problems like crime.

For several years, Maslow considered returning to the Blackfoot or another tribe for further cross-cultural psychological research. He hoped to verify his impressions of Blackfoot members by applying a variety of personality tests, like the Rorschach inkblots, to adults and doll-play measures to children. Such attempts at objective cross-cultural personality research were just beginning in the 1940s; had Maslow carried out his plans, he would have broken new and perhaps important conceptual ground.

He gradually abandoned the idea as impractical. Especially after the birth of his second daughter, Ellen, he realized that he felt too emotionally tied to his family to leave them even for a summer. While Maslow maintained an active interest in cross-cultural study through the early 1940s—corresponding with Margaret Mead on mutual concerns for instance—he never resumed his earlier involvement. Perhaps Ruth Benedict's departure from Columbia University in 1941, to work in Washington, D.C., for the government's war effort, contributed to Maslow's withdrawal from anthropological activity.

The other key influence in 1938 upon Maslow's evolving outlook was the birth of his first child, Ann. Just as the Blackfoot fieldwork had forced him to question his belief in cultural relativism, seeing Ann grow and develop made him doubt even more the notion that we are mere products of our upbringing or culture. As Maslow watched little Ann forcefully express her wants and dislikes—and, in so doing, very much influence those around her—he found himself rejecting John B. Watson's behaviorist perspective, which had meant so much to him as a young man. Watson's claim that he could take any child at birth and create whatever kind of person he wished through behavioral conditioning now seemed untenable and even a bit ridiculous. As Maslow and Bertha observed, matters were hardly that easy. The organismic conception of Kurt Goldstein, stressing that we bring to the world an integral biological makeup, began to seem more plausible. "Becoming a father," Maslow recollected, "changed my whole life. It taught me as if by revelation. It made the behaviorism I had been so enthusiastic about look so foolish that I couldn't stomach it anymore. It was impossible."

Ellen's birth in 1940 further strengthened his growing conviction in this regard. From birth onward his daughters appeared markedly distinct in personality and behavior. They had even seemed different before birth. While Ann had been calm and placid in the womb, Ellen had been active and restless. As children, their different personalities were just as salient. To Maslow, it seemed increasingly clear that any comprehensive theory of human nature must take into account our unique, individual, and innate qualities. By the early 1940s, therefore, he began to synthesize the biological or organismic approach with the behaviorist, Freudian, and Gestalt schools of thought that he had also found useful.

Maslow had become close to several psychoanalysts in New York City (see chapter 6). Aside from getting to know such leading European émigrés as Adler, Fromm, and Horney, he also became friendly with Bela Mittelmann, a Hungarian psychiatrist. Mittelmann soon learned that Maslow enjoyed intellectual parties and invited him regularly to his Manhattan salons. In this convivial manner, Maslow came to meet New York's most active psychoanalytic practitioners and writers, including Emil Oberholzer, Abram Kardiner, David M. Levy, and others.

Emigrating to the United States from Switzerland in 1938, Emil Oberholzer (1873–1958) lectured at the New York Psychoanalytic Institute while conducting a private analytic practice. Maslow eventually underwent a partial psychoanalysis with him. Maslow was still feeling much unresolved hostility toward his mother, Rose, who lived nearby in Brooklyn, for, much to his siblings' dismay, he shunned all contact with her. On occasion, one or another of Maslow's brothers would take Ann and Ellen to visit Rose, but he and Bertha never went along. Maslow also was interested in seeing what analysis was like from the patient's perspective. On both counts, he felt the sessions beneficial, although he continued to avoid his mother. It is not known what circumstances caused termination of the analysis.

Abram Kardiner (1891–1981) was another psychiatrist who strongly influenced Maslow. Kardiner was perhaps the leading psychiatric researcher in the field of anthropology through the 1930s and 1940s. Like Maslow, he was an American-born son of Jewish immigrants and had attended New York's City College. After specializing in psychiatry and undergoing analysis with Freud in Vienna, Kardiner returned to New York City and in 1930 founded the New York Psychiatric Institute, the first training school of its kind in the United States. Kardiner knew Maslow from his association with Ruth Benedict. With such mutual interests, the two men began to spend time together.

In 1939, Kardiner published *The Individual and His Society*, a work that interpreted several cultures in terms of their basic institutions like child-rearing and their control of sex, dependency, and aggression. Despite Kardiner's somewhat arrogant personality, Maslow felt awed by his brilliance, and they occasionally met at the latter's impressive home in Westport, Connecticut.

David M. Levy (1892–1977) was one of Maslow's closest intellectual companions during these years. Born in Scranton, Pennsylvania, he was educated at Harvard and the University of Chicago. A pioneer in child psychiatry, Levy had headed the New York Institute of Child Guidance for several years before Maslow met him in the late 1930s. By then, Levy had brought the Rorschach inkblot test to the United States from Switzerland and begun seminal theoretical work related to children's mental health. It was Levy who popularized the phrase sibling rivalry and helped develop activity-play therapy, in which children are encouraged to act out their emotions through play with dolls or puppets. Down-to-earth and unassuming, Levy enjoyed sharing with Maslow exotic eating places in New York City, from obscure Jewish dairies to fancy French restaurants. As an experimentally trained researcher, Maslow liked Levy's empirical emphasis on understanding children's emotional disorders.

Before long, Maslow began to contemplate writing his first book. Although he preferred to work on short research papers, he learned that the Brooklyn College administration considered the publication of a book an important indicator of professorial excellence and worthiness for tenure and promotion. Therefore, around 1940, Maslow decided to author a textbook on abnormal psychology. Having taught the subject for several years, he had extensive notes and a solid familiarity with over-all theory and research. With Mittelmann as collaborator, Maslow developed an outline and sought a publisher. On May 9, 1941, the two received a contract from Harper Brothers with an advance of $300. It was published later that year.

Maslow's interest in psychotherapy was not merely intellectual. Soon after coming to Brooklyn College in 1937 he found himself assuming the role of a lay psychotherapist. The students were academically gifted but beset with normal adolescent problems. They were perhaps even more prone to emotional difficulties than their college peers in other parts of the country, Maslow observed. Because they lived with their parents, privacy was virtually nonexistent. Many felt it difficult to develop a sense of autonomous adulthood when questioned each evening about their schoolwork and social activities. Conflicts with parents were almost inevitable, especially concerning religion, morality, and values. For some, parental pressures for obedience and constant bickering at home led to emotional distress.

In its early years, the school did not provide much academic counseling, let alone assistance with personal problems, and it lacked the sense of community typical at most colleges. Inevitably, some students turned to Maslow for personal advice. Warm and outgoing, he was a trained psychologist, and virtually the only faculty member interested in issues of personality and social behavior.

Maslow became resourceful and innovative in this helping capacity. With no formal training in psychoanalysis, he could not offer in-depth emotional assistance. But even had he acquired expertise as a lay, nonmedical psychoanalyst, like Erich Fromm or Theodore Reik, true psychoanalysis would not have been possible with his students. For one thing, he lacked the time for such involved one-to-one therapeutic work. Besides that, most students would not have committed themselves to the prolonged effort necessary for a successful analysis. But in the late 1930s, no proven therapeutic alternatives to psychoanalysis existed. It was not until Carl Rogers's pioneering work in developing nondirective counseling several years later—he published *Counseling and Psychotherapy* in 1942—that any coherent alternative to psychoanalysis was advanced. Thus, relying mainly on his intuition, reading, and conversation with analyst friends, Maslow offered informal therapeutic services to students.

For the most part, their emotional problems were minor. As Maslow remarked in an unpublished paper dated July 12, 1941:

> Most of my experience has been with only those cases that a lay psychotherapist would handle. I have not ordinarily dealt with severe neuroses and certainly not with psychoses except as an observer and friend. I have usually taken on only cases that I felt some confidence about. Since there are so many more cases than I can handle anyway, my time was always fully occupied.

Some of Maslow's cases involved mothers, probably attending evening classes, who were worried about their children's behavior at home. Typically, he would make a quick judgment as to whether the mother was herself emotionally stable and mature. If so, Maslow would tell her to throw away her parenting books, ignore the suggestions of her doctors, and not seek out psychologists, but simply follow her own intuition. Such a course of action, Maslow would say reassuringly, would work better than any advice she would get from experts. However, if the mother seemed emotionally unstable and immature, Maslow recommended a list of books on child psychology and referred her to a child psychologist or a psychoanalyst for herself.

Sometimes Maslow was sought out by students who had low self-esteem. Although academically bright, they felt shy, timid, or inadequate with others, especially the opposite sex. In such instances, Maslow intuitively developed an approach, based on his studies of dominance-feeling and ego-security, that is similar to the cognitive-behavioral method widely practiced by therapists today. Typically, Maslow would first elicit from the individual a list of specific anxiety-producing situations, such as being complimented by a stranger or being introduced to someone at a social gathering. Then Maslow would organize the list into a series of "steps" and provide instructions on how to act more forcefully, starting with the least anxiety-arousing situation or step. He would coach the student on what to do and say. After the student successfully behaved in a more outgoing manner, Maslow would focus on the list's next step, and so on, until all had been mastered.

In other instances, Maslow sought to develop alternatives to the lengthy and time-consuming Freudian technique of free association. He introduced an approach called "lifting the lid off the repression." In essence, this involved helping the individual to accept into conscious awareness some long-repressed impulse, like sexual feelings toward an attractive neighbor or hostility toward a parent. To accomplish this, Maslow sometimes described for the student many cases involving such an impulse, thereby emphasizing its normality. Or he would offer repeated assurance, as a kind of flattery, that only very courageous people dare recognize such an impulse. At times, Maslow was more indirect. In an offhand, oblique way he would comment that if the individual ever experienced such an impulse in the future, it should be regarded as something perfectly acceptable. In this manner, the student might gradually, or even suddenly, realize that the impulse had existed all along, or might recognize it for what it really was. This entire therapeutic process, Maslow stressed, depended upon the permissive, accepting attitude of the therapist.

Partly in response to time pressures at Brooklyn College, he also began to develop what he termed supplemental therapies as short-term or mild alternatives to psychoanalysis. One of his favorite methods involved the case history. As he recounted in March 1942:

> If somebody comes to me for help and I have no time, I say so, and then sort of as an afterthought I suggest that if they write out their problems and what they think about them, I would be glad to read them and comment. I give them some sort of outline.

> They are instructed to bring in their installments about once a week, at which time I look over the installment, criticize it, make whatever interpretive comments are necessary, and add more things to write about.

> I have had some very good success with this method when I have had enough time to talk with them at length. It seems never to have done any harm. I also ask them usually to keep a dream diary.

Maslow also recommended a variety of day-to-day activities to help students cope with stress. He valued dancing as a healthful and sociable way to let go of bodily and emotional tension. He also suggested that involvement in a creative activity like art or music could be uplifting and calming. For those who did not feel talented in either realm, he advised that simply listening to music or going to an art museum could be mildly therapeutic.

Most important to the impact on Maslow's later theoretical system, this work convinced him that we have certain inner needs unrecognized by Freudians and members of other psychological schools of thought—especially the need to experience meaning and purpose in life. A few innovative analysts like Fromm and Horney had touched on this issue, but it remained outside the bounds of mainstream psychoanalysis. A turning point in Maslow's thinking about therapy came around 1938, when a college woman desperately sought his help. She complained of insomnia, lack of appetite, disturbed menstruation, and a chronic feeling of boredom. Nothing aroused her interest or gave her any pleasure.

These symptoms seemed similar to those described by Abraham Myerson in his book *When Life Loses Its Zest*, which Maslow had found fascinating. As the woman went on talking, her situation seemed even more intriguing. She had graduated from Brooklyn College about a year before and had a lucrative but dull job as a personnel supervisor at a chewing-gum factory. In those Depression days, she was supporting her whole unemployed family and was envied by her friends for her income.

So what was the problem? In pouring out her heart to Maslow, she said she felt that her life lacked meaning. She had been a brilliant psychology student planning to go on to graduate training. She loved intellectual matters. But her family's financial straits had forced her to abandon her studies. At first, she had tried to convince herself that she should be happy and grateful for the well-paying job and its material rewards. But slowly, the image of a lifetime of such work began to oppress her, and she now felt totally empty inside.

Maslow, relying on his intuition, did not treat her by the classic Freudian approach. He was uninterested in her childhood, its conflicts and fantasies. Rather, he sensed the real issue to be the woman's sense of meaningless and wasted talent. In a later article, "The Need to Know and the Fear of Knowing," he wrote:

> I suggested that she might be feeling profoundly frustrated and angry because she was not being her own very intelligent self, that she was not using her intelligence and her talent for psychology and that this might be a major reason for her boredom with life and her body's boredom with the normal pleasures of life [like eating]. Any talent, any capacity was also a motivation, a need, an impulse. With this she agreed, and I suggested that she could continue her graduate studies at night after work . . . She was able to arrange this, and it worked well. She became more alive, more happy and zestful, and most of her physical symptoms had disappeared at my last contact with her.

This case and others like it had a profound effect on Maslow's view of human motivation, not only in regard to psychotherapy and counseling. Several years later, he would develop his theory of self-actualization based in part on such encounters.

Shortly after returning from the Blackfoot fieldwork, Maslow became increasingly interested in the larger social implications of his experience with the Blackfoot. He was strongly convinced that Ruth Benedict's criticism about the harmful competitiveness within American culture was correct. Clearly, the Blackfoot were far more emotionally secure than those he had studied at Brooklyn College and elsewhere. But what to do about the situation? Over the next two years, he gave this question considerable thought and wrote several polished though unpublished papers, such as "Security as a Religion" and "Technique of Changing a Society in the Direction of Security."

In those New Deal days, Maslow, like many social scientists, was intrigued with visions of benevolent centralized planning. Particularly interested in promoting greater emotional security, and thereby happiness and harmony, among Americans, he speculated about several methods to accomplish this end. One involved a radical overhaul of the U.S. educational

system to enhance cooperation among students. Maslow called
for abolishing competitive grading, especially on a curve, and
for changing the teacher's role from authority figure to ally in
the child's quest for emotional and intellectual growth.

To help foster more emotional security in our culture, he
advocated an extensive governmental program to guarantee
medical and disability insurance for all citizens. He stressed too
that we should begin to value such traits as generosity and
cooperation, rather than self-aggrandizement, as a definition
of success. "Ours is a money and power society," he noted,
"and so long as it is, it is thereby insecure. People must be
taught in the schools and in the psychological clinics and in
books, newspapers, and articles just what their hunt for power
means . . . that they are only seeking security."

Finally, he saw the American family as a key institution
badly in need of transformation:

> Our family is organized hierarchically. Also it is much
> too small in the social sense. Kinship systems and obligations
> do not spread wide enough, there is too much dependence
> upon one or two individuals, i.e., the mother or the father.
> In a word, too many eggs are put into one basket. The mother
> is far too important in the life of the child. Anything that
> happens to the relationship of the mother and child is very
> apt to bring insecurity.

> This is avoided in primitive societies by having many [care-
> givers among relatives] . . . Perhaps one way to do this is to
> create many warm emotional ties outside the home so that
> there is not too complete dependence upon the parental tie.
> This would involve [for the child], of course, much more
> visiting, more sleeping in other homes, much more camping
> out. In a word, much more independence of [the nuclear]
> home and family.

Although Maslow never sought direct political expression
for his intense beliefs about changing American society, particularly its mores involving sexuality and competitiveness, he
managed to put his ideas into effect in one regard. For several
years after his daughters were born, he participated in an
unusual communal living arrangement with extended-family
members.

The three-story house on Ocean Avenue in which the Maslows lived held several apartments, and gradually these began to fill up with their relatives. Over a period of seven or eight years, the commune at various times included his father, younger brother Paul, Bertha's mother and father, Bertha's divorced sister Anna and her two college-age sons—together, of course, with Maslow, Bertha, and their two daughters. For several years, Maslow was the only one of the entire group with a steady full-time job. His small salary at Brooklyn College had to help support them all.

For the commune to function effectively, each relative had specific day-to-day household chores and responsibilities. These were taken seriously by all concerned. For instance, even little Ann Maslow had a daily task: going to the different apartments in the house and waking everyone. Apparently, they all got along well and enjoyed a wonderful quality of life on meager earnings. When Maslow's colleague and friend Gardner Murphy came to visit, Maslow gave him a tour of the apartment. Pointing to one appliance and piece of furniture after another that had been bought on installment credit, Maslow suddenly spied one of his daughters. Sweeping her into his arms, he happily commented, "And this one we own outright."

Maslow always looked back fondly on this communal experience with relatives—which he called, in mock anthropological terms, his cliff-dwelling period. It also provided many lessons on how to create and sustain intimacy and warmth among members of a group. Maslow believed that many emotional problems common to our society stem directly from the absence of shared intimacy in our lives. Regarding the contemporary nuclear—or, increasingly, subnuclear—family as almost a prescription for loneliness and unhappiness, he commented, "I have no doubt that . . . present-day youngsters . . . suffer from having been deprived of grandparents; for that matter, they [have] often been deprived of parents, too." On the basis of his own experience, he believed that successful group living depends on two conditions: that the people are all fairly stable emotionally, and that there is one person "who is willing to go to a lot of trouble to be the clan mother or father and to hold the whole group together." For Maslow's family, Bertha's mother was such a figure.

At about the same time, Maslow was involved in another unconventional endeavor, a food cooperative in his Flatbush neighborhood. It represented his effort to create a viable alternative to profit-oriented supermarkets, and he was committed to seeing it succeed. However, despite volunteer labor, the co-op kept losing money and eventually closed. Maslow later regarded the experiment as a failure, affirming the necessity of organization and sound management for even the most selfless, not-for-profit enterprise. "The manager was lousy," he recalled, "and since then, I've come to appreciate the good entrepreneurs, managers, and businessmen—and efficiency and competence—rather than just good will and nice à priori doctrines."

Despite the enjoyment Maslow reaped from his small-scale attempts at alternative living in Brooklyn, he felt increasing frustration and sadness as he watched the steady triumph of fascism in Germany, Italy, Japan, and Spain. Like many sensitive people of his time, he reacted to Franco's brutal victory over the supporters of democracy as almost a personal tragedy, and felt more and more helpless before the sweep of ominous international events. Things were going well for him professionally—*Principles of Abnormal Psychology* had received glowing reviews and was on its way to becoming the standard work in the field—but he wondered what such achievements really accomplished against the darker forces in the world.

One afternoon shortly after the United States entered World War II, Maslow experienced a sudden inner transformation that gave him a sense of mission for the rest of his life. This vision filled him with direction, purpose, and energy, and he never forgot it. The catalyst was a humble, ragtag veterans' parade near Brooklyn College. The experience is best described in Maslow's own words:

One day just after Pearl Harbor, I was driving home and my car was stopped by a poor, pathetic parade. Boy Scouts and fat people and old uniforms and a flag and someone playing a flute off-key. As I watched, the tears began to run down my face. I felt we didn't understand—not Hitler, nor the Germans, nor Stalin, nor the Communists. We didn't understand any of them. I felt that if we could understand, then we could make progress."

I had a vision of a peace table, with people sitting around it, talking about human nature and hatred and war and peace and brotherhood. I was too old to go into the army. It was at that moment that I realized that the rest of my life must be devoted to discovering a psychology for the peace table. That moment changed my whole life.

From this day on, Maslow's work in psychology would steadily become more innovative and far-reaching, yet also more unorthodox. By setting course for undiscovered territory involving human nature and our unrealized potential, Maslow was taking on the lonely and arduous—but exhilarating—task of explorer.

CHAPTER NINE

Glimmerings of Self-Actualization

> My investigations on self-actualization were not planned to be research and did not start out as research, [but] as the effort of a young intellectual to try to understand two of his teachers whom he loved, adored, and admired and who were very, very wonderful people. I could not be content simply to adore, but sought to understand why these two people were so different from the run-of-the-mill people in the world.
>
> —A.M.

As the United States entered World War II and the international situation grew more ominous, Maslow saw one path toward realizing his vision of the peace table: developing a comprehensive theory of human motivation. The key questions for humanity, he thought, were really few in number: What do people really want in life? What do they need for happiness? What makes them seek certain goals? And, in more concrete terms, why do they flock to a Hitler or a Stalin?

In concentrating on these issues, Maslow found much in his previous psychological studies that made sense. He reviewed the theories of Alfred Adler and Sigmund Freud, Karen Horney and Erich Fromm, and the "new ego psychologists" Abram Kardiner and David M. Levy. Kurt Goldstein's work on the organism, especially his concept of self-actualization, seemed relevant. The experimental psychologists, too, had their insights. But no single approach offered more than a partial solution to understanding human nature; it would be necessary to assimilate and integrate them all.

Maslow was excited and confident about his emerging theory of motivation. No one else was synthesizing the elements of modern psychology—Freudian, neo-Freudian, behaviorist, Gestalt, and organismic—as he was doing. If his approach were successful in rigor and scope, centuries of speculation about our inner nature and behavior would become obsolete and, perhaps, a new vision would emerge to change civilization. In a representative research memo dated February 13, 1942, he confidently wrote, "I have no doubt that one by-product of modern motivation theory and research will be the overthrow once and for all of classical hedonistic theory."

Maslow also turned to anthropology for insights. On February 21, he wrote to Gregory Bateson, Margaret Mead's husband and collaborator, for information on Bateson's recent fieldwork among the Balinese.

A lecture by Max Wertheimer on "Being and Doing" that year also affirmed the intriguing possibility of unmotivated behavior, such as playfulness and esthetic enjoyment, unrelated to physiological needs. This was another aspect of human nature that none of the dominant theories had seriously addressed.

In developing his integrative approach to human motivation, Maslow kept thinking about his years of therapeutic work with Brooklyn College students. In trying to help them, he had been guided by personal intuitions about life's meaning and the way to happiness, but Maslow had never been very explicit about his own values. Certainly, he had never sought to effect merely an adjustment to society's mores in those he counseled, but to catalyze something deeper, involving the individual's goals and aspirations. He recognized that some students had benefited greatly from his therapeutic activity, while others had not. What aspects made the successes emotionally healthy and fulfilled? By musing in this way, Maslow concluded that people's needs could be grouped into several categories, and that some seemed more innately fundamental than others.

As Maslow began to pull together the strands of his new theory of motivation, he recognized its biological basis with regard to human nature. But by now he felt confident that cultural relativism was obsolete as an overriding principle for understanding human makeup and behavior. There is something about every person's life desires and goals, Maslow noted in his research memos that year, that transcends cultural pressures. As he would write in a major paper the following year,

"People, even in different societies, are much more alike than we would think from our first contact with them, and as we know them better we seem to find more and more of this commonness. We then recognize the most startling differences to be superficial rather than basic, [like] differences in style of hair-dress [or] tastes in food."

Meanwhile, Maslow began to seek a way to comprehend the motivations of emotionally healthy persons as well as neurotics. As he later recalled, "I went about it by trying to understand great people, the best specimens of mankind I could find." This particular search would soon become the capstone of his developing theory. Maslow's interest in highly fulfilled persons had been germinating ever since his first encounters with Ruth Benedict and Max Wertheimer back in 1935. As he later recollected:

> They were puzzling. They didn't fit. It was as if they came from another planet . . . Everything I knew didn't explain them. They were mysteries. They were also very nice and parental with me, and answered questions and let me hang around . . . And I had all sorts of notes on them, sort of journal notes, and I kept on trying to figure them out. That was an entirely personal enterprise. It didn't even occur to me to think of it as an exploration or a research.

One impetus had been a party at Maslow's home which Benedict and Wertheimer attended. The mood had been so warm, exuberant, and intellectually stimulating that Maslow began to wonder "what kind of culture would be generated by self-actualizing people in bulk." He had kept numerous notes about Benedict and Wertheimer, but he had been so busy with other projects that not much had developed over the years. He had not tried to organize his speculations into any larger theoretical context.

In 1940 Maslow first crystallized these musings. During his coauthorship with Bela Mittelmann of the book *Principles of Abnormal Psychology*, Maslow had deemed it necessary to devote an entire chapter to an overview of the normal personality. None of the others involved with the work-in-progress had expected such an unorthodox topic, but Maslow was given his way. In identifying what he called the manifestations of normality, he identified twelve broad qualities and several dozen specific ones. In using the term *normal*, Maslow was obviously referring to desirable or healthy traits. These included adequate self-esteem and self-knowledge, the ability to receive and express love, and the capacity to question the rules or ethics of one's society.

In the same chapter, he wrote a brief section subtitled "The Ideal Personality and Goals." Here Maslow asserted that while the question of the ideal personality is definitely related to values, he hoped that "science in its onward march will eventually take over the whole problem of values for study. We see no reason [not] to believe that most of our values, perhaps even all of them, will eventually come within the jurisdiction of science; but until this is true, any discussion of the ideal personality must be postponed."

When writing these sections, Maslow had been disappointed by the lack of information about such important considerations in psychology. He had been willing to wait for "science in its onward march." Now, with the world plunged into war and with the spreading triumph of Hitler and fascism around the globe, it was no longer possible to wait patiently for scientific progress concerning human nature. It was time to develop a comprehensive study of human motivation, encompassing our highest values and ideals.

The final catalyst for Maslow's work on motivation came in 1943. His psychiatrist friends Kardiner and Levy, both members of the Society for Research in Psychoanalysis and Psychosomatics in New York, invited him to present a paper based on his new integrative approach to human motivation. Maslow was pleased, for he always enjoyed their stimulating discussions and knew that the invitation would force him to formalize his scattered notes. That year he published his concept in two related papers. The first, "A Preface to Motivation Theory," appeared in January; the second, a far more powerful piece, "A Theory of Human Motivation," in the fall.

The latter article, which Maslow published at the age of thirty-five, became the most influential work of his career. The model of human nature that he advanced in it has largely replaced the Freudian, the behaviorist, and many others, and now guides understanding of the individual in a host of fields, ranging from psychotherapy and marriage counseling to education, from business management and marketing to nursing and health care, and even theology.

Maslow centered his theory of motivation on what he called the hierarchy of human needs. In essence, he contended that every person is born with a set of *basic needs* encompassing the physiological and including needs for safety, belongingness or love, and self-esteem. In a complex but lucid formulation, he argued that these basic needs can be seen as making up an unfolding hierarchy. He declared:

> It is quite true that man lives by bread alone—where there is no bread. But what happens to man's desires when there *is* plenty of bread and when his belly is chronically filled?

> *At once other (and "higher") needs emerge* and these, rather than physiological hungers, dominate the organism. And when these in turn are satisfied, again new (and still "higher") needs emerge, and so on. This is what we mean by saying that the basic human needs are organized into a hierarchy of relative prepotency.

One key implication of the theory is that a satisfied need no longer motivates our behavior. That is, a hungry man may willingly surrender his need for self-respect in order to stay alive; but once he can feed, shelter, and clothe himself, he becomes likely to seek higher ends. Maslow recognized that even such an apparently simple case has exceptions, such as people who engage in great personal sacrifice to help others or who demonstrate clear heroism. At the very time Maslow was developing his theory in New York, there were those dying of disease and starvation in German concentration camps who were selflessly sharing their last crumbs with fellow inmates and helping them to maintain hope in a nightmare. How can we explain such conduct? Although Maslow was not thinking of such extreme situations, he wrote:

> These [altruistic] people may be understood, at least in part [as having been] satisfied in their basic needs throughout their lives, particularly in their early years. [They] seem to develop exceptional power to withstand present or future

thwarting of these needs simply because they have strong, healthy character structure . . . It is just the ones who have loved and been well loved, and who have had many deep friendships, who can hold out against hatred, rejection, or persecution.

Finally, Maslow outlined the existence of another inborn human need—the need for individual fulfillment, or what he preferred to call self-actualization. He wrote:

> We may still often (if not always) expect that a new discontent will develop, unless the individual is doing what he is fitted for. A musician must make music, an artist must paint, a poet must write, if he is to be ultimately at peace with himself. What a man *can* be, he *must* be. This need we may call self-actualization . . . It refers to man's desire for self-fulfillment, namely, to the tendency for him to become actualized in what he is potentially. This tendency might be phrased as the desire to become more and more what one is, to become everything that one is capable of becoming.

The extent to which Maslow would come to focus on self-actualization is not obvious from this brief comment, but this was because he had nothing more definite to say—yet. Now, having completed what he proudly viewed as his most important contribution in psychology to date, Maslow was ready to turn his attention more closely to understanding self-actualization. The Freudians and neo-Freudians, he thought, had developed an accurate portrait of what we are like when thwarted and frustrated in our lower needs, and he therefore saw no need to pile up further details about neuroses and psychoses. The depths of human nature did not interest him much; for nearly fifty years psychiatry and abnormal psychology had been investigating them. Maslow preferred to explore uncharted psychological territory, and the challenge of studying "the best of humanity" appealed immensely to him. His motivation articles were attracting little attention so far, but he was unshakably convinced that he was engaged in work of historic importance and that widespread recognition would come in due time.

Initially, Maslow began to lecture to his psychology class

about his musings. "Finally, those two pictures [of Ruth Benedict and Max Wertheimer] clicked into one," and he saw them as the composite of the self-actualized person rather than just individuals. He shared his exciting new insight only with his students and close friends; the very concept of studying healthy people was too alien to be aired publicly in professional gatherings.

Between late 1943 and mid-1944, Maslow began to ask his Brooklyn College students to write about the "most self-actualized" person they knew. He used several terms more or less interchangeably at this point, including *good human being, almost ideally healthy human being, saintly person, basically satisfied person* (that is, one satisfied in his or her basic needs), and *self-fulfilling person.* In framing the assignment to his students, he presented several broad traits of self-actualization, such as "peace, contentment, calmness, the full utilization of capacities, full creativity and the like . . . [and] success of interpersonal relationships." Some described a favored grandparent or other relative, a friend, teacher, or other person who seemed to fit the model. Maslow read these reports carefully, hoping to gain a more detailed picture of the self-actualizing individual. But the topic was so unconventional that Maslow held off from exploring it vigorously for several years.

During those years, Brooklyn College was a center of political radicialism. It was known by many in the area as The Little Red Schoolhouse—a description that did not refer to the color of its buildings. Even before its separate campus was established in Flatbush, the school had become a focal point for left-wing radical activity. It was a part of Brooklyn College life that Maslow, as a democratic socialist, disliked intensely but could not wholly avoid.

When faculty members checked their mailboxes on May Day, 1935, they were greeted by the first issue of *The Brooklyn College Staff,* the self-proclaimed new organ of "The Brooklyn College Unit of the Communist Party of America." Its anonymous editors and publishers, apparently faculty and other employees of the school, demanded that the Communist party line be followed. They announced, "We believe that the capitalist system is doomed . . . And while fascism grows in the capitalist world and bloody wars are planned, in the Soviet Union we see the victorious working class building socialism, creating a better life for all." Published until 1939, the *Staff* became a familiar presence at Brooklyn College.

In other ways that Maslow found more troubling, Stalinism manifested itself on campus. A favored tactic was to infiltrate student clubs and use them to advance the Communist party line under the unwitting protection of the school's administration. The pattern became consistent, even predictable. Typically, a science or language club would suddenly find that many new, unfamiliar students had registered as members. Since campus clubs were open to all students, the newcomers were welcomed, if somewhat uneasily. At the next meeting, the new members would introduce resolutions to elect new officers and discuss international events. As soon as possible, they would vote as a bloc and take over the club's leadership. By packing meetings in this way, and by other tactics, a relatively small core of Stalinist students, combined with a few sympathetic faculty actively providing advice, exerted tremendous influence at Brooklyn College. Opposing them was a small but equally Machiavellian group of student Trotskyites, with their own tabloids, leaflets, organizing tactics, and faculty advocates.

This campus atmosphere reflected the political turmoil of the surrounding community. The Depression had marked Brooklyn's poor and working-class inhabitants, many of immigrant backgrounds. Many were receptive to the outcry against American capitalism, and felt they had little to lose if radical change swept through American society. By some local standards, a New Deal Democrat was no more than politically middle-of-the-road, if not conservative. It was the borough of Brooklyn that elected the lone Communist party member on New York's City Council, and it was Brooklyn that provided half the total U.S. circulation of the Communist party's *Daily Worker* newspaper.

Stalinist and Trotskyite activity at Brooklyn College peaked in 1939 and 1940, when the new president, Dr. Harry D. Gideonse, fought it head-on. Soon after, the United States and Soviet Union became allies in World War II, a situation that provided a new and temporary respectability for Communist influence on campus.

Brooklyn College's psychology department was by no means the center of far-left faculty sentiment, but it too was beset by ideological factionalism. With his gentle, socialistic outlook and predilection for mild alternatives such as food cooperatives, Maslow came under attack by both the Stalinists and the Trotskyites among his colleagues. Many were angered by his seeming aloofness from major international issues. At times, they challenged him directly: Why was he, as a fellow Jew and the son of immigrants, so smug, so indifferent to the plight of the world's exploited? Didn't he know he was just being used as a tool by the capitalists? For a while, Stalinists accused Maslow of being a hidden Trotskyite in their midst. Although he found the charge amusingly absurd, he was dismayed by their loathing for what he valued most about life in America: its personal freedoms, especially the Bill of Rights. In a general way he shared their vision of a world without war or hunger, but he could never share their contempt for individual civil liberties.

In his own manner, Maslow sought to apply the research findings of psychology to promoting social harmony and justice. Perhaps his chief mentors in this regard were Max Wertheimer and Erich Fromm, both of whom prized political democracy while recognizing many economic flaws in the American system. Even when closest to Fromm, though, Maslow never shared an admiration for Marxist thought. In such articles as "Liberal Leadership and Personality" and "The Authoritarian Character Structure," Maslow relied instead on anthropological and psychological work to guide his thinking. Undoubtedly, it was the latter paper, published in 1943, that represented Maslow at his most cogent and contributed conceptually to the landmark work *The Authoritarian Personality* (Theodore Adorno et al.), commissioned by the American Jewish Committee in the late 1940s.

In "The Authoritarian Character Structure," Maslow offered an innovative—and still highly relevant—approach to understanding the *authoritarian personality*. Rather than enumerating typical personality traits or political attitudes of such persons, Maslow insisted that a different method of comprehension was crucial, one rooted in phenomenology—that is, in the authoritarian's unique world view. "Many characteristics of the authoritarian person are already well known," he noted, "but these . . . have not been tied together under a unifying principle . . . of the total personality. This has encouraged many to consider an authoritarian as simply an eccentric or 'crazy person' who is ultimately impossible to understand. But this is not so."

For Maslow, the key feature of the authoritarian's world view is what he called the *jungle outlook*, a term he would employ for the rest of his life to refer to the view of human existence as a sort of jungle, "in which [each] man's hand is necessarily against every other man's . . . the whole world is conceived of as dangerous, threatening, or at least challenging." Once a person adopts this world view, Maslow contended, *everything* that he or she does becomes logical and indeed sensible. "We can easily see this for ourselves," he explained, "if we only imagine ourselves to be in an *actual* jungle peopled with *actual* wild animals." What would our appropriate response be, then, to a visitor who sanctimoniously urges us to befriend the ferocious lions and tigers? Well-founded incredulity and skepticism. In precisely the same way, the authoritarian reacts with contempt when admonished to love humanity and be kind to others. "If the world is actually jungle-like for an individual, and if human beings have behaved to him as wild animals behave, then the authoritarian is perfectly justified in all his suspicions, hostilities, and anxieties," Maslow asserted.

He listed a variety of authoritarian personality traits, including a tendency to relegate others into a personal hierarchy of bosses and underlings, an intense drive for personal power, hostility and prejudice, sadomasochistic tendencies, and, perhaps most important, an identification of kindness and compassion with weakness. Altering the authoritarian world view, Maslow argued, is necessarily a slow and difficult process, for it involves basic personality change.

In other related articles, Maslow drew from his own research findings to address issues of political psychology. While always affirming liberal democratic ideals, he consistently referred to the reality of antidemocratic—that is, genuinely hostile and vicious—individuals who must be recognized for what they are. Many idealistic, well-meaning people of the time, he believed, were psychologically naive when dealing with authoritarians, particularly skillful ones like Hitler and Stalin.

Much later in life, Maslow came to criticize many Western intellectuals in our own era for precisely this same naiveté.

A brief unpublished paper by Maslow entitled "Memorandum: Personality and Communists" was rather unique in its attempt to analyze the personality makeup of the American Stalinist advocate, as represented by the several dozen Maslow had met or treated at Brooklyn College. Nearly all the Communist party members he had encountered were hostile and embittered individuals who espoused an abstract love of humanity while inwardly seething with hatred for themselves and others. "They have ordinarily led miserable lives," Maslow observed; "they were cases of love starvation." He also identified a relatively small proportion of Communist party loyalists who were compassionate and kindly and practiced what they preached.

During the war years, Maslow began to apply his evolving theory of self-actualization to the issue of world improvement. The ideal society, he speculated, is one that enables each member to achieve his or her full potential. Even at that time, he wondered whether his theory, so strongly emphasizing individual fulfillment, could serve as an adequate blueprint for group welfare and happiness. Maslow worried that too great a stress on personal development might hamper group cohesion and harmony. Yet he saw the Soviet Union as an undesirable example of a system that embraces collective actualization at the expense of individual fulfillment. Was there a way to resolve this seeming conflict? Possibly, Maslow believed. His findings suggested that we become increasingly devoted to the happiness of others as our own basic needs become satisfied and as we begin to actualize our inmost potential. "It would seem, therefore, that there is no incompatibility between self-actualization and collective actualization," he wrote in an undated paper. "But we must stress that it only *seems* so: we do not know for sure."

Despite Maslow's interest in political psychology he stayed aloof from real-life politics at Brooklyn College and elsewhere. He never got politically involved in professorial union activities or larger causes. With his scholarly temperament, he simply tried to avoid the inevitable and often petty wheelings and dealings among his colleagues and school administrators. He lacked the slightest predilection for Machiavellian intrigue. What satisfied him was to write, do research, and inspire students. To come home each evening to his family was his other main desire in life. Having achieved such a lifestyle was just what he wanted. Sometimes, however, his colleagues regarded his indifference to faculty politics with misgiving and irritation.

It was never a question of Maslow's personality; he was never confrontational with peers. None of his former colleagues at Brooklyn College can recall his ever losing his temper at a student or fellow academician. At times, though, Maslow's strong sense of his own intellect was interpreted as smugness or even arrogance by others, even those who generally liked him. In an illustrative episode, Maslow one day watched a young colleague painstakingly wiring some equipment designed to measure human response to visual stimuli. With a smile that seemed haughty to the younger man, Maslow remarked, "That's what I call real anal-compulsive behavior!" To his credit, the colleague retorted, "Abe, that shows how much you know. It's just good engineering practice." But Maslow's comment, probably meant only as a jest, conveyed a condescending air that long rankled his junior colleague.

Maslow's steadily developing humanistic stance also isolated him from most of his peers. As he gradually became more philosophical in orientation, his implicit criticism of conventional psychology research sometimes seemed high-handed to others. Not only was his keen interest in a topic like self-actualization highly unorthodox by the standards of the field; even his regular courses, abnormal psychology and personality, lay outside the discipline's mainstream. Experimental studies of perception, learning, and animal behavior were the standard, favored areas for psychological research, both at Brooklyn College and elsewhere. In his own department, most faculty were either social psychologists like Solomon Asch or experimentalists like Edward Girden, who felt little kinship with Maslow's work.

Thus, when Daniel Katz became the first departmental head in 1943, he met resistance in seeking Maslow's promotion. The faculty committee viewed Maslow as egotistical and not a team player. They kept vetoing his advancement. Not until January 1946, nine years after Maslow had joined the school and demonstrated consistent productivity, was he finally promoted to assistant professor. At times, Maslow's brothers, dismayed by the never-ending financial woes that he and Bertha faced, urged him to quit teaching and join their increasingly lucrative cooperage corporation, but he always declined. Half-seriously, his father suggested shortly before his death in the late 1940s, "Abe, you like teaching so much! Why don't you make some real money and start your own college?"

While Bertha may have regarded her husband's position at Brooklyn College as something of a monetary dead end, he was content. He loved the intellectual excitement of New York City and enjoyed living near his brothers and other relatives like Will Maslow and Bertha's mother. By temperament a solitary thinker, he did not really mind the absence of close colleagues at Brooklyn College with whom to share his ideas. He simply enjoyed teaching there tremendously. He even devoted considerable energy in the mid-1940s to designing Brooklyn College's system of student evaluation of faculty. In creating one of the first college programs of this kind in the nation, Maslow believed that competent, even inspiring, teaching is an essential part of professorial responsibility.

By the mid-1940s, Maslow was more determined than ever to produce socially important research. The war's end had not diminished his sense of personal mission or his urgency in developing a new approach to psychology. He finally decided to publish the complete findings of his 1938 fieldwork among the Blackfoot Indians. By now, Maslow realized that his vague hope for follow-up fieldwork was unrealistic. He was no longer close to Benedict, Mead, and the anthropology group at Columbia University; his interests had shifted. Collaborating with John J. Honigmann, a former Brooklyn College student and researcher at Yale University, Maslow devoted only modest effort to the paper and requested his younger colleague assume senior authorship. Although still quite influenced by his exposure to the Blackfoot tribe, Maslow was no longer much interested in cross-cultural comparisons of personality and behavior, and his old field notes seemed cold.

In 1945 the two men submitted the paper to several journals, but none accepted it for publication. Perhaps too much time had elapsed for the data to look fresh and convincing. In a way, too, the social science zeitgeist had changed since the late 1930s, and articles about culture and personality no longer appeared to be timely or exciting. Maslow continued to re-count his valued Blackfoot experience in lectures and articles, but he never again attempted to publish his findings.

Soon after embarking on the study of self-actualization, Maslow began to develop a keen interest in the nature of science. Ever since he had turned to experimental psychology from philosophy, as a twenty-year-old at Wisconsin, he had loved science, perhaps a bit naively, as the noblest and most idealistic enterprise of modern life. Now, having embarked on the study of self-actualizing people, he felt tremendous excite-ment at being a path-maker; it became increasingly important to him to better understand the essence of scientific discovery and the true scientist. In an unpublished paper dated Decem-ber 1943, entitled "Nature of the Scientist," Maslow criticized those who are unable to take risks, chances, or attempt leaps of intuition in their climb toward knowledge. Perhaps thinking of his own colleagues, he compared such persons to those who sneered at the early model of the airplane because it could not fly well. Perhaps thinking, too, of his own fledgling efforts to map the heights of human nature, he wrote:

> I consider it quite scientific to work with vague concepts, doing the best we can in the face of complex problems . . . The true scientist lives in the land of possibility, the land of questioning rather than the area of final and complete answers. He is not content to rest on the achievements of his predecessors . . . The true scientist continually tries to extend the areas of knowledge, and therefore . . . works primarily with questions rather than with answers.

> Every true scientist is an inventor. Every great achievement of every great scientist has always been an invention. He invents new techniques, new concepts, new words, new ways of looking at things, new classifications. He creates an audience. In this sense then, he is always a rebel, a revolu-tionary.

> Each new invention, each great discovery creates turmoil behind the lines. The people who have settled down com-fortably are shaken and disturbed out of their comfort. They must learn new ways of doing things. They must see things

in a different way . . . It is clear then that any great discovery,
any new invention . . . anything which will require a reorganization of the conquered territory will be fought against,
will not be accepted easily.

Over the ensuing months, Maslow further developed his
notion of the nature of the ideal scientist. In a brief unpublished paper dated May 19, 1944, entitled "Note on the Ability
to be Passive," he insisted that childlike curiosity and openness
to experience are essential qualities in the search for truth.
"Most of the people who call themselves scientists have lost
. . . this ability . . . to see the world in [a] dionysian, romantic,
accepting fashion," he argued. "The effect of the scientist who
can retain his ability to be passive in the face of chaos of puzzling facts is that he will thereby be enabled to see things that
most other[s] will be blind to."

Never given to false modesty, Maslow began to see himself
as precisely such a trailblazer, especially after starting a new,
book-length project. For nearly fifteen years, ever since his
graduate days in Madison, he had hoped to write a definitive
overview of the entire psychology discipline; his youthful
dream had been to produce a work as influential as William
James's *Principles of Psychology*, which had virtually established the field's purview in the late nineteenth century. It was
time for another landmark work to guide the discipline, Maslow believed, and he would do the job. The ambitious project
fitted Maslow's sense of mission and capability. Shortly after his
collaborative text on abnormal psychology was published in
1941, Maslow began to plan the magnum opus. In mid-1942,
he developed a sketchy outline, but progress was slow. Nearly
two years elapsed before he drafted the introduction on May
19, 1944. Never published, the brief section sheds light on
Maslow's emerging outlook now at the time, with its bold,
sweeping vision and optimism:

This book is oriented around the basic psychological
problems, around the questions which thoughtful men have
asked for thousands of years. It is not oriented around the
esoteric, guild-like questions which the technical psychologists have concerned themselves with. When we come down
it, the outlook of modern, technological psychology on man

makes him out to be a blind, helpless, stupid, even vicious wanderer without purpose in a meaningless world. Even his wanderings [are portrayed as] being random, senseless products of accidental forces completely external to him, over which he has no control.

[But] the truth which we can see more and more clearly is that man has infinite potentiality, which, properly used, could make his life very much like his fantasies of heaven. In potentiality, he is the most awe-inspiring phenomenon in the universe, the most creative, the most ingenious. Throughout the ages, philosophers have sought to understand the true, the good, and the beautiful, and to speak for its forces. Now we know that the best place to look for them is in man himself.

In June 1944, Maslow completed a detailed outline for the twenty-one-chapter work. Its breadth of subject matter was immense. Despite Maslow's lofty ambition, he wrote only bits and pieces of chapters, and those only fitfully. These ranged from short typed notes on "The Animal Nature of Man" to others on "Formation of the Character Structure in Infancy." Nevertheless, Maslow rarely discarded anything he wrote and neatly filed each piece of writing away, to be expanded or refined at some future date.

One of the most important of such sections from the magnum opus-in-progress was "Problem-centering vs. Means-centering in Science." For many months, he labored to perfect this article before sending it off. The iconoclastic piece expressed his growing conviction that modern science, as exemplified by psychology, had become nearly obsessed with *methods* to the exclusion of innovative *ideas* about our inner makeup. Portraying the true scientist, as distinct from the technocrat, as an explorer and even something of a visionary, Maslow insisted that psychology had to become far more open to diverse sources of knowledge. The rat laboratory is not a very useful place, let alone the only place, to find truths about human nature, he insisted. Appearing in 1946, this article marked Maslow's first publication devoted to the philosophy of science, an area that would increasingly absorb his attention.

Shortly after completing this paper, Maslow was browsing in Brooklyn College's library when he chanced upon David Lindsay Watson's new book, *Scientists Are Human*. Its moving chapter on the scientific innovator as a lone wolf impressed him and reinforced his intuitive belief that the scientific pioneer is often lonely and misunderstood, sometimes viewed with suspicion and even alarm by those more timid. By this time, Maslow had begun to see himself as such an explorer. For the rest of his life, he preferred the self-characterization of "reconnaissance-man"—one who embarks on exciting and adventurous missions into the uncharted realm of the landscape within.

As Maslow slowly worked on his all-inclusive book on the normal personality, he began to believe ever more strongly that we are tremendously affected by childhood experiences. Basing his view most heavily on Karen Horney's neo-Freudian outlook, he increasingly argued that early deprivation or frustration of any basic need, such as for safety, love, esteem, or belongingness, almost inevitably damages or emotionally cripples us in adult life. Psychotherapy can be helpful as a corrective, Maslow readily acknowledged. (A few sessions with psychoanalyst Emil Oberholzer had helped him enormously.) But it cannot wholly restore what we have been denied during these crucial years. If true self-actualization is rare, Maslow emphasized, it is because most adults are still seeking to satisfy these lower, unmet needs.

No doubt, Maslow's growing attention to childhood stemmed at least partly from the presence of his daughters, Ann and Ellen, at home. As they grew to elementary school age, he continued to marvel at their temperamental differences as well as their joint emotional traits. He found infectious their buoyant energy, curiosity, and joie de vivre, and often wondered why so few adults had such qualities. He began to speculate that retaining a child's sense of wonder and exuberance, as Ruth Benedict and Max Wertheimer seemed to have done, might be an important attribute of self-actualizing people.

Maslow rarely sought to play the role of objective psychologist with his own children. However, he did practice one clever ploy, suggested by his friend David M. Levy's play therapy innovations. Every so often, Maslow asked Ann and Ellen

to put on a puppet show, offering to pay them for their wonderful entertainment. It was not until many years later that the
girls realized he had been able to "read their minds" through
the self-revealing puppet stories they enacted.

Maslow had little extra money in those years, but he always enjoyed small pleasures with his children. In warm
weather, he loved driving up to Derby, Connecticut, with the
family for a few hours away from New York's pavements. On
sultry summer nights in their Flatbush neighborhood, he
sometimes took Ann and Ellen, together with fifteen or twenty
of their fellow tots, on a short hike up Ocean Avenue to a
favorite luncheonette on Avenue H. Holding hands, the
youngsters would enter the store together, and Maslow would
treat each to an ice cream cone. The adolescent counterman
was a Brooklyn College student and neighbor named Robert
Rothstein, who knew the esteemed Professor Maslow by reputation. As Rothstein, now a college dean, recalls, "It was really
something to see the joy in his face as the children's eyes
danced at the extra-large scoops of ice cream I used to put on
their cones."

Sometimes, at about ten at night, the luncheonette's
phone would ring and a gentle voice on the other end would
say, "Hello, this is Dr. Maslow. I'm sorry to be calling so late,
but some friends have just come over, and I'd like to order
some ice cream." Despite Maslow's modest professorial income, he was known as a big tipper, and Rothstein would
bicycle to Maslow's building several blocks away before the ice
cream melted. Sometimes Maslow came into the luncheonette
on his way to or from a class and would always exchange a few
friendly words with Rothstein or other students there whom
he recognized. In such impromptu conversations, Maslow
rarely talked about himself but offered a warm solicitude about
the students' activities and plans.

Although by the mid-1940s Maslow had left sexual research behind, he returned for one last study under the request of Alfred Kinsey (1894–1956). Trained as a biologist specializing in the taxonomy of gall wasps, Kinsey had established
himself as America's foremost sexologist. Beginning with a
course on the family that he co-taught at the University of
Indiana in 1938, Kinsey had amassed hundreds, then thou-

sands, of sexual histories obtained through face-to-face interviews across the country with men and women from all walks of life. In 1941, Kinsey published his first article on human sexuality; his two most famous, landmark works were *Sexual Behavior in the Human Male* (1948) and *Sexual Behavior in the Human Female* (1953). Based upon the findings of his voluminous interviews, these books have probably been the most influential sexual reports of our time. Translated into every major language, they continue to be cited for their wide-ranging information on modern sexual behavior.

Soon after Kinsey initiated these interviews, he contacted Maslow, then teaching at Brooklyn College. Maslow had acquired only a modest national reputation for his seminal studies on female dominance and sexuality. To many of his more prudish colleagues, the subject was indelicate if not salacious, and consequently made less stir upon the academic psychology world than had his earlier work with monkeys. However, as a biologist interested in primate as well as human sexual behavior, Kinsey found both phases of Maslow's research career provocative and therefore sought him out. Maslow recalled:

> Kinsey, in his pre-pontifical days while he was still able to learn, was making rounds of all the people who had done research with sex—damned few there were. I liked him then, and we spent a great deal of time together, working over the proposed interview and bull-sessioning generally. Also, in my innocence he taught me a great deal. For instance, I remember his taking me to Forty-second Street [in Times Square] to actually point out the hustlers, whom I had passed a thousand times without even noticing.

Maslow followed with considerable interest Kinsey's career as a sexologist. But he gradually become concerned about one important aspect of Kinsey's extensive sexual interviewing. Apparently without realizing it, Kinsey was attracting a disproportionate percentage of highly dominant people as volunteers and hence was developing a statistically inaccurate picture of "normal" or *average* sexual behavior among Americans. In his own research, Maslow had found, at least with women, that the more dominant the individual, the more willing she was to talk about sex as well as engage in sexual activity of all kinds. Since Kinsey was basing his sexological studies solely on the results of detailed interviews with volunteers, Maslow was certain that Kinsey's work to date was seriously flawed.

With characteristic openness, Maslow contacted Kinsey to alert him to the sampling error that seemed pervasive in his research. Kinsey disagreed; he insisted that his method of interviewee selection was adequate. To resolve their scientific dispute, they decided to conduct a mutual research project.

Around 1945, Kinsey set up an office near Brooklyn College with his chief collaborator, Walter Pomeroy. At the same time, Maslow made a heartfelt appeal in the name of science to five of his psychology classes, urging them to participate in an important sexological study being conducted by Kinsey. Without informing his students of the precise nature of the research, Maslow urged them to volunteer for Kinsey's detailed sexual interviews. Maslow had already administered his Social Personality Inventory to them and therefore knew their scores on dominance-feeling.

Kinsey and Maslow recorded the names of the students who showed up for the interviews. Since Maslow's appeals had been made to classes as a whole, the external pressure had been identical on those who volunteered and those who did not. Through statistical means, the two researchers analyzed whether a disproportionate percentage of the volunteers had been those with highly dominant personalities. In addition, Maslow and Kinsey planned to correlate the volunteers' scores of dominance-feeling with their sexual conduct, as revealed by Kinsey's detailed interviews. Here again, Maslow anticipated that more dominant individuals would prove to be more sexually active, with greater sexual variety in their behavior.

Just as Maslow had predicted, the "volunteer effect" was confirmed: a disproportionate percentage of the Brooklyn College volunteers had high scores of dominance-feeling. This suggested that Kinsey's entire sampling method was distorted.

But the story does not end here. Enraged by these unflattering findings, Kinsey refused to publish the results of his collaboration with Maslow. He denied Maslow access to the sexual reports of the Brooklyn College students who had been interviewed, so that the second part of their research—correlating dominance-feeling and sexual conduct—could not be undertaken. Kinsey also refused to mention in any of his subsequent writings the collaboration with Maslow and its troubling implications. He even refused to mention anything that Maslow had ever written, thus consigning his research on women's sexuality and personality to nonexistence.

After several years of silence from Kinsey, in late 1950 Maslow decided that Kinsey would never turn over the rest of the data and that the collaboration was indeed over. He went ahead and published the available results himself. The 1951 paper, entitled "Volunteer-error in the Kinsey Study," appeared in the well-regarded *Journal of Abnormal and Social Psychology*. Thereafter, Maslow's few contacts with Kinsey, until the latter's death five years later, were not cordial. To Maslow, the once open-minded and innovative scientist had substantially changed in character.

In mid-1945, Maslow was ready to embark more energetically on his study of self-actualizing men and women. Since formulating the concept some three years before, he had given a fair amount of thought to it and kept many notes—certainly enough to publish a theoretical paper. But as a trained experimental psychologist, Maslow was uneasy about presenting anything formal on such a radical and unproven notion. To satisfy his empirical-minded colleagues—and himself—he knew he needed hard data to support his concept. It was time for sustained research that would be worthy of publication and wide dissemination.

On May 6, 1945, Maslow established a research log he called the "Good Human Being [GHB] Notebook." In his first entry, he wrote, "After fussing along for some years, I have decided today to dig into GHB research and do it more formally and rigidly. It's all very difficult, though. Lots of problems. As things stand now, I try to be as conscious as possible of insurmountable difficulties, and then I go ahead anyway."

What were Maslow's insurmountable difficulties? Even at this early juncture he had encountered a number of problems in conducting his research. From the outset, he had known that to study emotionally healthy, self-fulfilled people would not be easy, but he had not expected it to be so much more difficult than all of his earlier work on dominance, sexuality, emotional security, and related topics. First, there was the issue of sampling. Where would he find self-actualizers or "good human beings" to interview? Of course, he had access to a large and generally eager group of young men and women in his classes. But while his students had served admirably as research subjects in the past, they did not appear promising to provide clues about humanity's best specimens.

Maslow also found that the various personality tests he had found so helpful in the past, some of which he had developed, were of little use in measuring emotional *health* rather than illness. The Rorschach Inkblot Test was of minimal aid in this regard, as was Maslow's security/insecurity test. Much to his dismay, too, he found that in the case of particular students he suspected of being especially "good human beings," their scores on the personality tests did not correlate with his hunches. Perhaps the tests were accurate only in a limited way, failing to provide a full portrait of the individual. After all, Maslow's models for self-actualizers had been middle-aged adults like Ruth Benedict and Max Wertheimer. Maslow mused:

> Is it *possible* in our culture for a twenty-year-old to be a Good Human Being? With only superficial techniques at my disposal, how can I talk about character structure—the presumably unchangeable part of the person? . . . But such youngsters might be standing on their ears at [the] age of twenty. Maybe *just* because they're essentially fine people in a cockeyed world.

After several months of time-consuming interviews and testing, Maslow felt no closer to a solution to this dilemma. Twenty-year-olds just did not seem to possess the traits of self-actualizers to much extent. To find large numbers of willing adults to interview and test appeared out of the question. On October 29, 1945, he commented, "Saw X today [for an interview] and experienced my usual disappointment and scaling down of expectations. They're all well enough adjusted . . . but they have no flame, spark, excitement, goal-dedication, feeling of responsibility."

Maslow came to the unsettling conclusion that his other, early suspicion had likewise been correct: emotional security was not a very good predictor of one's degree of self-actualization. Some students who had tested as very secure were arrogant and smug when interviewed; one young woman had even flirted with him in a self-assured manner that irritated him. Could he find some other measure, then, to screen for basic psychological health? He knew that he was handicapped by serving as the sole selector of the personality criteria. If that were simply the problem, he could have others conduct the face-to-face interviews. In particular, he knew that he was biased in favor of attractive female students, tending initially to judge them as more self-actualizing than others their age. Their youthful beauty lent them an aura that did not necessarily indicate inner radiance, Maslow had come to realize. But the real issue lay deeper than that, as he had suspected earlier. On November 11, he wrote:

> Upon examining all these data, I came to the conclusion that I've been picking "fine" people whom I could respect and in whom I saw some sort of promise. But many high security scorers are just the opposite of this—smug, self-satisfied, "lumpish" in the sense of just not wanting or doing much, almost torpid . . . Then, some people are definitely insecure, even neurotic, and still I respect them and expect good developments.

> As the work goes on, my objectives shrink more and more. Out of the dozens of subjects, there's only *one* I'm *sure* of . . . the rest seem just to be "nice kids" and some of them not even that.

At the same time, Maslow faced another roadblock. Not only were many of his interviewees turning out to be far from self-actualizing but others whom he had chosen to study simply refused to participate. They kept putting him off or failed to show up for their interviews. Maslow had experienced the same puzzling phenomenon some years earlier, with creative older individuals, and even discussed it with Ruth Benedict. He began to wonder whether an intense desire for privacy might not itself constitute a characteristic of emotionally healthy people. Perhaps, he reasoned, one without a pressing need for self-validation would feel little desire to bare his or her soul in a psychology interview.

Despite the formidable research obstacles, Maslow did not

feel discouraged. He had known that studying "the best of humanity" would be no easy matter, and he was certainly not about to abandon such trailblazing work. If anything, Maslow's strong sense of personal mission and his intellectual pride prohibited giving up. Indeed, in the late fall of 1945, he began to view the study of self-actualizing people as even more vital a task than he had originally imagined.

It is hard to say what specifically quickened Maslow's approach. Certainly, his years of admiration for Benedict and Wertheimer had already convinced him that some remarkable people may serve as beacons for the rest of humanity. But these two friends, even when considered alongside other highly fulfilled people Maslow had met, had represented only intriguing oddities for him. It was not until he began to read biographies of great historical figures, especially of saints and sages, that his intellectual outlook decisively shifted. Maslow started to turn his prior question on its head: the issue was no longer "What makes for a genius like Beethoven?" but "Why aren't we *all* Beethovens?" Slowly and unexpectedly, Maslow's self-actualization research had become the basis for an entirely new vision of psychology, with the premise that each of us harbors an innate human nature of vast potential that usually becomes blocked or thwarted through the deprivation of lower needs. This inner potential, Maslow believed, had not been taken into account by any existing school of psychology. On January 6, 1946, he commented:

> Certainly a visitor from Mars descending upon a colony of birth-injured cripples, dwarfs, [and] hunchbacks . . . could not deduce what they *should* have been. But then let us *not* study cripples, but the closest thing we can get to whole, healthy men. In them, we find qualitative differences, a different system of motivation, emotion, value, thinking, and perceiving. In a certain sense, only the saints *are* mankind. All the rest are cripples.

The following week, Maslow put the matter more broadly:

> The notion I am working toward is of some ideal of human nature, closely approximated in reality by a few "self-actualized" people. Everybody else is sick in greater or lesser degree, it is true, but these degrees are much less important

than we have thought . . . There seems no *intrinsic* reason why everyone shouldn't be this way [self-actualizing]. Apparently, every baby has possibilities for self-actualization, but most get it knocked out of them . . . I think of the self-actualizing man not as an ordinary man with something added, but rather as the ordinary man with nothing taken away. The average man is a human being with dampened and inhibited powers.

In the same diary note, Maslow first reported the finding that self-actualizers seem to experience mystical-like episodes in their lives. It is not clear from his note what precipitated this observation, nor did Maslow follow it up at the time. As a confirmed atheist, he must have found the idea perplexing, but he was never one to ignore scientific evidence. His observation on "naturalistic mysticism" would flower some fifteen years later into his influential work on peak-experiences and the psychology of religion.

By early 1946, Maslow had thus uncovered two significant traits that seemed common to self-actualizing people: their intense desire for privacy and their tendency to experience mystical-like moments. He also had a hunch about a third trait: that emotionally healthy people see the world more accurately than their more anxiety-ridden peers. Based upon these additions to his developing conception of self-actualization, he decided to pursue several new lines of empirical research. Ruth Munroe, his friend and colleague at City College, had offered to help him score Rorschachs by means of a standardized checklist she was devising. One of the leading Rorschach experts in the country, Munroe was married to psychiatrist Bela Mittelmann, Maslow's former collaborator. Her new scoring system might prove more objective and hence more accurate in screening for mental health. Maslow also planned to rely more extensively on his emotional security test for screening purposes.

Finally, Maslow intended to carry out several wholly original experiments. He wished to prove that self-actualizers indeed perceive more accurately—not only in judging other people but also in discerning the world of light and sound. Some of the experiments that Maslow envisioned had their origin in decade-old discussions with Max Wertheimer as to why some people see things more accurately than others; thus, Maslow planned to test individual sensitivity to slight electric currents, odors, fine shades of color, and musical tones. He also planned to assess the intuitive ability of self-actualizers by having them judge people's personalities by looking at their photographs. His colleague Werner Wolff suggested yet another interesting study to validate his own belief that self-actualizing persons can be recognized by their facial expressions and body language—that happy, fulfilled people *look* different from those who are chronically frustrated or embittered.

Maslow felt especially excited about this latter experiment, for he too had long suspected that we can spot "good human beings" by their very demeanor. But he had begun to feel a persistent and disquieting fatigue lately, and in his diary entry of January 16, 1946, he obliquely wrote, "As soon as I feel healthy enough, we'll try it."

CHAPTER TEN

California Interlude

*Suppose I'd stayed at the Maslow Cooperage.
Would my psychology now be different? I
don't think so.*

*If you deliberately plan to be less than
you are capable of becoming, then I warn you
that you'll be deeply unhappy for the rest of
your life. You will be evading your own capacities, your own possibilities.*

—A.M.

*M*aslow found himself unable to continue
his experiments with self-actualizing people, for his health
began to deteriorate in early 1946. He had never been a physically vibrant person. Since his teenage years, his favorite pas-
time had been to read while lying on a couch or against a
cushion propped on the floor. Aside from an occasional spring
softball game among Brooklyn College faculty and students, he
participated in no athletics or regular exercise. He disliked
physical exertion of any sort.

Now in his late thirties Maslow began to find that his
already meager bodily energy was strangely diminishing. At
times he felt so exhausted after lecturing that he was on the
verge of fainting. He brought a cot into his office to allow him
to nap between classes, but it did not help much and even
provoked gossip among his colleagues. Increasingly, he felt
faint and weak, barely able to stand for more than a few minutes at a time.

Finally, under Bertha's worried prodding, Maslow sought
medical advice. He went from physician to physician, hospital
to hospital; everyone seemed baffled by his condition. Meanwhile, his physical vitality continued to dwindle. At last, Maslow was informed that he was probably suffering from a gen-

eral hormonal breakdown, brought on by a possibly malignant pituitary or adrenal tumor. No effective treatment existed. He was advised to make out his will, which he did.

The news was devastating. As an intellectually vital man, he found it difficult to face his own mortality at the age of thirty-eight. He was saddened at the prospect of leaving Bertha a widow and never seeing Ann and Ellen grow to maturity. He was also crushed by the realization that he might never bring his life's work to fruition. He had been so intent on bringing values and ideals into the field of psychology, in helping to build a better world. Nevertheless, Maslow confronted his potentially impending death with clear eyes. Years later, he wrote, "There was one thing I wanted to do before I died, and I did it. And my feeling was, 'Okay, now I can die.' And then I was not nearly as frightened or sad. It was like a closure . . . It was a good place to end." However, he never divulged what the "one thing" he wanted to do was.

Then, suddenly, Maslow's brothers came to the rescue. Harold, Lew, and Paul were skeptical that his medical condition was as serious as he had been led to believe. But clearly he was weak and unable to teach. They had opened a branch of the family business (the Maslow Cooperage Corporation) in the little town of Pleasanton, California, and needed a manager. As they explained the situation to him, they had rented out a big barn to store and repair barrels for a winery in Fresno. Pleasanton was in a lovely rural part of the state where the pace of life was quiet and relaxed. They insisted that he and Bertha could benefit from leaving Brooklyn for a while. Of course, his brothers emphasized, he would have a good salary; they would also give him a car and find them comfortable housing.

He could not refuse the offer, since he lacked the vitality to support Bertha and the girls by any other work. He took a medical leave of absence from Brooklyn College effective February 2, 1947. Maslow and his family went to the West Coast for the first time.

Today Pleasanton is one of the fastest-growing ex-urban areas in the United States. A former haven for gold rush desperados, its landscape has been transformed in recent years into a web of new subdivisions, office complexes, and bustling shopping malls. But when Maslow arrived in 1947, he found a sleepy, rural countryside about an hour's drive east of San

Francisco and Berkeley. The brothers had rented the family an attractive home. Ellen and Ann, seven and nine years old respectively, were enrolled in the local elementary school.

The Maslow Cooperage branch in Pleasanton was a small operation, one of about a half dozen barrel-repair plants they owned throughout the United States. It consisted of a single, large barnlike building in which about a dozen coopers worked. His brothers set up a makeshift office in a corner of the barn and soon left him on his own.

Maslow gave himself the title of plant manager as he took over day-to-day responsibility for the business. His brothers passed through the area only occasionally during their business travels. They had given him the well-paying post to help him relax and return to better health—and they did not expect him to be energetic on the job. In this respect, they were not disappointed. In later life Maslow tended to exaggerate the responsibilities of his position, especially when conversing with business people, but the reality was far more mundane. It did represent his first foray into the pragmatic world of business since his teenage odd jobs as delivery boy, hotel waiter, and night watchman, but the post was a sinecure by anyone's standards.

Each morning Maslow drove through the countryside from his home to the cooperage and opened it for business. As the coopers arrived and went to their work stations, Maslow wandered around, occasionally speaking with one or another, making sure they were doing their work. After about half an hour, he would become faint and lie down on a cot in his office. After an hour or two he would get up, wander around some more, and then lie down again. In today's business vernacular, this was his "managerial style."

As Maslow's strength began to return, he conducted sales work for Maslow Cooperage, initiating phone calls, following up customer inquiries, keeping track of accounts, and even making a couple of business trips to Mexico. As a salesperson, he demonstrated real prowess, and his brothers were impressed. After all, for a man who had been able to convince college women in 1935 to talk about their most intimate sexual feelings, selling barrel-repair services must have been easy.

Maslow soon found that the business world, as represented by the cooperage, was no place for the innocent. Shortly after taking the job, he told his suppliers that he did not wish to spend his time carefully inspecting whatever they shipped him. He indicated that he would forgo the customary inspections and simply trust them to supply adequate materials. But if the materials later proved second-rate or defective, he warned, he would not only demand his money back but end all purchases from them.

Sure enough, one of Maslow's suppliers shipped him some wholly inadequate materials. After discovering this, Maslow got his money back and told the firm that regardless of their prices, he would have nothing further to do with them. The supplier then tried to underbid his competitors, but Maslow kept his word.

In his own business dealings, his scruples and integrity proved beneficial. For instance, one of his duties entailed delivering the finished products of the Maslow Cooperage to a local winery. When Maslow first stopped at the winery, he had to wait in his delivery truck while someone at the gate counted the barrels on the trucks ahead of him. When his turn came, he told the gatekeeper how many barrels he had on board, and the gatekeeper's count verified that figure. This procedure occurred a second time, and perhaps a third. Eventually, when Maslow approached the gate, the keeper simply asked for the count and then waved him on through. The moral of this story, Maslow would chuckle as he later told his colleagues, is "If you want to succeed in business, get into a field like auto repair noted for its chicanery—and then proceed to practice complete honesty."

Aside from the work at the cooperage, Maslow generally enjoyed the slow pace of Pleasanton and found it conducive to physical recovery. As his brothers had anticipated, the sunny days and wide-open spaces were therapeutic. He and Bertha especially loved scenic drives through the countryside.

But one aspect of small-town life he detested: the subtle but pervasive anti-Semitism. There were few other Jews in the area. As an intellectual and a newcomer not merely from "back east" but from Brooklyn, he was visibly different from Pleasanton's other inhabitants and merchants. Initially, Maslow had expected a plethora of social invitations from local business and community groups. The prospect of regular gladhanding and socializing with American Legion, Chamber of

Commerce, and Rotary Club members filled him with dread. But the invitations never came.

In later years, Maslow used to joke that in Pleasanton he discovered that the name Abraham served admirably as a "semipermeable membrane," filtering out the prejudiced "bastards" from his life but allowing in those who accepted him for who he was.

One day, Bertha and Maslow learned that their landlord too was anti-Semitic. They knew that he was an alcoholic and that his wife kept their family together, but he had seemed friendly enough. Later, his wife let slip some of the vicious anti-Semitic slurs he had been making about his tenants from Brooklyn. After this rude awakening, Maslow and Bertha began to wonder about the real, unspoken sentiments of many non-Jews they had met in the area.

In Pleasanton, Maslow continued to devote time to psychological research. His fatigue, coupled with the pressures of relocating his family and undertaking a new job, prohibited any significant writing at first. In 1947, he published only a minor, two-page article, his least productive year since he had been a graduate student. Too weak to do any other publishable work, he kept up an intermittent flow of notes relating to self-actualization. He continued to read many biographies for clues about this highest state of human individuality. Thoughtful novels like Ayn Rand's *The Fountainhead* were another source of inspiration. Published in 1943, this story of a brilliant, idealistic, and uncompromising architect exerted a lifelong attraction for him.

Gradually, Maslow developed a list of several dozen people—historical figures, contemporary celebrities, personal friends, and relatives—who seemed to embody some of the traits he associated with mental health and strength. This was a new, critical step, for Maslow was no longer simply dealing in vague impressions and disembodied abstractions. He knew that he was coming to an important juncture in his evolving system of human personality. But with no one except Bertha to help maintain his intellectual momentum, he felt his work lay in abeyance.

Toward the end of the year, Maslow managed to complete a brief but important paper entitled " 'Higher' and 'Lower' Needs." Building on his emerging theory of motivation, he presented fourteen propositions to better delineate the differences between our loftier versus our more physiologically oriented needs. With a philosophical tone unusual in a professional psychology paper of the time—a tone characteristic of all his later writing—he emphasized that true fulfillment in life comes from satisfying our higher needs, especially the need for self-actualization. The more we pursue and realize our loftier needs, Maslow contended, the happier and even physically healthier we will be. Paradoxically, he observed, gratification of our higher needs also benefits others:

> People who have enough basic [need] satisfaction to look for love and respect (rather than just food and safety) tend to develop such qualities as loyalty, friendliness, and civic consciousness, and to become better parents, teachers, [and] public servants . . . People living at the level of self-actualization are, in fact, found simultaneously to love mankind most and to be the most developed idiosyncratically.

In early 1948 Maslow's health improved significantly, and he increasingly left the cooperage for the Berkeley area to enjoy something of an extended vacation or sabbatical. He and the family rented a house on Vallejo Street in Berkeley, not far from the University of California campus. Maslow became friendly with several social science faculty members there, especially Else Frenkel-Brunswik, from whom he learned a great deal. She impressed him with her warmth and intelligence.

Frenkel (1908–1958) had been born in Austria and received her doctorate in psychology from the University of Vienna. She taught there until the Nazi invasion in 1938, when she fled to the United States. She had married Egon Brunswik, her former colleague at the University of Vienna. With her husband, Frenkel had taken a faculty position at the University of California at Berkeley. In 1944 she had become a senior staff member of the Berkeley Public Opinion Study. This group, in collaboration with the Institute of Social Research at Columbia University under Theodore Adorno's leadership, was developing the landmark treatise *The Authoritarian Personality*, published in 1950.

Maslow had published several like-minded articles on personality and political attitude, and the two quickly became friends. Frenkel-Brunswik shared Maslow's passionate concern for world improvement as well as his interest in making psychology an effective tool for this purpose. In Europe, her most important study had involved the biographical examination of the lives of 400 persons, living and dead. In the phenomenological tradition, she and her coworkers had relied upon self-reports culled from diaries, letters, and, if possible, interviews to compare trends and thereby arrive at a new picture of the psychological stages of adult life. Since coming to the United States, Frenkel had written several papers on the nature of human motivation and on the relevance of psychoanalysis to understanding the "normal" personality. Like Maslow, she was eclectic in her intellectual outlook and held the Gestalt school in high esteem.

She organized an informal seminar that met with Maslow. It included her Berkeley colleagues David Krech, Donald MacKinnon, David Mandelbaum, Nevitt Sanford, and Edward Tolman. The circle of social scientists was a stimulating one for Maslow, and he spent hours each week engrossed in discussions with them. Maslow always prized and sought out such friendly meetings, even with those who did not share his philosophical outlook or even his field of interest. To participate in lively intellectual discourse was among his greatest delights.

As an anthropologist, Mandelbaum was the only nonpsychologist of the group. Having done his initial fieldwork in India in 1937, he had just returned from wartime duty and was eager to share his experiences. The cultural study of India would become one of his chief professional interests. Krech and MacKinnon were both interested in a broad range of topics, from experimental to clinical and social psychology.

Tolman was one of America's leading behaviorists. Although his extensive experimental research had been on rats, he possessed a strong social and humanitarian awareness. Like Maslow, he believed that a synthesis among the disparate and often warring schools of modern psychology was sorely needed. As an animal researcher, he was especially impressed with Maslow's earlier work on primate dominance and sexuality. Soon after the outbreak of World War II, Tolman had written *Drives Toward War*, a work that sought to advance a psychologically based approach to ending warfare. His notion of a world federation to override nationalist hatreds became important to Maslow over the ensuing decades.

Nevitt Sanford was another socially conscious psychologist and a collaborator with Frenkel-Brunswik on her project investigating *The Authoritarian Personality*. He found Maslow's writings on the subject relevant and incorporated them into his own approach.

In stimulating discussions with this group, Maslow sought to develop and refine his conception of human motivation: what are our real inner needs, and how are they satisfied? That year, he published two more professional papers related to these intriguing questions. They were entitled "Cognition of the Particular and of the Generic" and "Some Theoretical Consequences of Basic-need Gratification." In these articles, Maslow continued to argue forcefully that we have higher needs beyond the physiological ones posited by the Freudians and behaviorists. Once more integrating the insights of both psychological schools, as well as those of the Gestalt thinkers, Maslow spelled out more precisely the qualities of people whose basic needs have been fulfilled or gratified. For the rest of his life, such theoretical and philosophical issues would guide his work and interests.

Although he had not yet finalized his notion of the self-actualizing person, he contended that individuals whose lower needs have been gratified are qualitatively different from the rest of humanity. When we are no longer driven by the needs for safety, approval, and acceptance, and when we feel really secure about ourselves, then we become more serene, relaxed, generous, and even more optimistic and physically healthy, Maslow insisted. Our perceptions and intuitions also become more accurate and we become better learners, because we are emotionally able to see the world as it really is. At the core of Maslow's developing theory of human nature was his hierarchy of needs. He wrote:

> The physiological needs, when unsatisfied, dominate the organism . . . Relative gratification submerges them and allows the next higher set of needs in the hierarchy to emerge, dominate, and organize the personality . . . The principle is the same for the other sets of needs in the hierarchy, i.e. [safety] . . . love, esteem, and self-actualization.

Maslow experienced a curious and decisive falling-out with Ruth Benedict, his old mentor, during this time. Since 1941 she had been busy with intercultural work for the United States government and had not communicated much with Maslow. Learning that Benedict would be visiting Berkeley, Maslow sought her out, but she refused to see him. Shocked and hurt, he wrote her several letters asking how he had offended her and apologizing for anything he might have unwittingly said or done. But Benedict never replied. She died the following year.

During this time, Maslow's health greatly improved and his debilitating fatigue mostly disappeared. Apparently, whatever illness he had been suffering from was almost gone. As he considered the prospect of returning to Brooklyn College, his brothers asked him to become a permanent partner in the Maslow Cooperage Corporation. They made the offer not so much because of the business acumen he had demonstrated, but to give him greater financial stability than he had known as a career academician. The salary and benefits were tempting, compared to what he was receiving as an assistant professor at Brooklyn College, but Maslow gratefully declined the offer. He enjoyed teaching and research far too much to give them up.

In early 1949 Maslow moved back east with Bertha and the girls, eager to enjoy a few remaining months of leisure before resuming his academic career.

CHAPTER ELEVEN

Back to Brooklyn
and Onward

> *If we want to answer the question, how tall
> can the human species grow, then obviously
> it is well to pick out the ones who are already
> tallest and study them. If we want to know
> how fast a human being can run, then it is no
> use to average out the speed of the population;
> it is far better to collect Olympic gold medal
> winners and see how well they can do. If we
> want to know the possibilities for spiritual
> growth, value growth, or moral development
> in human beings, then I maintain that we can
> learn most by studying our most moral, ethi-
> cal, or saintly people.*
>
> —A.M.

Officially still on medical leave from Brook-
lyn College, Maslow began making plans to resume his teaching and research career in the fall of 1949. He and Bertha
rented half of a small red-brick two-family house on Avenue I,
just around the corner from the school. It was not an ideal
arrangement, but housing had become scarce in New York
City after World War II, and Maslow was intent on living close
to work. Although he was thankful to have come back to his
professorship in good health, Bertha and the children felt a
sense of dismay about their return to Brooklyn. Its concrete
pavement and brusque pace seemed even worse than they had
remembered after two years in California.

Eager to make the most of the leisure months remaining,
Maslow devoted much of his time to traveling up and down the
East Coast to visit friends and colleagues he had not seen since
his baffling illness began in 1946. In catching up on news about

their personal and professional activities, he was strengthened in his determination to transform modern psychology into a new discipline vitally concerned with values and human betterment. On a cross-country train ride earlier that year, he had been at work on an article when suddenly he saw a vision of human nature as a vast, many-roomed house, and he saw his task as exploring its highest reaches and leading others out of its lower depths.

At Cornell University that March, Maslow spoke in a forceful and confident tone that would become characteristic for him:

> The psychology of 1949 is largely a psychology of cripples and sick people . . . I see a large portion of the theoretical structure of current psychology as based upon the study of men at their worst, men in dire and acute emergency, men reeling under constant threat and frustration.

> Under such circumstances, how could it possibly be discovered that man had capabilities higher than . . . the neurotic? This is a little like [Wolfgang] Kohler's [Gestalt cofounder] comment on the maze . . . as an instrument for measuring intelligence. He said, "Even the greatest human genius could not show his intelligence in a maze."

Maslow was starting to advocate an iconoclastic approach to the field in such speeches, but he had yet to publish anything so decisive. He had kept his sweeping vision of a new psychology mostly to himself. After nearly six years of delving into the nature of self-actualization, he still felt timid about submitting this work to the scrutiny of his peers. Having begun his career as a rigorous experimentalist, he knew that his investigation of "humanity's best" was scarcely definitive. Yet he believed intuitively that in his quest for the loftier qualities of human nature, he had penetrated into an important unknown territory of psychology.

Coincidentally, Maslow heard from Werner Wolff, his friend and colleague at Bard College. Wolff was a kindly émigré psychologist interested in unorthodox subjects like handwriting, facial expression, and gait as hidden keys to understanding human personality. He shared Maslow's interest in extending neopsychoanalytic insights to the empirical study of normal people. Several years before, Wolff had collaborated briefly with Maslow on his self-actualization studies of Brooklyn College students. Maslow's strange malady had aborted their research, and the two had gone their separate scientific ways. Now Wolff was starting an innovative journal and wanted to publish something about the psychology of self-actualization.

If not for this invitation, Maslow recalled later, he might never have published anything about this compelling yet radically unconventional topic. But because Wolff's journal was neither empirically oriented nor a mainstream organ of the academic psychology world, Maslow agreed to write the paper. In June, he organized his ideas into a detailed outline and a few months later completed "Self-actualizing People: A Study of Psychological Health," which appeared in *Personality Symposia: Symposium #1 on Values* in 1950. Wolff's journal soon folded, but it had served one major purpose: to bring Maslow's theory of self-actualization into the open.

In terms of its philosophical boldness, Maslow's paper was among his most influential. Identifying thirteen common features of self-actualizers under his professional scrutiny since 1942–1943, he sampled from two groups: historical or public figures like Thomas Jefferson, Albert Einstein, and Eleanor Roosevelt; and personal acquaintances like Ruth Benedict and Max Wertheimer. He made no attempt to justify the selections on any grounds other than his claim that they exemplified the two criteria of optimal mental health: the absence of significant inner problems, and the "full use and exploitation of talents, capacities . . . [and] potentialities." Such people, he said, seem to be fulfilling themselves and to be doing the best they are capable of.

Maslow was challenging the fundamental premise of modern psychology: that we can devise accurate theories about human nature by studying the mentally ill or the statistically average. Among the specific traits of self-actualizers that he listed and briefly discussed were greater self-acceptance and acceptance of others, autonomy, spontaneity, esthetic sensitivity, frequent mysticlike or transcendent experiences, a democratic rather than authoritarian outlook, and involvement in a cause or mission outside oneself. Self-actualizing people, too, seemed to possess a good-natured rather than a cruel sense of humor and an earnest desire to improve the lot of humanity.

In addition, they tended to seek privacy and detach themselves from much of the petty and trivial socializing taking place around them.

He also found that, regardless of their particular occupation or station in life, self-actualizers tend to be highly creative as an outpouring of their very personality, not limited to activities like writing or composing music. "In this sense," Maslow noted, "there can be creative shoemakers or carpenters or clerks. Whatever one does can be done with a certain attitude, a certain spirit which arises out of the nature of the person . . . One can even *see* creatively, as the child does."

Finally, Maslow suggested that although self-actualizing people are not emotionally flawless, they can serve as exemplars in the values by which they lead their lives. Most individuals, driven by unfulfilled needs for safety, respect, or esteem, construct value systems that express selfishness or anxiety about others; but those who are satisfied in their basic needs "can devote [themselves] to higher gratification [and are] more identified with humanity than any other group yet described."

Maslow viewed his paper as a theoretical offering, not as a truly empirical study. In an unusual personal foreword, as he called it, he stated that his purpose was self-motivated rather than aimed at proving a hypothesis. But, he insisted, "I consider the problem of psychological health to be so pressing that *any* leads, *any* suggestions, *any* bits of data, however moot, are endowed with a certain temporary value . . . It seems that the . . . only thing to do is to not fear mistakes, to plunge in, to do the best that one can, hoping to learn enough from blunders to correct them eventually." Perhaps fearing the inevitable criticism from experimentalists, he wisely refrained from detailing his frustrating attempts in the mid-1940s to use the Rorschach Inkblot Test, the dominance scale, and other psychological tests to measure superior emotional health. But Maslow felt sure that he was intuitively correct and that new research methods would eventually validate his ideas.

The response to Maslow's article was immediate and favorable among social scientists who shared his ideals. Contemporaries like Carl Rogers at the University of Chicago, who was developing one of the nation's first counseling centers, considered it a conceptual breakthrough and enthusiastically shared it with colleagues and graduate students. At last, Rogers thought, someone had been courageous enough to describe the "far goals" of psychotherapy and counseling in moral terms, distinct from the mere social adjustment that Freudians tended to stress. Encouraged by such reactions, Maslow began to circulate privately a mimeographed copy of the article to interested colleagues in psychology, psychoanalysis, anthropology, and related disciplines. In this somewhat underground manner, its influence steadily grew around the country.

Meanwhile, Maslow continued to find teaching at Brooklyn College stimulating, especially after having been away for several years. He still taught popular courses in personality and abnormal psychology. Reflecting his search for a health-centered psychology, he deemphasized the classic Freudian approach to neurosis and psychosis and spoke increasingly about character, values, and social trends. Influenced partly by his mentors Karen Horney and Erich Fromm, Maslow began to stress his notion of *value disturbance*—that certain characterological tendencies reveal serious inner imbalance, although these may not be diagnosed in the orthodox psychiatric texts. He identified as real emotional illnesses authoritarianism, prejudice, chronic boredom, anhedonia (or lack of zest), and especially the loss of life-purpose and meaning.

In a typical lecture in the summer of 1950, Maslow described the authoritarian character structure as "the most important single disease afflicting man today—far more important than . . . medical illnesses. These come from cultural malarrangements. They are the most widespread of all diseases . . . pandemic . . . even in the United States, even in this classroom."

At Brooklyn College, Maslow also became involved in an innovative integrated social science course offered to five hundred freshmen, in which scholars in various disciplines spoke on contemporary issues. Maslow lectured on such subjects as the hierarchy of human needs, the effect of culture on personality, and the relationship between emotional health and values. He enjoyed this chance to dialogue with colleagues in sociology, philosophy, economics, and political science. Unlike many of his fellow academicians, he was never disdainful about teaching freshmen but regarded their education as an exciting challenge.

More and more, Maslow began to theorize that human nature encompasses many higher qualities unrecognized by orthodox psychology, including esthetic sensitivity. The psychology of art and music, an almost totally unexplored realm, had intrigued him for many years. Bertha, long an amateur sculptor, had often pondered with him the nature of the esthetic experience. When their older daughter Ann showed artistic talent and considered art as a career, Maslow's interest became more pronounced.

Relying mainly on intuition, he began to speculate that humans have an inborn need to experience and express esthetic emotions. In an unpublished paper dated January 10, 1950, he commented, "Very little is known empirically about esthetic pleasures, needs, impulses, creativeness, or indeed about anything esthetic. And yet, esthetic experiences can be so poignant and esthetic hunger so desperate that we are irresistibly tempted to postulate concepts to correspond to these subjective experiences." He rejected the idea that the esthetic experience is ineffable and therefore impossible to study scientifically, pointing out that our subjective feeling of awe or delight in the presence of art must have specific, measurable physical correlates like faster pulse, holding of the breath, or shivers on the spine. He raised a host of brief questions that might help to focus the interest of psychologists studying esthetics.

Maslow felt too unsure of such speculations to publish anything on the subject until the mid-1950s, when he and Bertha collaborated on a test of artistic sensitivity and other research. Still later he came to argue that our day-to-day outlook is affected by the amount of esthetic fulfillment we typically experience. As he put it, exposure to beauty tends to make us happier and even physically healthier, where chronic exposure to ugliness or blight has a corresponding adverse effect.

In 1951, Maslow coauthored one of his most comprehensive articles to date, an overview of his approach to personality that sketched many of the ideas that would later became synonymous with his position in the field. He argued that modern psychology, partly for ideological reasons, had become skewed in favor of an extreme cultural-relativist view of human nature. Although he acknowledged that a turning-away from the discipline's overly biological approach had been necessary and helpful, he insisted that a balance was sorely needed, or else the concept of an individual personality would evaporate into a mist shaped only by cultural forces.

He also condemned the two major schools of the field, Freudianism and behaviorism, for their fragmented and ultimately useless images of human nature: "Most important for a motivation- and value-theory is the introduction of a positivistic force to supplement the Freudian pessimism and the neobehaviorist relativism." Both approaches had for too long sidestepped the higher achievements of humanity, such as science, art, and philosophy, by studying "mainly crippled people and desperate rats."

Maslow did not simply criticize, but outlined his vision of a positive psychology, which would stress aspects like growth and creativity. The zeitgeist was beginning to change, and he was able to identify more than a half-dozen allied thinkers, including Erich Fromm, Karen Horney, Kurt Goldstein, and Carl Rogers. He also named psychiatric mentors Abram Kardiner and David M. Levy, as well as general semanticists like S. I. Hayakawa, as important leaders in the emerging psychology. The émigré psychiatrist Andras Angyal was yet another significant figure. These people, Maslow predicted, were helping to create a new science of psychology with profound implications for a host of endeavors ranging from political science, government policy, and social improvement to the scientific study of values.

Maslow continued his informal counseling of students who sought him out. Many not only venerated him intellectually but trusted him with their most intimate problems. One young woman, troubled by the desires she was feeling toward a handsome friend, asked Maslow's advice: should she become sexually involved with this man or wait until she felt more certain about his long-term intentions? At the time, social mores dictated that "proper" women were virgins upon marriage. But Maslow had never cared much for what he considered mere convention. If you really feel that attracted to him, he replied, have the affair and let matters take their course.

Maslow was beginning to resist the new conservatism sweeping through social science. He viewed with growing discomfort the Freudian-led emphasis on adjustment as the marker of emotional health. It was dismaying to him that the most ominous thing a parent could hear was, "Your child is maladjusted." His self-actualization studies offered a different picture of what mental health is all about.

In 1951, Maslow published several articles addressing this and related themes. Among the most interesting was a short piece entitled "Resistance to Acculturation." Citing sociologist David Riesman's idea of the "saving remnant" of inner-directed people in mass society, Maslow also drew from his own study of self-actualizers to claim that maladjustment or lack of conformity may not signify emotional immaturity, but rather truly superior social functioning. Quoting from his earlier paper in Wolff's journal, he offered more evidence that the "best of humanity" tend to be critical-minded rather than slavishly devoted to their culture's norms. Yet—and this was equally important to Maslow—self-actualizers are not wild-eyed rebels or cranky misfits; they can live in their culture, but not uncritically.

Self-actualizing people, with their sense of mission, live *in* their culture but not *with* it. Generally, he found, "they settled down to . . . an accepting, calm, good-humored, everyday effort to improve the culture, usually from within, rather than to reject it and fight it from without." He gave the example of a man who in his younger days had been a union organizer under dangerous conditions. He had given up in disgust and hopelessness but, becoming resigned to the slowness of change at that time and place, turned finally to education of the young. Maslow speculated, though, that self-actualizers were not necessarily quiescent and that if faced with dire emergencies would be ready to fight resolutely and courageously, such as by joining the wartime anti-Nazi Resistance in Europe. "My impression is that [self-actualizing people] were not against fighting," he observed, "but against ineffective fighting."

Maslow also raised the intriguing thought that such individuals, who act upon higher inner impulses and not always conventional mores, may constitute a special worldwide subgroup of their own. "If this turns out to be a tenable hypothesis," he wrote, "then . . . those individuals in different cultures who are more detached from their own culture should not only have less 'national character,' but also should be more like each other in certain respects than they are like the less developed members of their own society." Such persons can survive well enough in cultures that allow divergence from the norm, he observed, such as in America. Elsewhere, their lives might become endangered by their iconoclasm.

Finally, in a passage that may be interpreted as partly autobiographical, Maslow noted that "since only few people can attain health in our culture, those who do attain it are lonely for their own kind and therefore again less spontaneous and less actualized." In later years, he would believe ever more strongly—with reluctance for its elitist implications— that while every newborn has the capacity to self-actualize, only a few, the small "saving remnant," ever reach their true potential in life. Why this is so was an issue that occupied his last years and was never resolved. But he also came to feel that history teaches us one crucial, relevant lesson: for their own self-protection, great figures like Socrates, Spinoza, or Galileo in every generation and culture must somehow learn to camouflage their superiority or suffer the painful consequences.

While seeking to develop his emerging system of psychology, Maslow found little opportunity for intellectual interchange among his peers at Brooklyn College. He had no close friends on the faculty, and even in the psychology department his humanistic concerns isolated him from his more conventional, experimentalist-minded colleagues. Yet he was not particularly interested in moving to another academic institution. He liked the students at Brooklyn College a great deal, and with few administrative pressures placed upon him, he enjoyed having the relative freedom to devote to his writing.

In the spring of 1951, Maslow received a phone call from political columnist Max Lerner on behalf of Brandeis University a new school near Boston. Its administrators, aware of Maslow's innovative work, wanted Lerner to meet with him to discuss heading its psychology program. Maslow knew little about Brandeis, other than that it was somehow associated with the American Jewish community. He thought it might be a seminary or yeshiva, and he had no desire to become involved with any religious institution, Jewish or not.

But if Maslow had heard little about Brandeis, he certainly had heard much about Lerner, a nationally syndicated writer for *The New York Post.* As editor of *The Nation* and a writer for other liberal periodicals, Lerner's pungent analyses of domestic and international issues were widely quoted. He was also a respected scholar who had written extensively on American government. Perhaps mostly out of curiosity, Maslow agreed to meet Lerner.

At their meeting at his home, Lerner recounted that he had come to Brandeis in 1949 to head its new Division of Social Science and to teach courses in American civilization. The hectic pace, he explained, involved commuting every week from New York City to Waltham, Massachusetts, to spend two days on campus. The university president had given Lerner virtual carte blanche to hire new faculty, and he was seeking a forward-looking and energetic scholar to develop their almost nonexistent psychology program.

Lerner related the school's brief history to Maslow. It had started with Middlesex University, a small, privately owned and supported institution that was primarily a medical and veterinary school but also granted liberal arts degrees. Middlesex had been founded in 1926 by a Boston surgeon, Dr. John Hall Smith, who had committed several million dollars of his real estate fortune to establishing a school free from racial and ethnic discrimination. Its campus had occupied ninety acres in Waltham, about fifteen miles west of Boston.

From its inception, Middlesex had trouble maintaining accreditation and economic stability. Smith died in 1944, and for two years his son abandoned a law practice to assume presidency of the struggling university. In 1946, bankruptcy and collapse seemed inevitable until an unlikely figure came to the rescue: Dr. Joseph Cheskis, a Jewish immigrant and the dean of liberal arts, saw the school's collapse as an unprecedented opportunity for the establishment of a nonsectarian, Jewish-sponsored university. A hastily assembled Jewish group started gathering funds. It included Rabbi Israel Goldstein of New York, Albert Einstein, and George Alpert, a wealthy Boston attorney and father of Richard Alpert, who would later become famous as a Harvard psychologist turned counterculture guru known as Ram Dass.

The group decided to name the proposed school after the late U.S. Supreme Court Justice Louis D. Brandeis, one of America's most illustrious Jewish figures. It chose as president Abram L. Sachar of California, who had just completed a fifteen-year stint as national director of the B'nai B'rith Hillel Foundations, informal religious societies for Jewish college students. In a tiff over decision-making power in the group, Einstein withdrew. But by 1948, through Sachar's brilliant fund-raising ability, the school had amassed a respectable endowment.

In October, Brandeis University had opened with a faculty of only 14 and 107 enthusiastic freshmen, but it had grown steadily. The leadership had attracted, either as visiting or permanent faculty, historian Henry Steele Commager, composer Leonard Bernstein, and novelist-critic Ludwig Lewisohn. "We want to be certain of having some star in each area," Sachar had boasted to a reporter. "I tell students, 'Don't take courses—take people.' "

With similar pride, trustee George Alpert had commented, "For years, six hundred major educational institutions by Protestants, and two hundred by Catholics, have invited Jews to become part of their student bodies. Now at least one university created by Jews will invite Protestants and Catholics. We hope it's just a beginning."

In the fall of 1951, Brandeis would have a student body of 600 and would graduate its first class the following spring. Administrators were confident that accreditation would be granted in 1953, after two consecutive senior classes had graduated. They hoped that same year to establish a graduate school with doctoral-level training in psychology.

At the time, Lerner knew little about psychology but found Maslow intellectually impressive, despite his lack of interest in the effort of American Jews to build their own nonsectarian university. Lerner assured him that Brandeis would be open to students of all faiths and backgrounds. From the beginning, scholastic records had been the determining factor for entrance; students' names were detached from applications so they could not influence acceptance or rejection. The trustees' models were not Yeshiva University or Catholic University of America, but Harvard, Princeton, and Columbia. In the abstract, Brandeis would seek to promulgate the Jewish ideals of learning and knowledge. On a practical level, it would provide a haven for gifted Jewish faculty who were still encountering prejudice across the United States in academic promotions and appointments.

To win Maslow's personal interest in the position, Lerner

described the opportunity it offered a farsighted scholar to build his own psychology program. Maslow could mold the program exactly the way he wished: bring in innovative faculty of his choice, train graduate students in his own way, and acquire a national reputation as the leader of a community of like-minded psychology researchers and theorists. Lerner invited Maslow to visit the campus and be formally interviewed by the faculty hiring committee.

Maslow found the offer exciting. In a way, it reminded him of the 1930s at the New School for Social Research, when an entire brilliant faculty had been assembled virtually overnight. As a loner in Brooklyn College's psychology department, he knew that his influence there was limited. Just a few months before, he had finally been promoted to associate professor after fourteen years at the school. Certainly, he might someday be offered a position at a more prestigious university like Harvard or Columbia, but he would still be one isolated faculty member in a large, well-entrenched institution with its inevitable departmental politics. To head his own program at Brandeis at the age of forty-three would be a tremendous step in his career.

Despite his affection for his students, he was tiring of endless teaching. He still taught five classes per semester and would be required to do so until he retired. As his friend and mentor Heinz Werner had commented shortly before leaving Brooklyn College for Clark University, "As I grow older, the one thing I cannot look forward to here is a lighter teaching load."

Yet, Maslow realized, Brandeis was not even accredited. It had no alumni base and could easily collapse financially as had Middlesex University, its predecessor. And what if Brandeis turned out to be a thinly disguised, however well-intentioned, Jewish seminary or parochial school?

Maslow talked it over with Bertha. Almost any offer that would get them out of Brooklyn sounded attractive to her. "Why not just go for a look, Abe?" she urged. "They're paying your way, and just look at it as a little vacation to see the Boston area."

At Brandeis, Maslow spent most of his time with Lerner and historian Frank Manuel, its senior social scientists, and chemical researcher Saul Cohen, a Harvard graduate and di-

rector of the physical science division. All were of Jewish background, brilliant scholars in their respective disciplines. As
they toured the pastoral campus above Waltham, the unfinished nature of an institution only three years old was evident.
The campus was beautifully landscaped in places, but con-
struction was going on everywhere. The school did not yet
have a separate library building. In an obviously hasty manner,
the cadaver-dissecting room of what had been Middlesex University had been converted into a cafeteria, the stable into a
library, and the animal hospital into a speech clinic.

But Maslow was not much concerned with campus esthetics. After all, Brooklyn College was hardly a venerable, ivy-
draped campus. It was the life of the mind that excited Maslow,
and in a curious way, the ambition and raw chutzpah of Brandeis' trustees and founders in creating a major university
within a few years matched his own vision and sense of personal mission.

Maslow's interview was an odd affair. At first, Frank Manuel tried an old and effective ruse, in which he fabricated the
names of several "research psychologists" and asked the applicant what he thought of their work. Had Maslow tried to bluff
his way, the interview would likely have ended right there.
But Maslow knew most of the productive psychologists in the
country. Puzzled at the names Manuel mentioned, he innocently replied, "I've never heard of them. What is their research about?"

Satisfied of Maslow's integrity, Manuel launched into a
lively discussion of ideas, with Lerner and the others joining in.
Maslow began to offer his own thoughts, delighted to be among
such intellectuals, who seemed the antithesis of narrow ped-
ants. Eventually, the subject returned to the opening for which
Maslow was being considered. They reminded him that they
were seeking someone who had the vision and energy to build
an entire program, and they offered him the position. In a
burst of enthusiasm, he immediately accepted without even
negotiating for the salary—much to Bertha's chagrin when he
returned home with the exciting news.

Maslow notified Brooklyn College of his new post, and his
family prepared to move to Boston. He felt some remorse and
even some guilt about leaving Brooklyn College after fourteen
years. He had always immensely enjoyed teaching there and

from the beginning had experienced great empathy for its eager, hard-working students, with whom he shared a common ethnic and socioeconomic background. Maslow almost felt as if he were abandoning them, but he anticipated a far more challenging faculty position at Brandeis.

The Maslows bought a house in the historic old town of Newtonville, about a fifteen-minute drive from Waltham. Quiet and tree-lined, it was made up of white, mostly working-class families. This was the first house he and Bertha had owned in their twenty-three years of marriage. His brothers, doing well financially in their business, were happy to help them with the purchase. However, whenever Maslow accepted money from them, he vowed to pay them back, and kept a strict account in a ledger for this purpose.

For Ann and Ellen, now thirteen and eleven respectively, it was their third out-of-state move in five years and another severing of ties to friends and relatives. But Bertha was delighted to be out of Brooklyn and hopeful about the future.

CHAPTER TWELVE

Pioneering at Brandeis

> Until I became chairman [at Brandeis], I too
> could play adolescent and be against commit-
> tees, dates, schedules, organizations, laws,
> and rules. But the intrinsic necessities of the
> role of chairman taught me much.
>
> The pioneer, the creator, the explorer is
> generally a single, lonely person, struggling
> all alone with his inner conflicts, fears, de-
> fenses against arrogance and pride, even
> against paranoia. He has to be a courageous
> man, well aware that he is a kind of gambler
> who comes to tentative conclusions in the ab-
> sence of facts and then spends some years
> trying to find out if his hunch was correct. It
> is in this sense that I am presenting personal
> hunches, intuitions, and affirmations.
>
> —A.M.

As Maslow settled into his new position at Brandeis in the fall of 1951, he realized how big a challenge he had taken on: to build an almost nonexistent psychology faculty into one with a national reputation. But Brandeis itself was an unusual place in those early years, and Maslow was delighted to be there.

From its inception, the school had gained a widespread reputation for excellence, especially in the arts and humani- ties. It provided a forum for the avant-garde and attracted many brilliant thinkers in diverse fields. Under President Sachar's aggressive recruitment, such distinguished people as physicist Leo Szilard, anthropologists Alfred Kroeber and Paul Radin, and men of letters James Cunningham, Irving Howe,

and Ludwig Lewissohn responded to the call. Sociologist
Philip Rieff and composers Arthur Berger and Irving Fine also
came to teach there. Max Lerner continued to commute
weekly from New York City; so did the first head of the music
department, Leonard Bernstein. "We had about as much right
asking him to take this job as we would asking Winston
Churchill to teach history." Sachar announced gleefully.
Though Churchill never graced the classrooms, Eleanor
Roosevelt taught international affairs and doubled there as a
trustee.

To many observers, Brandeis possessed the most exciting
faculty for its size in the world. Sachar and his administrators
were not afraid to hire bright people who lacked a doctorate,
or who had European credentials little honored in the United
States. Brandeis was the bucolic New School of the 1950s.
Although many of its faculty had formerly been active in left-
wing, even pro-communist, causes, when Wisconsin Senator
Joseph McCarthy brought his traveling witch-hunt to Boston
in 1953, he terrorized every school but Brandeis. Perhaps he
was afraid of being labeled anti-Semitic.

One event that Maslow found especially stimulating was
the school's celebration of its first commencement in June
1952. A four-day Festival of the Creative Arts included a music
program led by Bernstein, ballet performances, jazz, art films,
readings by poets Karl Shapiro and William Carlos Williams,
and a symposium on the state of the arts.

Because Brandeis initially had no official academic departments but broader divisions like social sciences and humanities, Maslow had the unusual opportunity to become close with
colleagues in diverse fields. Most faculty members considered
the arrangement ideal in theory, a way to avoid intellectual
overspecialization. But in practice it proved unworkable. For
instance, a senior sociology professor might recruit a promising
young scholar for an interview, only to find colleagues hurling
questions relating to economics and history at the bewildered
candidate. Under intense faculty pressure, therefore, Brandeis' administrators abandoned the experiment and established in 1953 traditional departments with their well-guarded
territories.

Another innovation was somewhat more successful.
Sachar and Lerner set up an interdisciplinary seminar for sen-

ior students in which famous scholars were invited to speak frankly about their lives, rather than about their specific work. Many other students and professors regularly attended the talks, where guests included mathematician Norbert Wiener, psychologist Carl Rogers, and sociologist C. Wright Mills. After the visitor's presentation, a panel of Brandeis faculty would offer their insights. Maslow participated eagerly in such panels and generally made a forceful impression. Unfortunately, there was often little coherence between the guest's talk and the panel members' comments, and the format was eventually changed.

Maslow had taken directorship of the new department not because he wanted personal power, but because he was inspired by a vision of what psychology in midcentury might become. But he refused to hire mediocre scholars who might agree with him out of deference, submission, or even indifference. Following Sachar's lead, he sought to bring in promising young people seeking their first academic position, and well-established people who were at retirement age but were unwilling to be put out to pasture. In the first category, he hired gifted experimentalists such as Richard Held, Ricardo Morant, and Ulrich Neisser. In the latter group, he attracted veteran theorists like Kurt Goldstein and George Kelley. However, not one of these can be considered a "Maslovian" in any sense; nor did any share his impassioned approach to the field. Even the more humanistically oriented clinicians, such as Eugenia Hanfmann, Richard Jones, James Klee, and Walter Toman, generally had far more conventional interests such as alcoholism treatment, dream analysis, and the effect of birth order on family dynamics. None of the people Maslow hired became professionally close to him, and in view of the authority he wielded in these early years, this situation cannot be seen as accidental. He perhaps went out of his way to avoid recruiting his own followers.

From the beginning, Maslow's department included an experimentalist faction and a clinical faction, but in deference to the gentle man who had hired them, the members kept infighting to a minimum. They respected Maslow's broad vision and his embrace of all psychology as the key to human understanding. The growing department tended to be convivial and relatively free from typical academic politics. Maslow, perhaps naively, believed that researchers of perception could amicably meet with personality theorists and psychotherapists for the common advancement of the larger field. And, in a way, he realized his vision: at departmental colloquia, visiting lecturers were surprised to see the entire psychology faculty show up. Inevitably, however, squabbling over funds and positions would surface, and Maslow had to learn to say no, to set departmental priorities, and to make difficult decisions. As he later mused, "My attitude toward all these things started changing when I came to Brandeis as chairman, the boss. I had to learn to do all the unpopular and love-losing things."

Aside from Maslow's goal to attract gifted academicians, he hoped to set up several research institutes to probe the roots of psychology. These included an infant-study center, a neurophysiology laboratory, a primate facility, and a student counseling center. Of these, only the counseling center came to fruition, but it was highly successful.

In 1952, Maslow appointed Eugenia Hanfmann, a respected émigré psychologist, as director of the counseling center and gave her an academic post in his department. He insisted that the center be an independent administrative unit, with its own budget and housing, and that its files be kept confidential from both faculty and administration. This policy was unusual in protecting student rights, for elsewhere parents were immediately notified when their children sought formal counseling. Over the next few years, the center became known as the most dynamic of its kind in the United States.

In the early 1950s, still interested in research, Maslow became involved in an administration-sponsored program of psychological testing of freshmen. Each entering class was given the Rorschach Inkblot Test and Sentence Completion Test specially adapted for this age group. Maslow's goals were twofold: to identify students who scored as "troubled," and then compare their names with those who subsequently sought counseling; and to monitor the academic and extracurricular performance of those students who scored "healthiest" on the same tests. With these data, he hoped to collaborate with Morant to verify the theory that self-actualizers "see the world more accurately."

Unfortunately, the tests proved much less valuable than

had been anticipated. The subjective impressions of dormitory counselors proved more reliable in predicting students' emotional problems than did scientific personality scales. In addition, Hanfmann and others on campus resented the notion of gathering personality data on students without a specific need to do so. For these reasons, the mass testing was terminated. Similarly, Maslow and Morant found the notion of "seeing the world as it really is" to be difficult to study experimentally and therefore shelved that research project.

Maslow did not personally provide counseling to students at Brandeis, but his interest in psychoanalysis remained more than merely intellectual. Largely for personal reasons, he became a patient of psychiatrist Felix Deutsch, husband of well-known psychiatrist Helena Deutsch. Felix Deutsch, associated with the Boston Psychoanalytic Institute, had a strong research interest in psychosomatic medicine, a subject that Maslow had found fascinating since the early 1940s. He believed Deutsch to be a skillful analyst who helped him deal with his persistent hostility toward his mother, and with other childhood experiences, such as anti-Semitism, that seemed to affect his relations with others. Close relatives, like Will Maslow, noticed that he now seemed more relaxed and at peace with himself. To pay for the expensive sessions on his modest salary, Maslow worked out a creative arrangement: if another patient canceled, Deutsch would phone Maslow to come in, and charged him considerably less than the standard fee.

During Brandeis' pioneering years, Maslow had little time for scholarly work, and he reluctantly relegated research and writing to the background. But by temperament he could not remain intellectually idle for long. He published pieces based on earlier work, such as his Security-Insecurity Inventory, and the results of his abortive collaboration with Alfred Kinsey in the mid-1940s.

Around 1953, Maslow and his young colleague Morant began plans for a joint project, a definitive introductory textbook on how modern psychology had progressed since William James's *Principles of Psychology* in 1890. The plan was to examine James's chapters methodically and then show the extent to which the field had grown. Maslow was eager to demonstrate that little had been learned about esthetics, altruism, or religious experience over the past sixty-odd years. He also wanted to affirm psychology's real gains in animal behavior, learning theory, and testing.

The two men began work. Maslow's publisher, Harper & Brothers, was impressed enough to offer a contract, which the two promptly signed, but it was an uneasy collaboration. Certain topics, especially in Morant's domain of sensory perception, were too complex to be explained easily to freshmen. Further, Maslow was mainly interested in extrapolating freely from available findings to make broad philosophical statements about human nature, while Morant wanted to keep to statistics and hard data. Eventually, they notified Harper & Brothers of an amicable parting of the ways.

Maslow was successful in completing another work: he pulled together his own diverse articles from the past thirteen years since he had coauthored *Principles of Abnormal Psychology* with Bela Mittelmann. The basic format of the new book, *Motivation and Personality*, came out of his undergraduate course on this subject at Brandeis. Published in 1954, the work of eighteen lucid chapters was dedicated to his brothers at the Maslow Cooperage. The early chapters included refinements of his writings on the hierarchy of needs and self-actualization, particularly its manifestation in such areas of human functioning as love, cognition, and motivation.

Several of the later chapters were original formulations and revolutionary in their import. With titles like "Normality, Health, and Values" and "Toward a Positive Psychology," Maslow set forth his vision of transforming the field into something morally and scientifically exhilarating. Among the most crucial, widely quoted statements in the book:

> The science of psychology has been far more successful on the negative than on the positive side; it has revealed to us much about man's shortcomings, his illnesses, his sins, but little about his potentialities, his virtues, his achievable aspirations, or his psychological height. It is as if psychology had voluntarily restricted itself to only half its rightful jurisdiction, and that the darker, meaner half.
>
> In a word, I contend that psychology has not stood up to its full height and I would like to know how this pessimistic

mistake came to pass, why it has not been self-correcting, and what to do about it. We must find out not only what psychology *is*, but what it ought to be, or what it *might* be, if it could free itself from the stultifying effects of limited, pessimistic, and stingy preoccupations about human nature.

Perhaps the most encouraging aspect of the book lay in its appendix, "Problems Generated by a Positive Approach to Psychology," in which Maslow laid out more than a hundred projects for humanistic research, including perceptual studies focusing on esthetics, intuition, and "good taste"; research on emotions like ecstasy, elation, and mysticism; exploration of topics taboo to clinical research, such as love and friendship, creativity, courage, and compassion. Speaking of social psychology, he commented, "Brotherhood and equalitarianism deserve as much attention as class and caste and domination . . . Why not study the religious brotherhoods? The consumers' and producers' cooperatives?" He observed:

> We spend a great amount of time studying criminality. Why not study law-abidingness, identification with society, social conscience? . . . In addition to studying the [therapeutic] effects of . . . good life experiences, such as marriage, success, having children, falling in love [and] education, we should also study the [therapeutic] effects of bad experiences, particularly of tragedy, but also illness, deprivation, frustration, and the like. Healthy people seem able to turn even such experiences to good use.

Upon completing *Motivation and Personality* in May 1954, Maslow felt tremendous pride. Never one for false modesty, he believed he had written one of the most important works in the history of psychology. His only doubt lay in how soon his colleagues would wake up to this realization.

As he was strolling through Harvard Square one evening, browsing in bookstores, he spied Max Lerner in a restaurant having dinner with his two college-age sons. Maslow stepped in and they exchanged greetings. "What have you been up to lately?" Lerner asked.

Maslow related that he had just authored a book about human values and the higher life within.

Smiling, Lerner said, "Plato already wrote that book, Abe."

Maslow, also smiling, replied, "Yes, Max, but I know more than Plato did."

The casual remark stunned Lerner and his sons. Years later, Lerner realized that his colleague had been correct: modern psychology can indeed offer greater insight into human nature than even the greatest philosophers of old.

Motivation and Personality quickly attracted widespread attention in the field and catapulted Maslow to national prominence. The book was nearly universally acknowledged as a major psychological achievement of the 1950s. More significantly, its compelling ideas began to penetrate a host of other realms, ranging from business management and marketing to education, counseling, and psychotherapy. To many interested in psychology and its practical application in everyday life, Maslow's name began to stand for an approach to human nature that was innovative, radical, and optimistic in a uniquely American way.

The book carried none of the pessimism that marked Freud's later outlook, or the inward brooding of Jung's symbol-laden writings. Nor was the weight of history seen to be as heavy upon us as psychoanalyst Erik Erikson believed. *Motivation and Personality* brought Maslow a multitude of speaking engagements and consulting opportunities for the rest of his life. If he had published nothing else afterward, his name would be secure in the field.

Despite such acclaim, Maslow was still prone to anxiety attacks before addressing certain audiences. One of the worst episodes occurred when he was asked in mid-1954 to be one of six psychologists participating in a national symposium at the University of Nebraska devoted to motivation. Maslow was initially delighted with this official recognition of his work—the greatest honor of his career to date. He would receive a large honorarium, and an impressive publication was guaranteed. But he began to worry: What if his paper were poorly received, even ridiculed by his peers? He was going to say unorthodox things and criticize the dominant outlook. If he botched it, would he ever get another chance at such influence? Word would surely get back to his colleagues at Brandeis and might even undermine his position as department head.

Perhaps, rather than risk humiliation, he should decline the offer and get back to his usual writing. Or should he go through with the talk?

Part of Maslow's problem was that his self-image in midlife had begun to change, perhaps inevitably. In his earlier days, he had adopted the persona of a precocious young researcher with filial respect for his mentors and elders. Even when presenting his ground-breaking paper in 1943 on the hierarchy of human needs, he had been surrounded by fatherly figures like psychiatrists Abram Kardiner and David M. Levy, who treated him with indulgent encouragement. Now, at the age of forty-seven and as the department head of a growing university, he could no longer act precocious, and he feared real professional embarrassment and damage to his steadily built reputation.

Maslow became progressively more apprehensive about the speech. He tried to find excuses to back out, procrastinating until the last minute, thinking he might say he had no time left to complete it. But his better instincts won out, and he went to Nebraska for the symposium on January 13–14, 1955.

At the outset of the speech, Maslow set his tone by declaring his militant position:

> I must warn you, this paper is very frankly in a different tradition from the ones you have heard in previous years in this series. For one thing, I am not *only* the disinterested and impersonal seeker for pure cold truth for its own sake. I am also very definitely interested and concerned with man's fate, with his ends and goals and with his future. I would like to help improve him and to better his prospects. I hope to help teach him how to be brotherly, cooperative, peaceful, courageous, and just. I think science is the best hope for achieving this, and of all the sciences, I consider psychology most important to this end. Indeed, I sometimes think that the world will either be saved by psychologists—in the very broadest sense—or else it will not be saved at all.

He criticized both the behaviorist and Freudian approaches for their faulty models of human motivation, based on their research samples of lower animals like laboratory rats and emotionally disturbed people. It is no wonder that the images of human nature generated by such study are foolish distortions, he insisted. Only by studying healthy persons, "who are predominantly growth-motivated," can we develop an accurate portrait of what we are really like.

In describing our basic needs for safety, belongingness, esteem, and the like, he drew an analogy to vitamins: emotional disturbance is "at its core . . . a deficiency disease, that [arises from] being deprived of certain satisfactions which I call needs in the same sense that water and amino acids and calcium are needs, namely that their absence produces illness." In coming years, he would stress this comparison throughout his writings and public talks.

As our basic needs are satisfied, he explained, our growth-needs—aimed at self-actualization—become dominant. Because such higher needs—those for creativity or esthetics, for example—have no permanent end point, psychological growth is a lifetime rewarding process, involving the "fulfilling of yearnings and ambitions, like that of being a good doctor . . . or a good carpenter . . . or, most important, simply the ambition to be a good human being."

Finally, Maslow highlighted several major traits that distinguish the growth-motivation of the healthy from those he called deficiency-motivated. Although clearly implying that we all possess varying degrees of both tendencies, he emphasized that the more we understand what motivates self-actualizers, the better equipped we are to solve such ancient philosophical mysteries as selfless love and mystical descriptions of the cosmos. By studying unhealthy individuals, he implied, we simply cannot gain insight into higher or non-neurotic human experience of the universe. "Do we see the real, concrete world, or do we see our own system of rubrics, motives, expectations and abstractions, which we have projected onto the real world? Or, to put it very bluntly, do we see or are we blind?"

To Maslow's relief, the paper was well received. It soon became one of the most important theoretical components of his evolving system. The presentation also helped to advance his reputation in American psychology, and he found himself part of a small but growing movement of people in the social sciences who shared his commitment to values and world betterment. That year, he circulated a list of "Creativeness, Self, Being and Growth People" of some forty scholars—including Gordon Allport, Andras Angyal, Charlotte Buhler, Erich

Fromm, Kurt Goldstein, Paul Goodman, Rollo May, Ashley Montagu, Charles Morris, Lewis Mumford, Harry Overstreet, David Riesman, Carl Rogers, Pitirim Sorokin, and Paul Tillich.

There was nothing yet resembling the movement that would develop into the so-called Third Force of existential-humanistic psychology in the early 1960s. Indeed, it would be several years before this list would expand to provide the mailing base for the *Journal of Humanistic Psychology,* finally flowering into his "Eupsychian Network" of several hundred groups and organizations devoted to humanistic social change in the late 1960s. Nevertheless, this initial list was important to Maslow during the intellectual quietude of the 1950s. He encouraged members to write to one another and often sent his latest writings to them for private circulation long before they were published.

Maslow was socially happier at Brandeis than he had been at Brooklyn College. He became part of a circle of friends who remained together for close to fifteen years. These men, nearly all of whom shared his secular-Jewish background, included historian Frank Manuel, sociologist Lewis Coser, and political philosopher Herbert Marcuse, together with psychologist Ricardo Morant and practicing psychiatrist Harry Rand.

Manuel was one of Maslow's closest friends and intellectual confidants. Born in Boston in 1910, he received his doctorate in history from Harvard at the age of twenty-three. A Marxist radical in his youth, he fought in the Spanish Civil War against fascism. After becoming disillusioned with the Communist left, he became a strong advocate of democratic socialism. Despite his Harvard degree, anti-Semitism made it difficult for him to land an academic position, and he worked in New Deal governmental agencies for several years. During World War II, Manuel served as a combat intelligence officer with the United States Army, receiving the Bronze Star for bravery. After teaching briefly at Case Western in Cleveland, he joined the Brandeis faculty in 1949, its second year of existence. There he taught European intellectual history, with a specialty in utopian thought, and had many lively debates with Maslow on this evocative topic. Manuel was known for his cynical brilliance and caustic manner with students and colleagues alike.

Maslow's other intimate friend during these years was

Harry Rand. Born in Boston to Jewish immigrants, he had been a professional jazz drummer before attending medical school at Middlesex University, the precursor to Brandeis. After doing his psychoanalytic training at the Boston Psychoanalytic Institute under Felix Deutsch in the late 1940s, Rand became well known in the area for his psychiatric skill. Although he published few writings, he impressed Maslow with his delightful personality and therapeutic insight. The two men, close in age and background, formed a tight bond. In 1957, Maslow brought in Rand to advise the Brandeis student counseling center staff and to teach clinical psychiatry part-time. His interests ranged from psychoanalysis and literary criticism to the wider social implications of his psychiatric case studies. Tall and balding, the extroverted Rand was a popular figure among graduate students and faculty. By far the wealthiest of Maslow's social group, Rand often provided the drinks and poolside space at his home for parties. Aside from being a vital link to the psychoanalytic world for Maslow, Rand in later years became his closest confidant.

Sociologist Lewis Coser, another friend, was born in Berlin and attended the Sorbonne in the 1930s, where he became active in left-wing politics. After emigrating to the United States, he taught at the University of Chicago, then came to Brandeis in 1951. A skilled, meticulous scholar, yet active in the democratic socialist cause, Coser received his doctorate from Columbia University shortly after publishing his first book, *The Functions of Social Conflict*, in 1954. That same year, as McCarthyism began to wane, he joined with Irving Howe, then teaching at Brandeis, to publish *Dissent*, a lively democratic-left periodical in New York City.

Perhaps the most famous member of Maslow's social circle was political philosopher Herbert Marcuse, who came to Brandeis in 1954. German-born and a member of the Frankfurt Institute's inner sanctum, he served with the U.S. Office of Strategic Studies during World War II and then with civilian federal agencies for a time. The year Marcuse arrived on the Waltham campus, he published *Eros and Civilization*, one of his most influential works and a provocative attempt to synthesize Marxist and Freudian thought.

Marcuse and Maslow, sharing an interest in psychoanalysis and culture, quickly became friendly although never intimate. They often lunched together on campus. Ideologically a staunch Marxist, Marcuse possessed a much darker vision of America. In *Eros and Civilization,* he argued that Erich Fromm and Karen Horney, Maslow's mentors in New York City in the 1930s, had oversimplified Freud's outlook and undercut its inherent political radicalism. Marcuse became especially close to Frank Manuel. One Sunday morning each month, Maslow joined them for a swim at the Newtonville YMCA, followed by spirited conversation over a leisurely breakfast.

Maslow was a good friend to them all. A sparkling and witty conversationalist, he could regale them for hours with stories and anecdotes. His forte was the bon mot, delivered at just the right conversational moment to evoke maximum laughter and delight. Acting on his own theory, he deliberately sought to bolster his friends emotionally, on the premise that few people ever have their needs for self-esteem and self-respect sufficiently met for self-actualization to occur.

He loved praising them warmly, emphasizing their originality and brilliance. His friends recognized his motive for doing so, but his manner was so gentle and well-meaning that they nevertheless found it uplifting. Above all, he encouraged them to aim for the heights of creative achievement and to see themselves as he did, each a potential genius with tremendous ability and value to the world. Perhaps Maslow's one personality flaw, they thought, was his own corresponding grandiosity, his sense of great personal mission to change the human condition. As Manuel recalls, "He had a messiah complex, but he never sought to impose it on others."

Despite the high affection they felt for Maslow, none of these scholars shared his intense, rather unorthodox interests. Morant, the only psychologist of the social group, was an experimentalist with mainstream pursuits who did not follow Maslow's passionate vision of a new psychology. The others were shocked by Maslow's ignorance of Marxism, economics, and sociological theory. Since he never made an effort to learn their disciplines and they did not care to learn contemporary psychology, little cross-fertilization of ideas took place. As sophisticated and widely traveled cosmopolitan thinkers, they were equally puzzled by his reluctance to visit Europe. He had never spent time abroad; the farthest he had ventured from New York City was Mexico.

The intellectual prejudices of Maslow's friends at Brandeis, however, blinded them to the potential importance of his work. In particular, those who were European-educated and steeped in the rich academic traditions of history, sociology, and political philosophy looked askance at the curious amalgam of Maslow's career—encompassing monkeys, women's sexuality and dominance, emotional security and hierarchies of inborn needs, Blackfoot Indians, and self-actualizing people. They would never have said it to his face, but to them such subjects smacked of the simplistic and had little bearing on the important issues of the day.

For instance, Coser recalls that Maslow sometimes asked him to explain a major international incident or domestic political issue. When Maslow voiced his own opinion about such affairs, Coser would detach himself completely. Although Maslow, as an Adlai Stevenson Democrat, had joined the "correct" left-liberal organizations (the American Civil Liberties Union, Americans for Democratic Action, The Committee for a Sane Nuclear Policy), his friends viewed him as hopelessly naive and idealistic about world betterment.

Maslow was acutely aware that his friends had little interest in the work that meant so much to him. But he was by temperament an intellectual loner and did not find this situation oppressive. For one thing, his friends obviously enjoyed his companionship. For another, Bertha was showing increasing interest in his professional activity as Ann and Ellen grew into adolescence and required less supervision at home. Several years later, he stated in an interview, "I have no real colleagues in the Boston area. My closest one is Frank Manuel, with whom I have good debates, and he thinks all my work is a lot of shit."

As if playing up to their image of him, Maslow often told the following story, perhaps apocryphal, about himself. To his friends, it delightfully portrayed the man they affectionately regarded as a sweet but ineffectual innocent among the harsh realities of the world. One evening, as Maslow used to tell it, he rode the ferryboat that ran from New York City to Boston. Standing on the deck and gazing out, he noticed an attractive woman smiling in his direction. As he absentmindedly smiled back, she strode over and initiated conversation in a friendly manner. Never one to ignore such female attentions, Maslow reciprocated warmly.

After a good deal of conversation, the woman asked, gazing meaningfully into his eyes, "How would you like to come to my cabin for a party?" Not one to miss a party, Maslow agreed, and she asked him to wait a few minutes before joining her. When he got there, he discovered that the cabin was empty except for the two of them. As she shut the door behind him, he turned to her puzzled, and asked, "Where's the party?"

The woman explained that she was a prostitute, and while she certainly had enjoyed their conversation, she was obliged to charge him for her time. Maslow, embarrassed, dutifully paid her.

Although not religiously observant or interested in Jewish culture, Maslow was an early supporter of Israel, at a time when such a stance was unfashionable among many of his faculty friends. To express his commitment, he diligently purchased Israeli savings bonds—much to his brother Harold's surprise, in view of their paltry interest rate. Perhaps Maslow's sentiment toward Israel was influenced by his cousin Will Maslow, who had become a dynamic leader of the American Jewish Congress and was related by marriage to Israel's first prime minister, David Ben-Gurion.

Before long, he was presented with a far greater opportunity to help Israel, when his reputation reached that nation's premier institution of higher learning. In early 1955, he received the first of several offers to join the faculty of the Hebrew University in Jerusalem. Psychologist David Wechsler, then at New York University and a frequent visitor to Israel, communicated the invitation from the school's president to Maslow to head its nascent department and do for them what he had accomplished for Brandeis.

"At present, the University has no psychology department to speak of," Wechsler wrote, "[but] the situation would be very challenging to a person minded to start things from a beginning." Maslow was promised a liberal salary and a free hand at hiring, but turned down the offer, which required at least a three-year commitment. Having been at Brandeis only four years, he was unwilling to move his family again, and he considered himself a pioneer with much work yet to be done.

In 1955 Brandeis was bustling. Around the expanding campus, modern lecture halls, dormitories, libraries, and museums were going up, part of a massive building program.

Every building bore the name of a philanthropic family; even benches and trees bore plaques listing donors' names. A bronze statue of Justice Louis Brandeis stood watchfully on one of the hills. Eleanor Roosevelt conducted the ceremonial unveiling. But the proud centerpiece of the school was its set of three chapels, each designed to resemble an open Bible: one for Jews, one for Catholics, and one for Protestants. The gray stone Bibles were calibrated precisely to the same thirty-foot height, so that none of the religious denominations should feel slighted.

This feverish building was attributable to the remarkable fund-raising success of one man: Brandeis President Abram Sachar. As early as his hiring in 1948, he had shrewdly recognized that the older, more established German Jews in America would not contribute substantially to the school until it was self-sufficient. The key to Brandeis' survival and growth, Sachar believed, lay in the untapped pool of well-to-do, first-generation American Jews of Eastern European origin. Proud of their heritage, devoted to education even when they lacked it themselves, these self-made businessmen, lawyers, accountants, and physicians represented the hope of the school, and Sachar deftly pursued them. He also helped sponsor the National Women's Committee for Brandeis University, an energetic volunteer organization with a local chapter in virtually every Jewish community in the United States. At the school's numerous fund-raising events, faculty members were typically put on display, as it were, to lend an intellectual tone. Former Brandeis professor Irving Howe reminisced in his autobiography, *A Margin of Hope*: "Sachar would [ask] with a grin that I 'speak above their heads just a little,' " to make potential donors feel even more impressed with the faculty's erudition.

Maslow willingly participated in such fund-raising efforts around the country. Despite the precious time they took from his scholarly activity, he adopted a good-natured and often whimsical paternal attitude toward such functions, which he scheduled in conjunction with travel for conferences and other professional meetings. Once he was asked by the Cincinnati chapter of the National Women's Committee of Brandeis University to speak at a luncheon. In accepting the invitation, he sent the following draft to be used in their publicity flyer:

How has Freud transformed our lives?
Why does a psychoanalyst use a couch?
Why do women join clubs?
Why is being a good parent so difficult today?
Why the deluge of "escape pill" users?
Why is Elvis Presley?

For the answer to these and many other questions

COME AND BRING A FRIEND TO THE

Midwinter Meeting
January 28, 1957
and hear

DR. ABRAHAM H. MASLOW

• eminent authority
• fascinating personality

Important: There will be a True or False quiz at the meeting.
Test your knowledge of psychology—it will be fun!

Sometimes Maslow took a more serious attitude toward these speeches and regarded them as an opportunity to help familiarize others with his approach to the human mind. For example, in mid-1955 he addressed the Worcester, Massachusetts, chapter of Brandeis' National Women's Committee in a talk entitled "Personality Problems and Self-Help."

As he typically did in such speeches, he expressed his conviction that modern science in the form of psychology has much to offer us today, even in the seemingly abstract realm of morality and ethics. "The more we learn about [our] natural tendencies, the more closely we may formulate a system of what might be called natural values."

Maslow also emphasized that each of us has an intrinsic core of personality—what he called a "real self"—unique and yet possessing traits in common with all humans. This core is not inherently evil, as the Freudians and theologians believe, but good or neutral. Reflecting his belief in the biological essence of human nature, he also assured his audience: "Cultural differences, although seemingly very marked, are actually only superficial. As one goes deeper into personality, it is apparent that men have more in common than in difference."

Finally, Maslow gently railed against the conformist ideology of the times. We can learn one key lesson from self-actualizers, he said: fulfillment in life never comes from following the crowd, but only from being faithful to one's yearnings and talents. Social adjustment should under no circumstances be seen as the way to happiness; rather, the path may lie in resisting prevailing values. As he often asked rhetorically, "The question is—adjusted to what?"

CHAPTER THIRTEEN

Disappointments and New Dreams

We fear our highest possibilities. We are generally afraid to become that which we can glimpse in our most perfect moments, under conditions of great courage. We enjoy and even thrill to the godlike possibilities we see in ourselves in such peak moments. And yet we simultaneously shiver with weakness, awe, and fear before these very same possibilities.

Obviously the most beautiful fate, the most wonderful good fortune that can happen to any human being, is to be paid for doing that which he passionately loves to do.

—A.M.

M aslow enjoyed the company of his colleagues at Brandeis during the 1950s, but from the outset his relations with students were strained. It was an unexpected situation, quite the reverse of his years at Brooklyn College, where he had generally admired the students more than the faculty. For Maslow, the problem with the Brandeis undergraduates was not in their intellectual caliber, for the school had a rigorous selection process. Rather, he felt they lacked real drive and ambition. In a manner that he had never found necessary at Brooklyn College, he sometimes resorted to direct challenge in his classes at Brandeis.

One day, feeling particularly frustrated by a roomful of blank expressions after he launched into one of his favorite descriptions of self-actualizing people—their commitment to a cause or mission in life—he suddenly asked the class, "How many of you plan to become psychologists?" A number of hands shot up. "How many of you plan to become great psychologists—another Freud?" No hands. "Why not?" Maslow demanded. "If you don't want to be a great psychologist, why bother going into the field at all? Who do you think will be the great leaders in psychology, or history, or medicine, thirty years from now, if not you here in this room?"

Maslow's hard-working students at Brooklyn College had shown an ambition, an unabashed desire to shake the world, that he missed among the students at Brandeis. No doubt he communicated his disappointment, albeit unwittingly, to them. As a result, Brandeis students never flocked to Maslow. Gone, for the most part, were the grateful, adoring youngsters who had taken down every piece of advice he gave in Brooklyn. Maslow was popular enough on campus, but simply one of a number of provocative lecturers and thinkers. For the first time in his life, he was shocked to see that students were voluntarily dropping his courses.

Maslow recognized that part of his discontent reflected the changing times. In the Eisenhower years, international events no longer ignited much passion on campuses. The American economy was booming, suburbs were sprouting across the land, and students everywhere were placing a premium on enjoying their college years, having fun rather than grimly seeking to get ahead or transform the social order.

In the 1940s, Maslow had recommended Budd Schulberg's novel *What Makes Sammy Run?* for its vivid portrayal of Sammy Glick, the archetypal young man hurriedly and crudely clambering up the American ladder of success without regard for others. Maslow had regarded the story as a warning to his students to be less driven for personal achievement at any cost. But the 1950s was the time of the "organization man," and brash Sammy Glicks were anathema to corporate recruiters. Maslow was chagrined at the small number of truly ambitious youngsters at Brandeis. Far too many seemed complacent, a quality he abhorred.

Perhaps, too, he unconsciously resented the greater affluence of his Brandeis students; most came from well-to-do Jewish families. Naturally he had felt greater kinship for his Brooklyn College youngsters, whose origins and values lay closer to his own. Also contributing to the problem, no doubt, was Maslow's entrance into middle age. He had less classroom energy and patience, and with two teenage daughters going through their rebellious years at home, he was finding the stage of adolescence less appealing.

By now, Maslow had tremendously high, perhaps unrealistic, expectations for his students. He was not content merely to see them learn the subject matter well. He wanted to uplift them morally as well as intellectually, to see them visibly mature on the path to self-actualization. Even with this ambitious goal, he was often successful. His introductory psychology course, far more morally and intellectually challenging than others taught elsewhere, was popular and influenced a high proportion of students to major in the subject. Decades later, many former students still recall Maslow's inspiring, unique voice amid the doldrums of the 1950s.

Political activist Abbie Hoffman, for example, was a psychology major at Brandeis during the mid-1950s and a good friend of Ellen Maslow in those years. In his autobiography, *Soon to Be a Major Motion Picture*, he reminisced, "Most of all [my professors], I loved Abe Maslow. I took every class he gave and spent long evenings with him and his family. There was something about his humanistic psychology (considered radical at the time) that I found exhilarating amidst the general pessimism of Western thought. A hundred years of examining the dark side of human experience, chiefly because of the influence of Darwin and Freud, would be set in perspective by Maslow's insights regarding healthy motivation."

Another Brandeis student of the early 1950s remarked, "I think of Abe Maslow . . . as the beacon that pulled me into safe harbor, a refuge from which I could sail full speed ahead. Having 'got' the message, I have dedicated my life to passing it on."

But, perhaps inevitably, some did not get the message, and Maslow tended to take such occurrences as personal rejections and a measure of his own failure. In an illustrative episode, Maslow addressed his introductory psychology students on the last day of class in mid-1954. In his quiet but intense manner, he exhorted them to be aware of themselves as individuals with unique talents and vast potentials. It was up to each of them to become all he or she could in life. Virtually everyone found Maslow's fatherly, earnest comments moving; some felt an almost palpable spirit of inspiration in the room.

One young woman raised her hand. Gazing thoughtfully, Maslow acknowledged her.

"I'm wondering about the final exam. Could you give us some idea about the questions on it?"

Every head turned toward her, in bewilderment, surprise, or disgust. Maslow became angry for the first time since the course had begun. As his face reddened, he replied rather heatedly, "If you can ask a question like that at this moment, then I'm concerned about how much you've really understood here this semester."

There was an embarrassed silence. Maslow stood there silently, his expression turning from anger to dismay and disappointment. The student rose, hurriedly gathered her things, and left. After a few moments, her classmates slowly and quietly filed out of the room as Maslow stood there with a rueful, enigmatic look on his face.

Maslow's involvement with his graduate students was much more problematic. Beginning in 1953 when its psychology doctoral program was founded, Brandeis accepted about a half dozen applicants during each of the next few years. Most came for the innovative learning atmosphere that Maslow had created, and many sought to train with him on a one-to-one basis. Especially after *Motivation and Personality* was published in 1954, Maslow—and, by association, Brandeis University—acquired a national reputation in psychology. The department was small, an idyllic setting in which to guide bright, intellectually congenial young men and women through the thicket of advanced study into the clearing of humanistic endeavor. Having had excellent, supportive mentors like Harry Harlow and William Sheldon at the University of Wisconsin, followed by Ruth Benedict, Edward Thorndike, and Max Wertheimer in New York City, Maslow had valuable personal experience to prepare him to be a mentor. Yet his relationship with his graduate students was perhaps the only real failure of his career. Many remain bitter toward him to this day.

What went wrong? The answer appears both complex and simple. In later years, he conceded that matters had not turned out well, but his own explanation conflicted with that offered by the students themselves. He attributed their poor performance largely to their personal weaknesses, not to his own supervisory style.

Maslow had decided to offer unprecedented freedom to doctoral students and therefore abandoned much of the traditional grading procedure such as frequent examinations, formal lectures, even required courses. To train effective future social scientists, he believed, it was vital to foster skills such as writing papers and to engage students in as much independent fieldwork and research as possible. Students were encouraged to choose their own pace and focus; self-discovery was emphasized over close supervision.

This somewhat laissez-faire system worked well with doctoral students who were self-motivating and autonomous, and disastrously with others. But Maslow believed, perhaps a bit coldly, that the latter were better off discovering at age twenty-five that they lacked the ability for a successful career in psychology than learning it fifteen years later.

Before allowing his doctoral students to pursue their idealistic interests, he was adamant that they learn subjects like statistics and laboratory design to analyze human perception. Many of those who had come to Brandeis expecting to learn some innovative ways to study motivation and personality thought Maslow was giving a mixed message: urging them to be creative, yet requiring that they take the same experimental courses that he attacked in his writings as fragmentary and shortsighted.

Maslow saw no contradiction. He sometimes replied vehemently that at Wisconsin he had studied the most "hardnosed" subjects possible—anatomy, embryology, animal behavior—and had even done his dissertation under Harry Harlow on monkeys. Twenty-odd years later, he was studying self-actualizing people. Clearly, rigorous scientific training is not incompatible with humanism, and learning statistics will not turn students into brutal monsters.

On both these points, Maslow knew he was at least partially right. His sink-or-swim approach threw students back on their own resources more than conventional graduate programs; and courses like statistics were hardly a betrayal of the humanistic spirit. But the real gripe of his doctoral students cut deeper than these two issues, and it was one they could not express directly to him for fear of repercussion: he was no longer conducting empirical research and therefore offered them only the most cursory direction. The rigorous experimentalist courses he advocated would have been more palatable had it been clearer what their purpose was from Maslow's own perspective. He had indeed pointed the way in *Motivation and Personality* to dozens of intriguing and potentially important avenues of humanistic research, but he was not personally involved in that kind of empirical work.

The truth was that he simply did not accept the responsibility of serving as guide and mentor to advanced graduate students. By the mid-1950s, he had decided that conducting empirical research would draw valuable time and energy away from his quest to transform psychology's purview. He did his intellectual work by reading, taking long solitary walks, jotting down ideas on file cards, and then typing rough drafts more encompassing in scope. It was an intuitive approach to psychology that provided almost no concrete guidance to others.

Some of his doctoral students would have felt less betrayed had he at least shown interest in their efforts, which were often designed to test various aspects of Maslow's multifaceted theory of human nature. But even in this regard, he showed little interest in their ideas. At best, some doctoral students came to regard Maslow as unintentionally too self-absorbed to become involved with their training. They either worked autonomously or chose to train under someone else on the faculty. "If you want to get your doctorate," was the inside saying among advanced students, "don't work under Abe Maslow. You'll never get out of here if you do." At worst, they muttered that he hypocritically espoused a whole agenda of humanistic and socially relevant research while neither attempting it himself nor guiding anyone else who wished to accomplish it.

Maslow's colleagues tended to adopt a more conciliatory attitude. To them, he seemed to genuinely believe himself perpetually on the verge of undertaking some major, significant empirical work validating his ideas. He did not intend to betray doctoral students, they believed, but in the challenging area of humanistic, value-laden research, he was intellectually honest enough to neither endorse nor accept flawed proposals from them.

During the course of Maslow's fifteen years of doctoral-level supervision, he did lend his attention to a few graduate-student research projects that interested him. One study, initiated by Norbert Mintz (who later became a psychotherapist), sought to test the hypothesis that we are emotionally affected by the esthetics of our surroundings. With Bertha Maslow's artistic assistance, Mintz designed three rooms: one attractive, one deliberately repulsive, and one a typical professorial office. Each of forty-six students was randomly assigned to one of the three rooms and asked to rate a photographic set of faces as either zestful or weary, content or irritable. As Mintz and Maslow had predicted, those in the most attractive room saw the faces as more energetic and happy than did those in the less attractive rooms. In short, Maslow's notion that we are by nature esthetic creatures received some empirical validation. Completed in mid-1955 and published the following year, the well-executed study is still cited today.

The other empirical investigation on which Maslow collaborated during this period was initiated by clinical psychologist Joseph Bossom. He was interested in testing the idea that our degree of emotional security strongly affects how we perceive other people. Using Maslow's security test, he first rated students' emotional security and then asked them to judge two hundred photographs of faces according to their degree of personal warmth. The least emotionally secure students tended to see the faces as less warm, while the most secure students found more warmth in the photographs.

The finding was inconclusive. Because the faces had not been "objectively" measured, it was not clear whether the most secure students were perceiving these more accurately or simply projecting their own feelings just as much as were their insecure peers. Still, it was an interesting and well-crafted study. Published in 1957, it too suggests that Maslow could have been far more productive empirically at Brandeis had he put his mind to it.

During this time, however, Maslow's sights were turned to a different aspect of psychology, to what he would soon call peak-experiences. This term, which he coined, steadily penetrated beyond academia's confines in the 1960s into everyday language. Maslow's work on peak-experiences stands among his most famous and influential.

His inquiry began after he completed *Motivation and Per-*

sonality in 1954. He decided to explore in depth a realm virtually unknown to social science, which had first intrigued him more than a decade before: ecstatic or mystical experience. At Brooklyn College, he had discovered one basic attribute of self-actualizers to be their frequent experience of unusual moments of great joy, serenity, beauty, or wonder. For some, lovemaking triggered such episodes; for others it was the wilds of nature or exalted music. Whatever the catalyst, the experience itself seemed to possess striking features that seemed to Maslow to be germane in his quest for the heights of human nature.

However, his mysterious illness in 1947 and his subsequent moves around the country had delayed his inquiry into the subject. Now he was ready to look at transcendent experience in depth.

As a lifelong atheist who had always associated religion with dogma and superstition, Maslow did not find the path emotionally easy, and his academic milieu offered little help. Conventional psychology had virtually nothing to say about religious experience, other than to spout the old Freudian dictum that it is merely a neurotic sublimation of the sexual urge. Maslow's circle of faculty friends at Brandeis—fellow atheists, with an added Marxist contempt for religion—were of no intellectual support. Braving their good-natured sneers, he ventured into this territory alone.

Initially, he did a great deal of background reading on Eastern religious thought, including such books as *The First and Last Freedom* by Indian philosopher J. Krishnamurti and *The Wisdom of Insecurity* by Alan Watts, British theologian and popularizer of Zen Buddhism. Maslow also became interested in the work of Swiss psychiatrist Carl Jung, which was receiving its first wide translation into English.

Maslow's unpublished notes show that in the summer of 1954 he began to list specific examples of transcendent experience, under the heading of (inner) "timelessness." These included the mystic state, hypnotic trance, esthetic absorption, and intense sex. The following year, he began to ponder yogic descriptions of the ecstatic state known as samadhi. Soon he chose a phenomenological approach with which to examine such lofty experiences more closely; that is, to understand how we see the world in such moments. Then, to buttress his religious readings, he solicited personal reports from self-actualizing people he knew, and began to incorporate unsolicited reports from colleagues and others who heard about his new work. In this manner, he amassed perhaps more up-to-date material on the subject of mysticism than any major American psychologist in more than fifty years, since William James's *Varieties of Religious Experience.* By the spring of 1956, Maslow was so excited by his preliminary findings that he decided to share them with his colleagues.

To his shock, the paper was rejected by one highly regarded journal after another: *Psychological Review, American Psychologist, Psychiatry.* He was stunned and angry but not defeated. He wisely decided to offer the article as his address at the upcoming convention of the American Psychological Association, which had just elected him president of its prestigious Division of Personality and Social Psychology. As a keynote speaker, he did not need to win approval for his presentation; otherwise, it might have been refused for this forum, too.

The series of journal rejections, unprecedented in Maslow's twenty-five-year career, left a bitter impression. He realized how unorthodox his work had become. To avoid any more professional humiliation and waste of productive time, he never again submitted his major articles to the American Psychological Association's prestigious periodicals. Instead, he turned to minor or maverick professional publications, or those unconnected with the discipline.

That summer, he became quite anxious about his impending address. He regarded his work on peak-experiences to be so unconventional that he feared ridicule among his audience of peers.

Presented on September 1, 1956, Maslow's paper was entitled "Cognition of Being in the Peak Experiences." It was indeed highly unorthodox by the standards of the time, incorporating no experimental techniques or statistics but simply setting forth his analysis of an exotic and superior mental state never before identified in the scientific literature. As with Maslow's earlier paper on self-actualization, he recognized the tentative nature of his inquiry but viewed it nevertheless as vital, scientific "reconnaissance work." He began his address:

Self-actualizing people, those who have come to a high level of maturation, health, and self-fulfillment, have so much to teach us that sometimes they seem almost like a different breed of human beings. But because it is so new, the exploration of the highest reaches of human nature and of its ultimate possibilities . . . is a difficult and tortuous task.

He described nearly twenty common features of the peak-experience, which he associated with extreme inner health. Based on his sample's phenomenological reports, these included temporary disorientation with respect to time and space, feelings of wonder and awe, great happiness, and a complete though momentary loss of fear and defense before the grandeur of the universe. People typically mentioned that polar opposites, like good and evil, free will and destiny, seemed transcended in such instants; everything in the cosmos was connected to everything else in a unity of splendor.

To what extent do such peaks reflect *real* perceptions of the world, and not mere wishful, infantile fantasies as Freud believed them to be? Maslow answered this question by saying, "If self-actualizing people can and do perceive reality more efficiently, fully, and with less motivational contamination than others do, then we may possibly use them as biological assays. Through *their* greater sensitivity and perception, we may get a better report of what reality is like . . . just as canaries can be used to detect gas in mines before less sensitive creatures can."

Finally, perhaps constituting the most important aspect of his paper, Maslow noted that peak-experiences often leave profound and transformative effects in their wake. He alluded to two reports, one from a psychologist and one from an anthropologist, of mystic experiences so intense "as to remove certain neurotic symptoms forever after." Generally, Maslow commented, "the person is more apt to feel that life . . . is worthwhile, even if it is usually drab, pedestrian, painful, or ungratifying, since beauty, truth, and meaningfulness have been demonstrated . . . to exist." Such conversion experiences, he declared, "are of course plentifully recorded in human history but so far as I know have never received the attention of psychologists or psychiatrists." He ended his address by emphasizing the need for further study into this highly intriguing but little-understood phenomenon of healthy functioning.

The presentation was received well by Maslow's more open-minded colleagues. Others viewed the concept as an interesting but dubious venture outside of science and into the domain of unprovable religion. Maslow was pleased by what he had been able to say publicly. Yet because the address was not published until 1959, it did not gain much immediate attention in the field beyond his network of allies.

Although Maslow very much wanted to see his psychological work put to larger, humanitarian ends, the mood of the early-to-mid-1950s conspired against it. McCarthyism frightened most American scholars away from involving themselves in anything that might be viewed by the government as even remotely socially critical or iconoclastic. But after nearly five years of defaming thousands and ruining many lives with the taint of communism, Senator McCarthy fell from grace. The downfall began with a Senate investigation into McCarthy's alleged attempts to gain preferential treatment by the army for his young assistant. The televised hearings gave millions the opportunity to see McCarthy's unprincipled conduct, and on December 2, 1954, the Senate censured him. Although he retained his seat, his power quickly dissipated.

The possibility of constructive change beckoned once more to many innovative thinkers. In the fall of 1955, Maslow was contacted by Pitirim Sorokin, renowned Harvard sociology professor, whom he knew only by reputation. Sorokin was organizing a group of socially minded scholars seeking to foster greater altruism in America and around the globe. The first meeting would take place in a few weeks, Sorokin explained, and Maslow's presence would be welcomed.

Maslow was excited by the invitation. Sorokin, already close to seventy, was respected as perhaps the most eminent, if eccentric and irascible, living sociologist. He also possessed a colorful personal history. He had established an international reputation while living in czarist Russia more than forty years before. When political events during World War I plunged Russia into chaos, Sorokin joined with the liberal socialists against the Bolsheviks and served in Alexander Kerensky's brief democratic government. This action nearly cost Sorokin his life, for when the Bolsheviks seized power in 1918, they arrested him as a traitor and decreed his execution. After six weeks in jail awaiting death by firing squad, Sorokin was freed by Lenin. In 1922 he again found himself labeled an enemy of the Revolution. This time he fled the country, emigrating with his family to the United States. After teaching at several colleges, he secured a faculty position at Harvard in 1930. Over the ensuing years, he continued to write many provocative books of sociological theory. After the horrors of Nazism, Stalinism, and World War II, he became seized with the belief that humanity's only hope for survival lay in what he called creative altruism.

Inspired by this outlook, industrialist-philanthropist Eli Lilly made possible the establishment of the Center for Creative Altruism under Sorokin's direction at Harvard in 1949. Sorokin had longed for a research component to the modest center, and in mid-1955 he felt the time was ripe for action. He contacted a select group of thinkers whose idealism and intellectual rigor he admired, including Maslow.

The meeting on October 29 at Harvard's Emerson Hall brought together some fifteen academicians, including physicist Henry Margeneau and philosopher Francis Northrop, and Vermont Senator Ralph Flanders. Sorokin made an impassioned appeal stressing the urgent task before them: to join together for scientific study into the "mysterious, powerful grace" of altruism. He envisioned not only ground-breaking research concerning altruism but also educational work such as publications and conferences. Their ultimate end was to effect a radical transformation in worldwide consciousness, eliminating the causes of war and strife. After serious discussion, the group voted unanimously to incorporate itself as the Research Society for Creative Altruism.

From the first meeting, Maslow was one of the most excited and committed members. The lofty goal matched precisely his personal vision of applying scientific reason to promote a better world, and he had high hopes for what they could accomplish. Unfortunately, he soon found, the society seemed to do little other than hold meetings and discuss ambitious but vague plans for the triumph of altruism over the forces of selfish egoism. In March 1956, Sorokin issued a compelling statement-of-purpose for the society, entitled "Why and What of the New Association." The following month, he helped incorporate it as a legal entity in Massachusetts.

That spring, Maslow devoted considerable energy to developing a plan for specific research the society might sponsor over the next several years. They had practically no research funds, but this seemed only a minor problem. Sorokin, after all, had philanthropic ties. The plan identified five broad, long-range areas of investigation:

1. A careful study of all the main forms of creative unselfish love and of destructive selfishness . . . in human relationships as well as among the non-human species.

2. What kind of a general system of values is particularly conducive to altruistic and egoistic transformation of persons, groups, institutions and culture?

3. What are the factors and sources of altruism and egoism?

4. What sort of basic social institutions are conducive to altruism and egoism generally, and for what particular individual or group specifically?

5. What kind of techniques are most efficacious for altruistic transformation of persons and groups . . . generally and for a particular person or group specifically?

Within these general topics, Maslow listed more than twenty specific research projects suggested to him by Society members. The proposals ranged tremendously in scope, but all mirrored his faith in the creative application of science as the ultimate key to world peace and harmony. Some of the most intriguing involved studying the mass media and the major religious denominations for their influences on American social values and morality; identifying ways of strengthening the declining family; devising experimental methods to teach altruism to children; and measuring the physiology of such divergent human emotions as love, compassion, and hatred. Such innovative research—cutting across the fields of psychology, sociology, economics, and even biology—was intended, according to Maslow, "to enrich the existing knowledge of creative, unselfish love in all its essential aspects and . . . to furnish . . . ways for altruistic transformation of persons, groups, institutions, and culture."

To conduct work of such magnitude would require a well-funded institute, so Maslow energetically set to work planning its administrative structure. It seemed most sensible to him and his colleagues that the society form an independent Values Institute with a small permanent group engaged in teaching, research, and dissemination of information to the public—similar to Princeton's Institute for Advanced Study, where Albert Einstein had made his intellectual home for many years. In a memorandum, Maslow gave his frank impressions of seven possible candidates for the core faculty: biologist Ludwig von Bertalanffy, psychologist Else Frenkel-Brunswik, composer Aaron Copland, artist Gyorgy Kepes, anthropologist Dorothy Lee, psychologist Ross Mooney, and economist Walter Weisskopf. Maslow added, "Finally, I may say that I have not proposed some of the top people living, simply because they are already in such good places that I think it very unlikely that we could seduce them away. However, it might do no harm to try such people as Gordon Allport in psychology, David Riesman in sociology, Clyde Clukhorn in anthropology, Erich Fromm in psychoanalysis, Henry Murray in psychology, Andras Angyal in psychiatry, Charles Morris in philosophy, [and] Paul Tillich in theology."

Based largely on these proposals, the society's administrator Frances Bowditch initiated contacts in 1956 and early 1957 with foundations and private philanthropic sources. To win the necessary funding, the plan (partly developed by Maslow) was first to set up a national advisory board of scholars, industrialists, and labor, governmental, and religious leaders who would publicize the Values Institute, serve as trustees, and help raise the money to carry out its mission. In January 1957, the society opened a permanent office in the Sheraton Building in downtown Boston, with two full-time employees and a part-time assistant.

During Maslow's often frustrating initial months, he became friendly with academician Robert Hartman. Friendly and jovial, Hartman shared Maslow's vision of reshaping modern social science into a powerful moral force in the world. Hartman had received a degree in international law in his native Germany. After becoming involved in politics, he served as a judge in Berlin for several years. When Hitler came to power, Hartman was forced to flee the country, for he had known and opposed many of the Nazi party's inner sanctum in his student days. After brief stays in Paris and London, Hartman served in Sweden from 1934 to 1941 as the Scandinavian representative of Walt Disney Productions. There he married and had a son. After brief study at the University of Mexico, he emigrated to the United States in 1942.

Shortly after the war, he received a doctorate from Northwestern University. His thesis, influenced by psychologist Kurt Lewin, had been titled *The Moral Situation: Can Field Theory Be Applied to Ethics?* In 1948, he wrote his first book, *Profit Sharing Manual*, which brought him to the attention of American industry. He viewed employee profit-sharing as an important ingredient of what he called democratic capitalism. Hartman served as chairman of the Commission on Peace for the International Council of Community Churches and wrote for UNESCO. In 1956, after teaching as a visiting professor at the Massachusetts Institute of Technology (where he met Maslow), he accepted a position at Mexico's National University.

The two men felt like comrades-in-arms, committed to making the Values Institute a reality, but progress was slow. More than a year after Maslow had drafted his proposals, on February 11, 1957, he wrote with frustration to Hartman in Mexico:

> Things are still diddling along with the Institute. Sorokin is a nuisance and [Francis] Northrop is a dope, as you predicted. I have tried successfully to detach myself from the whole thing emotionally, and I suggest that you do this too. Sometimes it looks as if something good will come of it, sometimes not. The thing to do is to wait until there are definite offers. Then we'll examine them very carefully and see what we wish to do.

At last, something concrete emerged from the committee meetings. The Society, in large part through Maslow's perseverance, organized The First Scientific Conference on New Knowledge in Human Values, October 4–5, 1957, at MIT. The symposium drew several hundred scientists and scholars from around the country and was among the most noteworthy interdisciplinary gatherings of its kind during the decade. Its impressive roster of speakers included Maslow, Fromm, Goldstein, and Allport in psychology; and Bertalanffy, D. T. Suzuki (the influential scholar of Zen Buddhism), Tillich, and Sorokin representing such disciplines as biology, philosophy, and theology. These scholars sought to advance a greater professional sensitivity to values. Except for the more activist Fromm, most were rather apolitical although of liberal sentiment. They believed that an essentially secular-humanistic outlook could best guide humanity. Under Maslow's editorship, their presentations were published in 1959 as a book entitled *New Knowledge in Human Values.*

In Maslow's presentation, he offered a view advanced earlier in his works such as *Motivation and Personality.* Citing his self-actualization research and evidence from psychotherapy and counseling studies, he stressed that psychology had finally become a useful tool for the study of human values. The topic could no longer be dismissed as mere philosophical banter but could now be pursued scientifically. He also affirmed his theory that when people are denied gratification of such basic needs, as for belongingness and self-esteem, they suffer emotionally and develop unhealthy values. Perhaps reacting to the presence of the many sociologists and philosophers who lacked training in natural science, Maslow emphasized the uniquely biological thrust of his approach to human nature. He criticized the cultural-relativist orientation:

> Man is ultimately *not* molded or shaped into humanness
> . . . The environment does not give him potentialities and
> capacities; he *has* them in inchoate or embryonic form, just
> exactly as he has embryonic arms and legs. And creativeness,
> spontaneity, selfhood, authenticity, caring for others, being
> able to love, yearning for truth are embryonic potentialities
> belonging to his species-membership just as much as are his
> arms and legs, brain and eyes.

For this reason, he urged his colleagues to grapple with the complexities of human instinct and the

[partially] hereditary-determined needs, urges, and . . . values of mankind. We can't play both the biology game and the sociology game simultaneously. We can't affirm *both* that culture does everything and anything, and that man has an intrinsic nature. The one is incompatible with the other.

Maslow continued to devote thought to his still controversial theory of self-actualization. He wrote many short, unpublished papers on the subject during 1956 and 1957. One concerned the importance of firm limit-setting for children to help provide a solid emotional basis for their higher development. Focusing specifically on the safety need in his hierarchy of innate human needs, he commented, "Children . . . need, want, and desire controls, decisiveness, and discipline. Primarily, this is because they need and want safety." Children may superficially appear to crave complete freedom and resent adult restrictions, but to give in to such demands results in the "contempt and disgust that the overindulgent child has for his weak parents." Such a child, lacking fulfillment of the safety need, will find it harder to grow to adulthood with a sense of inner security, a prerequisite for self-actualization. In this regard, Maslow agreed with Adler's view that spoiling children has long-term pernicious effects on their emotional development.

In another paper, entitled "Problems Inherent in Self-Actualization," he addressed "the big tasks for the self-actualizing person." The typed notes reflect his view that even self-actualizers experience personal difficulties in everyday life and that inner growth therefore never stops. In his perspective, the self-actualizing individual is not a mythical being free of problems, but one who has simply met his or her basic emotional needs for safety, belongingness, love, and esteem. What kind of difficulties could such a person have?

To Maslow, these difficulties stem from the self-actualizer's very superiority. For example, how do you relate to your family members if you go through your days happier and more fulfilled than they are? How do you avoid overshadowing intimates, particularly your children? Learning to cope with success and actually enjoy your talents and accomplishments in the face of envy, jealousy, and even hostility from others is another difficulty for self-actualizing men and women. Finally, Maslow noted, the self-actualizer must deal with the reality that because of this superiority, he or she is "essentially alone . . . [and] can look only within" the self for direction in life.

The issue of masculinity and femininity in relation to self-actualization occupied much of Maslow's attention during this period. One of the few to give such questions much thought in the 1950s, he was particularly interested in whether we experience growth and self-fulfillment differently depending on our gender; and, if so, whether this difference is due to cultural or innate forces. Maslow's position on this question was characteristically complex and creative. At least as far back as his friendship with Karen Horney in the 1930s, he had considered Freud's view of women both inaccurate and demeaning; clearly, there was more to female psychology than procreative anatomy. Yet, with Maslow's increasingly biological view of human nature and its potential, he was unwilling to embrace totally the view that there are no intrinsic male-female differences with regard to emotions and behavior.

Although he never published anything on the subject, he amassed copious notes, incorporating reactions to various books; he found Philip Wylie's surrealistic novel *The Disappearance* especially stimulating. It explored the possible innate emotional differences between the sexes. In a letter dated October 9, 1956, Maslow wrote to a female colleague who inquired about his perspective on women's actualization: "I have been grappling with these problems for a good twenty years now, and have huge mounds of writing on the subject. Unfortunately, I still feel too uncertain about the answers to publish them." However, in the same letter he went on to say that definite inborn psychological differences exist between men and women, regardless of their particular culture. He suggested that separate male and female basic needs must be fulfilled prior to self-actualization and that "this actualization [also] takes place differently for men and for women." He added that men and women differ somewhat emotionally, cognitively, and even perceptually. Because our culture denigrates the feminine modes, "our conceptions of the universe, of science, of intelligence, [and] of emotion are lopsided and partial because they have been constructed by man."

Since Maslow's ground-breaking 1930s study of female sexuality and dominance, he had been an advocate of the right of women to assert themselves in many areas of life including the intellectual. This was not just an abstract value. Among his closest colleagues over the years had been Ruth Benedict, Else Frenkel-Brunswik, Karen Horney, Margaret Mead, and other women whose brilliance he had greatly admired. He had always been sensitive to the uphill battle women had waged to realize their potential among men who feared bright, decisive women. Yet Maslow thought that hormonal influences might dictate an inherently feminine mode of being in the world, although scientific evidence was lacking. He felt it would be a mistake if women seeking legitimate improvement in their economic status emulated the masculine mode and abandoned their own.

"If only women were allowed to be full human beings, thereby making it possible for men to be full human beings," Maslow concluded in this detailed letter, then our culture might finally generate a balanced, rather than masculine-oriented, approach "to philosophy, art, and science. If I ever get up courage enough to write anything on the subject," he promised, "I shall send you a copy."

Throughout the postwar era, Maslow believed fervently that American culture had steadily come to devalue women's traditional work—namely, child-rearing and homemaking—and that a much-needed revolution between the sexes would take effect only when the activities of nurturing were elevated to their rightful important status. He believed that such traditional women's professions as teaching and nursing were slighted as well. Yet Maslow rarely tried to romanticize the role of motherhood or suggest that women are by nature superb caretakers of children. Having experienced his own mother's cruelty and indifference, he often told his teenage daughters that raising children well comes only from emotional maturity, not simply from what most of his colleagues dubbed the maternal instinct.

Although Maslow believed that some innate psychological differences exist between men and women, he also felt strongly that self-actualization involves a synthesis of traits associated in our culture with both masculinity and femininity. In an intriguing unpublished paper dated July 7, 1957, he wrote, "Granted that males and females come to . . . self-actualization via different paths, it nevertheless seems to be becoming clearer and clearer that the next step in personal evolution is a transcendence of both masculinity and femininity to general humanness." In this lofty state, the differences between the "healthy male" and "healthy female" become insignificant: "Both males *and* females then become decisive, able to say 'no,' stern, strong, initiating . . . *and also* passive, yielding, accepting, and eager to please. . . . They *both* become 'motherly' and 'fatherly.' "

A chief social task for our time, Maslow suggested, is to demonstrate through scientific research, education, and psychotherapy "how childish and inaccurate and unbiological our current definitions of masculinity-femininity are and to peel away . . . one spurious attribute after another: to like music is *not* feminine." Such scientific inquiry, he said, should involve not only psychology but biology and endocrinology as well, since these fields bear upon the issue of gender differences. Finally, he advocated that social research be carried out to determine "how . . . cultures have to be changed to permit [greater] self-actualization for women."

In the mid-1950s, Maslow began to acquire a national reputation outside the academic world for his work on creativity. In a sense, he earned this accolade by default; as he had observed in *Motivation and Personality*, conventional psychology had almost nothing to contribute to this important subject. With rare exception, neither the Freudians nor the behaviorists had shown the slightest interest in understanding our creative nature. Much to Maslow's surprise, he found himself sought after by corporations and governmental agencies interested in fostering creativity in their employees, especially in such fields as engineering and research and development.

One of his first consulting positions took place in the summer of 1954, when he spent a week with officers at the Maxwell Air Force Base in Alabama to help improve their problem-solving abilities. Unexpectedly, he came away from the experience with a powerful respect for their decisiveness and emotional strength, a far cry from the personal qualities of the socially timid, querulous academicians he had known nearly all of his professional life. Many years later, he could vividly recall how the colonels and majors had unknowingly taught him "that really strong and mature people can say 'no,' can stick to their guns, can debate, but don't get small or trivial in the process."

Over the next few years, as Maslow's name began to spread through the halls of business and public service, consulting offers became more frequent. One project involved assisting an insurance company that wanted to predict the health of college students. His recommendation was to examine closely their attitudes and values, because he believed that the mind strongly affects the body. In another project, a major toy company asked Maslow to suggest new toys to develop and market; he suggested that they stop manufacturing so many military toys and concentrate on those that stimulate children's creativity.

Such consulting activity helped to supplement a modest professorial salary. Perhaps more important, Maslow immensely enjoyed this work as a "real-world" challenge and a vindication of his system of psychology. In a pattern that began in the mid-1950s and continued in accelerated form through the rest of his career, his ideas were embraced by those in a host of practical fields, from business management and marketing to nursing, long before they would find wide acceptance among his psychological colleagues, who felt that scientific proof was still lacking. At times, though, he could not help but feel a certain ironic amusement at being venerated by laypeople as an expert in such nascent scientific realms as the study of creativity.

Particularly after the Soviet launching of the Sputnik satellite in the fall of 1957, American educators and industrialists awoke to the issue of creativity and how to foster it. As a result, Maslow was frequently asked to speak before professional associations on this topic suddenly in vogue. In such talks, he often emphasized that American men not only misunderstand but even fear their own creative impulses. They mistakenly regard traits such as artistic sensitivity, playfulness, tenderness, and imagination as innately feminine and somehow indicative of homosexuality.

As a result, many men suppress these qualities that constitute the wellsprings of creativity. His favorite extreme example was the man so emotionally rigid that he is unsure whether he's fallen in love, or seldom allows himself to laugh heartily or cry, since love, laughter, and tears lie outside the province of rationality. Until American men learn to cherish rather than deny their natural, softer impulses, they are not likely to improve their creative abilities, he stressed.

Maslow was hardly oblivious to the larger social issues that affect workplace creativity. In the conformist era of the 1950s, he was one of the few established psychologists to speak out on the tendency of large organizations, whether governmental or private-sector, to stifle individual self-expression. Creativity cannot flower in the deadly atmosphere of bureaucratic inertia, he insisted. Despite their fears about Soviet scientific advances, corporate and governmental leaders cannot simply mandate greater creativity. It can arise only when people feel free to be themselves and express what they feel. The completely well-adjusted and docile employee—"the man in the gray flannel suit," as portrayed by Sloan Wilson's popular novel—is rarely the most creative.

However, Maslow—perhaps by nature more optimistic than his Brandeis colleagues like Herbert Marcuse—believed that American corporations and public organizations could successfully change to allow more room for the unfettered individual. "In the early stages of creativeness," he declared at a seminar for U.S. Army research and development engineers in 1957, "you've got to be a bum, and you've got to be a bohemian, you've got to be crazy."

In the same address, Maslow advocated the importance of developing, even in the army's intensely bureaucratic system, a commitment to individual self-expression. "I have no doubt that the [conformist] standard of practice which has worked . . . in large organizations absolutely needs modification and revision of some sort. We'll have to find some way of permitting people to be individualistic in an organization. I don't know how it will be done, [but] . . . we've got to face it."

Brandeis scarcely resembled the United States Army. But having devoted much of his personal energy since 1951 to building the new school, Maslow was starting to feel the need to nurture his own creativity in the best possible way.

CHAPTER FOURTEEN

Slow Rhythms of Mexico

I love working as I have been here in Mexico, all alone, no helpers but no responsibilities either.

[On my] Mexican vacation, I learned a different way of working—timeless, placeless, primary-process.

—A.M.

After more than six vigorous years at Brandeis, Maslow was eager for a rest and a change of scenery. In early 1958, he and Bertha made plans for the summer and upcoming sabbatical year: nearly fourteen precious months of leisure. But where to go? They decided to spend the time together in Cuernavaca, Mexico.

Ten years earlier, when Maslow had done sales work for his brothers' business in Pleasanton, California, he had liked what he had seen of Mexico, especially its slow and easy pace of living. It also had the virtue of being inexpensive; while they were struggling to put both daughters through college at the same time, this financial consideration was uppermost in his and Bertha's minds. They hardly dared believe the rumors about how royally one could live in Mexico on a moderate income of American dollars, but they knew it would be cheaper than any comparable place in the United States. Although Maslow planned to cloister himself for unhurried reading and writing, he looked forward to having at least one close friend, philosopher Robert Hartman, close by in Mexico City. Ann Maslow decided to join her parents and enrolled in the junior-year-abroad program at Bennington College to study art in Mexico.

Following a leisurely cross-country drive, visiting friends

and stopping at points of interest, the Maslows arrived in Cuernavaca early that summer. They rented a comfortable cottage with a swimming pool, hired a maid-cook and a handyman-gardener at a very low cost, and began to settle in. Cuernavaca was renowned as one of Mexico's most beautiful cities, and Maslow was delighted with his choice. At five thousand feet above sea level, Cuernavaca enjoyed much warmer, balmier weather than Mexico City, which lay some fifty miles to the north; yet it was not unbearably hot even in summer. Cuernavaca, capital of the state of Morelos, had little industry. It was a vacation spot for affluent Mexico City residents who owned weekend homes there and for American tourists and other foreigners. Everywhere, picturesque old homes with red-tiled roofs and flowering gardens nestled among huge old trees that shaded the quiet streets.

During Maslow's first sunny weeks in Cuernavaca, he relaxed by the pool and began to catch up on his reading. He wanted to bring himself up-to-date concerning the growing body of European existentialism translated into English, as well as other current philosophical writings. Otherwise, Maslow had few definite plans for his sabbatical year, except to put his teaching and administrative duties at Brandeis wholly out of mind. He felt considerable pride in reflecting on the growth of the psychology department since he had become its head in 1951. But lately he had been feeling increasingly exploited in this role and resentful of the valuable time he was giving away to others. In Mexico, he hoped to concentrate on his scholarly work virtually free of external demands. While Bertha and Ann explored Cuernavaca and the surrounding countryside, he spent most of his hours in solitary poolside reading, frequently jotting down his reactions or typing rough responses to books and ideas. This was his personal heaven.

For a few weeks, Maslow tried to master conversational Spanish. He found the effort time-consuming and difficult and gave up. However, he could read Spanish newspapers and books fairly well. Bertha developed proficiency in what the locals called "kitchen Spanish," so she could communicate effectively with their maid-cook.

In late August, Maslow came out of his seclusion to attend the International Conference of General Semantics in Mexico City, where he had been invited to give a luncheon address on creativity. Over the past decade, he had maintained a strong interest in the philosophical work of the conference's founder, Alfred Korzybski, and other semanticists like S. I. Hayakawa. He enjoyed getting together with this group of innovative, like-minded social scientists. The day before his own talk, Maslow sat in on an interesting luncheon address on culture, family values, and psychotherapy. The speaker was a good-humored Mexican professor of psychiatry in his late thirties, Rogelio Diaz-Guerrero.

As a cross-cultural researcher, Diaz-Guerrero offered the view that Mexicans have a very different set of family values than do people in the United States and Canada; such values, he insisted, strongly affect the way therapy can be done. For instance, Mexicans believe that the truthfulness of a statement made between husband and wife should not be measured in terms of its *objective* reality but rather in terms of the degree to which it constructively *benefits* the couple and the entire family. Unlike most North American psychiatrists and their lay public, Mexicans reject the Freudian notion of the inevitability of the Oedipal complex and other supposedly immutable conflicts among family members. Instead of regarding people as passive and helpless beings, Diaz-Guerrero argued, Mexicans believe that we *create* our social reality by the way we choose to live.

Impressed by this presentation, Maslow rose and told the assembled gathering a story, conveying his own related outlook:

> One day, a traveling family came into town X. They found an important local man, and explained that they had left the town of Y because people there were most unfriendly and uncooperative. How are people in this town? they wanted to know. "Unfortunately," the important local man replied, shaking his head, "they are just the way you described those in town Y." Upon hearing this, the family continued on their journey.
>
> Immediately afterward, a second traveling family arrived. They likewise found the same man, and related that they wished to settle there. They explained that they had come from the town of Y, where everyone was most friendly and cooperative. However, for the wife's health reasons,

their doctor had advised them to leave immediately. How are people here? they wished to know. Nodding his head, the local man replied, smiling, "Just like those you described in town Y—friendly and cooperative."

Diaz-Guerrero felt moved by Maslow's tale and, after the session, introduced himself. He related that as a Mexico City psychiatrist in private practice and research, he had found Maslow's *Motivation and Personality* immensely stimulating. As the two men conversed about their mutual interests, both felt an immediate spark of friendship.

Beginning that September, Maslow and Diaz-Guerrero and their wives met socially nearly every other weekend. Bertha quickly became close to Ethel, who was originally from Australia. Ethel usually brought their two preschool children, Rolando and Cristina, to the get-togethers, and their exuberant curiosity often reminded a wistful Maslow of the days when Ann and Ellen had been that tender age. The Maslows and Diaz-Guerreros spent their weekends together in one of three places: the Diaz-Guerreros' home in Mexico City, their weekend house about forty minutes south of Cuernavaca, or at the Maslows' home. They rarely dined at formal restaurants or even casual cafés but spent most of their time in lively conversation over the home dinner table.

Although Diaz-Guerrero was at heart a cross-culturalist, he respected Maslow's theory of motivation and the hierarchy of needs as the most comprehensive yet developed in science. He also shared Maslow's optimism and affinity for an existentialist, values-oriented approach toward their field. In their discussions, Maslow often emphasized his notion of *instinctoid needs*—our innately good tendencies for compassion, altruism, and the like—which can be easily crushed in early upbringing. They agreed, too, about the importance of understanding the individual's will-to-power, and they frequently debated these contrasting trends within the human personality. Diaz-Guerrero tended to be more insistent about our inborn potential for aggression, but their similarities of thought far outweighed their differences.

A particularly lively topic was Maslow's theory of self-actualization. His colleague argued that while self-actualization is probably a worldwide phenomenon, its specific manifestation inevitably differs from one culture to the next. Thus, while a self-actualizer in the United States or Canada might embody the traits of autonomy and a strong need for personal privacy that Maslow had identified in his research, a Mexican counterpart would be far more committed to serving family members, friends, and community.

After such discussions with Diaz-Guerrero, and after reading Dostoevsky's *Brothers Karamazov*, which Maslow found evocative, he decided to record his developing thoughts on this issue. In an unpublished paper dated January 1, 1959, he commented, "So far, I have been studying self-actualization via autonomy, as if it were the only path. But this is quite Western, and even American." Realizing that in a relatively poor country like Mexico few people could find self-fulfillment through their livelihood, Maslow speculated that perhaps renunciation and cloistered piety were more viable avenues for self-actualization than he had previously recognized. For example, in czarist Russia and such contemporary dictatorships as Batista's Cuba and Duvalier's Haiti, the opportunity to self-actualize through public activity was almost wholly eliminated. Thus, Maslow observed, "If a man is forbidden to *Be* by his times, apparently he can get *some* of the effects of *Being* via yearning, dreaming, fantasying, idealizing, utopianizing . . . [or through] writing . . . or painting, or being religious." In this way, one could at least partially express one's highest or noblest qualities by transcending the existing social order, however wretched and corrupt it might be. However, Maslow noted, in a country like the United States, with its many individual opportunities for constructive and creative work, to seek self-fulfillment through the pathway of renunciation is neither necessary nor desirable.

Another frequent topic of conversation, one in which Bertha, Ethel, and sometimes Ann Maslow participated, concerned the nature of femininity, masculinity, and family relations in Mexico versus North America. Maslow was especially intrigued by the social traits of Mexican women, especially the middle-aged, whom he admired as noble. He found young Mexican women vibrant and graceful, more so than their better-educated counterparts in the United States. Yet, as they grew older and married, these same women seemed to become so totally devoted to their families, especially their children, that they lost their spark and became uninterested in the outer world. Middle-class women in North America, Maslow noted, seemed to experience a different but similarly incomplete process of maturation. They strove so hard for self-development that they lost the real pleasures of motherhood and marriage.

A related subject of lively discussion was how Mexican parents, as opposed to those in the United States, raised their children. To Maslow, the Mexican father appeared to be an important psychological if not physical presence in the home. He was respected by all family members, and though he tended to be stern, even harsh, as a disciplinarian, his children always knew where they stood with him. They developed a sense of right and wrong. In contrast, Maslow believed, the typical North American father of the 1950s was a weak and ineffectual figure who enjoyed little respect among his children. This situation was bound to lead to familial and larger social problems, especially affecting children's emotional growth, Maslow thought. He and Diaz-Guerrero also found interesting the parallels that seemed to exist between Jewish-American and Mexican families. In both ethnic groups, the mother appeared the dominant emotional figure; however, in the Mexican family, she lavished her love upon her children unconditionally, while in the Jewish family, she strove to foster in them achievement and success.

Before long, such discussions motivated Maslow and Diaz-Guerrero to embark on formal research. They collaborated on an article entitled "Juvenile Delinquency as a Value Disturbance." This little-known but intriguing paper marked Maslow's first published effort to apply his emerging theory of value disturbance to a specific social problem: in this case, juvenile delinquency. In later years, he approached the issues of crime, drug addiction, and penal recidivism from this same vantage point. The subject of juvenile delinquency had been in the news of late—Leonard Bernstein's musical *West Side Story*, for example, had recently opened on Broadway—and Maslow felt that none of the politicians or social analysts really understood the troubling phenomenon.

The key to comprehending youthful delinquency, Maslow and Diaz-Guerrero asserted, is to recognize that it mainly represents the expression of male adolescent rage toward adults and their culture. Central to this hatred is a vengeful contempt for the weak, indecisive, or absentee fathers who have let them run wild without guidance, who have thus failed to provide models for appropriate male conduct. The two researchers emphasized that setting limits and employing consistent discipline—punishment when necessary—were essential qualities of being a responsible parent. When parents abdicate their authority over children and adolescents, a vacuum of power results. In this situation, boys show defiance through such acts as vandalism, bullying, joining gangs, engaging in duels as a test of manhood, and, finally, violent and criminal delinquency.

At the end of their paper, Maslow and Diaz-Guerrero listed several key principles that emerged from their collaboration. These included:

1. All humans, including children, need a coherent value system.

2. Lack of a value system in the larger culture breeds certain forms of psychological disorder.

3. Individuals will crave and search for a coherent value system.

4. People prefer having *any* value system, however unsatisfying, to none at all—that is, complete chaos.

5. If there is no adult value system, then a child or adolescent will embrace the value system of peers.

Over the next decade, as the level of violent juvenile crime steadily escalated in the United States, Maslow increasingly emphasized this line of reasoning in his private writing. However, he rarely publicized his viewpoint, fearing that, amid the black struggle for political and economic equality in the 1960s, it might be misunderstood as an endorsement of the status quo. His fear was probably well founded. Several years later, when Harvard sociologist Daniel P. Moynihan issued a report on the pathology of the black American urban family, he was roundly attacked as a racist, a label that stuck well into his New York Senatorial campaign.

Maslow and Diaz-Guerrero produced no other papers together. Both preferred their convivial dinner-table discussions to the more demanding task of putting their ideas into print. Indeed, Maslow found that the slow pace of life in Cuernavaca induced in him a more casual attitude toward systematic intellectual work than he had felt in many years. He loved the new feeling of having no set schedules, no superimposed deadlines; under sunny Mexican skies, he no longer felt the urge to create self-imposed ones. While he enjoyed visits from relatives like his brother Harold and Brandeis colleagues James Klee and Frank Manuel, what he liked most about his sabbatical was the freedom from external obligations of any kind, even those of a social nature.

One of Maslow's rare forays into society took place when he and Bertha joined Erich Fromm and his wife for dinner in Mexico City. For nearly a decade, Fromm had been teaching at the National Autonomous University of Mexico, having moved to Mexico for his wife's health. Fromm had built a department of psychoanalysis in the medical school and had founded the Mexican Psychoanalytic Institute. He was also commuting to Michigan State University, where he taught psychology.

Even before Maslow's sabbatical, he had been looking forward to meeting with Fromm in Mexico, perhaps even collaborating with him. That evening, he enjoyed the company of his mentor from the late 1930s. The discussion was lively and stimulating, centering on Ernest Jones's recent biography of Freud. But to Maslow's disappointment, Fromm was as aloof and reserved as ever, and nothing further developed between the two.

Sometimes Maslow got together socially with Robert Hartman, the German philosopher he had gotten to know while collaborating on the Values Institute. From his new home in Mexico City, Hartman traveled frequently to consult for major American companies engaged in management training and other projects.

Although her parents basked in the serenity of their Mexican sojourn, Ann became increasingly bored and depressed.

On her father's recommendation, she saw Diaz-Guerrero for private psychotherapy and found him supportive and empathic. She decided there was nothing productive for her to accomplish in Mexico and it would be wisest to return to New York City, where she had friends. At their final session, Diaz-Guerrero, in true Latin style, gave Ann a warm good-bye hug that she always remembered fondly.

In early December 1958, Maslow visited the California Institute of Technology (Caltech) as a guest of its YMCA-sponsored Leaders of America program; John Weir, Caltech's administrator, was responsible for bringing Maslow to campus. He met with many groups of interested students and a few faculty members. He found the young engineering students to be a cluster of extraordinarily bright young minds, perhaps the best student body he had seen (next to MIT's) on the more than one hundred college campuses he had visited in the past ten years. Most of his conversations with the students centered on creativity, motivation, and sexuality and dating.

Despite their intellectual level, Maslow saw definite problems among these science-minded high-achievers. In particular, many young men seemed to be emotionally immature, expressing their masculinity in an aggressive and competitive rather than affectionate way. The most psychologically unhealthy students, Maslow thought, were those who seemed superficially poised, self-assured, and smug, for in his view they had stopped developing within.

Before Maslow left Caltech, he agreed to Weir's request to write his impressions and offer recommendations to improve the quality of student life. In a characteristically frank report dated March 7, 1959, Maslow responded. After praising much of what he had seen on campus, he cautioned Weir that emotional immaturity often accompanies intellectual precocity and that the growth process of young adults must be respected. Maslow encouraged Weir to provide more liberal arts courses at Caltech, especially those highlighting the ethical, esthetic, and psychological dimensions of modern science; such a curricular change would not only better educate students but would reduce the dropout rate by offering more emotionally relevant subjects.

Maslow reported that Caltech's resident house system, offering an alternative to large-scale dormitory living, was a good idea; even better, he suggested, would be the presence of a resident family for each group of students. In this way, they would feel less emotionally isolated from the normal stream of social life. This innovation was especially desirable since Caltech had no women students. Maslow suggested, too, that a more extensive counseling program was needed, especially to deal with "the problems of high IQ and creativity in immature people." Sometimes all that gifted students need is a sympathetic older figure, or an opportunity to collaborate with one, Maslow said. Perhaps he was thinking back to his apprenticeship under the fatherly Edward Thorndike.

Maslow's final suggestion was consistent with his overall educational and moral philosophy: the goal at Caltech should be to turn out not merely competent or good engineers and scientists, but great ones—creators, innovators, and leaders. "This is a qualitatively different job, not just a matter of degree," he insisted, one requiring further educational research as well as commitment to teaching.

In March 1959, Maslow began keeping a daily journal, which was to be one of his most significant projects for the rest of his life. His impetus came from several sources, including the journals of Danish philosopher Soren Kierkegaard and of his former mentor Ruth Benedict.

For years, Maslow had jotted down on three-by-five cards every idea that came to him, at any hour of the day or night. Later he filed the cards within several dozen folders with titles like Dominance, Masculinity/Femininity, Values, and Self-Actualization. To express more sustained thoughts, he typed rough drafts of short papers, often making a number of copies for cross-indexing. Whenever he began formal research for a presentation, article, or book, he reviewed the contents of his files.

The files were now so extensive that it was difficult to keep track of his ideas. He hoped that keeping a journal would enable him to better organize his work and develop his insights more systematically. He also wished to examine how his thoughts germinated within the context of specific events in his life. "Every intellectual used to keep a journal," he commented, "and many have been published and are usually more interesting and instructive than the final format."

Curiously for a man only fifty-one years old, Maslow also mused that a journal would help promulgate his work after his demise. "The sad thought I've so often had," he recounted, "[is that] whenever I die, it will [leave] many things half done. The journal system is better for salvaging incomplete stuff for someone else to finish."

Another reason for initiating the journal was his realization that he was not a systematic scholar or scientist; he was what was popularly known as an idea man. Several weeks later, as he prepared for a demanding lecture tour in California and the East before his return to Brandeis in the fall, he became pensive. Five years had elapsed since *Motivation and Personality* had been published. Since then, he had not only failed to complete any major writing but had not even begun any important, sustained projects. His year in Mexico had been happy but, by the standards of his Brandeis colleagues, not very productive.

In a revealing journal entry dated June 15, Maslow looked hard at his own method of scholarship. Accurately describing the bulk of his published work since 1954, Maslow lamented:

> Practically none of my papers in the last five years have been written specifically as scientific papers. They've all been started by a solicitation or call from the outside, not from within me. Practically all have been well paid for. Most of them were for general rather than specific audiences. They all had deadlines . . . They were all about an hour long—that is, had an externally and artificially imposed length rather than an intrinsic length. None of them were "scholarly" in the way most of my previous papers were.

His psychoanalyst Felix Deutsch and his psychiatrist friend Harry Rand had called his attention to his lack of disciplined scholarship, but he felt too secure in his self-image as a pathmaker, and too productive in this role, to change his style of work.

Ironically, Maslow still clung to his hope of writing the definitive psychology text but finally wondered whether he possessed the vigor and patience for such an extensive project. Referring to his upcoming lecture tour, he mused, "It looks as if I'd like to do this same thing for another two years until the girls get through college. I *must* earn the extra money I get by these lectures . . . I doubt whether I'll have time the next two years to do any other kind of writing."

In the winter of 1959, an anthology edited by Maslow, *New Knowledge in Human Values,* was published. He was pleased with it, particularly his own paper in it. Intellectually, he felt increasingly drawn to philosophy, especially existentialism, and his reading preferences began to decisively shift from experimental psychology to the "softer" areas of social thought. Some of the books he found thought-provoking during his sabbatical included *From Death Camp to Existentialism* (later renamed *Man's Search for Meaning*) by Holocaust survivor Viktor Frankl, *The Sane Society* by Erich Fromm, and essays by psychologist Rollo May, philosophers Jean-Paul Sartre and Alfred North Whitehead, and others. For less demanding fare, Maslow enjoyed science fiction for its bold speculations and utopian themes.

Maslow was disenchanted with the traditional leftist outlook espoused by Fromm, Herbert Marcuse, and others still drawn to Marxist thought. Maslow rejected as overly cautious, if not groundless, their worry that the growing effort among corporate managers to make employees feel creative or happy was just a clever ruse to maintain power over them. Real changes were finally occurring in the American workplace, he believed, and should be praised and encouraged, not condemned.

In a journal note dated May 15, Maslow commented after reading Fromm's *The Sane Society*: "These old socialists are overdoing it. For them industry is still as villainous as it used to be, even though it has changed its nature entirely." But how could well-meaning business leaders, government officials, and educators best promote creativity and self-fulfillment in our highly complex society? "If our Values Institute goes through," he observed, "these are all basic problems to work with: What economic structures are needed to help the real individual to develop—what social theories, politics, [and] education?"

The spring of 1959 found Maslow still laboring to get the Values Institute off the ground. Several months before, he had sent Brandeis President Sachar a detailed proposal concerning an Institute for Research in Human Values. Its mission would encompass teaching, publishing, consulting, and, especially, research devoted to values, morality, and ethics. Religious studies would also come within its purview. He had described the envisioned administrative structure and even stipulated the salary ranges for its core faculty. But Maslow had yet to receive a reply. He received an encouraging letter dated March 9 from Robert Hartman, who reported that five major corporations—AT&T, General Electric, IBM, General Foods, and Nationwide Insurance—were prepared to support the project financially. Since there was a dearth of competent scholars in the field of values, Hartman indicated that only one Values Institute could be established for many years to come.

Armed with this news, Maslow sent off another letter to Sachar with a copy of *New Knowledge in Human Values*. In a reply dated March 25, Sachar still gave no definite answer. "Let's wait until you return for a discussion about a proposed Institute. We're up to our ears in financial problems now, and in a harassed climate, I really wouldn't do justice to what may be a very valuable project."

On April 13, Hartman, consulting with General Electric's Management and Research Institute in the New York City area, wrote to Maslow brimming with excitement. Several days before, Hartman reported, he had seen Sachar and their meeting had gone splendidly. Not only had Sachar greeted him "like a long-lost friend," he had shown great interest in the plan for a Values Institute housed on the Brandeis campus. He had read Maslow's detailed proposal and was ready to offer total commitment to the project. "As soon as you return . . . Sachar will ask you to call a conference of some ten people interested in and willing to work with the new Institute," Hartman wrote.

Hardly believing this apparent stroke of good fortune, Hartman continued, "I didn't really know what was happening to me, nor do I understand right now what it all means . . . I feel he means it but can't really understand how this came about so suddenly . . . He treated the whole thing as a foregone conclusion, and as one of the things Brandeis is bound to do."

Although he was more familiar with Sachar's enthusiastic manner as well as Brandeis' precarious financial situation, Maslow was hopeful upon receiving the news. The study of values was beginning to attract widespread interest, not limited to a small coterie of social scholars and philosophers. There was much that the Values Institute could accomplish, especially with an active research program, and Maslow hoped that after more than two and a half years of planning, his dream might soon be realized.

For lack of funding, the Values Institute would never materialize. To Maslow's regret, Sachar soon relegated the proposal to low priority in the face of more immediate needs. Brandeis was scarcely ten years old, and Sachar felt obligated to defer the project until more secure times. With a poetic and bitter irony, Sorokin, originator of the whole idea, later wrote of the abortive effort, "The prevalent worldwide climate of blood belligerency and interhuman strife, with their individual and tribal egoisms, turned out to be exceedingly unfavorable for the cultivation of the garden of an unselfish creative love."

Still invigorated by prospects of Sachar's support for a Values Institute, Maslow went to Santa Barbara, California, the weekend of June 20. He had been invited by the Southern California Association for Group Therapy to be chief speaker at an Interdisciplinary Conference on Values. Although he had not prepared a polished paper, he spoke forcefully and from the heart. In coming years, this freewheeling, almost exhortatory style of address before popular and professional groups would become characteristic.

He expressed his sense of ignorance and humility in light of the magnitude of the task before them. Reading from his essay in *New Knowledge in Human Values,* he expounded his belief that the times were critical, for humanity's traditional value systems were rapidly collapsing. "We are in the midst of a historical period in which we are shifting from a search in the world for values, from religious, political, and economic systems—from them to ourselves. This quest for identity . . . has never been true before, not even in the East. Psychology must become conscious of it, so that it can organize this in the most fruitful fashion."

He spoke of the importance of avoiding a philosophical quagmire in the study of human values. Rather than trying to decide what people ought to do, we should find the most psychologically healthy individuals and then empirically see what values they actually live by. In this way, Maslow explained, he and his fellow practitioners might one day be able to say definitively that certain values, such as prejudice or chronic cynicism, are emotionally bad for us, in the same way that physicians can confidently state that smoking is bad for the heart.

Maslow offered his California colleagues two pithy aphorisms as his parting words: First, that "there is no conflict between religion and science, but [only] between stupid science and stupid religion." And second, in the context of psychotherapy and values, he urged them to think of Freud, "as a friend, not as a father."

On August 20, Maslow's Mexican holiday came to a close. He and Bertha began a leisurely cross-country drive, one of the few sustained activities, Bertha found, in which her husband would participate without absorbing himself in a book or writing. Even while driving, however, Maslow had the habit of jotting down ideas on cards that he kept in his pockets. If necessary, he would pull over to the roadside to record a new insight that he did not wish to lose; it was one of his eccentricities that Bertha had long ago learned to accept.

On the way back to Boston, they stopped briefly at Louisville, Kentucky, where Maslow had a speaking engagement. They continued to Cincinnati to spend several days at the annual American Psychological Association convention. Maslow was one of five psychologists participating in a Symposium on Existential Psychology, which he had helped organize. The other speakers included Gordon Allport, Rollo May, and Carl Rogers, all of whom knew one another well. In a sense, they regarded themselves as among a vanguard of those seeking to humanize the discipline. It was an exciting gathering, and one that was intellectually significant. Out of this symposium would emerge an anthology edited by Rollo May entitled *Existential Psychology*, a work that brought existential thought to the attention of many psychologists and lay readers for the first time.

It was eminently characteristic of Maslow that his symposium speech on existentialism was direct and informal rather than obscure or pedantic. He chose a provocative title: "Existential Psychology: What's in It for Us?" The "Us," of course, referred to Maslow's fellow psychologists, whom he knew were typically indifferent (if not openly hostile) to philosophical discourse. In this respect, little had changed in mainstream American psychology since he had been a student at Wisconsin.

Maslow therefore presented as pragmatic a view of European existentialism as possible. At the outset, as if to reassure them of his intentions, he declared himself neither an existentialist nor an ardent observer of the movement. He had studied existentialism not for its own sake but for its psychological relevance. Now, he wished to announce that European existentialism had much to say to psychologists—not so much through its revelatory insights, but through its confirmation of what American theoreticians and clinicians were already beginning to discover about human nature. In particular, Maslow praised several of his former mentors and colleagues for their role in this growing movement devoted to self-identity and growth: they included Allport, May, and Rogers at the Symposium, and also Erik Erikson, Erich Fromm, Kurt Goldstein, Karen Horney, and those in allied groups such as the Jungians, Gestalt therapists, and certain neo-Freudians.

Maslow offered a series of brief but explicit statements pertaining to existentialism and psychology. While rejecting the European emphasis on anguish and despair as central to human existence, he highlighted existentialism's attention to the serious or tragic dimensions of life, and its focus on what makes the individual unique. In this regard, not only might the existentialists help to enrich existing psychology, but, far more than the Freudians or the behaviorists, they might also provide "an additional push toward the establishment of another *branch* of psychology . . . of the fully evolved and authentic self and its ways of being." Although he had no name for it yet, within a year or two this budding branch would come to be known as *humanistic psychology,* a term he helped coin.

Of all the existential literature he had read, Maslow said, he had been most touched by the notion of "future time." In the core of our being we each carry the seed of our becoming, of our latent potential. "No theory of psychology will ever be complete that does not centrally incorporate the concept that man has his future within him, dynamically active at the present moment."

After fourteen serene months in Mexico, Maslow was ready to return to work. At the edge of a new decade, in the fertile intellectual ground of the United States, it was time to germinate some seeds of his own.

CHAPTER FIFTEEN

Enlightened Managers, Mystics, and Entrepreneurs

If we lose our sense of the mysterious, of the numinous, if we lose our sense of awe, of humility, of being struck dumb, if we lose our sense of good fortune, then we have lost a very real and basic human capacity and are diminished thereby.

What conditions of work, what kinds of work, what kinds of management, and what kinds of reward or pay will help human stature to grow healthy, to its fuller and fullest stature? Classic economic theory, based as it is on an inadequate theory of human motivation, could be revolutionized by accepting the reality of higher human needs, including the impulse to self-actualization and the love for the highest values.

—A.M.

R eturning to Brandeis from his sabbatical, Maslow was ready to embark on a long-envisioned major project: a thorough critique of modern science from a humanistic perspective. For more than fifteen years, he had given thought to this issue, and with his newfound vitality, the time seemed right to attack science's value-free ideology and statistical emphasis on trivializing the most meaningful aspects of human experience. Especially in his own field of psychology, he viewed the experimentalists' obsession with method over purpose as hopelessly irrelevant to humanity's pressing concerns. To this statistical emphasis, he applied a favorite aphorism: "What's not worth doing is not worth doing well."

Almost immediately, however, Maslow found himself burdened by administrative and teaching duties. As head of the psychology department, he shouldered many tasks out of a sense of obligation but resented them as infringements upon his writing. "Now, as I do get into a big job," he wrote in his journal, "I find I have to give up many interests such as reading, friends, students, colleagues. Can't scatter my forces, my inadequate vigor, my limited time."

During the next few months, Maslow was frustrated by his slow progress on new projects. He had trouble sustaining energy for his critique of science, and by the summer of 1960 he decided to shelve that project temporarily. Despite the interest aroused by his work on peak-experiences, he also was having a hard time getting his proposed anthology of articles accepted for publication. Editor after editor sent him this polite rejection: Your papers are too scattered to comprise a coherent book without substantial rewriting. Maslow knew the editors were right; many of the articles had been speeches rather than carefully crafted theoretical or empirical contributions. However preparing short addresses for professional gatherings occupied a good deal of his time. With two college-age daughters requiring substantial financial support, he regarded his speaking engagements as a necessary source of extra cash.

One such stimulating event was an existentialist meeting in New York City whose participants included psychiatrist Viktor Frankl and psychotherapist Rollo May. Both gave Maslow helpful suggestions about his work. He found particularly useful Frankl's comment that we never self-actualize in a vacuum, but always in relation to people and circumstances around us. Maslow agreed that self-actualization involves a "calling" to service from the external, day-to-day world, not only a yearning from within.

Meanwhile, the nature of peak-experiences absorbed much of Maslow's research. In gathering additional accounts from students about their peak moments of life, he became more convinced that these rare, transcendent episodes are a key to our unrealized potential. He published an article based partly on such reports, entitled "Some Dangers of Being-cognition." He intended it as one piece in a broader personal critique of his own theory of self-actualization, which he felt was being too uncritically accepted as scientific truth by many humanists.

He first sought to rectify the growing "misunderstanding

of self-actualization as a static, 'perfect' state in which all human problems are transcended, and in which people 'live happily ever after' in a superhuman state of serenity or ecstasy. This is empirically not so." Rather, he insisted, self-actualization is "a development of personality which frees the person from the deficiency problems of growth, and from the neurotic . . . problems of life, so that he is able to face, endure, and grapple with the 'real,' [existential] problems [of] the human condition."

Reaffirming the poetic, ecstatic knowledge that peak-experiences bring, which he called *Being-cognition,* Maslow stressed that they also carry the inherent danger of instilling passivity. Achieving the mystic's sense of cosmic unity can be tremendously uplifting, but such a state must always be balanced by action in the daily world. Therefore, *Deficiency-cognition,* seeing the flaws and disharmonies around us, has its place too.

Maslow contended that the world's great religions have always preached against overreliance on inner contemplation at the expense of action, and that Buddhism, for example, distinguishes between two kinds of mystics: the lesser, privatist *Pratyeka Buddha,* "who wins enlightenment only for himself," and the nobler *Bodhisattva,* who, having attained enlightenment, regards his own salvation as imperfect as long as others remain lost in confusion and ignorance. Over the next few years, as more widespread interest in Eastern mysticism and meditation grew, Maslow increasingly emphasized the point that too much inwardness is neither psychologically healthy nor socially desirable.

Clearly, he identified more strongly with the active mystic. With his restless temperament, he never felt personally drawn to reclusive contemplation or esoteric bodily practices like yoga. Nor did he seek exotic travel for a sense of wonder. Rather, he felt most at peace and uplifted when listening to classical music, especially the Romantic composers, or when bird-watching on Audubon Society nature walks in pastoral New England. Sometimes, at night, to reach a desired inner state, he listened to recordings of birdcalls. Lovemaking with Bertha was another source of revelatory joy for him, as he sometimes told her. However, he rarely talked to others about his own peak-experiences, and Bertha by nature was even more private.

In an August 1960 radio interview for the Pacifica Foundation in Berkeley, Maslow advanced an innovative notion: *eupsychia*, or "realistic" utopia. Since his experience among the Blackfoot Indians more than twenty years earlier, he had been intrigued by the question, How ideal a culture does human nature permit? Clearly, we are not angels; yet studies of self-actualizers showed that some people do operate at humanity's highest ideals of altruism, creativity, and purpose. Several science-fiction books triggered further thoughts in this realm. After lively discussions with Frank Manuel, Maslow arrived at his own definition of utopia, or eupsychia: the community produced on a desert isle "by one thousand self-actualizing people and their families."

Such a place interested him as a thought-experiment—not only for its absence of social negatives such as robbery, fraud, or murder but especially for its positives. What would the community's arts, sciences, aspirations be like? How might its sexual mores differ from our own culture? Would it create a structured religion? If so, what would be its teachings and practices? How would decision-making be carried out? He considered it of great importance that society start to think about such questions; but he observed that any such vision of earthly heaven is, in a sense, a projection of our own unfulfilled needs and longings.

For example, as he and Manuel noted, most utopian books through the ages have been written by men. Vivid depictions of utopia as a sexual paradise, with unlimited beautiful, willing partners, seemed a peculiarly male rather than female fantasy. If so, What sort of utopian portraits might women have created through the centuries, had they been given the opportunity?

During the radio interview, Maslow stressed his biological view of human nature. "Instead of cultural relativity, I am implying that there are basic, underlying standards that are cross-cultural, which transcend cultures and which are broadly human. Without these standards, we would simply have no criterion for criticizing, let us say, the well-adjusted Nazi in Nazi Germany."

He also contrasted his utopian focus with that of classic philosophers and theologians. "Throughout history, [humanity] has looked for guiding values, for principles of right and wrong outside of [itself], to a God, to some sort of sacred book perhaps, or to a ruling class. What I am doing is to explore the theory that you can find the values by which mankind must live . . . by observing the best of humanity." Emphasizing the pragmatic character of his own approach, he stated, "Our task is to create an environment where more and more of these innate instincts can find expression. This is what I would characterize [as] Eupsychia."

That same month, utopia seemed to beckon personally to Maslow when Richard Farson, codirector of the newly founded Western Behavioral Sciences Institute (WBSI) in La Jolla, California, offered him a financially generous eight-month fellowship to begin in January 1961. WBSI was a non-profit organization devoted to innovative research in human relations. The fellowship would provide complete scholarly freedom in a congenial atmosphere without bureaucratic entanglements. Maslow would help facilitate learning free from grades, exams, course credits, and degree requirements.

Farson's offer delighted Maslow, who was already starting to miss the quiet freedom he had enjoyed in Mexico. Deferring tentative plans to visit Japan later in the year with Bertha, he accepted, hoping that Brandeis President Sachar would soon allow him to take a second sabbatical.

A few days after receiving the invitation, Maslow attended the American Psychological Association's annual convention in Chicago. He was voted one of the top twenty most creative psychologists in the country and received several attractive job offers. He was already president of the Massachusetts Psychological Association; now he was nominated for national board membership of the American Psychological Association and the presidency of the Society for the Psychological Study of Social Issues (SPSSI). But he refused to be considered for the positions because of the extra administrative work they would entail. Nevertheless, he felt honored by the respect shown by his peers. It seemed his twenty-five years of effort to transform American psychology were finally showing results.

Returning from the convention, he was stunned to learn that Sachar had vetoed his sabbatical request, "suggesting" that he take off one semester, not two, and wait nearly a year, until June 1961, before leaving. Angered, Maslow contemplated resigning to make his way as an independent scholar living on grants, fellowships, and visiting professorships. However, having suffered with his family through the Depression, he was not about to let personal pride cost him the security of tenure and full professorship. He restrained his impulse to quit.

In the early fall, Maslow went through intense soul-searching regarding a paper he was scheduled to present at a Karen Horney memorial meeting on October 20 in New York City. This was no ordinary address for him, as Horney had been a key mentor during the 1930s and 1940s and had greatly influenced his career. Nor had the eight years since her death diminished his admiration for her psychoanalytic innovations. His paper was entitled "Peak-experiences as Acute Identity Experiences" and he worked hard through September and October to summarize several years of important research.

About three nights before the speech, Maslow himself had a peak-experience. In the middle of the night, he awoke in a state of inspired euphoria. Coming downstairs in his pajamas, he started writing in his journal. He wrote for hours, consumed in a timeless moment of creative fervor. Finally the mood passed and, somewhat dazed, he realized his teeth were chattering from the dawn's cold and his bladder was ready to burst.

When Bertha awoke, he related his unusual experience. She suggested, "Abe, why not read them what you just wrote, and toss away your academic paper? This is the real stuff. The other is just talk *about* peaks."

Bertha's idea was intriguing, for he had long insisted on the legitimacy of experiential reports in psychological inquiry. Certainly, his full description of a personal peak-experience would be instructive. But could he bare his soul in this way, especially to relative strangers? For the next few days, he thought about this constantly. The morning of his talk, he had still not decided. He mounted the podium holding both papers, uncertain which to read.

Gazing at the audience, he decided not to share his own peak-experience. He did not feel particularly close to most of them, and to be so personal seemed as inappropriate as "taking a bath in public" (his words). Nevertheless, he mentioned this quandary in his preparatory remarks, which were later published. In modern science, he said, our subjective experiences are too often slighted or ignored. Statistics and quantifiable methods are not the only paths to understanding the human mind. It was time to "enlarge the jurisdiction of science" by embracing "the problems and data of personal and experiential psychology." He praised such self-revelatory accounts as Marion Milner's *On Not Being Able to Paint* for their scientific usefulness.

Maslow then presented his formal paper on peak-experiences. In such moments, we achieve our most intense awareness of being and purpose in life. Carefully denying any supernatural or theistic connection in peaks, he insisted that they arise naturally out of human nature itself. When we enter into such experiences, we gain the fullest appreciation possible of our precious uniqueness in the universe, our strengths and talents: we accept what we are. For this reason, he explained, peaks are accompanied by feelings of spontaneity, joy, and openness, and can even change our habitual outlook on life.

Despite the praise Maslow received for this seminal paper, he was upset for weeks afterward about his reluctance to read his more personal account. More than a month later, he wrote in his journal, "How the hell am I going to be able to bare myself before those not worthy of it? Or am I making this act of baring myself too intimate, or more than it need be?" He raised the issue with his analyst, Felix Deutsch, but without resolution.

In early January 1961, Maslow participated in a lively meeting at the First Annual Conference on Personality Theory and Counseling Practice, held at the University of Florida. In attendance were Carl Rogers, Sidney Jouard, and others associated with what was being called humanistic psychology. With President-elect John Kennedy promising to get the country moving again, there was a buoyant optimism in the air. Within their own discipline, Maslow and his colleagues no longer felt quite so isolated but, rather, at the forefront of a new movement.

His address, entitled "Some Frontier Problems in Mental Health," was one of his most provocative and exciting to date. Since most of the audience was already familiar with his work, he chose to be somewhat speculative. But first he issued a cautionary note, a reminder that true inner growth is a lifelong process. "Some of my students," he wryly observed, "read a paper or two on self-actualization, and then have a kind of

sudden conversion experience, and on Thursday at two
o'clock, they decide they're going to be self-actualized *as of
that moment*. Then, I find I've let loose in the world people
who have jumped to the goal too quickly."

Maslow devoted much of his paper to the importance of
humor in emotional health. Citing self-actualizing people as
exemplars in their playful creativity and capacity to laugh at
themselves, he observed that we often ignore the power of
humor to uplift us through life's deep realms, even sexuality:

> If a Martian were reading the sex books, he'd think this
> is a very grim business. I'd like to announce that [sex] is also
> fun. And I've found that [among self-actualizers, physical]
> love at its best is also a kind of silly thing . . . They report a
> great deal of little secret jokes . . . [and this is] part of . . .
> intrinsic, full functioning.

Reflecting his growing interest in the psychology of religion, he noted too the relevance of humor for theology:

> It's interesting that the Western conceptions of God
> don't permit him any humor. Think about that a little. We
> tend to think of the religious person mostly as humorless.
> [But] some of the mystics do take into account humor, jok-
> ing, gaiety, and laughter, and will make jokes as *part* of reli-
> gion . . . I would [emphasize] humor as one of the ultimate
> values.

Finally, he stressed the vast unknown realm of human
potential. Down through the centuries, we have been dominated by our lower emotional needs because of the pressures
of poverty, war, and disease. Now that civilization is striving
to overcome such forces, there may be unfolding soon an unprecedented opportunity for human growth.

> Our spiritual height, our characterological height . . . is
> in principle unlimited . . . I have no idea how far it is possible
> for the human to develop . . . [As for the future], what kind
> of culture would be generated by one thousand self-actualiz-
> ing people, and their families?

If world conditions improve as we all hope they will, then it may be very well that the conceptions of health which we talk about at this conference may be obsolete in twenty years. Human beings may turn out to have been much more brilliant than we can now conceive, much more creative, much more wonderful. We're stuck now in our own culture ... stuck in a silly world which makes all sorts of unnecessary problems. Supposing they are solved, then what? Who knows what we will develop and what our grandchildren will be like?

The winter semester at Brandeis passed quickly, but Maslow felt increasingly pressured by administrative and teaching duties. He now recognized the legitimacy of student complaints about his indifference toward their work. In a journal entry dated January 22, he noted, "I guess one big factor underlying everything is the feeling that I have so much to give the world—the Great Message—and that this is the big thing. Anything else that cuts it or gets in the way is 'bad.' Before I die, I must say it all."

Shortly thereafter, Van Nostrand Press agreed to publish his book of articles on Being-psychology, and he excitedly began organizing his material. He was also pleased that the *Journal of Humanistic Psychology,* of which he was cofounding editor, had finally been published, and he was proud of his colleague Anthony Sutich for spearheading this achievement.

Maslow and Bertha arrived at WBSI in La Jolla in mid-May. It was to be their first prolonged stay in the West since they had lived in Pleasanton and Berkeley. Before departing Brandeis, Maslow made two important decisions: to resign the chairmanship of the psychology department and turn it over to his friend Ricardo Morant, and to quit smoking. Both decisions had been long in coming, and both were permanent.

Maslow was elated to have so much scholarly freedom at WBSI. Andy Kay, the engineer-entrepreneur who had funded the fellowship, seemed friendly enough, but Maslow felt a bit perplexed as to why he had been so generous. Another man Maslow met that summer became an important intellectual influence and a good friend: Henry Geiger, the editor-publisher of MANAS, an avant-garde periodical of essays. MANAS inspired Maslow, and he soon began buying gift subscriptions for friends and like-minded colleagues.

Over the summer and fall at La Jolla, he kept busy polishing his book on Being-psychology. He found Mircea Eliade's *The Sacred and the Profane* a useful work, yet longed for a scientific way to talk about such qualities as awe, wonder, and ecstasy. Deeply held childhood associations involving religion, superstition, and his punitive mother made it hard for him to approach theological vocabulary.

Perhaps his most important insights came during further analysis of the narrations of great mystics and sages and those who reported peak-experiences to him. From these accounts, he identified seventeen universal values, which he termed *Being-values*, or *B-values*, that seemed to be mentioned again and again: truth, beauty, justice, goodness, wholeness, perfection, uniqueness, simplicity, order, aliveness, self-sufficiency, necessity, completion, richness, effortlessness, playfulness, and dichotomy-transcendence. All appeared equally important in the mystics' narratives; they could not be ranked in a hierarchy. In a journal entry dated August 12, he mused:

> Why are the B-values more right than any other kind?
> . . . How to answer the accusation: "You like them—that's why you think they're so good. How can you prove they're good?"

> The main reason I got into them was through peak-experience work. That's the way the world looks in the peak, in B-cognition . . . [But] B-values overlap very much with the description of self-actualizing people.

Not surprisingly, Maslow's long-standing disdain for religion initially made him uneasy in the company of clergy and religionists who flocked to his lectures on peak-experiences and the B-values. It was strange to him to speak in churches, but the admiration he felt from his audiences—mostly liberal Protestants, including Unitarians, and some ecumenical Catholics—was very real. Later, a few maverick rabbis sought him out; they enjoyed discussing the convergences between classic Jewish values and his own approach to the mind. Although he never abandoned his atheistic contempt for ritual observance, such conversations convinced him that his unpleasant child-hood experience of Judaism had blinded him to the wisdom within it and the world's other great religions, especially their views of human nature.

Before leaving La Jolla, Maslow received an invitation from Andy Kay to spend the following summer observing managerial operations at his company, Non-Linear Systems. Kay promised a lucrative stipend and assured Maslow that he would find the visit stimulating.

Maslow returned to Brandeis in January 1962. Busy with teaching again, he also found time for new reading and chanced upon a fascinating book entitled *Ecstasy* by English-woman Margharita Laski. Her empirical study of people's ec-static moments during everyday life—a walk in autumn woods, a dazzling sunset at sea—independently confirmed much of Maslow's earlier work on peak-experiences. He was so excited by her book that he planned to devote a seminar to it. He also found exciting the writings of another English thinker, Colin Wilson, the self-educated young author of *The Outsider* and *The Stature of Man*. Wilson's lively philosophical writings, of-fering an optimistic, even exhilarating view of humanity's un-realized greatness, inspired Maslow, and the two began to correspond.

Closer to home, he was intrigued by the work of another iconoclastic optimist, Harvard psychologist Timothy Leary. Together with research associates Richard Alpert and Ralph Metzner, Leary was conducting ground-breaking work on the effects of psychedelic drugs like psilocybin on the mind. Since arriving at Harvard in 1960, Leary and Maslow had become quite friendly, and spent many hours discussing their mutual interests in creativity, superior mental functioning, and peak-experiences. After hearing her father's admiration for Leary, Ellen Maslow went to work for Leary as a research assistant.

On a few occasions, Maslow brought Leary to Brandeis' psychology colloquia as a guest speaker. As a result, Ricardo Morant and Harry Rand became intrigued by the possibility of collaborating on psychedelic research, which was then re-spectable and publicly funded by various agencies. Maslow was interested in psilocybin as a trigger of peak-experiences, Mor-ant in its influence on perception, and Rand in its therapeutic potential as part of psychoanalysis. But Maslow himself was unwilling to try any of Leary's experimental drugs. "It's too easy," he would say. "To have a peak-experience, you have to sweat."

During their frequent lunches together, Leary liked to tease his friend a bit. "All right, then, Abe, you want to sweat? Well, do you plan to walk back from Harvard Square to Brandeis, or are you going to drive? You mentioned going to California next month. Do you plan to walk there, or take a plane? You want to sweat, don't you?"

Leary believed that psychedelics were providing a unique new technology for mind exploration and might shed light on the unknown territory Maslow had first surveyed in his work on peak-experiences. Leary called his own experimentation "applied mysticism," and was grateful for Maslow's encouraging words about the travails of being a path-blazer far from the conventional halls of academia.

That spring, Maslow's *Toward a Psychology of Being* was published, a collection of his essays and addresses over the past eight years. Despite its academic style, the book became extremely popular, eventually selling 200,000 copies before a trade edition was issued in 1968. The book opened on a stirring note:

> Every age but ours had its model, its ideal. All of these have been given up by our culture: the hero, the gentleman, the knight, the mystic. About all we have left is the well-adjusted man without problems, a very pale and doubtful substitute. Perhaps we shall soon be able to use as our guide and model the fully growing and self-fulfilling human being, the one in whom his potentialities are coming to full development, the one whose inner nature expresses itself freely, rather than being warped, repressed, or denied.

Toward a Psychology of Being was the kind of book, passed around from person to person, that not only inspires but changes people's lives. Many more were affected by its message than actually read it. Terms like *peak-experience* and *self-actualization* began to penetrate the popular vocabulary and help shape the zeitgeist of 1960s America. Before long, nearly every college student in the country was hearing such phrases, as legions of admirers promoted Maslow's approach.

In late May, the Maslows moved out of Newtonville into a home they had purchased in scenic Auburndale. The Charles River meandered behind the house, and the view included a wooded island in the distance. For the Brooklyn-reared thinker, it was utopia. Initially he felt overwhelmed. "The first time I saw [the river view], I almost died . . . It was a very, very great experience, profoundly esthetic . . . I remember collapsing in a chair and looking at all this in just perfect wonder . . . The place was so beautiful that it would crack your skull open, it was almost painful." Moments later, he began to make plans to put in a birdhouse and other additions. With a shock, he realized that he was in a sense trying to "improve paradise." This experience led him to believe that humans are by nature never permanently content, but seek higher and higher "heavens."

He and Bertha did not have much time to enjoy their dream house, for Kay awaited their arrival at Non-Linear Systems (NLS) in early June. Maslow was curious about what he might find at NLS, but little more. His main reason for going had been Kay's generous offer: a large consulting fee in return for visiting the plant only one afternoon per week and talking with Kay. If anything developed from the consulting, well and good, Maslow thought; if not, he intended to devote his energy to refining his system of Being-psychology. He had brought his books, papers, and file cards pertaining to the subject.

On Monday, June 6, Maslow made his first visit to NLS and spent time with Kay, who acquainted him with its history. A slender, self-assured man of medium build, Kay recounted his own background. The son of an East European–born couple who worked as weavers in New Jersey, Kay had frequented New York City's radio and chemical shops as a teenager to stock his home basement laboratory, where he repeated Nikola Tesla's experiments and nearly blew off his leg making rockets. After finishing high school in 1938, he enrolled at MIT, where he received a general science degree and competed on the wrestling team. In 1942, Kay joined the Jack and Heintz Company, a Cleveland instrument manufacturer. There, under the pressures of World War II, he worked close to eighty hours per week building and testing equipment.

Kay learned more than engineering at Jack and Heintz. He observed that the company employed only a few hundred managers for 9200 workers in eight plants. Believing that workers should police themselves, cofounder William Jack had instilled a team spirit that led employees to criticize peers who arrived late for work. Jack also supplied vitamins and free lunches and handed out fifty-dollar bonuses to all workers, at a time when the average assembly line operator earned a dollar an hour. Jack gave a pep talk over the loudspeaker twice a day, once during the 4:00 A.M. graveyard shift. "He was the greatest persuader I ever met," Kay recalled admiringly.

After World War II, Kay resettled in California and joined Pasadena's Jet Propulsion Laboratory. In 1949 he went to work for his former mentor as vice-president of the Bill Jack Scientific Instrument Company in Solana Beach, on the outskirts of San Diego. Kay helped supervise the building of aerial reconnaissance cameras. Determined to develop as much mastery in management as in engineering, he avidly read nearly everything written in this new field.

Three years later, Kay started his own firm, which he called Non-Linear Systems. He took over a former navy blimp hangar in nearby Del Mar, where the company's chief product was the first commercial digital voltmeter. From the outset, NLS garnered a reputation among engineers for product excellence. But before long, it became better known throughout the American business world for its managerial innovations.

In 1957, Kay met Richard Farson at a management seminar, hired him as a consultant, and began exploring better ways to run NLS. "I had watched people assemble our voltmeters," Kay recollected, "and they seemed unhappy. Everybody wanted to be at the tail end where it was finished." After three years of tinkering, Kay embarked on one of the most radical and far-reaching managerial experiments in the United States. Relying heavily on Maslow's *Motivation and Personality* as his bible, and on other motivational texts, Kay decided that to make his employees happy—and, he hoped, more productive—he would effect sweeping changes. He believed, based partly on Maslow's ideas, that each worker benefits from a sense of closure, of seeing a finished product that he or she has personally built. With happier and healthier employees, Kay felt, his company would likewise be happier and healthier.

He dismantled the assembly lines and replaced them with production teams of six or seven workers. Each team learned every aspect of productivity and exercised participatory management, deciding with a team leader how to best produce its share of products. Each unit also took complete responsibility for assembling, inspecting, "debugging," and packing the instruments. Every employee learned the entire assembly process for several products. Breaks were not taken at scheduled times but whenever convenient for the team. Each team worked in a private workroom whose decor they chose.

Kay implemented a host of other innovations at NLS. Besides paying his employees twenty-five percent more than San Diego's prevailing wage, he dispensed with time cards, penalties for lateness or sickness, and salesmen's expense accounts. He gave departments more autonomy by allowing them to keep their own financial records, thereby freeing him and his top managers for long-range planning. He also offered small-group sensitivity-training for managers and aptitude testing for those who requested it. He even created the post of vice-president for innovation.

Since these changes, employee morale was superb, turnover was a fraction of the national average, customer complaints had plummeted, and sales and productivity were soaring.

Maslow was intrigued by Kay's laudatory account but quickly became even more impressed by what he saw as he wandered around the grounds. With growing excitement, he found himself putting aside his papers and books on Being-psychology and religion, and turning full attention to what was happening at NLS. Just as Kay had described, a radically democratic atmosphere permeated the company; employees looked happy and interested in their work. Maslow also wanted to interview employees in their homes, but time did not permit. Within his first week there, he began to spend many hours conversing with Kay, observing management training classes, and occasionally sitting in on meetings.

Kay provided Maslow with a tape recorder for dictation and a secretary to transcribe his comments. At the same time, Maslow kept busy reading management texts, starting with Peter Drucker's *The Practice of Management.* Impressed with its brilliance, he next read Douglas McGregor's *The Human Side of Enterprise,* which Maslow found powerful for its ethical, democratic view of the workplace.

Each week, Maslow dictated hours of thoughts in reaction to NLS and his reading. His subjects were wide-ranging: methods of enhancing employee motivation, the psychology of leadership, and entrepreneuring as a form of self-actualization. He devoted special attention to elaborating the concept of *synergy*, originated by anthropologist Ruth Benedict in unpublished lectures in 1941, referring to cultures in which cooperation is rewarded and advantageous to all. Benedict's notion was almost unknown except to Maslow, Margaret Mead, and a few others who had known her personally. Now he saw the concept as relevant to the business world, as an underlying principle of management and human relations. NLS was demonstrating that organizational and worker interests could converge through what he called enlightened management.

He and Bertha had an enjoyable time socially that summer, attending many parties in the San Diego and Los Angeles areas. Especially memorable was a get-together with novelist Aldous Huxley, author of *Brave New World*. During the past decade, Huxley had written with increasing conviction about the vast unknown range of human potentiality. He praised such esoteric traditions as yoga for their insights into the human mind. In 1954, his controversial book *The Doors of Perception* had poetically highlighted his mystical-like experience upon ingesting mescaline. Maslow enjoyed Huxley's gentle manner and regarded him as a saintly visionary and self-actualizer. Other friends Maslow also spent time with in California included management theorist Robert Tannenbaum of UCLA and Henry Geiger.

One of Maslow's most stimulating experiences that summer came when he spent a few days on Tannenbaum's invitation at the University of California's Conference Center at Lake Arrowhead. There he observed sensitivity-training sessions run by Western Training Labs (WTL), which Tannenbaum directed. This field of human relations grew from work done in 1946 and 1947 at MIT by Gestalt psychologist Kurt Lewin and his colleagues, who were experimenting with methods of leadership training that ultimately became focused on small, intensive groups as the vehicle for learning. Lewin found that, in the absence of a formal agenda, a group could study its own development—patterns of communication, dynamics, and leadership—as a powerful way to learn leadership skills. Within a few hours, group members usually gained vivid insight into how they reacted to different forms of social interaction such as flattery, direct challenge, or hostility. With helpful feedback from one another, they could make tremendous progress in developing appropriate leadership skills. After Lewin's death in 1947, his colleagues continued to develop this method. The small groups became widely known as t-groups (t for training), and the overall approach as human relations training and sensitivity training.

During the past fifteen years, Lewin's original group had organized itself as the National Training Laboratories (NTL), based in Washington, D.C., and held national workshops each summer in Bethel, Maine. Along parallel lines, Carl Rogers at the University of Chicago in the late 1940s had developed small-group methods to facilitate personal growth among members. More emotionally intense than NTL's, Rogers's approach had begun to catch on in the late 1950s, especially in California. Tannenbaum at Western Training Labs was one of its leading West Coast progenitors.

NTL and WTL ran "laboratories" for school executives, community and student leaders, and college faculty, as well as a special human relations program for alumni of previous labs. It was this last group Maslow observed in California, and he was excited by what he saw, especially the openness and mutual helpfulness. But he wondered whether this training method could work "under really bad conditions, that is, with really authoritarian, paranoid, or immature people." For this reason, he felt it important to regard the t-group "as a kind of limited experiment under especially good conditions."

A few weeks after the Lake Arrowhead conference, Tannenbaum arranged for an informal get-together between Maslow and UCLA Graduate School of Business Administration faculty. The gathering offered the opportunity to exchange views with such leading management theorists as James V. Clark, Charles Ferguson, Fred Massarik, and Arthur Shedlin. These men, along with Tannenbaum and Warren Bennis, had all been influenced by Maslow's theory of human nature. They have become identified as among the founders of organizational development. As a result of this group's influence, a number of American companies and nonprofit associations in recent years have become involved in efforts to improve the efficiency and morale of their organizations.

A fortuitous event occurred that summer as Maslow and Bertha drove on Highway 1 along California's breathtaking coast near Carmel. Growing tired, they decided to find an inn to spend the night, but the road offered no lodgings. Noticing a light, they gratefully drove onto the grounds of Big Sur Hot Springs, later renamed the Esalen Institute. Entering the lodge, they found at the desk a rather gruff Oriental man, Gia-fu, who sharply asked, "What do you want?"

Explaining that they needed a room for one night, they were handed a pen and curtly asked to sign the register. Bertha wanted to leave immediately, but her husband was too exhausted to care about the service. Gazing at the signature, the desk clerk suddenly stared with intense interest at the tired, middle-aged couple. "Maslow?" he asked with excitement. "*The* Abraham Maslow?"

Animatedly, he began bowing and repeating loudly, "Maslow! Maslow! Maslow!" Richard Price, the cofounder of Esalen, rushed in and introduced himself. Smiling with delight, he told Maslow that the entire staff was sharing several copies of *Toward a Psychology of Being* and explained that Big Sur Hot Springs was a new venture hosting workshops led by writers and therapists interested in humanistic psychology and its ramifications. Its other young cofounder, Michael Murphy, was away that weekend, but he and Maslow began corresponding in the fall and eventually became close friends.

Of all the people Maslow met that summer, he found Kay the most intriguing. Initially, he suspected that Kay's managerial innovations were purely profit-oriented, but he soon saw that Kay was sincerely interested in making the world a better place, not only through his business but also through his Unitarian fellowship meetings. Maslow came to regard creative entrepreneurs like Kay as potentially important figures. Later he mused in his journal, "A couple dozen . . . would be enough to change a whole darned country. It's not so much foreign capital that is needed in most poor countries, it's entrepreneurs of this self-confident type."

Nevertheless, he was quick to turn down Kay's offer at summer's end for a full-time, permanent position at NLS. Maslow had no desire to devote himself solely to managerial psychology, nor did he feel comfortable about leaving Brandeis' intellectual atmosphere for the day-to-day pragmatism of the voltmeter world. A telling episode occurred one day when Maslow and Kay got together with Henry Geiger, who was clutching a thick book.

"What do you have there, Henry?" Kay asked the scholarly editor.

"It's Dostoyevsky," was the reply. "You really ought to read him, Andy."

Bemused, Kay retorted, "What do I need Dostoyevsky for when I've got Abe?"

Maslow also turned down Kay's offer to return for two months the following summer, but he agreed to make three one-week visits during the coming year, at an attractive salary.

As Maslow prepared to leave California and gathered together his books and notes on Being-psychology, he wondered what had made him abandon his plans to write that summer. Several explanations came to him. First, he had been excited to realize that his theories, especially of motivation, were being put to the test. With his experimentalist training, he had long felt chagrined about not being able to verify his theories of motivation and self-actualization. To his delight, Kay and his management consultants were attempting to do precisely that: NLS was one big laboratory.

But NLS was something potentially even more important: a working example of eupsychia, a deliberate effort to be utopian in the most positive sense. Maslow had criticized most modern utopian writing as anti-industrial, an unrealistic movement back to the farm, but at NLS the highest principles of motivation were being applied in a factory environment. Having long despaired of individual therapy as a means of social change, he had viewed education as perhaps the most effective means of world betterment. But that year the workplace seemed even more promising.

Ever the scientist, Maslow worried that Kay and his consultants were too readily espousing his ideas. In a journal entry dated September 6, he wrote, "They're being taken as gospel truth, without any real examination of their reliability, validity. The carry-over from clinic to industry is really a huge and shaky step, but they're going ahead enthusiastically and optimistically, like Andy Kay, as if all the facts were in, and it was [already] proven scientifically."

To Maslow's intense pleasure, Kay offered to print a sizable number of Maslow's *Summer Notes* manuscript about enlightened management. Maslow gave a copy to Tannenbaum, who enthusiastically decided to share its provocative insights with colleagues in management theory and consulting.

The following January (1963), Maslow's ideas began to circulate even more widely when an immensely influential book, *The Feminine Mystique*, was published. Its author, Betty Friedan, was a Smith College psychology graduate and housewife-turned-journalist who had met Maslow several years before to discuss his theory of self-actualization as it might apply to women's psychology. She had found him congenial and supportive, and the two became friends. Arguing that post–World War II women in America had been placed in an intellectual and social straitjacket, her cogent work became a best seller and soon was a rallying point for the new feminism.

The Feminine Mystique devoted nearly a chapter to Maslow's humanistic aproach as an alternative to Freud's demeaning view of women. Friedan highlighted, too, Maslow's little-known yet seminal studies from the 1930s on female sexuality and dominance. Above all, she embraced his notion of self-actualization, and its rejection of mere social adjustment, as the key to women's emotional health. To buttress her argument, she related, "Professor Maslow told me that he thought self-actualization is only possible for women . . . if one person can grow through another—that is, if the woman can realize her own potential through her husband and children. 'We do not know if this is possible or not,' " he said. Maslow much admired the book and thereafter often advised his female graduate students to speak with her about her ideas. His one criticism was that its author should have built on "the feminine mystique" by stressing the vital importance of nurturing activities rather than downplaying these as trivial compared to masculine work pursuits. Later, Friedan partially came to adopt this outlook in "the second phase" (as she called it) of her feminist writings.

During the next few months, Maslow learned that his *Summer Notes* manuscript was gaining wider attention. With

Kay's financial support, Tannenbaum had distributed copies to National Training Laboratories' national network of trainers. On April 16 he wrote Maslow, "In recent weeks, I have received letters from a number of them and your ears should be burning, so many of our colleagues have found your *Notes* to be most exciting and stimulating. I personally admire your willingness to publish your 'Flow of Thoughts' in this manner. I believe these *Notes* will have a considerable impact on the thinking of a large number of individuals."

In the spring of 1963, Maslow and Bertha agreed to participate in NTL's Continuing Program led by Tannenbaum and others in Maine. However, only a few days before they were to leave, Maslow was diagnosed as having gallstones, and his summer plans were canceled. He was admitted into Faulkner Hospital on July 1 for surgery and was discharged twelve days later. His convalescence was slow, and he worked only intermittently on his writing.

As the weather cooled, his vitality returned. His major project now was a short book on his approach to the psychology of religion. The national fraternity Kappa Delta Pi had offered him an honorarium for a lecture on the subject, to be presented in the spring of 1964, and he was eager to crystallize his thinking. Initially, he worried whether he would have much to contribute beyond what other psychologists had already said, notably William James in his classic *Varieties of Religious Experience,* but by late fall, Maslow had nearly completed the manuscript. He proudly judged his work on peak-experiences to constitute a major empirical breakthrough in the field, because it was based on hundreds of carefully elicited reports.

Working on the book aroused his interest in new questions: Why don't more people have peak-experiences? Do some individuals unknowingly suppress them from memory? If not, what accounts for those who cannot recall a single moment of bliss or ecstasy in their lives? Maslow suspected that peakers and non-peakers may differ emotionally in some important way.

Developing his theory of metapsychology, focusing on our highest needs and aspirations, became increasingly important to Maslow. Therefore, he expanded the technique he had used earlier when interviewing scientists about their motivation:

"What are the biggest kicks and rewards and high moments you get of your work? When do you feel best and happiest about it? And when do you feel worst about it? What are the moments of depression, of failure, when you wish you were in some other work, when you feel like giving it up?"

Most ambitiously, Maslow prepared a thirty-page document entitled "General Researches," outlining several dozen innovative research projects, few of which he would live to attempt, let alone complete. These included investigations into the psychology of philanthropy; how men in comparison to women experience being in love; and how our facial attractiveness as we age reflects our emotional health. He was also interested in studying reformed criminals, those who undergo genuine moral conversion in prison, for the lessons they might teach us about how to overhaul our grossly ineffectual criminal justice and penal system.

As the year progressed, Maslow grew increasingly interested in social and educational change. Hoping to influence business managerial practice, he awaited publication of his *Summer Notes* in book form; his publisher had agreed to title it *Eupsychian Management*. Attending the American Psychological Association Convention in Los Angeles in September 1964, he startled many colleagues by holding up Michael Murphy's catalogue and announcing, "I want to tell you about Big Sur Hot Springs. The operative word is *hot*. This place is hot." While at the convention, he received an offer to become a permanent staff member at Western Behavioral Sciences Institute. Carl Rogers had already been lured there from the University of Wisconsin, and Maslow found the proposal intriguing. However, Bertha was opposed to her husband's quitting Brandeis for a less secure post, so he continued to search half-heartedly for other possibilities.

In the fall, *Religions, Values, and Peak-experiences* was published and was favorably reviewed. Psychological humanists as well as liberal theologians and clergy praised the book for its incisive view of human nature, its ecumenicism, and its ethical and non-supernaturalist emphasis.

In this slender volume, Maslow placed the peak-experience at the heart of organized religion. "The very beginning, the intrinsic core, the essence . . . has been the private, lonely, personal illumination, revelation, or ecstasy of some acutely sensitive prophet or seer," he wrote. For millennia, such intense moments have been attributed to an external, supernatural force; but, he reported, the study of peaks clearly showed that religion can be approached rationally and ultimately scientifically. The mystic's experience reflects a real perception of the B-values that lie deep within us.

In this regard, he warned against stripping such wondrous episodes from religion:

> Some perceptive liberals and non-theists are going through an 'agonizing reappraisal' very similar to that which the orthodox often go through, namely a loss of faith in their foundation beliefs. Just as many intellectuals lose faith in religious orthodoxy, so they also lose faith in positivistic, nineteenth-century science as a way of life. They too often have the sense of loss, the craving to believe, the yearning for a value-system . . . I believe this need can be satisfied by a larger, more inclusive science, one which includes the data of transcendence.

Throughout the book, Maslow rejected religious supernaturalism. By this he meant anything that cannot be verified empirically. While still an atheist, he therefore stressed a kind of naturalistic mysticism, denying the traditional trappings of religion such as an afterlife, a personal God, and a divine order. For Maslow, none of these is necessary to be religious, to live the B-values to their fullest.

He also suggested that peak-experiences have important therapeutic value; hence they might be deliberately triggered by the use of psychedelic drugs under proper supervision:

> The power of the peak-experience could permanently affect [one's] attitude toward life. A single glimpse of heaven is enough to confirm its existence even if it is never experienced again. It is my strong suspicion that one such experience might be able to prevent suicide, for instance, and perhaps many varieties of low self-destruction, [such as] alcoholism, drug-addiction, and addiction to violence.

Sales of *Religions, Values, and Peak-experiences* were slow initially, but Maslow was confident that his message would be carried to the appropriate pulpits and classrooms around the country. He received many invitations from seminaries and sectarian associations to speak about his fresh approach to religious experience. But by the winter of 1965, he was busy with another project: trying, after five years, to complete *The Psychology of Science.*

In the course of much reading about scientism and technocratic science as a worldview, he began to argue that a chief psychological plague of modern civilization was what Mircea Eliade called *de-sacrilization:* the disappearance in our lives of a sense of the sacred. With nothing to evoke awe, wonder, or devotion, we inevitably feel empty within, Maslow contended, for these are intrinsic human needs. In a similar way, we have lost genuine heroes; the very concept of heroism has become suspect, old-fashioned, and seemingly obsolete. The same has occurred with such traditional virtues as courage, fidelity, and reverence.

He decried the growing trend in American culture of cynicism and debunking, or sneering at innocence, as another symptom of underlying *valuelessness,* brought on by the breakdown of religion's traditional moral influence upon society. In many impassioned journal notes, he railed against much of the mass media, both its advertising and editorial content, for furthering this trend. His common epithet in this context was "the malice and despair" outlook: that is, the ridiculing of traditional moral values.

Perhaps more strongly than in anything he published on this issue, he expressed his view in an impassioned lecture to students in March 1965 entitled "The Taboo of Tenderness: The Disease of Valuelessness." Because many Brandeis students were pre-med majors, he wisely began with a relevant example:

> [I wish to talk about] the fear of appearing corny, square, sentimental . . . This whole business is an illness . . . De-sacrilizing [is] a defense, a flight from something, a fear of confrontation with, a fear of consciousness of [the sacred].

[I recently asked students] in a major medical school, "Why did you go into medicine?" Everybody looked uncomfortable. You never say that you went into medicine to help people. That would be corny. That would not be cool. That would be admitting to a high motive of some kind . . . The correct thing is to make a joke—stethoscopes are very becoming on you, or "well, it's a good living."

But if you are a psychologist and have dealt with people [therapeutically], you know that it is absolutely phony. It's just a big fake. A good half or two-thirds . . . have gone into medicine for the reasons that a corny man might think, that he's touched by the possibility of helping people to remain alive . . . Or that he gets a great shiver of awe and wonder and amazement when he delivers a baby, or he's shaken to his roots when somebody dies under his hands. No, you can't say that, even in the medical school. You have to make a joke about it.

We are all acquainted with people who cannot stand intimacy, nakedness, honesty, defenselessness, those who get uneasy with close friendship, those who can't love or be loved. Running away from this disturbing intimacy or beauty is a usual solution.

One way people do this, Maslow suggested, is to debase or de-sacrilize these qualities:

Innocence can be redefined and called stupidity. Honesty can be called gullibility. Candor becomes lack of common sense. Interest in your [work] can be called cowardice. Generosity can be called softheadedness, and observe: the former word is disturbing, the latter is not. It can be dealt with. You can deal with a jerk or a fool or a pollyanna or something of the sort. [But] nobody knows how to deal with an honest man.

In evading our own growth, our potential for greatness, we all engage in such ploys from time to time, he said. Especially adolescents, but also adults adopt the stance of being "cool" and free from intense feeling of any sort. But such *counter-valuing* is another form of suppressing our highest nature:

> If you are a man and you are not struck dumb by your woman once in a while, you're missing something, you're being blind to something which is there—and vice versa, of course. As a matter of fact, there is as much de-sacrilizing of the male by our females as there is the other way around. It's quite rare to find a wife adoring her husband. It just isn't done. It's permitted, I think, still for a husband to adore his wife: that is, to get really sloppy about it in a nice way. I don't think it's possible anymore for women to get sloppy about their husbands. I think that's forbidden now.

He briefly reminded his students of "the defenses against maturity, the defenses against becoming a father [or] a mother—as [opposed to] the wish to remain [a kid] forever." He ended the remarkable lecture on a note of exhortation:

> [The basic] value question is, what vision do you aspire to? . . . If you really look in the mirror, what kind of person do you want to be? Obviously, this doesn't happen by accident. You have to work for it, train for it. If you get a picture of yourself being a good physician, for instance, and of bringing babies into the world, [such a profession can become] a religious experience. Just simply an awe-experience. Well, having that kind of thing means work, very hard work. Medical school is tough. Anything is tough if you want to be good . . . It's like asking, what do you want to grow into? What does self-actualization mean to you?

During the spring, Maslow fulfilled a long-held dream of co-teaching with Frank Manuel a course on utopian thought. While Manuel assigned students such classic works as Plato's *Republic* and Thomas More's *Utopia*, Maslow found himself reading science fiction also. He enjoyed the genre for its imaginative exploration of utopian issues involving science, social trends, and the future. To him, its top writers evinced a creative concern for new ideas and their impact on the world. One visionary novel that he recommended to his students was Aldous Huxley's *Island.*

Maslow respected Manuel enormously as a scholar, but the team-teaching heightened their differences in temperament and outlook. Maslow felt frustrated and at times angry at Manuel's razor-sharp cynicism and contempt for those who still idealistically believed in world betterment. Long embroiled in Brandeis faculty politics, Manuel announced that he was leaving for New York University. Crushed, Maslow had frequent dreams of rejection for several months after this news.

Although Maslow continued to complain about the time-consuming pressures of advising graduate students, several proved to be serious researchers. One study he supervised was Deborah Tanzer's concerning natural childbirth as a trigger of peak-experiences in women. Later published as a popular book entitled *Why Natural Childbirth?,* the research, which involved personality tests and clinical interviews with child-bearing women, was perhaps the first empirical effort of its kind. It helped spur the trend toward natural childbirth, initially fought by the medical establishment. Another study was Joel Aronoff's social and psychological validation of Maslow's hierarchy-of-needs theory, carried out on the Caribbean island of Saint Kitts. It too was published. Later, both Tanzer and Aronoff recalled that, aside from encouragement, Maslow provided them with little direct guidance.

By mid-1965, he was deliberately withdrawing himself more and more from campus affairs. In part, he felt isolated by his political outlook, which was more centrist than was fashionable among students and faculty. In a journal entry on May 1, he wrote, "I've been keeping my mouth shut at Brandeis on current politics, because generally I agree with [President Lyndon] Johnson, which is a very unpopular stance here. But if we had a weak, vacillating president, then I'd *have to* speak publicly and take the attack."

He also felt isolated from most of his colleagues in a psychology department that was becoming increasingly experimentalist and conventional. He was even becoming restless with the limitations of humanistic psychology, sensing the

need for a new "Fourth Force" devoted to religious and
spiritual issues. He noted on July 12:

> The Third Force is like Sweden, Norway, and Denmark,
> where God died and there *is* no god, where everything is
> sensible, rational, commonsensical, logical, empirical but not
> yet transcendent. You can admire and respect Scandinavia,
> but you can't love it, much less worship it! Everything that
> a good, mundane, this-worldly, reasonable . . . intelligence
> could do has been done there. But it's not enough!

Soon, he would coin the term *transpersonal psychology*
for this approach and would help sponsor an association and
journal to promote it.

During the summer of 1965, two events absorbed Maslow's attention, both involving drugs. The Ethics Committee
of the American Psychological Association (APA) had brought
charges of ethics violations against Timothy Leary and Richard
Alpert (Alpert later became known as Ram Dass) for their
sensationalist and loosely supervised experiments giving
psychedelics to volunteers. Both men had been fired from
Harvard two years before, and the APA's intended expulsion
of them from membership would be merely a symbolic gesture. Nevertheless, Leary hired a top-notch civil liberties lawyer in New York City to defend them, and Alpert asked Maslow to speak on their behalf at a hearing to be held at APA
headquarters in Washington, D.C. Maslow had been far less
friendly with young Alpert than with Leary, but he felt some
obligation: For one thing, Alpert's father, George, a prominent
Boston attorney, was a trustee and cofounder of Brandeis.

Before flying to Washington on July 16, Maslow briefly
regretted having gotten involved in the dispute. On the plane,
he scrutinized the APA's list of documents pertaining to the
case. While Leary and Alpert had possibly violated APA's code
of ethics, he realized, the code itself was clearly discriminatory
against those who sought to be trailblazers in science. "Is it
ethical to be timid, fearful?" he wondered in his journal.
"Maybe I'll have to a write a code of ethics for revolutionary
science."

As it turned out, Maslow's testimony was not needed. For
reasons never clear to Leary and Alpert, the APA Ethics Com-

mittee dropped its charges just before the hearing was to begin, and the protagonists found their would-be accusers friendly and disarming.

Maslow's other drug-related episode had far greater impact on his career and outlook. For several months he had listened to reports about an unusual new drug rehabilitation program based in California, called Synanon. It was led and staffed by former addicts, who were successfully forming local treatment centers throughout the country and winning the endorsements of prominent people in the arts and government. The journal MANAS praised Synanon, which seemed to combine toughness and candor with genuine compassion in a highly structured group-treatment format. In contrast, orthodox psychiatry was having meager success in treating drug addicts. The more Maslow read about Synanon, the more it seemed that this new approach was potentially very important, beyond simply curing addicts. When his Brandeis students informed him that a Synanon offshoot called Daytop Village had been set up on New York's Staten Island, he decided to investigate.

On August 13, Maslow flew to Daytop for an overnight visit. After a brief tour of the facility, he participated in an encounter group involving former addicts and "straight" people like himself. Group process lay at the heart of Synanon's success; far more intense than the t-groups promulgated by NTL and WTL, encounter groups were aimed at accelerating members' emotional growth through extremely, even brutally, candid remarks about one another's flaws or "hang-ups." It was Maslow's first exposure to an encounter group, and he was impressed by the toughness with which members took criticism from their peers.

The next day he spent several hours talking with staff and clients and gave an impromptu talk on his impressions. He found much to praise at Daytop Village, especially its intense group cohesion, which seemed to offer the addicts a sense of belongingness coupled with direct feedback about their immaturity or evasions. Yet he was not uncritical; he wondered aloud about Daytop-Synanon's failures: those who dropped out, and those who did not even try the program.

Returning to Boston, he commented in his journal, "Very remarkable experience—much learned, many questions.

Probably would have stayed on if I had the free time." Over the next few weeks, in conversations with Harry Rand and others, he sought to better understand the nature of drug addiction and its cure. One insight he gained was that it is predominantly a male phenomenon, and that in most cases, the addict's father has been physically or psychologically absent. In Maslow's last years of life, he began to regard the self-help and support-group model of Alcoholics Anonymous, Synanon, and similar organizations as a key to personal growth, not only for those with addictive disorders but for all people in our fragmented society.

In the fall, Maslow was granted another sabbatical. He and Bertha spent it driving leisurely through the South and Midwest. To prevent squabbling about where to go and what to do, he established a simple rule: she would set the itinerary, and he would defer to her every choice. The autumn months went by pleasantly for both. Other than working on *The Psychology of Science*, he did little sustained writing. He spent his time socializing with friends and visitors like Michael Murphy of the Esalen Institute. The two men spent nine hours together one day at Maslow's home, planning Maslow's first weekend workshop at Esalen, to take place in the winter of 1966. Although impressed with Esalen's humanistically oriented lecture program and therapeutic orientation, Maslow had put off Murphy's invitations to speak there. Now his schedule was free enough to accept.

By mid-1965, Esalen was attracting national attention for its innovative programming. Its galaxy of presenters included photographer Ansel Adams, general semanticist S. I. Hayakawa, Nobel Prize chemist Linus Pauling, theologian Paul Tillich, historian Arnold Toynbee, and philosopher Alan Watts. There was no particular "party line" underlying Esalen's programming, but cofounders Murphy and Richard Price believed that a synthesis of humanistic psychology and Eastern thought might provide the path to world transformation and peace. Half-jokingly, Murphy called it "the Vision," but his idealism and sense of purpose were appealing to Maslow, who may have seen something of himself in Esalen's youthful co-president. Maslow's one misgiving was that Esalen was becoming increasingly enamored with experiential methods to quicken self-actualization, and pulling away from intellectual rigor. He planned to address this trend in his workshop.

Also at this time, a tense event arose at Ellen's marriage ceremony at Lew Maslow's home. Lew and his siblings had invited their mother, Rose, to the wedding. The night before, Maslow lay awake for hours with acute anxiety. It would be the first time he had seen his mother in decades, and he feared that she might create a scene. At the ceremony, however, she was as distantly polite toward him as he toward her. But no reconciliation took place. Maslow refused to attend her funeral a few years later.

In October, *Eupsychian Management: A Journal* was published. Maslow had wisely decided to preserve the extemporaneous style of the original *Summer Notes*, written at NLS three years before. To this end, he had not modified or revised his initial impressions. In contrast to the dry, academic tones that dominated the field of management, Maslow's book had a unique immediacy, freshness, and vitality. It showed his inquisitive mind at its best. The book raises questions of what Maslow's influence might have been had he done a similar freewheeling account while observing a large hospital, prison, or big-city welfare or unemployment office.

Despite its formidable title, *Eupsychian Management* brought Maslow immediate attention among the leaders of America's business schools. Many in the management field viewed it as his most important book to date, providing concrete recommendations specific to his compelling theories of human nature. His novel concepts concerning employee motivation, "human assets" accounting, the psychology of entrepreneuring and leadership, and, especially, synergy exerted tremendous influence as they reached a receptive generation of managerial theorists and organizational consultants in the 1960s. *Eupsychian Management* soon went through a series of reprintings and was translated into Japanese.

This reception surprised Maslow. For once in his life, he had badly underestimated the potential impact of his ideas. Although gratified by the response, he felt business people seemed to be forgetting that the humanistic approach depends in large part on good conditions and that a sudden downturn in the international economy or domestic markets might make such principles, at least temporarily, less relevant than many realized.

Maslow also foresaw many problems before enlightened management could become a national, not to mention worldwide, reality. Decades of racial and economic injustice urgently needed to be redressed; mutual suspicion and outright war among nations further hampered this dream. Companies like NLS were hardly typical, Maslow realized, but they were promising:

> The old-style management is steadily becoming obsolete ... The higher people get, the more psychologically healthy, the more will enlightened management policy be necessary in order to survive in competition, and the more handicapped will be an enterprise with an authoritarian policy ... That is why I am so optimistic about eupsychian management ... why I consider it to be the wave of the future.

CHAPTER SIXTEEN

Uneasy Hero of
the Counterculture

In recent years, and to this day, most human-istic scholars and most artists have shared in the general collapse of all traditional values. And when these values collapsed, there were no others readily available as replacements. And so today, a very large proportion of our artists, novelists, dramatists, critics, literary and historical scholars are disheartened or pessimistic or despairing, and a fair propor-tion are nihilistic or cynical. [They believe] that no "good life" is possible and that the so-called higher values are all a fake and a swindle.

[We are in] a chaos of relativism. No one of these people now knows how and what to choose, nor does he know how to defend and to validate his choice. This chaos may fairly be called valuelessness.

—A.M.

American society in 1966 was becoming engulfed in rapid and violent change. Over a quarter of a million U.S. soldiers were fighting an undeclared and appar-ently unsuccessful war in South Vietnam. To a growing num-ber of people, the military draft seemed insatiable and the political system grossly unresponsive. Some opponents of the war called for civil disobedience; supporters raised the possi-bility of using tactical nuclear weapons against North Vietnam. The civil rights movement was split in its own ranks between staid lobbying groups and black-power advocates who scorned compromise. Environmental issues like air and water pollution occupied the media's attention. For the first time since the Depression, the ability of politicians to deal effectively with a host of domestic and international problems seemed questionable.

Simultaneously, there arose the beginnings of what would soon be known as the counterculture of America's late 1960s: a movement of intensely disaffected, predominantly young people who looked toward the tenets of humanistic psychology, Eastern religion, and psychedelic drugs for direction. The number who actually followed Timothy Leary's advice to "Tune in, turn on [with drugs], and drop out" was never very large. But millions more, especially college-educated people in their twenties and thirties, sought meaning and guidance in the writings of philosophers and social thinkers like Paul Goodman, Aldous Huxley, Rollo May, Bishop James A. Pike, Carl Rogers, Alan Watts, and, later, Richard (Ram Dass) Alpert, R. D. Laing, and others. To many, one figure stood out for his long-standing intellectual rigor and stirring vision of individual potential: Abraham Maslow. His name began to assume heroic proportions, nowhere more so than in California.

Sponsored by the Episcopal Diocese of California and Esalen Institute, on January 6, 1966, Maslow gave a public address at Grace Cathedral in San Francisco before a capacity crowd of more than five hundred. Esalen's young co-president Michael Murphy and journalist George Leonard, who spent most of the evening with Maslow, witnessed him trembling with nervousness before the talk. He calmed visibly once he launched into his impassioned speech, "Toward a Psychology of Religious Awareness."

His theme: psychology and religion are building an important bridge joining two previously separated shores of human nature. At last, Maslow declared optimistically, these territories are being linked. He wished to report what the building process looked like from science's shore. He proceeded to highlight such topics as self-actualization and the values of healthy people, the nature of peak-experiences and value disturbances like chronic boredom and cynicism, and the role of science in fostering a sense of wonder about the cosmos. During the question-and-answer period, he touched on a variety of intriguing topics ranging from male-female differences in peak-experiences to the urgent need to transform American education.

By all accounts, the lecture was a huge success. The next day, an excited Maslow was driven to Esalen to lead his weekend workshop. The catalogue announced, "Discussions with Dr. Maslow of the major themes of his work, such as Being vs. deficiency motivation, peak-experience, self-actualization, eupsychia, and a psychology of health and growth."

Because Maslow's name has remained misidentified with the excesses of the 1960s counterculture, particularly its experiential center at Esalen, it may be worthwhile to recall what he regarded as his most memorable, unpleasant encounter there.

Since his early work on the scientific study of transcendent experience in the 1950s, Maslow had been convinced that the English language is inadequate for precise discourse about the higher life. Aside from the classic vocabulary of theologians, which had become highly abstruse, there is no accurate way to discuss what he called the psychology of Being, the range of exalted emotions like awe, bliss, ecstasy, euphoria, reverie, and wonder. His own research on peak-experiences had shown that we need not be starry-eyed mystics to undergo such sensations; they are as near and familiar as the mother who gazes lovingly into the eyes of her child, or the nature-lover who beholds a mountain sunrise. "These happenings are in truth mysteries," he had written in *Religions, Values, and Peak-experiences.* "Even though they happen a million times, they are still mysteries."

Perhaps overambitiously or naively, Maslow believed that by bringing together a group of congenial people personally familiar with peak-experiences and Being-psychology, he could help build a scientifically meaningful language of transcendent experience. Michael Murphy, who was by now a close friend, had assembled a group of scholars, therapists, and well-wishers, including actress Jennifer Jones, an Esalen devotee.

Murphy and co-president Richard Price had reluctantly invited Fritz Perls, the irascible Gestalt therapist who resided at Esalen. Born in Germany in 1893 and trained as a psychiatrist before World War II, Perls had become internationally renowned at Esalen for Gestalt therapy, which he had developed with Paul and Laura Goodman in the mid-1950s. Unquestionably a brilliant and a masterful therapist, Perls was nevertheless well known among the Esalen community as an aged womanizer with a vulgar tongue and enormous ego. With his large, unkempt beard and predilection for jumpsuits, Perls strolled around Esalen as if he owned it. He turned the auspicious weekend into one of the worst experiences of Maslow's life.

Some twenty-five people assembled in the Esalen lodge Friday night after dinner. The invited participants sat in a circle before the fireplace, and the workshop observers seated themselves audience-style around them. Murphy offered a few words of greeting, then turned the meeting over to Maslow, who briefly reviewed his theory of Being-motivation and its implications for the field of psychology. Then he plunged directly into the task at hand. Some of the invitees were confused about precisely what Maslow wanted them to do. As for the observers, most had come for camaraderie, if not a peak-experience in the presence of the man who had inspired them, and were put off by the intensely academic tone of the workshop.

"Take 'duty,' " Maslow earnestly began. "Now, how would you define duty in a nontraditional way, a psychological meaning that conveys self-actualization or health?"

There was an embarrassing silence. Then Hobart Thomas, a psychology professor at California's Sonoma State College, suggested that duty can be thought of as fulfilling one's personal destiny; that is, one's innate potential.

"Right," replied Maslow, "that's a good example."

"This is just like school," Perls exclaimed in a loud, sarcastic voice. "Here is the teacher, and there is the pupil, giving the right answer."

Maslow ignored this first jab, and the rest that Perls would level that evening and the next day. By nature, Maslow avoided confrontation as much as possible, and he refused to respond in kind to Perls or permit himself to be unnerved. Perls, however, neither ceased his needling nor departed gracefully. He had rarely shown interest in anything intellectual at Esalen, for he viewed such philosophical discussions as a waste of time. With his strong sense of self-importance, Perls could not bear to see Maslow coolly leading the gathering in seminar style.

As Saturday wore on, the atmosphere became increasingly tense. The sensible procedure might have been to halt the meeting and, as a group, openly address Perls's behavior.

But Murphy did not want to challenge Perls; nor did anyone else. Maslow was unwilling to end his discussion and turn it into the emotional free-for-all of an encounter group, which would have pleased Perls.

On Saturday night the atmosphere grew even more strained as Maslow doggedly continued his effort to develop a "B-language" despite the mood. Suddenly, Perls dropped to the floor and began to make whining, infantlike sounds before the astonished gathering as he slowly wrapped himself around Maslow's knees. That did it. Staring down in disbelief at Perls, Maslow tersely announced to Murphy, "This begins to look like sickness."

The meeting broke up in confusion. Seething with unexpressed rage, Maslow stayed up for hours in his room. Writing down his angry thoughts calmed him, and eventually he fell asleep.

Sunday morning, he was more composed and ready to dispense a tongue-lashing. As he had realized while reflecting in his journal, Perls had gotten away with his atrocious behavior because the others had allowed him to.

Maslow began by emphasizing that the well-intentioned workshop had failed miserably because the members had proved ineffectual in working together. "Good individuals can form a lousy group," he remarked. "The procedures for forming good groups are separate, different from [those] for becoming a nice man. They're not the same thing . . . Every marriage I've come to think of as a political situation; there is the harmonization of the interests of two human beings. Now first of all, this means structure, agenda, programs."

How do you create a good working group? The issue has little to do with spontaneity or self-expression, those traits cherished at Esalen. "I have worked with people I hated, so long as . . . they were good workers," Maslow said. "And now we have a situation with people I'm very fond of, individually, and found we couldn't work. It is not really essential that we love each other in order to work well. It's a different set of rules. You can work with your enemies if you have to, so long as you share the rules."

The key rule, Maslow stressed, is that a work group must have both a strong leader and a structure. "A work party means . . . you're building a house. First you make foundations, and then somebody wants to work on the roof first. The chairman has to tell him no. Structure, order, agenda, and, most particularly, the strong chairman [are necessary]."

Maslow began to berate them personally, in the manner of an angry father. "I must urge you to meditate on the fact that Esalen, and many of the people of Esalen . . . are fleeing from overinhibition, overintellectualization . . . and going through a transitional phase . . . But what's self-actualization for anyway? If you don't just want to be a selfish person contemplating your navel . . . you put your shoulder to the wheel."

He proceeded to scold Esalen's staff and its regular visitors for smug indifference, even contempt, for those less "liberated" in their lifestyles. "I'm not a square, and I'm not conventional, and I'm not part of the establishment," Maslow contended. "I repudiate that label. [Yet] I don't despise the establishment. If you have compassion, you don't. If you really like . . . the people you're trying to teach, you don't speak above their heads . . . If I go talk with a group of people who are not college people, and I talk like a big, academic professor, that's hypocritical, that's show-off, and [it means] I don't love them enough."

If they continued to show such childish behavior in the name of spontaneity, he warned, he would have no choice but to advise his colleagues to avoid Esalen. This remark hardly won the favor of the Esalen staff, but Maslow was in the midst of a rare public display of temper and intent on venting his sentiments. Their refusal to value reason—specifically what he had tried to accomplish with the B-language workshop—was becoming intolerable to him and beginning to cost them his support, he declared. He turned to codirector Murphy and asked, "You know this place has a reputation for being anti-intellectual? . . . Hating science? Against research?"

As though lecturing a class of confused students, Maslow became more impassioned: "We've got brains . . . And that's part of spontaneity. And when your brain is free to work spontaneously, it's a very nice feeling . . . I'm a good worker. I work hard, I try to achieve things, and this is out of ultimate affection for other people. I would like to do good. I'd like to help my [unborn] great-grandchildren. I'd like them to come into existence instead of having the whole damn-blasted earth blown away. And this is my way of doing it. It's the best thing I can do . . . If you don't use your brain, you're not fulfilling your potential.

"I have the feeling of historical urgency . . . that there's a fire that we have to put out. The world is burning up. It's literally possible there [will be] atom bombs next week. God, we have to hurry. You know there's a fire to be put out. You're firemen. And get going. You have good hoses, use them. You've got lousy hoses, okay, that's the best you've got, use them . . ."

Some of those in attendance found Maslow's exhortation annoyingly paternalistic, though well intentioned. They also rejected as overly academic his criticism of Esalen's strong embrace of experiential methods to enhance personal growth. Other participants, like Murphy, respected Maslow for accurately diagnosing Esalen's chief weakness: its lack of intellectual vitality.

After the fiasco at Esalen, Maslow was glad to be back home and spent the next few months of his sabbatical leisurely driving with Bertha through the southern and eastern United States. He gave occasional lectures but spent most of his time visiting friends and exploring out-of-the-way places. Having completed *The Psychology of Science: A Reconnaissance* after nearly seven years, he felt little desire for sustained writing but wanted to relax and enjoy himself socially.

He was astonished in May to learn he had been nominated, among a handful of candidates, for president of the American Psychological Association, with balloting to take place that summer. It was an ironic turn of events, for Maslow had come to regard his critique of science as so radical that he had actually dreamed several times of being expelled from the organization.

He was also feeling politically more and more at odds with many of his academic colleagues. Part of the problem lay in his unwillingness to condemn totally the American presence in Indochina, just as in the 1930s and early 1940s he had been far more anti-communist than was fashionable on campus. Simultaneously, as violent crime sharply increased in U.S. cities and, for the first time, many citizens began to fear walking the streets after dark, Maslow became puzzled and then disturbed by the seeming indifference of most left-liberal politicians and writers. That month, he quit the American Civil Liberties Union because of what he considered its overzealous defense of criminals. Not long after, he resigned as a board member of the pacifist-oriented SANE (Committee for a Sane Nuclear Policy), founded in the 1950s by Erich Fromm. Both associations represented for him the increasing inability of mainstream liberals to cope with the reality of human aggression, either domestically, in the form of random and organized crime, or in international affairs.

Political ideology was becoming a heated issue for Maslow. His younger daughter, Ellen, had developed into a New Left activist. Living in New York's Greenwich Village, she was close to prominent figures like pacifists David Dellinger and A. J. Muste, writer-therapist Paul Goodman, and former Brandeis psychology student Abbie Hoffman. Maslow had greatly admired Ellen's bravery in joining the Freedom Riders to fight for black voter registration in the Deep South several years before, although he had feared for her safety. Now he felt dismay and sometimes anger at what he considered her simplistic social outlook. Occasionally they clashed openly over their differing viewpoints, but they generally adopted an uneasy silence whenever current events came up for discussion. In a journal entry dated June 3, Maslow commented:

> Ellen's political and work position is in effect a nonposition, nonideological, even anti-intellectual. They have no heroes or sacred texts . . . The Communists and Socialists and other "parties" they consider ridiculous and laugh at . . . One thing seems clear about this group. They reject *society* itself, *any* society, the machinery, the structure, the necessities . . . Poor kids. They're all doomed to depression, disillusionment, and eventually feeling stupid . . . [unless they] compromise.

On July 8, Maslow was stunned to learn of his election to the presidency of the American Psychological Association. He realized that he was hardly the intellectual loner he had believed himself to be; thousands of his colleagues had voted for him. He also felt embarrassed to attain an honor that so many of his own mentors had been denied, among them Erich Fromm, Kurt Koffka, Kurt Lewin, Max Wertheimer, and contemporaries such as social psychologist Solomon Asch, personality theorist Henry Murray, and behaviorist B. F. Skinner. Yet he was genuinely proud that he, as a Jew, had received this distinction and felt that President Sachar and others at Brandeis would be pleased. He knew that the APA presidency would burden him with extra administrative duties and siphon time from his writing, but he was willing to shoulder such responsibility for the greater impact his ideas might exert.

That fall brought greater public adulation than Maslow had ever experienced. He was chosen Humanist of the Year by the American Humanist Association; almost daily he received invitations from around the country and abroad to speak at academic and public conferences, to accept honorary degrees, and to collaborate on a multitude of community, educational, and research projects. Certainly, the optimism and social energy of the mid-1960s was giving Maslow's work a push that would have been unthinkable during the quietude of the Eisenhower years. More specifically, a catalyst for his new influence was the publication of *The Psychology of Science: A Reconnaissance.*

A slender, provocative book, it constituted a strong attack on conventional science as exemplified by experimental psychology. Developing ideas that had appeared in works like *Motivation and Personality,* Maslow argued that mainstream science had produced a pathetically inadequate image of human nature and its vast possibilities as a consequence of its overreliance on methodology and statistics and its avoidance of values.

> This book is not an argument *within* orthodox science. It is a critique *of* orthodox science and of the ground on which it rests, of its unproved articles of faith, and of its taken-for-granted definitions, axioms, and concepts . . . It is my impression that the weaknesses of classical science show up most obviously in the fields of psychology and ethnology. Indeed, when one wishes knowledge of persons, or of societies, mechanistic science breaks down altogether.

Writing in a semiautobiographical way, referring to his impersonal medical training at Wisconsin and his later groping efforts to study self-actualizing people, Maslow ended the book by evoking his lifelong motivation as a scientist: to reverently explore the mysteries of the universe and thereby improve our lot on earth.

> I have got more "poetical" experiences from my own and others' researches than I have from poetry. I have got more "religious" experiences from reading scientific journals than I have from reading "sacred books" . . . Not only does science begin in wonder; it also ends in wonder.

The Psychology of Science evoked a good deal of praise from colleagues in counseling, psychotherapy, and education. Significantly, too, it received wide attention in the popular press. For example, a review in the *Boston Herald* called it "a quietly revolutionary book . . . [which] could be a milestone in the development of a more human, more complete and less alienating approach to the study of both nature and man."

Praise for the book was not universal. Most of Maslow's experimentalist colleagues saw it as naive, his weakest book in an otherwise distinguished career. Since he had stopped doing empirical research, they questioned his ability to offer meaningful criticism of their methods. They also regarded as misguided, if well-intentioned, his apparent view that rigorous experimentalism precludes the emotion of awe or wonder.

Thus, even before *The Psychology of Science* was published, B. F. Skinner at Harvard, who had long been friendly with Maslow despite their differing emphases, had written him:

> I suppose I am a neo-behaviorist, and to some extent, a positivist psychologist, and I certainly do not feel . . . that values and the life of value are none of my professional concern. I do not renounce all consideration of poetry and art or even religious and transcendent experiences. I do want to find something in all of these which goes beyond experience, however, and I would hold that experience is a by-product or epiphenomenon.

> So far as I can tell, I have had many peak experiences and they have not decreased as I have become more rational or materialistic or mechanistic . . . I do not feel that I am more

at home with the cognitive than with the emotional, impul-
sive, and volitional as you imply . . . You ought to get to know
a behaviorist better!

Maslow felt comfortable in responding to contacts from
esteemed colleagues like Skinner, and valued their criticism as
well as their praise. But public adulation was a different matter. He found it hard to refuse speaking engagement requests,
even when they came from schools or associations that held
little interest for him. Over the years, he had accepted such
invitations partly for financial reasons. Now, even though he
no longer needed the money, he could not easily bring himself
to reject them. Nor was he easily able to turn away the growing
number of professionals, business people, college students, and
lay readers of his books who contacted him by mail or phone,
or even trekked to Brandeis to see him personally. Some
wished to enlist his support for innovative social projects or
research; others desired career guidance. Some simply had a
burning curiosity to meet this gentle, inspiring man.

Despite Maslow's frequent complaints about such demands, he clearly enjoyed being admired for his work after
many years of relative isolation. Nevertheless, he lacked sufficient objectivity about many of those who sought him out.
Typically, he responded to their interest in his ideas by assign-
ing them library research or suggesting a pilot study of an
intriguing topic like the development of friendships, peak-
experiences in children, or self-actualization among non-
professional women. Almost invariably, to his continued puz-
zlement and frustration, his would-be "helpers" (as he called
them) would let him down, often disappearing. Among the
Brandeis psychology faculty and graduate students, such folk
were sarcastically known as "Abe's groupies."

But to Maslow this was no laughing matter. Increasingly,
he felt harried and overwhelmed, with no time for his own
needs, and his health began to suffer. He fell prey to frequent
bouts of fatigue, insomnia, and chest pains. After worried discussions of these symptoms with Bertha and his psychiatrist
friend Harry Rand, he underwent a complete physical examination, including an electrocardiogram. Everything proved
negative, but he continued to feel unwell. To his family members and close friends, he looked tired and overburdened, from

the way he sat slumped in his chair to his slow, stooped gait. They admonished him not to work so hard but could offer little specific advice.

Part of his exhaustion was emotional, for he was becoming drained by some of the contradictions he saw in his own theory of self-actualization. His Brandeis students, for instance, were bright, affluent, and physically healthy; they could take for granted the economic and social benefits that earlier generations had struggled for. Yet, to Maslow, they seemed far less actualizing than their predecessors, who had lived through a world war or the Depression. Why was this so? Why don't more people truly fulfill their potential? Maslow's journals are filled with accounts of many nights in which he lay awake for hours pondering this mystery.

Finally, in discussions with historian Frank Manuel, he proposed the existence of a previously unrecognized inner disturbance he called the *Jonah complex*, taking its name from the biblical tale. He described this syndrome as "an escape from greatness," a refusal to face up to our capacities for tremendous achievement, for changing the world. Speaking more globally than of a simple fear of success in the workplace, he referred to an almost willful failure to develop to full potential. "If you deliberately set out to be less than you are capable," he warned, "you'll be unhappy for the rest of your life."

At the same time, he wondered if some individuals might not be more innately likely to self-actualize than others, constituting what he termed "a biological elite." At a conference of business leaders and managerial psychologists at Palm Springs, California, in the winter of 1967, Maslow publicly voiced some of his uneasy thoughts on this issue. As his colleague Carl Rogers recalled, "I was very shocked to hear Abe talk this way. I couldn't believe he meant the elitist things he was saying."

In April 1967, Maslow served on a panel in nearby Cambridge, Massachusetts, to discuss the state of research into LSD (the psychedelic drug lysergic acid diethylamide). Notwithstanding his dislike for Timothy Leary's sensationalist approach to mind-altering drugs, Maslow upheld the scientific legitimacy of psychedelic research. But by that spring, an alarming increase in violence across the United States convinced him that our most pressing psychological issue was not unleashing creativity but understanding human aggression; and that a Manhattan Project type of effort was essential to cope with the dark side of human nature. In meeting with Robert Ardrey, author of the best-selling *The Territorial Imperative*, Maslow felt ever more strongly that a definitive work on human aggression—tying together the evidence from endocrinology, animal psychology, psychoanalysis, and social psychology—was necessary. He felt himself physically unequal to the task but believed that a team of experts collaborating with a popular writer like Ardrey could do the job if given sufficient resources.

Having worked relentlessly for several months on a new theoretical paper devoted to *metamotivation* (the state of yearning for the B-values), Maslow was feeling more and more urgency about his own mission in life. In the course on utopian thought he taught that spring, he made it clear to students that he viewed his system of psychology as vital to any coherent approach to world betterment—of greater import to humanity, in fact, than a cure for cancer. In a long diary entry of May 3, he commented:

I've become a kind of work-machine, responding to duty practically all the time, and not really having much fun, or relaxing, or vacationing, or even resting. I don't saunter much, as I used to, or just loaf. Have pretty well given up really listening to music. These all seem like self-indulgences, and I'm impelled to work, to read only that which is relevant or useful . . . I press on . . . [The] trouble is, I'm too grim about it.

For a man nearing sixty, such an attitude was not a good omen for his health. During the summer, Maslow struck up a brief but lively correspondence with A. D. Fisher, a young anthropologist in Canada who was studying the Blackfoot Indians. Maslow was shocked to learn that nearly all of the Blackfoot culture was gone. They had become one of Alberta's most impoverished Native American tribes. Many families had been broken up, with illegitimacy common and alcoholism rampant. Even murder took place on the once-quiet reservation. Precious little was left of the altruism or the warm fellowship and extended family closeness that had touched Maslow so deeply in 1938 and had given him important insight into human nature.

Intensely saddened, Maslow urged his younger colleague to publish in a personal way what he had witnessed, to show "how it is possible to destroy cultures and individuals."

Distressed by such developments, Maslow believed more strongly than ever that humanistic social science offered the world the best future. In this regard, he was especially pleased to receive the galleys of his metamotivation paper in late August. To him, the paper represented the culmination of twenty-five years of work since his peace-table vision in Brooklyn shortly after the United States had entered World War II. "There's [now] a whole comprehensive system of human nature available to whoever wants it," he proudly noted. "Of course, I'll keep writing, but if I died now, a really perceptive man could do with what I've finished."

"A Theory of Metamotivation: The Biological Rooting of the Value-life" was published later in the year. It summarized more than a decade of the author's theorizing about human motivation and needs. He contended that we all have inborn higher *metaneeds* for creativity, challenge, and the like, and we suffer from *metapathologies* if these motives are frustrated or blocked. Examples of these disorders abound: the alarming rise in violence, delinquency, drug addiction, and senseless crime among the impoverished, and the pervasiveness of boredom, thrill-seeking, and cynicism throughout our society. To Maslow, these spiritual illnesses were signs of a mass crisis born of frustrated idealism, a despairing reaction to the limited and pessimistic social theories of our times. With a strident call for change, he wrote:

> Not only does the whole of official science and orthodox psychology offer . . . nothing, but also the major motivation theories by which most men live can lead . . . only to depression or cynicism. The deepest and most real motivations are seen to be dangerous and nasty, while the highest human values and virtues are [denigrated as] essentially fake . . . Our social scientists are just as disappointing in the main . . . The "science" of economics is . . . a totally false theory of human needs and values, a theory which recognizes only the existence of lower needs or material needs.

In all, Maslow offered twenty-seven different propositions composing his theory of motivation. Among the intriguing notions: *existential* or *intrinsic guilt,* which is "deserved and biologically sound," as opposed to neurotic guilt, which involves unnecessary regret. We know that physical pain is desirable, he argued, because it tells us that part of our body is hurt; similarly, intrinsic guilt is healthful, for it communicates that we have betrayed or violated our higher nature in some way.

He also identified fifteen specific B-values and the spiritual disorders that result from the deprivation of each. When we are persistently denied the experience of justice, beauty, or truth, he said, we develop such metapathologies as chronic vulgarity, bleakness, cynicism, grimness, or loss of excitement about life.

Maslow was excited about the paper, which appeared that year in the *Journal of Humanistic Psychology.* To his surprise, it attracted little interest beyond his closest intellectual allies. He realized ruefully that, like his earlier writings, the metamotivation paper might take fifteen or twenty years to become accepted by the social science establishment.

In the fall of 1967, beginning a one-year Ford Foundation fellowship, Maslow went to California for a few weeks of speaking engagements. Bertha went with him. In mid-September, he gave a well-publicized lecture on "Farther Reaches of Human Nature" to an audience of one thousand at San Francisco's Unitarian Church. As usual, he overprepared for the talk, which went well, and used only a fraction of his notes. He felt so tense before addressing the enthusiastic overflow audience that he told Michael Murphy he wished to do no more lectures of that sort.

He and Bertha went down to Esalen for a couple of days. While Bertha admired Murphy's handsome charm and graciousness, she was unimpressed with the experiential and body-oriented goings-on there and especially irritated by the "dirty hippies" who hung around Esalen, despite Murphy's efforts to keep them away. Her husband, though, remained ambivalent. He felt somewhat fatherly affection for Murphy and respected his vision of creating a "hothouse" to help people grow to their full inner nature. However, he worried about the privatism, or self-centeredness, Esalen seemed to be encouraging. Speaking to its "resident fellows," he warned against experientialism. In his own mind, he "thundered like an Old Testament prophet—of duty, responsibility." He regarded Esalen as potentially the most important educational experiment in the world, but lacking intellectual rigor. "It still hovers on the knife-edge of self-indulgence, mere experientialism, [and] anti-intellectualism," he mused. "I really don't care much about helping a privileged few to lead happier lives on the edge of catastrophe. This factor of historical urgency . . . looms bigger with me all the time."

Returning to the East Coast, Maslow spent most of his fellowship that fall visiting old friends and colleagues with Bertha and finishing his presidential address for APA's convention in September 1968. Another major project concerned what he termed his Theory Z approach to management. Presenting his view before leading managerial theorists at Harvard, MIT, and Yale that fall, he wanted to break new conceptual ground beyond Douglas McGregor's classic Theory X and Theory Y approach, first outlined in *The Human Side of Enterprise.* McGregor had argued that managers have an implicit theory of human nature: Theory X managers view people as inherently lazy and selfish, while Theory Y adherents regard them as innately productive and cooperative.

In essence, Maslow contended that neither is really accurate. In a theory that has become immensely influential, he stated that, as people grow toward self-actualization, their psychological needs at work change correspondingly. For example, purely monetary compensation does not mean much to those propelled by higher needs. Instead, what Maslow called *metapay*—for example, compensation in the form of opportunity to be creative and work more autonomously—becomes increasingly important as a job motivator. Convinced that a new, humanistic ethos was rising through the American workplace, Maslow began to collect job advertisements for engineers, executives, Peace Corps volunteers, and others to dramatize his view that metapay and similar concepts were tacitly becoming recognized and implemented.

"The United States is changing into a managerial society," he wrote on November 19, after reading a socialist piece that seemed intellectually outdated. "Does capitalism exist here *at all* in the same sense that it did in London in 1844, or in the

Latin American oligarchies? These idiots have probably never talked to a man like Andy Kay, or my brother Lew [of the Maslow Cooperage], or even the small businessman like my father. It's all a priori for them, as also for Herbert Marcuse."

Meanwhile, Maslow felt more and more tired, sleeping poorly and suffering from a spastic colon. In late October, he underwent another comprehensive medical exam. Everything was diagnosed as normal except for anemia, and he was prescribed iron pills and belladonna. Yet he continued to experience dizziness and intense fatigue. Following Harry Rand's suggestion, he resumed psychoanalysis in Boston in early November to deal with possible emotional causes of his ailments.

On December 2, with Michael Murphy, Maslow participated in a conference on transcendence at the Episcopal Divinity School in Cambridge. Sociologist Robert Bellah, political activist Dorothy Day, and theologians Harvey Cox, Emil Fackenheim, and Huston Smith also presented comments. It was a stimulating event for Maslow, but he was dismayed to find himself misunderstood by several people there. Despite his disclaimer that peak-experiences must be verified by reason before being accepted as truth, most of the other speakers misinterpreted his position as a glorification of experience to the exclusion of rationality. To avoid future misunderstandings, he decided to be more explicit at such gatherings. Nevertheless, to some intellectuals, Maslow's name began to connote an experientialist, even narcissistic, bias.

Four days later, Maslow experienced severe chest pains and was rushed to a nearby hospital. He had had a serious coronary and was placed in intensive care, then moved to a recovery wing. He canceled his APA presidential speech for the coming September and, while in the hospital, immersed himself in hours of reading, including Leo Tolstoy's novel *Resurrection*.

Maslow's hospital experience was pleasant, almost embarrassingly so. He enjoyed a steady stream of visitors who helped him pass the time. He also felt freed from many professional commitments. Sensitive to the altruism and kindness of his nurses and nursing students, he kept himself intellectually busy with research: specifically, what made them choose and remain loyal to such demanding and financially unrewarding duties? He began to question them closely about their work satisfaction and motivation. Over the next few weeks, he interviewed more than a dozen nurses. When he gently asked one of the most kindly, "Why did you go into nursing? What are the greatest moments of reward?" she began to weep.

Their answers were initially superficial, such as, "Because I like people." However, when he probed for their peak-experiences—"a moment so wonderful it made you weep or get cold shivers of ecstasy"—their comments were revealing, especially from those serving on the surgical units. For example, one nurse stated, "When someone gets healthy and walks out and comes up to me and says, 'Thanks.' " Several replied, "Delivering my first baby." Most replied that receiving gratitude from patients made their exhausting work worthwhile; when gratitude was missing, they felt used and taken advantage of.

This pilot study confirmed for Maslow his suspicion that gratitude is a vital and perhaps psychologically basic dynamic in human relations. He became more certain that people who are unable to feel and express appropriate gratitude are disturbed or "crippled" in some way, perhaps suffering from a metapathology, just as are the chronically cynical or sarcastic. Maslow developed several ideas for further research, like comparing the personality test scores of nursing students with their New Left activist counterparts. He was sure that the future nurses would achieve considerably higher scores on such dimensions as altruism, compassion, and emotional stability, and that such a study "could be of very great importance in producing hope against . . . despair."

At times in the hospital, Maslow worried about his private journals and their posthumous fate. He compiled a list of well-wishers who might be willing, in the event of his death, to help publish his journals at a loss and donate copies to libraries. "I'm going to assume I'll live some more years, but just in case, I must make all these arrangements right away."

He also wanted to arrange, in case of his death, for publication of his newly planned anthology, *Farther Reaches of Human Nature*. After listing many other projects that needed work, he noted, "But these duties are precisely what I'm supposed to emancipate myself from now with a bad heart. How can one be calm when he sees a cure for cancer? Here I am panting to get home and work! But would such happy work hurt me? . . . I don't think I'll care too much. It's just too important." His post-coronary attitude did not bode well for his physical condition.

On December 27, Maslow was discharged and went home. Still on leave from Brandeis with the Ford Fellowship, he tried to maintain his productivity by catching up on his mail and planning a few short articles. But soon the reality of his heart condition began to affect him emotionally, and at times he became depressed and quarrelsome with Bertha. Familiar sensations of time pressure returned, especially from the APA presidency's administrative demands. "The old test," he reflected. "Supposing I had unlimited funds, what would I choose to do? No question about it: I'd get out of the world. Perhaps go to a small, warm Mexican town and hide."

During the next few weeks, Maslow underwent a series of tests at Boston's renowned Lahey Clinic. He learned to his shock that his strange malady twenty years before at Brooklyn College had probably been an undiagnosed heart attack; apparent scarring of his heart tissue had been found. He was advised that it would take two to three years for his heart to rebuild itself and, until then, he was at high risk for another, possibly fatal, coronary. He would have to live very, very carefully. The news was depressing, although not unexpected. Persistent chest pains in Boston's icy weather had convinced him that he was seriously ill. And yet, to casual visitors and even intimates, he appeared cavalier about his health. His experimentalist friend Ricardo Morant reminded him continually, "Abe, slow down, you've just gotten out of intensive care!"

Maslow's behavior may have reflected the fact that he had long ago come to terms with his own mortality, perhaps because of that erroneous diagnosis of a fatal tumor while he was still a young man. Since then, he had lived with a vivid intuition that his life would not be lengthy and that he had much to accomplish in a relatively short time.

In late January 1968, he felt well enough to do a small project: preparing another periodic mailing list. This one he called The Eupsychian Network. It included about fifty organizations, newsletters, and associations including the Esalen Institute, the American Association for Humanistic Psychology, the American Ethical Union, and the Unitarian Universalist Association. He identified these as "interested in helping the individual grow toward fuller humanness, and in helping the society grow toward synergy and health, and in helping all peoples move toward becoming one world and one species."

By March, Maslow felt strong enough to resume his weekly psychoanalytic sessions. He also granted a long interview to *Psychology Today*, a promising new scientific periodical for lay readers. Perhaps because of his recent brush with death, he increasingly pondered his career to date. In a journal entry dated March 7, he commented:

> If I ever write [my autobiography] in a personal way ... I consider also that [my] work was determined unconsciously by the Jewish passion for ethics, utopianism, messianism, the prophetic thundering. My whole value-laden philosophy of science could be called Jewish—at least by my personal definition. I certainly wasn't aware of it *then*. And maybe all of *these* trends are responses coping with anti-Semitism, trying (1) to understand it and (2) to cure it by making universal brotherhood.

Often depressed about his health, Maslow found work to be the best palliative. One of his most satisfying new projects emerged when Jonas Salk, director of the Salk Institute of Biological Studies in California, phoned him in late February and invited his comments about the relevance of his psychological work to contemporary biology. "My whole psychology is fundamentally biological," Maslow reflected as he began the project, which he hoped would help move the field away from a value-free, technocratic approach. Completed several months later, the paper pleased Maslow so much that he planned to expand it into a book entitled *Humanistic Psychology and Biology*. "In these memoranda," he wrote, "I leave aside all the obvious frontier questions in biology and confine myself to what I think is being neglected or overlooked or misinterpreted—all this from my special standpoint as a psychologist."

He advised Salk and his staff that the two vital challenges for our time are "to make the Good Person and to make the Good Society," both tasks that require the knowledge of biologists. More specifically, Maslow praised emerging areas of biology, in particular the fields of biofeedback and environmental health. But our environment always includes other people and their values, Maslow admonished, and certain social milieus may therefore be dangerous for physical and mental well-being. Arguing that the case for psychosomatic medicine was strong, he insisted that our bodily health depends not only on the satisfaction of our lower emotional needs—say, for love and self-esteem—but also on the satisfaction of our higher meta-needs, involving beauty and justice. In other words, chronic exposure to ugliness, dishonesty, or injustice can make us physically as well as emotionally unwell.

Besides calling for an end to the value-free approach in science, Maslow offered a few speculative remarks, mainly concerning the possible biological underpinnings of self-actualization and general personality. Maslow's comments were privately circulated among Salk's staff and were published in substantially condensed form in "Toward a Humanistic Biology" that year in the APA's monthly periodical.

By early May, Maslow's stamina was returning. He finished a paper for the *Harvard Educational Review* and began working on the revision for the trade paperback of *Toward a Psychology of Being.*

Another project he wished to begin had long been on his mental back-burner: a cross-cultural critique of the shallowness of American friendships. In an unpublished paper he decried the loss of intimate, lifelong relationships as one of our society's most serious problems, rooted in "the breakup of the permanent and enduring, face-to-face relationships common in the past, at least in rural areas, in villages, in extended families and clans, and in *real* neighborhoods . . . I think it comes now to the necessity of having some equivalent of the old family organization as a center, from which [can] fan out all sorts of other work relationships, acquaintances, colleagues, friendships, and the like." Seeking to produce a paper with real-life cases, he planned to ask either Harry Rand or Rogelio Diaz-Guerrero to collaborate.

Having resumed psychoanalysis, Maslow realized that he had a good deal of unexpressed anger, a situation his cardiologist warned was bad for his heart. His anger arose against many sources—the complacent psychologists who dominated APA and his own department at Brandeis and, more broadly, all those who seemed oblivious to the demanding social problems of our time. He noted on June 5, after Robert Kennedy's assassination, "this feeling of impatience to get on with the job that so urgently and obviously needs to be done . . . But what's the best way to *harness* this anger so as to be more effective? That's what I want—to have *effect*."

As president of the APA, he had energetically sought to involve his colleagues in the civil rights cause and had pushed for training of more black psychologists in the United States. He was disappointed to find that few of his peers viewed the issue as a priority. He wrote to his daughter Ellen, who had sought to arouse his concern, "I couldn't get anyplace in APA with the Negro education stuff, but I've learned how to handle it . . . Anyway, I've learned that they are of good will, not prejudiced. Just that they won't make any . . . concessions or special efforts beyond being scrupulously fair." That spring, following widespread black rioting in many cities, Maslow joined with Carl Rogers and eighteen other leading psychologists in drafting the following letter, which was circulated by "Psychologists for Social Involvement" to APA members:

> As psychologists we are particularly concerned with the influences of environment upon behavior. We endorse the conclusion of the National Advisory Commission on Civil Disorder that the recent disorders result largely from conditions of discrimination, poverty, and unemployment, which have their roots in racial prejudice. As *citizens,* we strongly urge that direct action be taken to combat these unjust conditions. Concrete evidence of changing conditions, rather than vague hopes for the future, must be apparent without delay in order to avoid the death and destruction that is incipient in our nation.

In mid-June, Maslow took a much-needed respite to participate in the National Training Laboratory's t-groups in Bethel, Maine. Visiting friends and colleagues, such as Erik Erikson and Robert Tannenbaum, he and Bertha spent two delightful weeks there. But his involvement was not only socially stimulating. He took copious notes on his t-group impres-

sions and began to speculate about their wider societal importance to help resolve problems like racial tensions. More than
ever, he felt that well-run t-groups, although hardly social
cure-alls as some were suggesting, have tremendous potential
to help people communicate more effectively and become
closer to one another. As a participant, he felt moved several
times by the healing power of genuine candor in the group,
where members could reveal and overcome their most painful
fears or weaknesses in a warm, empathic context.

Following an impromptu lecture on his emerging view of
t-groups, he was asked his opinion of the civil rights movement. All human beings have certain inner needs to fully develop, Maslow declared. Therefore, they should have, in every
society, the right to satisfy these needs, ranging from the most
basic—for food and shelter—up the hierarchy to dignity, self-
actualization, and the B-values.

Since t-groups tend to be direct, soul-baring affairs, Maslow was not surprised that his recent heart attack came up for
discussion: why had he let himself get so overworked, he was
challenged. Despite his predilection for self-reflection, this was
clearly not a subject he had faced often. On June 22, he mused
in his journal:

> Since [my] heart attack, so many people—and I myself—
> [have been] thinking of how hard I worked and how ex-
> hausted I got, and why I didn't take it easier . . . [There is]
> no question of my sense of responsibility for years, of duty,
> a kind of messianic quality, as if *only* I were available to bring
> the message.

Since publication of his metamotivation paper, he regarded his mission of constructing a new psychology as accomplished. As for his voluminous scattered notes, self-memos, and
files:

> If I live long enough, I'll structure them into a system of
> human nature and of society. But if I don't, others will for
> sure, even though I don't know when . . . So I consider my
> major duty done, and [I'll] be content as a preparer, a fore-
> runner, and relax and loaf as soon as I get strong enough to
> travel.

By late August he found his attention turning to a decidedly nontheoretical issue. His pregnant daughter Ann was nearing her term. He and Bertha flew to Columbus, Ohio, to await the birth of their first grandchild. They had long yearned for this momentous event, since well before either Ann or Ellen had married.

To pass the time, the future grandparents did a bit of sight-seeing. For Maslow, the most evocative experience of the two weeks was a visit to the Ohio State Fair. To his surprise, he felt deeply moved by the fair, especially by the farm animals and the rural people who proudly showed them. He thought of the contempt many of his Brandeis colleagues would have had for the scene as "the ultimate in amusing corn or camp," and mused once more about how sharply his values differed from theirs. He recalled, as another measure of their contempt for America, how shocked they had been when he announced his sabbatical plan to travel around the United States rather than live in Paris.

Ann's delivery was late, and Maslow regretfully returned home while Bertha stayed in Columbus. On September 18, a euphoric Bertha phoned to say that Ann had given birth to a healthy daughter.

By the beginning of the fall, Maslow considered himself in a curious position. He was admired throughout the world for his work. Two biographies were being written about him by Frank Goble and Colin Wilson; both would focus on his work rather than on his life. He gave frequent interviews to a variety of popular magazines and daily received requests for speaking engagements throughout the country and abroad. Despite his recent heart attack, he was doing more lecturing before governmental and professional groups, from NASA engineers and State Department officials to Department of Agriculture executives, on such "Maslovian" managerial topics as eupsychia, synergy, and metamotivation in the workplace. Yet, with all these honors, he felt misplaced at Brandeis and academia in general.

Fatigued, he wrote little except his journals, which became increasingly important to him. Anticipating a steady improvement in his stamina, he planned a variety of future projects. One of these, proposed by his editor at Harper & Row, was a revision of *Motivation and Personality*. Fourteen years had elapsed since he had written that seminal book, and he was excited by the prospect of incorporating much new material to help support his original, mainly intuitive outlook about human nature. Much work had been done in such new fields as managerial theory and organizational development; his chief problem might be how to limit his revised edition.

He also wanted to write a book applying his unique psychological system to political theory. All systems of government, including our own, he observed, are based upon certain specific but typically unstated views of human nature. Now that his theoretical system was steadily gathering empirical support and starting to replace the Freudian and behaviorist images, he felt the time might be right to put forth an explicit, scientifically rooted theory to justify democratic rule and law. He began to gather notes on everything relevant to the topic, from United Nations policy on newly developed nations to the need for a sweeping overhaul of the criminal justice and welfare system in America. The book would also refer to the growing body of writing by such managerial thinkers as Warren Bennis, Peter Drucker, and Douglas McGregor.

Maslow was especially interested in addressing the explosive racial situation in the United States. He found relevant much of the new educational reform writing, including James Herndon's *The Way It Spozed to Be* and John Holt's *How Children Fail*. Holt, teaching at nearby Boston University, invited Maslow several times to his classes. Maslow advised the students that American blacks, to achieve their full potential, must overcome not only socioeconomic discrimination and public school inertia but also the lack within their urban families of strong fathers, firm discipline, and healthy, attainable goals for children.

Maslow was excited by the possibility of helping to develop an independent "Esalen East" in the Boston or New England area. Several acquaintances were seeking philanthropic funds for such a project and were enthusiastic about prospects. Having witnessed the strengths and weaknesses of both the Esalen Institute and National Training Laboratory t-groups, Maslow had many pertinent ideas to offer in creating a "growth center" on the East Coast.

The major issue, as he saw it, was to build community and not simply to foster isolated self-expression. He envisioned an enormous range of programs, including a publishing house, a retreat center, a congenial meeting place for friends, a dating-marriage matchmaking program, a center to give natural childbirth training and help parents with young children, an institute for "well-marriage" counseling where couples could share experiences, an educational division offering teacher training, and adult classes on such topics as how to develop friendships and how to examine American folkways and mores from a cross-cultural perspective. He also envisioned a program of weekend visits with authors for lively discussion of their work. As he noted in his journal, the goal of all these activities was decidedly not self-absorption, but the creation of "better people, better groups, better citizens, better society, [and a] better species."

Maslow was far less enthusiastic about staying in academia as the 1968 fall semester neared. It would be his first teaching assignment since the spring of 1967. He had come to regard the university environment as outmoded and viewed the faculty as clinging to medieval guild privileges like tenure, while contributing little to the world's pressing problems. He harbored little respect for many of his psychology colleagues. As he wrote to his activist daughter Ellen, "I think if the world were going to end tomorrow, all they would think to do is to be 'scientific' and run the rats just one more time."

In the refusal of most social scientists to consider the possible value of creative ventures like Esalen and Synanon or the burgeoning field of organizational development, Maslow found a hostility to new ideas and, therefore, an anti-intellectualism in the true sense of the term. Several years of conversations with innovative businessmen and managerial consultants had also convinced him that America's colleges were among the worst-managed organizations in the country.

More personally, he felt isolated and unappreciated at Brandeis, most acutely in the department he had built. Even casual visitors could see that he was sad and dejected. In a journal entry dated October 15, he ruefully commented:

> In my department, as it gets more and more experimental, "rigorous," I find myself getting more and more shy, retiring, less at home ... and I realized that for the first time *ever*, I had not automatically put my reprints in all the faculty and grad [student] mailboxes this summer and fall ... I don't

feel valuable, or needed, or wanted by most of the department faculty or by most of the grad students. I haven't been asked about my work, my books or papers, or what I was thinking or planning to do.

His contact with students was especially upsetting. With the handful who impressed him by their motivation and creativity, he was delighted to spend hours chatting over coffee, offering guidance and encouragement. But few students now sought him out, and he was convinced that the vast majority remained self-indulgent and intellectually undisciplined. He felt so dismayed by the general campus mood that he began to develop a book about humanistic education; he intended it to be no idealistic paean but a tough-minded analysis. In fact, the project was overdue, for he had promised it to the Ford Foundation as part of his fellowship terms in early 1966. Feeling somewhat stronger since his heart attack, he hoped to write the book in the next few months.

Maslow's seminar on Experiential Approaches to Education, meant to be a close look at new developments in the field, corroborated his outlook. It became the worst experience in his thirty-five years of college teaching. Almost immediately, about a third of the class, mostly undergraduates, rebelled against Maslow's authority and demanded to form their own group to experience these methods instead of merely talk about them. He initially resisted their insistence that they had the right and ability to teach themselves, and sometimes they became rude and even insulting. He found the words "Abe is a big-mouth" scrawled across the classroom blackboard one day. Occasionally, after complaining of chest pains and leaving to lie down on a cot in his office, he heard sarcastic murmurings that "Abe is copping out on us again." In his diary entry of October 22, he railed against such students:

> I think of the contrast with my own way of learning at their age. I got whatever I could out of all my teachers, bad and good, even if only a little. [Here] I feel ineffective, not well used, not using my full power. It's as if I took a job in a chewing-gum factory ... What am I being paid for? Listening to *them*? This is a job in which I *cannot* grow, or enjoy myself ... I'm doing therapeutic work, not teaching psychology.

Matters improved after he let the malcontents form their own class. He now believed that they had craved fellowship so intensely that they had simply been unable to participate in serious intellectual dialogue. They were merely confused adolescents, not deliberately hurtful. He realized, too, that his own theory of human nature cogently explained their behavior: the need for belongingness is more pressing than the need for self-actualization. But he considered it a pity, and a waste of his intellect, that these young adults were still struggling to satisfy basic needs that should have been met when they were children. As he told Bertha, Ann, and a few trusted friends, "I'm too old for this sort of work anymore."

Yet he never seemed to realize that his teaching problem was partly one of personal style. His avuncular manner could not have been more unsuited to the student mood of the times, especially at an intellectually elite liberal arts school like Brandeis. Reacting hurtfully to their scorn for his political moderation and quiet optimism about the future, he had a tendency to lecture like a parent berating a recalcitrant child. This approach only heightened tensions in his class.

In mid-November, Ann and her husband, Jerry, together with newborn Jeannie, came for a two-week visit and helped raise Maslow's spirits tremendously. Jeannie was an attractive baby with a wonderful temperament—evidence of Ann's intuitive skill as a mother, Maslow thought. Decades of dreaming about what grandfatherhood would be like were nothing compared to the reality of this tiny child gazing trustingly into his eyes. She seemed to embody the B-values and imparted to him renewed optimism and faith in human nature. He was eager to live long enough to experience her childhood with her but suspected that this would not be.

After the visit ended, Maslow felt deeply frustrated at being on campus. On December 5, he noted with dismay that he had spent more time in his seminar that fall debating political theory than in discussing education. Commenting on the radical students' takeover of the library and administration building at Columbia University to protest institutional racism there, he tersely wrote, "I want more and more to quit teaching."

CHAPTER SEVENTEEN

California Rescue: The "Postmortem" Life

*I like to be the first runner in the relay race.
I like to pass the baton on to the next [person].*

*I have a very strong sense of being in the
middle of a historical wave. One hundred
and fifty years from now, what will histori-
ans say about this age? What was really important? What was going? What was finished? My belief is that much of what makes
the headlines is finished, and the "growing
tip" of mankind is what is now growing and
will flourish . . . if we manage to endure. His-
torians will be talking about this movement
as the sweep of history.*

—A.M.

*B*y the late fall of 1968, Maslow was on the
verge of leaving college teaching; partly for financial reasons,
partly out of inertia, he was unable to make the decisive break.
It was less than a year since his coronary, and he would have
been justified in taking an extended medical leave from Brandeis. At the height of his fame, he could well have supported
himself by writing and occasional speaking engagements. With
both his daughters past college age, there was less financial
pressure. But like many who had struggled through the Depression, Maslow could not bring himself to quit a secure position, however unsatisfying. He tried to resign himself to five
more years of teaching, after which, at the age of sixty-five, he
could retire from Brandeis and move on with his life.

Then, on December 9, everything changed. He received
a telephone call from William P. Laughlin, president and
chairman of the board of the Saga Administrative Corporation

based in Menlo Park, California. Maslow knew Laughlin, the wealthy cofounder of Saga, only slightly; a couple of years before, they had met at a sensitivity training workshop sponsored by the National Training Laboratory in Washington, D.C. Maslow had served as a speaker-observer at a training session for young corporate presidents, and Laughlin had expressed admiration for his fresh ideas about American business management. He had also spoken vaguely of bringing Maslow to California on a special fellowship, but nothing specific had developed from the conversation.

Now, Laughlin cheerfully informed Maslow, the fellowship was ready. He was prepared to offer Maslow a two-to-four-year commitment with the following conditions: a handsome salary, a new car, and a personally decorated private office with full secretarial services at Saga's attractive campuslike headquarters on Stanford University's suburban outskirts. What would Maslow have to do in return? Nothing. Laughlin explained that he had heard of Maslow's discontent with full-time teaching and simply wished to give him unlimited free time for writing and scholarly work. Maslow would not be expected to perform any duties at the company; the fellowship would be created out of Laughlin's personal funds, and there would be no connection with the Saga Administrative Corporation at all. Was Maslow interested?

As Bertha vividly recalls, her husband stood as if in a stupor, holding the telephone receiver and occasionally replying rather distantly, "Mmhm, mmhm." In an uncharacteristic manner, Maslow showed no emotion as he perfunctorily thanked Laughlin and hung up. Bertha asked, "Abe, what was that all about?" Open-mouthed after hearing him repeat the conversation, she urged him to call Laughlin back and apologize for his apparent coolness. "Even if you're not interested," she said, "that's no way to treat someone who means well and is only trying to help you." He then called Laughlin back, apologized, and discussed the offer a bit more animatedly before agreeing to continue their conversation the next day. He had been so stunned by Laughlin's offer, he explained to Bertha, that he had been rendered speechless.

All that evening, Maslow talked with Bertha about whether to accept the offer, and he thought about it long into the night. It appeared almost too good to be true. The next day, the two men spoke again and more details were clarified. It was just what Maslow had been dreaming of for years. But what do you do when your most alluring dream suddenly seems to come true? If you're Maslow, you pull back and take a long, hard look before acting.

For the rest of the week, he spent countless hours talking things over with Bertha and debating with himself. Would it really be wise to quit academia? True enough, he disliked teaching more and more, but he enjoyed the intellectual company of some faculty friends; perhaps the student situation would improve. And what about their lovely home on the Charles River? Could he give that up so easily? Boston was a stimulating place, culturally and intellectually. What would the San Francisco area be like? Whatever decision he made, he was confident that Bertha would be supportive.

During the next few weeks, events conspired to help Maslow make his decision. The Boston weather was cold and blustery; it went right through him, leaving him tired and weak with chest pains, barely able to walk across campus. He was demoralized and felt like an invalid. He knew that with his heart condition there was little sense in suffering through New England's harsh winters when he could be basking under California's sunny skies. Meanwhile, his undergraduate students were as immature and rebellious as ever. Perhaps emboldened by Laughlin's offer, Maslow lashed back at them and expressed his contempt for their adolescent arrogance and willful ignorance: "When you get older, you'll be nice people. But right now, you're immature jerks!" To his surprise, they seemed to treat him with more respect, if only temporarily, after this display of anger.

On December 31, Maslow and Bertha celebrated their fortieth wedding anniversary with friends and champagne. He had decided to accept Laughlin's fellowship and relocate to California as soon as possible, provided that the details could be agreed on. Several months before, Maslow had consented to lead a weekend workshop at Esalen in January 1969, and he hoped to finalize plans with Laughlin on the same trip.

On January 2, 1969, Maslow flew to San Francisco, where he was met by two Saga officials, William Crockett and James Morrell, director of management training and executive vice-president, respectively. Both men were somewhat awed by this famous writer-intellectual whose ideas were beginning to reshape managerial practices in boardrooms and factories across the country. Maslow did his best to put them at ease. They drove him to Saga headquarters in Menlo Park, where the fellowship terms were presented in detail. The landscaped site was beautiful and the contract terms were all in order. Maslow accepted and telephoned the news to Bertha. He was then driven down the coast to Esalen, accompanied by Morrell and his wife, Marylyn.

Esalen's course catalogue announced: "Dr. Maslow will discuss his most recent thinking about psychology, religion, eupsychia, education (especially in regard to self-actualization), and whatever else seems of interest." Although Maslow's name carried tremendous allure, his presentation (like his workshop of three years earlier) was at odds with Esalen's typically experiential programs. Maslow led no group encounters, taught no exotic methods of awareness or meditation, but simply talked about the ideas that excited him. To some of the audience, he seemed too cerebral, and perhaps too judgmental in his pronouncements. Especially to Esalen's regulars, like his wild nemesis Fritz Perls, Maslow had a paternalistic, almost rabbinic quality that challenged their "I do my thing, you do your thing" approach to values and social behavior.

On Sunday, Maslow decided to speak about democracy and politics, humanistic psychology, and the increasingly violent nationwide campus protests against the Vietnam War and domestic racism. He first alluded to the tendency among many in the counterculture, and some specifically at Esalen, to ridicule those with conventional values and lifestyles. Then he spoke forcefully about the importance in a democracy of respect for individual differences: In any political situation, even within marriage, this respect, coupled with the willingness to compromise for the greater good, is essential for our democratic way of life. He also condemned the justification of violence as a legitimate response to social problems like poverty and racism. Only as a last resort, and then only where is no rule of law—as in the Deep South before the civil rights movement—can lawbreaking be justified, Maslow contended; otherwise, the very nature of democracy is undermined.

On the drive back to Menlo Park, Maslow continued his heartfelt remarks with the Morrells and Esalen's cofounder Michael Murphy. In an impassioned tone, Maslow stressed that as their elder, he had lived through World War II and the near triumph of fascism in Europe and Asia. He had witnessed how close Western civilization had come to collapsing under the onslaught of Nazism, and he was not going to let the situation happen again. Burning buildings or shouting down campus speakers was not something he would accept as an expression of political protest, however sincere its motivation. The following year, he participated in the White House Task Force on National Goals as one way to influence federal policy-making. Having been a supporter of Hubert Humphrey's 1968 presidential candidacy, Maslow was skeptical about Richard Nixon's commitment to change. But he was unwilling to stand idle when so much needed to be done, especially concerning major social institutions like education and social welfare.

Maslow returned to Brandeis on January 7 and applied for immediate sick leave. That way, he reasoned, he could keep his faculty chair in psychology if Laughlin's fellowship did not work out. But if Maslow had any lingering doubts about whether to stay at Brandeis, these were quickly dispelled by campus events. A group of black militants took over a campus building in protest of what they perceived as institutional racism at the university. There was deliberate vandalism of scholarly work, such as students' theses, in the library. Especially because the protesters had received scholarships to study at Brandeis, Maslow was disgusted with their behavior and the timidity of his colleagues in responding to this assault.

His final meetings with his seminar were angry and confrontational. He announced that he was leaving Brandeis, partly because he was too old to put up with the students' adolescent nonsense. After attending a final session of the leaderless encounter group that had made up one faction of his class, Maslow remarked that he had heard only three statements there about the nature of humanistic psychology, and all three were wrong. One student retorted, "Who are *you* to tell us what's correct and what isn't?"—and seemed puzzled when Maslow burst out laughing.

Brandeis granted his sick leave. He and Bertha made some quiet good-byes and in late January threw a going-away party attended by the psychology department. Their house was up for sale, and they felt a bit depressed about being uprooted after nearly eighteen years in the Boston area. Before arriving in San Francisco, they visited management professor Warren Bennis and other friends in Buffalo, New York, then spent several days in Columbus, Ohio, with Ann and her family. Maslow spent hours caressing and playing with his granddaughter. Saying good-bye was hard. As always, writing was his best catharsis, and on the plane to California, he rhapsodized in his journal about his boundless love for Jeannie.

During the next few weeks, Maslow settled into his new life. He and Bertha had hoped to live in San Francisco, but they saw that the commute would be impractical. They rented a furnished apartment in the suburb of Mountain View, and while her husband became acclimated in his new work environment, Bertha house-hunted in the surrounding area. Living like transients bothered them, but they both enjoyed the balmy climate and their opportunities to socialize with interesting people.

Maslow was impressed with what he saw at Saga. The company, controlled by Laughlin and two cofounders, dated back to 1948 as a partnership among the three at Hobart College in upstate New York. They had pooled their financial resources and convinced the administration that they could run the college's previously money-losing cafeteria and manage it profitably. They did so well that they won a contract to run three dining halls at the nearby women's college.

By 1957, Saga had established itself on nineteen college campuses around the country. By 1961, the number was ninety-eight. The owners were clearly doing something right; Saga had never lost or dropped a college from its clientele. One key to Saga's success, Laughlin explained to Maslow, was its "unlimited seconds" policy, an attraction for hungry college students who enrolled in its meal plan. In 1965, Saga had completed its national headquarters in Menlo Park. In the mid-1960s, Saga had continued to grow and diversify in such areas as food services for hospitals and retirement communities. In 1968, the company had gone public by offering stock.

Such growth had exacted a heavy price from Saga, Laughlin conceded: a steady deterioration of employee morale. Two employee surveys conducted in the mid-1960s had revealed widespread job dissatisfaction; many felt shut out of decision making and helpless to initiate decisions on their own, a consequence of the centralized style of administration. Therefore,

Laughlin and his associates had brought in two management consultants from the new field of organizational development; one was Robert Tannenbaum, Maslow's friend at UCLA.

Since then, Saga's executives had sponsored two more programs in keeping with the goals that Tannenbaum had helped them formulate. The first was a thorough organizational diagnosis, especially surveying managers' complaints and problems. The second was a series of seminars for managers around the country to discuss the results of the survey. One outcome of this activity was the creation of teams of similar-level managers in each major geographic area of the United States, for the purpose of enhancing managerial problem solving. In addition, Saga's top executives sent out word that more open, frank communication was necessary between subordinates and their immediate supervisors at all levels of the company.

In the corporate world today, such an enlightened approach to management is well accepted, although not always put into full effect. Twenty years ago, such practices were radical. Maslow felt that Laughlin, Crockett, Morrell, and other Saga leaders were genuinely concerned with the quality of life there and not simply with the number of dollars flowing into the company's coffers. To Maslow, their pragmatic idealism was not unlike that of his friend Andy Kay, owner of Non-Linear Systems. He enthusiastically joined them for spirited discussions, often over meals with their wives, on such topics as the nature of effective management and leadership, organizational change, and the wider implications of such activity for building a just and creative society.

Meanwhile, Bertha found an attractive house for sale in the lovely Ladera section of Menlo Park. In mid-February, the Maslows signed the papers, with Laughlin lending them the down payment and serving as cosigner of the mortgage. As he had promised, he gave Maslow a new car for personal use—a Mercedes-Benz, the preferred automobile among Laughlin's well-to-do circle. Maslow was at first embarrassed to drive it. Before long, Maslow decided to install a swimming pool at their new home. Initially, a pool seemed like an extravagance, but he became convinced that swimming every day might strengthen his heart and prolong his life.

On March 4, the W.P. Laughlin Foundation issued a press

release with the title, "Dr. Abraham Maslow accepts Laughlin Foundation grant," announcing his acceptance of the agreement. Attached was Maslow's statement of purpose, outlining his immediate and long-range plans for the next few years.

He ambitiously identified seven short-term projects, including a brief, informal book on humanistic education; a new anthology of his recent writings, to be entitled *Farther Reaches of Human Nature*; a paper on racial relations and their improvement; another on social, institutional, and organizational change; and a psychologic-scientific inquiry into the nature of evil and its place in a comprehensive theory of human nature and ethics. His highest priority, he said, was to write a book on humanistic politics, "because of the current assault on American values, and loss of faith in them . . . I interpret much of the current turmoil, especially among the young, as an anguished cry for just such values, something to believe in that is also intellectually and scientifically respectable."

His long-range goal was to develop and promote an all-inclusive psychological approach to human nature and society. "A new image of man and a new image of society generates changes in all aspects of human life," he contended. "These new possibilities . . . are revolutionary in almost the same sense that the Darwinian, the Freudian, Newtonian, or Einsteinian revolutions were."

Maslow sometimes felt as if Laughlin had rescued him from the turmoil at Brandeis. After selling their house in Massachusetts, the Maslows moved into their new home in April. A few months later they enjoyed their first swim in the new pool.

On a typical day, Maslow took a morning swim and breakfast with Bertha on their patio. Then he drove to Saga and headed for his office, his pockets bulging with three-by-five cards and loose papers. His secretary would hand him the mail, which was usually extensive. He often visited colleagues in the building for long chats, or dictated notes for his various works-in-progress. For lunch, he casually joined a group at Saga's employee cafeteria; its executives had refused to segregate themselves by creating a separate executive dining facility. Nearly everyone at the company, from clerks through senior managers, was proud and delighted to have Maslow in their midst, for he was warm and unassuming to the staff. After lunch, he usually drove home, had a long nap, and did some reading and perhaps some more writing. In the evenings, he and Bertha were much-sought-after dinner companions in the San Francisco Bay area.

Aside from old friends in California's humanistic psychology community, Maslow particularly liked the company of Crockett and Laughlin. Crockett had been a career foreign service officer with the State Department and appointed by John F. Kennedy to be deputy undersecretary of state for administration. In this capacity, one of Crockett's innovations was to invite civilians into the State Department as advisers; Laughlin was among those who accepted. Shortly before offering Maslow his fellowship in 1969, Laughlin had invited Crockett to create and direct Saga's organizational development program. The three men engaged in many intense discussions on such topics as promoting world peace, government bureaucracy and public service, and the newspaper industry, with which Crockett was also familiar. On Maslow's suggestion, they formed a kind of permanent encounter group; they agreed to be completely open with one another in expressing their feelings.

Through this association, Maslow became increasingly interested in the nature of leadership. These strong, decisive business and governmental figures he called *aggridants,* a term he derived several years earlier when reviewing studies of aggrandizing, or highly dominant, animals. Such people seemed very different from the quiet academicians Maslow had known for most of his life, and he wondered what made them that way. He felt sure that such leaders are born, not made—that there is something innately unique in their ability to successfully manage or direct others. But he was troubled by the elitist implications of this notion and decided to give it much more careful thought before publishing anything on the subject of leadership.

Maslow also became friendly with several staff members of the Stanford Research Institute. These included Willis Harman and Arnold Mitchell, both humanistically oriented social scientists with interests in economics and business management. Maslow often talked with them about his theory of the hierarchy of needs and his interest in understanding the values by which people guide their lives. Mitchell and his associates went on to develop one of America's most successful and influential values-oriented think tanks devoted to market research and consumer behavior. It has become known as SRI International. Harman went on to head the Institute of Noetic Sciences, a research center devoted to human potentialities.

Maslow's contact with such figures prompted him to keep a constant flow of journal notes on the social and political implications of his concepts of psychology. He intended to organize these into a popular book, but he did not live to complete the project. Central to the effort was his view that democracy had been sold short for a long time. He felt that the American dream had not been expressed well for many years, perhaps not since Thomas Jefferson. Success in America was too often defined in material terms and, for this reason, young idealists here and around the world were finding little worth respecting about our country. He found it ludicrous—and ultimately dangerous for America's international status—that the Soviet Union, China, and other authoritarian nations had usurped the language of morality and justice by espousing idealistic motives for their actions. Especially in the impoverished places of the globe, Maslow insisted, there was a tremendous need for the masses to have a democratic equivalent to *The Communist Manifesto*—that is, an explicit statement and rallying cry for freedom and individual liberty.

He viewed the mass media as especially guilty in their political distortions, communicating only bad news to the world about the nature of a democracy like the United States. "Only that which is a catastrophe, an emergency, a horror of some sort . . . is considered to be worth a headline," he wrote. "The whole positive side of life is missing from the newspapers. We have huge amounts of space on juvenile delinquency and practically none on juvenile idealism and selfless service."

He also believed that American democracy had changed for the worse in recent years. "I feel strongly that we need to do some hard, realistic thinking about our political system," he wrote in a journal entry. "It is no longer working as . . . originally designed . . . Thanks to mass media and the decline of a critical public spirit, our political life is now largely election-winning, image-projecting, public relations, and advertising."

By mid-August, Maslow was finished with his revised preface to *Motivation and Personality*. He viewed it as his most important accomplishment since leaving Brandeis. Although he did not elaborate any new ideas in the piece, he noted a number of significant psychological developments that had occurred since the book was published in 1954. These included the emergence of humanistic and later transpersonal psychology as legitimate fields of study and the burgeoning of organizational development as an applied discipline. While expressing satisfaction with the acceptance of his ideas during the past fifteen years, he called for more research and patience in helping to advance a more hopeful yet realistic picture of human nature and its unrealized potential.

By this time, Maslow delighted in his new life in California. He did not miss Brandeis or college teaching. He enjoyed intellectual freedom, congenial company, and the Bay Area's wonderful climate. He also relished the excellent secretarial support services and beautifully decorated office at Saga. If his granddaughter Jeannie had been with him, he could have asked for nothing more. Maslow savored the days that followed his near-fatal heart attack less than two years before. On a cassette tape he mailed that summer to editor T. George Harris of *Psychology Today* (a magazine for which Maslow was a paid consultant), he spoke of his new outlook:

> My attitude toward life changed. The word I use for it now is the *postmortem* life. I could just as easily have died, so that my living constitutes a kind of an extra, a bonus . . . Therefore, I might just as well live as if I had already died.

> One very important aspect of the postmortem life is that everything gets doubly precious . . . You get stabbed by . . . flowers and by babies and by beautiful things—just the very act of living, of walking, breathing, eating, having friends, and chatting. Everything seems to look more beautiful rather than less, and one gets the much-intensified sense of miracles.

> If you're reconciled with death or even if you are pretty well assured that you will have a good death, a dignified one, then every single day is transformed because the pervasive under-

current—the fear of death—is removed . . . I am living an end-life where everything ought to be an end in itself, where I shouldn't waste any time preparing for the future, or occupying myself with means to later ends.

Sometimes I get the feeling of my writing being a communication to my great-great-grandchildren who, of course, are not yet born. It's an expression of love for them, leaving them not money but in effect affectionate notes, bits of counsel, lessons I have learned that might help them.

Although the generations of the future certainly concerned Maslow, he was far more interested in his own granddaughter and followed her every stage of development with interest and joy. To his friends and colleagues on the West Coast, he personified the doting grandfather. He and Ann traveled frequently to visit each other; about every eight weeks, he spent several days with Jeannie. He rhapsodized in his journals about the baby's good nature, innocence, and lively alertness. In a manner inconsistent with his usual intellectual rigor, he even compared Jeannie's happy, placid disposition to the qualities of sages and mystics. Sometimes, when his friends wanted to discuss major issues like educational change or world peace, he would repeatedly bring up Jeannie's accomplishments or antics. It was if he had suddenly rediscovered babies and was amazed all over again at the process of human growth. He told Bertha and Ann that after his heart condition improved, he hoped to conduct empirical research with infants and toddlers. He was especially interested in how such qualities as fear and selfishness develop in young children.

On November 10–11, a conference of ten college and hospital food-service directors was held at Saga's corporate headquarters. Sherman Moore, executive vice-president of the company, wanted to gain more direct information about administrative problems at Saga operations across the country. He invited Maslow to sit in on the meetings and to share his general impressions at the last session. Relaxed and friendly with the group of middle-managers, Maslow told jokes to put them at ease. In a serious vein, he urged them to continue their commitment to humanistic management—that is, to be open and self-revealing with their coworkers when they returned to their jobs. American men don't express their emotions for fear of being seen as vulnerable, he contended, but a real man is one who can be soft and tender with others.

Above all, Maslow said, their interest in enlightened management was uniquely American, in our country's best tradition and a promise of good things to come. With genuine emotion, Maslow declared his admiration for the nation that had given him so much; where, only one generation before, his father had arrived impoverished but possessing priceless freedom. He confided:

> I'm a sidewalk boy who's gone on to a marvelous vocation. I got to exactly the spot that I was born for . . . I don't know where you come from individually, but the fact is that it could be anyplace. None of you need any pull; you don't need a relative; you don't need any privilege; you don't have to go through a particular school . . . It depends on your capability and talents. I think that it's helpful, as it has been for me, to be very aware of simply our good fortune . . . in being part of this American dynamic . . . I feel this fact for myself, and I suggest that you become aware of it and just feel privileged to be an American . . . If America could fulfill [its] dream a little more, we, in turn, could build a world dream.

In the winter of 1970, as California's weather turned chilly, Maslow seemed to have more frequent thoughts of his own mortality. Watching the waves break over the shore at a seaside resort, he was moved to tears as he contemplated the beauty around him and the preciousness of such moments. Another intense experience came when he and Bertha visited the Pleasanton area, where they had lived briefly more than twenty years before; it evoked many memories. If at this time Maslow had intimations that he might die soon, he preferred to keep them to himself and not upset others.

On March 17, he met for several hours with an international group gathered at the Organizational Frontiers Seminar organized by Robert Tannenbaum and Warren Schmidt at the UCLA Graduate School of Management. Maslow spoke freely, without notes, about many topics that occupied his current interest: hopefulness versus despair about the future, the nature of science and the search for truth, peak-experiences and values, and the nature of leadership. He also directed anger toward the cynics of human nature "who are, unfortunately, given so much voice that they essentially have the microphone in our culture." Referring the audience to his new preface to *Motivation and Personality,* which he described as "a kind of personal credo," Maslow expressed optimism that organizations in America would change for the better; patience and dedication were needed to make our nation's founding dream of a just society come true. It was one of his most personally satisfying talks since leaving Brandeis, and the friendly, respectful mood of the UCLA students made him more certain than ever that he had made the right choice.

By early spring, Maslow began to organize his notes for a thorough critique of the Esalen Institute and its countless imitations; he hoped to publish the piece later in the year. Maslow knew that this article would undoubtedly lose him many devotees both in California and elsewhere. But he was so thoroughly disenchanted with Esalen's stress on experientialism and self-absorption that he felt it desirable to be ruthlessly honest in his assessment. When his friend Michael Murphy came to visit that spring, Maslow, half-expecting an angry confrontation, told him of his intentions. Much to Maslow's delight, Murphy replied that he did not fear the publication of such a frank and thoughtful report, but eagerly anticipated it.

Maslow did not live to finish this project, but he typed an interesting set of notes dated March 20 entitled "Esalen Critique: Memorandum." He expressed his fear that the search for mystical or exotic experience divorced from ethics leads ultimately to death, noting that sadomasochistic literature is filled with such examples. More specifically, he criticized Esalen's "big-bang" approach to personal transformation and suggested that the Institute should place more emphasis on hard work, discipline, and lifelong effort as essential to inner growth. Maslow also questioned its emphasis on sagelike emotional health, when many people in our culture are clearly disturbed and first need to be treated for their illness. "Esalen should not exclude Freud and psychoanalysis," he noted. Finally, Maslow faulted Esalen for its implicit anti-intellectual stance. "Experientialism must be taken only as a means to further ends. It is not enough. We must continue beyond that to seek knowledge, wisdom, values. Why is there no library at Esalen? . . . Again, all of this must be judged by the product . . . that is, does it make good persons or bad persons? Does it make society better or worse?"

That month, Maslow completed what would be his last published article, on humanistic education, a topic he was still planning to address in a short book. For some time, he had been disturbed by the widespread misuse of his ideas, as well as those of colleagues including Aldous Huxley, Carl Rogers, and Alan Watts, concerning creativity and self-expression. He felt ready to commit some of his thinking to publication. Drawing upon his unpleasant experience with Brandeis students in the fall of 1968, he insisted that to be creative in any field of endeavor, from chemistry to psychology, one has to first accept the yoke of discipline and the mundane learning of facts and methods. From our vantage point today, it may seem hard to understand what all the fuss was about. But Maslow wished to clarify his stance that encounter groups and other useful vehicles for encouraging self-expression had never been intended as substitutes for classic forms of education and were of decidedly minor importance in professional training:

> I think we can teach history, mathematics, astronomy, biology, and many other subjects . . . in such a way as to stress personal discovery . . . peak-experiences, illuminations, [and] the sense of mystery, and of awe. This is certainly one of the pressing tasks for professional educators. Even so . . . I worry when competence [is] considered to be irrelevant or unnecessary.

In mid-April, Maslow attended a transpersonal psychology conference in Council Grove, Iowa. He and psychologist James Fadiman flew to Kansas City, then boarded a bus to the conference site. Maslow enjoyed Fadiman's company a great deal, and they talked about their mutual interest in the psychology of religion. The conference brought together researchers focusing on such topics as meditation and the new integration of psychology and spirituality. They included Elmer Green of the Menninger Clinic, who was one of the first to investigate biofeedback as a therapeutic tool; Helen Bonner, who was exploring the use of music therapy; and Stanley Krippner, who was studying psychedelics and their effect on artistic creativity. Michael Murphy was there to discuss new developments at Esalen. Maslow was especially intrigued with Joe Kamiya's pilot biofeedback research on teaching people to control their brain waves to enhance relaxation and meditation. Psychiatrist Stanislav Grof's careful use of LSD therapy also aroused Maslow's interest.

Maslow began his presentation by mentioning some items in his revised preface to *Religions, Values, and Peak-experiences.* When he had written the book in the early 1960s, he had been somewhat naive, he confessed, about the dangers of an overzealous interest in mysticism and the purely experiential aspects of religion. Now, he was deeply concerned, even alarmed, about the widespread tendency to seek unusual sensations in the name of the spiritual. Such esoteric traditions as astrology, tarot cards, the I-Ching, and kabbalah were forms of superstition without any scientific evidence, Maslow stated. He planned to urge publicly that all sensible people reject these and similar subjects as nonsense.

To Maslow's surprise, many in the audience immediately protested. They argued that he knew little about the history of mysticism and the world's esoteric traditions. There *is* evidence for the validity of such systems, Fadiman and others insisted, although it may not conform to the dictates of modern Western science. Eager to speak on his main topic and wishing to avoid an unpleasant confrontation, Maslow agreed to rewrite his preface and refer only to nameless "fads and cults," not to specific esoteric practices.

Maslow then highlighted his developing notion of the *plateau-experience.* He proposed that the true mark of the sage or self-actualizing person is not so much the presence of intense moments of joy or ecstasy but of extended periods of serenity or rapture. Unlike peak-experiences, he added, these plateaus could be achieved through conscious, diligent effort. Maslow was developing exercises to help individuals attain the plateau state of consciousness. To dramatize his point, he plucked a tiny flower, placed it on his knee, and asked the audience to gaze at it intently, with their full attention. He recommended another exercise: look at a person you see all the time, such as a spouse, family member, or friend, and "make believe that you (or he/she) is going to die soon." Such methods, he indicated, can serve to break the dull, habit-worn way we relate to others and help us see the world once more with freshness and delight.

Unusual for Maslow in a public address, he spoke personally of his own transcendent experiences. He mentioned his poignant awareness of the evanescence of individual existence before eternity as he had stood watching the ocean waves and surf several weeks before. He found himself quivering as he talked. When he began to speak of his thoughts about his infant granddaughter, he became so emotional that it was hard for him to continue. He spoke too of a transcendent vision he had experienced at a Brandeis graduation ceremony some years back: in the distance of his mind's eye, he saw a long procession of scholars and thinkers—going all the way back to Socrates, Plato, and Aristotle and stretching far, far into the future of yet unborn generations—and he had felt a serene joy in seeing himself a part of this unbroken line. Perhaps more than anything else Maslow said that day, this rare, heartfelt self-disclosure moved his audience.

Energized by the conference, Maslow returned to Menlo Park with renewed vigor to finish his new preface to *Religions, Values, and Peak-experiences.* The writing went rather easily. As per his agreement with Fadiman and others, he refrained from criticizing any particular esoteric school of thought. But he clearly warned against the danger of indulging in mystical pursuit and the willful seeking of peak-experiences for their own sake. Such self-absorption is not only selfish, he wrote, but potentially evil. Alluding to the interests of many in the drug-and-hippie counterculture, he wrote that the quest for exotic sensations

> can sometimes wind up in meanness, nastiness, loss of compassion, or even in the extreme of sadism . . . The great lesson from the true mystics . . . [is that] the sacred is *in* the ordinary, that it is to be found in one's daily life, in one's neighbors, friends, and family, in one's backyard, and that travel

may be a *flight* from confronting the sacred . . . To be looking
elsewhere for miracles is a sure sign of ignorance that *everything* is miraculous.

Maslow was pleased with his productivity since moving to
California just over a year before. He had completed two important pieces of writing on schedule. His new anthology, *Farther Reaches of Human Nature*, seemed to be progressing
well. In planning future projects, Maslow felt torn between
writing more journalistically for a larger audience or maintaining his predominantly scholarly and scientific approach. In
either case, he decided, he would continue with his informal,
dictated-memo and short-paper style of self-expression, rather
than attempt anything more rigorous.

Through most of April and May, Maslow gave talks at local
universities and professional associations. He dictated his ideas
for books and empirical research, hoping that one day he
might have a staff under his direction to verify and extend his
innovative notions of human personality, its latent potential
and heights. He developed a special interest in what he liked
to call the *Taoist*, or sagely noninterfering parent, spouse, or
educator. Watching Jeannie develop under Ann's gentle mothering, he came to appreciate ever more strongly the innate
force for growth that lies within each child. Close observation
of his granddaughter also led him to greater interest in the
"wisdom of the body," our inborn processes for health and
self-healing.

After visits from several Israeli social scientists, Maslow
became enthusiastic about the possibility of studying intentional communities once his health improved. He was especially interested in understanding the human forces that contribute to the failure of most communes. This was a badly
neglected yet potentially ground-breaking subject for research, he was sure. He looked forward to his first trip abroad,
to visit an Israeli kibbutz to observe the dynamics of democratic and successful communal living.

Above all, Maslow planned to turn his attention to the
issue of human nature and evil. The world is filled with evil
events, he believed; yet the number of deliberately hurtful,
malicious people seems small. Perhaps most individual evil is
not intentional at all, he speculated in his journal, but caused

by ignorance. If so, then it might be fruitful to "change our image of the devil from a cruel, cold man with a pain-producing pitchfork to [one] stumbling down the stairs or ineptly breaking things in spite of his good intentions."

But Maslow was no pollyanna. In his last months, he felt it increasingly vital that any comprehensive theory of human nature accept our imperfection without falling prey to despair. Even the best of people—the self-actualizers he had long studied with admiration—are imperfect, Maslow observed. It is wrong and even dangerous to expect perfection from one another in any sort of relationship. "A good marriage is impossible," he flatly remarked in his journal, "unless you are willing to take shit from the other." He strongly believed, too, that the breakdown of traditional family ties today, as well as of intimate friendships, has come partly from the inability of many to live with human imperfection. Without such an acceptance, true give-and-take for the greater good cannot take place. To expect human perfection rather than improvement, either in the abstract or in everyday life, is an incalculable error. In this regard, "Nirvana now!" was a popular slogan of the counterculture that Maslow especially abhorred. To seek the perfect friend, the perfect job, or the perfect spouse, he felt, is a sure prescription for disappointment and unhappiness.

On the weekend of June 6–7, Maslow and Bertha enjoyed some rare moments of privacy at their Menlo Park home. On Sunday morning, Bertha telephoned the Morrells and invited them to visit. Marylyn Morrell agreed to sit for a sculpting session with Bertha. Meanwhile, Maslow worked busily on his writing. He temporarily excused himself from the company and mentioned that he was grappling with his emerging theory of human evil. He seemed to be having difficulty getting started and kept coming out of his seclusion to chat. Later, putting his work aside, he sat on the patio with Bertha and the Morrells to look at photographs. It was a beautiful day. As the Morrells prepared to leave, Maslow walked with Marylyn to the front door. There they noticed a neighbor's Siamese cat stretching sensually, and together quietly admired its graceful beauty for a few moments before their final good-bye.

On Monday, June 8, Maslow was out as usual by his pool. Meticulously following his cardiologist's orders, he glanced at his stopwatch and began to jog slowly. Suddenly, under California's sunny skies and with Bertha relaxing a few feet away, he collapsed without a sound. When she frantically rushed over to him, he was already dead of a massive heart attack. He was sixty-two years old.

In the wake of Maslow's unexpected death, many of his friends and colleagues sought to honor his memory in a suitable manner. Among the first of these were Robert Tannenbaum and Warren Schmidt of UCLA. On June 10, they distributed a notice to their Organizational Frontiers Seminar students, who had spent several exciting hours with Maslow just a few weeks before. The note informed them, "His great heart stopped suddenly, and from all that is known, without pain." Tannenbaum and Schmidt announced that they were helping to publish a memorial volume dedicated to Maslow's unique spirit and message and invited them to share their recent memories of Maslow. In this way, others might come to know something of Maslow's personality.

Maybe it was the idealistic time in America that evoked their unabashed, touching remarks; certainly, Maslow's own nature, too, enthralled them. One person commented, "I have never met a man more ready to die and yet more full of life than Maslow." Several mentioned an uncanny sense of reverence that they had experienced that day with him. Another participant observed poetically yet accurately, "There was something otherworldly [about Maslow]. He could have talked to Plato with ease, but would have felt just as elated in conversing with a janitor about the virtues of grandchildren."

Perhaps the most moving comment came from someone who had barely known Maslow but seems to have spoken for the many individuals whom he touched in his impassioned life and career: "It felt good to be human in his presence. In a disturbed world, he saw light and promise and hope, and he shared these with the rest of us."

Epilogue

Since Maslow's death in 1970, his influence has spiraled outward, beyond the edges of the humanistic psychology movement and its East and West Coast enclaves. In Europe and Japan, too, this influence continues to be felt. Through countless professional and popular interpretations, his ideas have come to affect powerfully how we view ourselves as individuals. His notions about self-fulfillment and emotional well-being have influenced the fields of psychology, counseling, education, health care, business management, marketing, and theology. They have helped overturn long-standing popular values about the way to lead a worthwhile life.

Through the impassioned ideas that Maslow advanced for nearly two generations, we have enlarged our beliefs about human nature and its untapped potential. As we move toward the twenty-first century, it seems undeniable that his image of innate human makeup—encompassing higher as well as lower needs—will stand as the most comprehensive to emerge in the social sciences. Indeed, Maslow's compelling views have subtly shaped, for better or worse, much of our daily expectations of love and marriage, work and leisure. Yet much of the specific content of Maslow's career has remained little known, and the evolution of his influential ideas untraced. Furthermore, Maslow's work has been widely misunderstood and distorted by many of his critics and advocates.

I hope that this biography has helped make clearer what motivated and excited him and what his vast legacy means for us today.

Glossary

Abraham Maslow coined many terms in developing his influential system of psychological thought. Over the decades, some of them have come to circulate through the wider world of social science and even American culture as a whole. Nevertheless, some of Maslow's most influential terms have been consistently misunderstood and misapplied. At the time of his death, he had begun to voice dismay over the increasingly distorted representations of his ideas. The following key terms are defined briefly here as he used them in his writings.

Aggridant. A biologically superior member of a species, human or otherwise; a better perceiver and chooser; tends to occupy a dominant or leadership position in the social world of that species. Also known as *alpha*.

Alpha. See **Aggridant.** Derived from Aldus Huxley's usage in *Brave New World*.

Apollonian mystic. One who experiences transcendence and the sacred through contemplation.

Authoritarian personality. An individual who has a basic *jungle-view* outlook and regards kindness and benevolence as signs of weakness to be exploited.

Basic needs. Inborn, *instinctoid*, lower psychological needs. In hierarchical order, from bottom to top, they are the needs for safety and protection, belongingness, love, respect, and self-esteem.

Being-cognition (B-cognition). Clear, contemplative knowing, especially of the transcendent, sacred, and eternal aspects of a person or thing. Occurs most often in *self-actualizing* people, especially, though not exclusively, during a *peak-experience.*

Being-humor (B-humor). Philosophical or enlightening humor, reflecting a high level of maturity and motivation; for example, the quality of humor associated with Abraham Lincoln.

Being-knowledge (B-knowledge).   Knowledge of the transcendent, unique, or sacred inherent in a person or thing, gained through *B-cognition* rather than through logic or rationality.

Being-love (B-love).   Unselfish, unconditioned regard for the nature and potentialities of the loved one, rather than use of the loved one to gratify one's own *basic needs;* loving something precisely the way it is, in its uniqueness.

Being-motivation (B-motivation).   See **Metamotivation.**

Being-needs (B-needs).   See **Metaneeds.**

Being-psychology (B-psychology).   Psychology concerned with human cognition, experience, and motivation during the highest states of awareness, such as in *peak-experiences.*

Being-values (B-values).   The intrinsic and ultimate human values, such as truth, beauty, and justice. They are the objects of our *metaneeds* and the goal of our *metamotivations.*

Belongingness needs.   Inborn psychological needs for feeling a sense of membership in a group, family, tribe, or society.

Bodhisattva.   Buddhist term for one who, having attained personal enlightenment, selflessly returns to the everyday world to serve as a teacher and helper for others; contrasted with **Pratyeka Buddha.**

Cognitive pathologies.   Sick or anxiety-based expressions of our need to know and understand the world around us. These include intolerance for ambiguity, the compulsive need for certainty, over-intellectualizing, *rubricizing,* and *pseudo-stupidity.*

Counter-values.   Fear, hatred, or resentment expressed toward the *B-values,* such as truth, goodness, and beauty, or toward virtue in general.

Counter-valuing.   Experiencing or expressing hostility toward the *B-values* or what embodies them, such as by debunking or devaluing. This is a psychological defense against feeling awe or wonder in the presence of the *B-values,* due to the resentment they can arouse in us because of our deficiencies.

Deficiency-cognition (D-cognition).   Ordinary knowing, such as through logic or rational analysis, in which people or things are seen in their isolated details.

Deficiency-humor (D-humor).   Hostile, cruel, or belittling humor, such as laughing at another's misfortune; reflects a low level of maturity or motivation.

Deficiency-love (D-love).   Regard for the loved one's capacity to satisfy our own *basic needs.*

Deficiency-motivation (D-motivation).   Motivation related to satisfaction of our *basic needs.*

Deficiency-needs (D-needs).   See **Basic needs.**

Deficiency-psychology (D-psychology).   Psychology concerned with human cognition, experience, and motivation in the realm of the *basic needs* and ordinary consciousness.

De-sacrilization.   A common psychological defense in our culture against being flooded by "softer" emotions. It involves a suppression or denial of such feelings as tenderness, kindness, awe, wonder, ecstasy, or a sense of the miraculous in any human endeavor.

Dionysian mystic. One who experiences transcendence and the sacred through wild exuberance.

Eupsychia. By formal definition, the culture that would be generated by one thousand *self-actualized people* on an isolated island; more broadly, the most perfect society that human nature can permit, which satisfies the *basic needs*, and presents the possibilities for *self-actualization*, of all its members.

Eupsychian. Moving toward *eupsychia*—that is, toward achievable psychological health; connotes real improvability rather than mere utopian traits. Also, the actions taken to foster and encourage such a movement by a teacher, therapist, or manager; refers to the mental, social, or organizational conditions that make health more likely.

Eupsychian management. By formal definition, the managerial principles generated if one hundred *self-actualized persons* became partners and invested their pooled savings in an enterprise, so that each person had equal say; more broadly, enlightened management in general, concerned with fostering the personal growth and creativity of organizational members, the quality of products and services, and the health and prosperity of the organization as a whole.

Existential gratitude. Appropriate, healthy gratitude, occurring when there is love or empathy between individuals.

Existential guilt. Appropriate, healthy guilt, which results from a betrayal of our higher nature or of the B-values, like justice or truth, in our lives. Also called **intrinsic guilt.**

Existential psychology. Psychology emphasizing individual identity and experiential knowledge as its starting points; deals with the real problems or dilemmas of human existence, such as the quest for meaning in life.

Existential therapy. Psychotherapy or counseling that focuses on treating people who experience value disturbances, or *metapathologies*.

Fourth Force. See **Transpersonal psychology.**

Growth-needs. See **Metaneeds.**

Hierarchy of needs. The inborn array of physiological and psychological needs encompassing the *basic needs* and *metaneeds*. As a lower need is fulfilled within us, a new and higher need tends to emerge.

Holistic. Concerned with things in interconnection rather than in isolation from one another; contrasted with the atomistic or reductionistic approach, which perceives in fragments or isolated details.

Humanistic psychology. Introduced in the 1960s, the term refers to the broad-based psychology that Maslow, Rollo May, Carl Rogers, and others helped to establish, which seeks to transcend the schools of Freudianism and behaviorism. Also known as the **Third Force.**

Instinctoid needs. Inborn psychological needs, encompassing *basic needs* and *metaneeds*. Although weak in nature, these cause us to desire and seek out certain values, such as beauty or truth, in our lives. The gratification of instinctoid needs is necessary for complete health.

Intrinsic guilt. See **Existential guilt.**

Intrinsic values. Those human values that are *instinctoid* and that we need to satisfy to avoid illness and to achieve full growth; deprivation of the intrinsic values leads to *metapathologies*. Also, the object of the *metaneeds*.

Jonah complex.   Based on the biblical figure Jonah, this emotional condition reflects a "fear of one's own greatness" and results in a fear of doing what we do best, and evasion of our own potentialities. In daily life, the Jonah complex can take the form of a low level of aspiration, or *pseudo-stupidity.*

Jungle outlook.   The outlook of the authoritarian individual, in which people are seen to be either "lambs" or "wolves," victims or potential predators; usually accompanied by an inability to empathize with anyone outside of one's limited blood-family.

Love-needs.   Encompassing the *basic need* to feel loved by others, such as by friends or family members.

Metamotivation.   Motivational state of yearning for the *B-values,* like truth, beauty, justice, perfection; the dominant motivation in a *self-actualizing* person.

Metamotives.   The motives of people who have had their *basic needs* met and who are therefore activated by the *B-values.*

Metaneeds.   Inborn though weak psychological needs that lie beyond the *basic needs;* these are our needs for the *B-values.* Their deprivation leads to *metapathologies*, or "sicknesses of the soul."

Metapathologies.   The spiritual-existential ailments that result from the persistent deprivation of *metaneeds*—the lack of fulfillment of *metamotivations.* They include cynicism, apathy, boredom, loss of zest, despair, hopelessness, a sense of powerlessness, and nihilism.

Metapay.   Compensation geared toward one's higher needs, such as the opportunity to be creative and work more autonomously.

Nadir experience.   A desolation experience, such as psychotic regression, failure or tragedy, confrontation with death, or an intense confrontation with an existential dilemma; may lead to a breakthrough or transformation of our values and outlook on life.

Non-peaker.   Person who fears and therefore inhibits or rejects his or her peak-experiences. This is usually done through denial, suppression, or "forgetting," so that such episodes disappear from awareness and memory. A *non-peaker* is usually overly rational, practical, materialistic, or obsessive-compulsive.

Normative psychology.   Psychology concerned with how people *should* emotionally or cognitively function.

Peak-experience.   An ordinarily brief and transient moment of bliss, rapture, ecstasy, great happiness, or joy. We usually feel such emotions as awe, reverence, and wonder in such moments; also, we feel more alive, integrated, "here-and-now," and yet in touch with the transcendent and the sacred; more frequent in *self-actualizing* people.

Plateau-experience.   A serene and calm, rather than intensely emotional, response to what we experience as miraculous or awesome. The high plateau always has a noetic and cognitive element, unlike the *peak-experience,* which can be merely emotional; it is also far more volitional than the *peak-experience;* for example, a mother who sits quietly gazing at her baby playing on the floor beside her.

Pratyeka Buddha.   Buddhist term for one who wins enlightenment only for himself, independently of others; contrasted with the **Bodhisattva.**

Proctological view.   The outlook of the cynic or one who is in despair; it typically involves belittling, debunking, or looking for the worst motives in the actions of others. One who has this outlook is suffering from one of the *metapathologies*.

Pseudo-stupidity. A *cognitive pathology*, a manifestation of the *Jonah complex;* it typically involves a defense against or denial of one's own intelligence.

Reality freshening. Consciously seeking to reawaken our experience of the *B-values*, such as of beauty, truth, and justice; a necessary antidote to "taking things for granted." See **Re-sacrilization**.

Re-sacrilization. Seeking to view a person or thing "under the aspect of eternity." Restoring the sense of wonder and the sacred in our everyday lives. See **Reality freshening**.

Rhapsodic communication. Poetic language, such as using metaphor and mythical symbols; this form of communication often occurs during a *peak-experience* and overcomes the limitations of purely rational, logical discourse.

Rubricize. To stereotype or categorize something or someone as a type rather than to perceive it as unique and one of a kind; for example, to categorize one as a waiter or policeman, not as an individual. Periodic *reality freshening* is necessary to overcome our tendency to rubricize.

Safety needs. Inborn psychological needs for feeling a sense of physical security; a type of *basic need*.

Self. The biologically based core of the personality.

Self-actualization. The apex of personal growth, in which we become freed from *basic needs* and *deficiency-motivation;* not an end point in most people, but a drive or yearning to fully develop. Also, the process of fulfilling our latent talents, capacities, and potentialities at any time, in any amount. Although we all have this drive, we also possess a fear of growth.

Self-actualized person. A psychologically healthy, mature, and self-fulfilled individual, whose *basic needs* are met and who is therefore motivated by *metaneeds* and an active seeking of the *B-values*. Such a person tends to have certain specific traits, including creativity, sagacity, emotional spontaneity, and commitment to a calling.

Self-esteem needs. Inborn psychological needs for feeling a sense of self-esteem and self-worth; a type of *basic need*.

Synergic. Having the quality of *synergy;* also, the extent to which individual and organizational/societal needs or goals are mutually enhanced. For example, a synergic society "is one in which virtue pays." A good marriage is also synergic.

Synergy. Term coined by anthropologist Ruth Benedict in 1941 and elaborated by Maslow to generalize about cultures. A high-synergy culture is one in which what is beneficial for the individual is simultaneously beneficial for everyone, and vice versa; for example, a culture that generously rewards altruistic behavior. A low-synergy culture is one in which what is good for the individual is harmful for others, and vice versa; for example, an organization in which one's success can occur only at the expense of others.

Taoist. Having the quality of receptivity and surrender; being nonintrusive and noninterfering.

Taoist science. Science having the *taoist* quality; also, making use of *Being-cognition*, not only *Deficiency-cognition*, in the pursuit of knowledge.

Theory Z. Managerial theory formulated by Maslow that seeks to synthesize and transcend the influential Theory X and Theory Y dichotomy advanced by Douglas McGregor in 1960.

Third Force. See **Humanistic psychology.**

Transpersonal psychology. An approach founded and introduced within *humanistic psychology* by Abraham Maslow in the late 1960s, which seeks to incorporate human spirituality into a comprehensive model of human nature and its potential. Also known as the **Fourth Force.**

Unitive perception. The ability to perceive the sacred through the secular; also, a fusion in perceptions of the Being-realm and the Deficiency-realm.

Value disturbance. See **Metapathologies.**

Valuelessness. The state of being without a system of values; leads to a variety of *metapathologies,* as well as to bodily illness.

Maslow's Publications

1932 "Delayed Reaction Tests on Primates from the Lemur to the Orang-outan." (With Harry Harlow and Harold Uehling.) *Jour. Comparative Psychol.* 13: 313–343. "Delayed Reaction Tests on Primates at Bronx Park Zoo." (With Harry Harlow.) *Jour. Comparative Psychol.* 14: 97–101. "The 'Emotion of Disgust in Dogs.'" *Jour. Comparative Psychol.* 14: 401–407.

1933 "Food Preferences of Primates." *Jour. Comparative Psychol.* 16: 187–197.

1934 "Influence of Differential Motivation on Delayed Reactions in Monkeys." (With Elizabeth Groshong.) *Jour. Comparative Psychol.* 18: 75–83. "The Effect of Varying External Conditions on Learning, Retention, and Reproduction." *Jour. Experimental Psychol.* 17: 36–47. "The Effect of Varying Time Intervals between Acts of Learning with a Note on Proactive Inhibition." *Jour. Experimental Psychol.* 17: 141–144.

1935 "Appetites and Hungers in Animal Motivation." *Jour. Comparative Psychol.* 20: 75–83. "Individual Psychology and the Social Behavior of Monkeys and Apes." *Intern. Jour. Individ. Psychol.* 1: 47–59.

1936 "The Role of Dominance in the Social and Sexual Behavior of Infra-human Primates: I. Observations at Vilas Park Zoo." *Jour. Genetic Psychol.* 48: 261–277. "II. An Experimental Determination of the Dominance Behavior Syndrome." (With Sydney Flanzbaum.) *Jour. Genetic Psychol.* 48: 278–309. "III. A Theory of Sexual Behavior of Infra-human Primates." *Jour. Genetic Psychol.* 48: 310–338. "IV. The Determination of Hierarchy in Pairs and in Groups." *Jour. Genetic Psychol.* 49: 161–198.

1937 "The Comparative Approach to Social Behavior." *Social Forces* 15: 487–490. "The Influence of Familiarization on Preferences." *Jour. Experimental Psychol.* 21: 162–180. "Dominance-feeling, Behavior, and Status." *Psychological Review* 44: 404–429. "Personality and Patterns of Culture." In Stagner, Ross, *Psychology of Personality*, McGraw-Hill. "An Experimental Study of Insight in Monkeys." (With Walter Grether.) *Jour. Comparative Psychol.* 24: 127–134.

1939 "Dominance-feeling, Personality, and Social Behavior in Women." *Jour. Social Psychol.* 10: 3–39.

1940 "Dominance-quality and Social Behavior in Infra-human Primates." *Jour. Social Psychol.* 11: 313–324. "A Test for Dominance-feeling (Self-esteem) in College Women." *Jour. Social Psychol.* 12: 255–270.

1941 *Principles of Abnormal Psychology: The Dynamics of Psychic Illness.* (With Bela Mittelmann.) New York: Harper and Bros. "Deprivation, Threat, and Frustration." *Psychological Review* 48: 364–366.

1942 "Liberal Leadership and Personality." *Freedom* 2: 27–30. *The Social Personality Inventory: A Test for Self-esteem in Women* (with manual). Palo Alto, Calif.: Consulting Psychologists Press. "The Dynamics of Psychological Security-Insecurity." *Character and Personality* 10: 331–344. "A Comparative Approach to the Problem of Destructiveness." *Psychiatry* 5: 517–522. "Self-esteem (Dominance-feeling) and Sexuality in Women." *Jour. Social Psychol.* 16: 259–294.

1943 "A Preface to Motivation Theory." *Psychosomatic Medicine* 5: 85–92. "A Theory of Human Motivation." *Psychological Review* 50: 370–396. "Conflict, Frustration, and the Theory of Threat." *Jour. Abnormal and Social Psychol.* 38: 81–86. "The Dynamics of Personality Organization I & II." *Psychological Review* 50: 514–539, 541–558. "The Authoritarian Character Structure." *Jour. Social Psychol.* 18: 401–411.

1944 "What Intelligence Tests Mean." *Jour. General Psychol.* 31: 85–93.

1945 "A Clinically Derived Test for Measuring Psychological Security-Insecurity." (With E. Birsh, M. Stein, and I. Honigman.) *Jour. General Psychol.* 33: 21–41. "A Suggested Improvement in Semantic Usage." *Psychological Review* 52: 239–240. "Experimentalizing the Clinical Method." *Jour. Clinical Psychol.* 1: 241–243.

1946 "Security and Breast Feeding." (With I. Szilagyi-Kessler.) *Jour. Abnormal and Social Psychol.* 41: 83–85. "Problem-centering vs. Means-centering in Science." *Philosophy of Science* 13: 326–331.

1947 "A Symbol for Holistic Thinking." *Persona* 1: 24–25.

1948 " 'Higher' and 'Lower' Needs." *Jour. of Psychol.* 25: 433–436. "Cognition of the Particular and of the Generic." *Psychological Review* 55: 22–40. "Some Theoretical Consequences of Basic-need Gratification." *Jour. Personality* 16: 402–416.

1949 "Our Maligned Animal Nature." *Jour. Psychology* 28: 273–278. "The Expressive Component of Behavior." *Psychological Review* 56: 261–272.

1950 "Self-actualizing People: A Study of Psychological Health." *Personality Symposia: Symposium # 1 on Values*, Grune & Stratton, New York, 11–34.

1951 "Social Theory of Motivation." In Shore, M. (Ed.), *Twentieth Century Mental Hygiene*, New York: Social Science Publishers. "Personality." (With D. MacKinnon.) In Helson, H. (Ed.), *Theoretical Foundations of Psychology*, New York: Van Nostrand. "Higher Needs and Personality." *Dialectica* (Univ. of Liege) 5: 257–265. "Resistance to Acculturation." *Jour. Social Issues* 7: 26–29. *Principles of Abnormal Psychology* (Rev. Ed.) (With Bela Mittelmann.) New York: Harper & Bros. "Volunteer-error in the Kinsey Study." (With J. Sakoda.) *Jour. Abnormal and Social Psychol.* 47: 259–262. *The S-I Test (A Measure of Psychological Security-Insecurity)*. Palo Alto, Calif.: Consulting Psychologists Press.

1953 "Love in Healthy People." In Montagu, A. (Ed.), *The Meaning of Love*, New York: Julian Press. "College Teaching Ability, Scholarly Activity, and Personality." (With W. Zimmerman.) *Jour. Educ. Psychol.* 47: 185–189.

1954 "The Instinctoid Nature of Basic Needs." *Jour. Personality* 22: 326–347. *Motivation and Personality.* New York: Harper & Bros. "Abnormal Psychology." "Normality, Health, and Values." *Main Currents* 10: 75–81.

1955 "Deficiency Motivation and Growth Motivation." In Jones, M. R. (Ed.), *Nebraska Symposium on Motivation: 1955*, Univ. of Nebraska Press. Comments on Prof. McClelland's paper. In Jones, M. R. (Ed.), *Nebraska Symposium on Motivation, 1955.* Univ. of Nebraska Press, 65–69. Comments on Prof. Old's paper. In Jones, M. R. (Ed.), *Nebraska Symposium on Motivation, 1955.* Univ. of Nebraska Press, 143–147.

1956 "Effects of Esthetic Surroundings: I. Initial Effects of Three Esthetic Conditions upon Perceiving 'Energy' and 'Well-being' in Faces." (With N. Mintz.) *Jour. Psychol.* 41: 247–254. "Personality Problems and Personality Growth." In Moustakas, C. (Ed.), *The Self*, Harper and Brothers. "Defense and Growth." *Merrill-Palmer Quarterly* 3: 36–47. "A Philosophy of Psychology." *Main Currents* 13: 27–32.

1957 "Power Relationships and Patterns of Personal Development." In Kornhauser, A. (Ed.), *Problems of Power in American Democracy.* Wayne University Press. "Security of Judges as a Factor in Impressions of Warmth in Others." (With J. Bossom.) *Jour. Abnormal and Social Psychol.* 55: 147–148. "Two Kinds of Cognition and Their Integration." *General Semantics Bulletin* 20 & 21: 17–22.

1958 "Emotional Blocks to Creativity." *Jour. Individual Psychol.* 14: 51–56.

1959 "Psychological Data and Human Values." In Maslow, A. H. (Ed.), *New Knowledge in Human Values*, Harper and Brothers. (Editor). *New Knowledge in Human Values*, Harper and Brothers. "Creativity in Self-actualizing People." In Anderson, H. H. (Ed.), *Creativity & Its Cultivation*, Harper and Brothers. "Cognition of Being in the Peak Experiences." *Jour. Genetic Psychol.* 94: 43–66. "Mental Health and Religion." In *Religion, Science, and Mental Health*, Academy of Religion and Mental Health, New York University Press. "Critique of Self-actualization. I. Some Dangers of Being-cognition." *Jour. Individual Psychol.* 15: 24–32.

1960 "Juvenile Delinquency as a Value Disturbance." (With R. Diaz-Guerrero). In Peatman, J., and E. Hartley (Eds.), *Festschrift for Gardner Murphy*, Harper. "Remarks on Existentialism and Psychology." *Existentialist Inquiries* 1: 1–5. "Resistance to Being Rubricized." In Kaplan, B., and S. Wapner (Eds.), *Perspectives in Psychological Theory, Essays in Honor of Heinz Werner*, International Universities Press. "Some Parallels between the Dominance and Sexual Behavior of Monkeys and the Fantasies of Patients in Psychotherapy." (With H. Rand and S. Newman.) *Jour. of Nervous and Mental Disease* 131: 202–212.

1961 "Health as Transcendence of the Environment." *Jour. Humanistic Psychol.* 1: 1–7. "Peak-experiences as Acute Identity Experiences." *Amer. Jour. Psychoanalysis* 21: 254–260. "Eupsychia—The Good Society." *Jour. Humanistic Psychol.* 1: 1–11. "Are Our Publications and Conventions Suitable for the Personal Sciences?" *Amer. Psychologist* 16: 318–319. "Comments on Skinner's Attitude to Science." *Daedalus* 90: 572–573. "Some Frontier Problems in Mental Health." In Combs, A. (Ed.), *Personality Theory and Counseling Practice*, University of Florida Press.

1962 "Some Basic Propositions of a Growth and Self-actualization Psychology." In Combs, A. (Ed.), *Perceiving, Behaving, Becoming: A New Focus for Education. 1962 Yearbook of Association for Supervision and Curriculum Development*, Washington, D.C. *Toward a Psychology of Being*, 2d ed., Van Nostrand, 1968. "Book Review: John Schaar, Escape from Authority." *Humanist* 22: 34–35. "Lessons from the Peak-experiences." *Jour. Humanistic Psychol.* 2: 9–18. "Notes on Being-psychology." *Jour. Humanistic Psychol.* 2: 47–71. "Was Adler a Disciple of Freud? A Note." *Jour. Individual Psychol.* 18: 125. "Summary Comments: Symposium on Human Values." Solomon, L. (Ed.), *WBSI Report* No. 17, 41–44. *Summer Notes on Social Psychology of Industry and Management*, Non-Linear Systems, Inc., Del Mar, Calif.

1963 "The Need to Know and the Fear of Knowing." *Jour. General Psychol.* 68: 111–125. "The Creative Attitude." *The Structurist* 3: 4–10. "Fusions of Facts and Values." *Amer. Jour. Psychoanalysis* 23: 117–131. "Criteria for Judging Needs to be Instinctoid." *Proceedings of 1963 International Congress of Psychology*, Amsterdam: North-Holland Publishers, 86–87. "Further Notes on Being-psychology." *Jour. Humanistic Psychol.* 3: 120–135. "Notes on Innocent Cognition." In Schenk-Danzinger, L., and H. Thomas (Eds.), *Gegenwartsprobleme der Entwicklungspsychologie: Festschrift für Charlotte Bühler*, Verlag für Psychologie, Göttingen, Germany. "The Scientific Study of Values." *Proceedings*

7th Congress of Interamerican Society of Psychology, Mexico, D.F. "Notes on Unstructured Groups." *Human Relations Training News* 7: 1–4.

1964 "The Superior Person." *Trans-action* 1: 10–13. *Religions, Values, and Peak-experiences.* Ohio State Univ. Press. "Synergy in the Society and in the Individual." *Jour. Individual Psychol.* 20: 153–164. (With L. Gross.) "Further Notes on the Psychology of Being." *Jour. Humanistic Psychol.* 4: 45–58. Preface to Japanese translation of *Toward a Psychology of Being*, Seishin-Shobo: Tokyo.

1965 "Observing and Reporting Education Experiments." *Humanist* 25: 13. Foreword to Andras Angyal, *Neurosis & Treatment: A Holistic Theory*, Wiley, v–vii. "The Need for Creative People." *Personnel Administration* 28: 3–5, 21–22. "Critique and Discussion." In Money, J. (Ed.), *Sex Research: New Developments.* Holt, Rinehart & Winston, 135–143, 144–146. "Humanistic Science and Transcendent Experiences." *Jour. Humanistic Psychol.* 5: 219–227. "Criteria for Judging Needs to be Instinctoid." In Jones, M. R. (Ed.), *Human Motivation: A Symposium*, Univ. Nebraska Press, 33–47. *Eupsychian Management: A Journal.* Irwin-Dorsey. "Art Judgment and the Judgment of Others: A Preliminary Study." (With R. Morant.) *Jour. Clinical Psychol.* 21: 389–391.

1966 "Isomorphic Interrelationships between Knower and Known." In Kepes, G. (Ed.), *Sign, Image, Symbol*, Braziller. Reprinted in Matson, F. W., and A. Montagu (Eds.), *The Human Dialogue: Perspectives on Communication.* Free Press, 1966. *The Psychology of Science: A Reconnaissance.* New York: Harper & Row. "Toward a Psychology of Religious Awareness." *Explorations* 9: 23–41. "Comments on Dr. Frankl's Paper." *Jour. Humanistic Psychol.* 6: 107–112.

1967 "Neurosis as a Failure of Personal Growth." *Humanitas* 3: 153–169. "Synanon and Eupsychia," *Jour. Humanistic Psychol.* 7: 28–35. Preface to Japanese translation of *Eupsychian Management.* "A Theory of Metamotivation: The Biological Rooting of the Value-life." *Jour. Humanistic Psychol.* 7: 93–127. "Dialogue on Communication." (With E. M. Drews.) In Hitchcock, A. (Ed.), *Guidance and the Utilization of New Educational Media: Report of the 1962 Conference*, American Personnel and Guidance Association, Washington, D.C., 1–47, 63–68. Foreword to Japanese translation of *Motivation and Personality.* "Self-actualizing and Beyond." In Bugental, J. F. T. (Ed.), *Challenges of Humanistic Psychology*, McGraw-Hill.

1968 "Music Education and Peak-experiences." *Music Educators Jour.* 54: 72–75, 163–171. "The Farther Reaches of Human Nature." *Jour. Transpersonal Psychol.* 1: 1–9. "Human Potentialities and the Healthy Society." In Otto, Herbert (Ed.), *Human Potentialities*, Warren H. Green, Inc., St. Louis, Mo. "The New Science of Man." In papers on *The Human Potential* for the Twentieth Century Fund, New York. *Toward a Psychology of Being*, 2d ed., Van Nostrand. "Conversation with Abraham H. Maslow." *Psychology Today* 2: 35–37, 54–57. "Toward the Study of Violence." In Ng, Larry (Ed.), *Alternatives to Violence*, Time-Life Books. "Some Educational Implications of the Humanistic Psychologies." *Harvard Educational Review* 38: 4, 685–696. "Goals of Humanistic Education." *Esalen Papers.* "Maslow and Self-actualization" (film). Psychological Films, Santa Ana, Calif. "Some Fundamental Questions That Face the Normative Social Psychologist." *Jour. Humanistic Psychol.* 8. *Eupsychian Network.* Mimeographed. (Included in No. 128).

1969 "Theory Z." *Jour. Transpersonal Psychol.* 1 (2): 31:47. "Various Meanings of Transcendence." *Jour. Transpersonal Psychol.* 1: 56–66. Reprinted in *Pastoral Psychol.* 19: 188, 45–49; 1968. "A Holistic Approach to Creativity." In Taylor. C. W. (Ed.), *A Climate for Creativity: Reports of the Seventh National Research Conference on Creativity, University of Utah. The Healthy Personality: Readings.* (With Hung-Min Chiang.) New York: Van Nostrand Reinhold. "Notice biographique et bibliographique." *Revue de Psychologie Appliquee* 18: 167–173. "Toward a Humanistic Biology." *American Psychologist* 24: 724–735. "Humanistic Education vs. Professional Education." *New Directions in Teaching* 2: 6–8.

1970 *Motivation and Personality.* Rev. ed. New York: Harper & Row. "Humanistic Education vs. Professional Education. *New Directions in Teaching* 2: 3–10.

1971 *Farther Reaches of Human Nature.* New York: Viking Press (Esalen Series).

Bibliography

Major Books About Maslow

Frick, Willard B. *Humanistic Psychology: Interviews with Maslow, Murphy, and Rogers.* Columbus: Charles E. Merrill, 1971.
Goble, Frank. *The Third Force: The Psychology of Abraham Maslow.* New York: Grossman Publishers, 1970.
International Study Project. *Abraham Maslow: A Memorial Volume.* Monterey, Calif.: Brooks/Cole, 1972.
Lowry, Richard. *A. H. Maslow: An Intellectual Portrait.* Monterey, Calif.: Brooks/Cole, 1973.
Lowry, Richard, ed. *Dominance, Self-Esteem, and Self-Actualization: Germinal Papers of A. H. Maslow.* Monterey, Calif.: Brooks/Cole, 1973.
———. *The Journals of A. H. Maslow.* Vols. 1 and 2. Monterey, Calif.: Brooks/Cole, 1979.
Wilson, Colin. *New Pathways in Psychology: Maslow and the Post-Freudian Revolution.* New York: New American Library, 1972.

Selected Bibliography

Adler, Alfred. *Social Interest.* Translated by John Linton and Richard Vaughn. New York: Capricorn, 1964.
Adorno, T. W.; Frenkel-Brunswik, Else; Levinson, Daniel J.; and Sanford, R. Nevitt. *The Authoritarian Personality.* New York: Harper & Row, 1950.
Agee, James. "Southeast of the Island: Travel Notes." In *The Collected Short Prose of James Agee,* edited by Robert Fitzgerald. New York: Ballantine, 1970.
Alexander, Franz; Eistenstein, Samuel; and Grotjahn, Martin, eds. *Psychoanalytic Pioneers.* New York: Basic Books, 1966.

Anderson, Walter Truett. *The Upstart Spring: Esalen and the American Awakening.* Reading, Mass.: Addison-Wesley, 1983.

Angyal, Andras. *Foundations for a Science of Personality.* New York: Commonwealth Fund, 1941.

————. *Neurosis and Treatment: A Holistic Theory.* New York: Wiley, 1965.

Ansbacher, Heinz L. "Was Adler a Disciple of Freud? A Reply." *Journal of Individual Psychology* 18 (1962): 126–135.

Ansbacher, Heinz L., and Ansbacher, Rowena R. *The Individual Psychology of Alfred Adler.* New York: Basic Books, 1956.

Ardrey, Robert. *The Territorial Imperative.* New York: Atheneum, 1966.

Argyris, Chris. *Integrating the Individual and the Organization.* New York: Wiley, 1966.

————. *Management and Organizational Development.* New York: McGraw-Hill, 1971.

Aron, Adrienne. "Maslow's Other Child." *Journal of Humanistic Psychology* 17, no. 2 (1977): 9–24.

————. "A Response to Hampden-Turner." *Journal of Humanistic Psychology* 18, no. 1 (1978): 87–88.

Aronoff, Joel, and Wilson, John P. *Personality in the Social Process.* Hillsdale, N.J.: Erlbaum, 1985.

Asch, Solomon. *Social Psychology.* New York: Prentice-Hall, 1952.

Benedict, Ruth. *Patterns of Culture.* Boston: Houghton Mifflin, 1961.

Bennis, Warren, and Nanus, Burt. *Leaders: The Strategies for Taking Charge.* New York: Harper & Row, 1985.

Berger, Brigette, and Berger, Peter. *The War over the Family: Capturing the Middle Ground.* Garden City, N.Y.: Doubleday, 1983.

"Blossoming Brandeis." *Time,* April 13, 1962, 73–74.

Bodkin, Maud. *Archetypal Patterns in Poetry.* London: Oxford University Press, 1934.

Bolman, Lee G., and Deal, Terrence E. *Modern Approaches to Understanding and Managing Organizations.* San Francisco: Jossey-Bass, 1984.

Boorstein, Seymour, ed. *Transpersonal Psychotherapy.* Palo Alto, Calif.: Science and Behavior Books, 1980.

Bottome, Phyllis. *Alfred Adler: A Biography.* New York: Putnam and Sons, 1939.

Bradford, Leland P.; Gibb, Jack R.; and Benne, Kenneth D., eds. *T-group Theory and Laboratory Method.* New York: Wiley, 1964.

Bugental, James F. T., ed. *Challenges of Humanistic Psychology.* New York: McGraw-Hill, 1967.

Buss, Allan R. "Humanistic Psychology as Liberal Ideology: The Socio-historical Roots of Maslow's Theory of Self-actualization." *Journal of Humanistic Psychology* 19, no. 3 (Summer 1979): 43–55.

Cheney, Sheldon. *Men Who Have Walked with God.* New York: Knopf, 1956.

Christenson, Cornelia. *Kinsey: A Biography.* Bloomington, Ind.: Indiana University Press, 1971.

Christman, Henry M., ed. *One Hundred Years of the Nation.* New York: Macmillan, 1965.

Coser, Lewis A. *Refugee Scholars in America, Their Impact and Their Experiences.* New Haven, Conn.: Yale University Press, 1984.

Coulton, Thomas Evans. *A City College in Action.* New York: Harper & Brothers, 1955.

Curti, Merle, and Carstensen, Vernon. "The University of Wisconsin: To 1925." In *University of Wisconsin*, edited by Allen G. Bogue and Robert Taylor. Madison, Wis.: University of Wisconsin Press, 1975.

Dalton, Melville. *Men Who Manage*. New York: Wiley, 1959.

Davis, John William, ed. *Value and Valuation, Axiological Studies in Honor of Robert S. Hartman*. Knoxville, Tenn.: University of Tennessee Press, 1972.

Davis, Keith, ed. *Organizational Behavior: A Book of Readings*. New York: McGraw-Hill, 1977.

Dennis, Lawrence J. "Maslow and Education." *Education Digest*, March 1976, 32–36.

Deutsch, Felix, ed. *On the Mysterious Leap from the Mind to the Body*. New York: International Universities Press, 1959.

Dreikurs, Rudolf. *Fundamentals of Adlerian Psychology*. Chicago: Alfred Adler Institute, 1953.

Drucker, Peter F. *The Practice of Management*. New York: Harper, 1954.
———. *The Frontiers of Management*. New York: Truman Talley Books, 1986.

DuBois, Cora. *The People of Alor*. With analyses by Abram Kardiner and Emil Oberholzer. Cambridge, Mass.: Harvard University Press, 1960.

Easley, Edgar M., and Wigglesworth, David C. "Jonestown in the Shadow of Maslow's Pyramid." *Humanist*, July 1979, 41–43.

Eliade, Mircea. *The Sacred and the Profane*. New York: Harcourt, Brace & World, 1959.

Elkind, David. "Erich Fromm (1900–1980)." *American Psychologist* 36, no. 5 (May 1981): 521–522.

Ellis, Willis D., ed. *A Source Book of Gestalt Psychology*. New York: Humanities Press, 1950.

Erikson, Erik. *Childhood and Society*. New York: W. W. Norton, 1950.

Esalen Institute Programs. Big Sur, Calif.: Esalen Institute, 1966–1970.

Etzioni, Amitai. "A Creative Adaptation to a World of Rising Shortages." *Annals of the American Academy* 420 (July 1975): 98–110.

Ewers, John C. *The Blackfeet: Raiders on the Northern Plains*. Norman, Okla.: University of Oklahoma Press, 1958.

Fernandez-Marina, Ramon; Maldonado-Sierra, Eduardo; and Trent, Richard C. "Three Basic Themes in Mexican and Puerto Rican Family Values." *Journal of Social Psychology* 48 (1958): 167–181.

Fernberger, Samuel W. "The American Psychological Association: A Historical Summary, 1892–1930." *Psychological Bulletin* 29, no. 1 (January 1932): 1–89.

Fine, Reuben. *A History of Psychoanalysis*. New York: Columbia University Press, 1979.

Fisher, A. D. "Indian Land Policy and the Settler-State in Colonial Western Canada." In *Essays on the Political Economy of Alberta*, edited by David Leadbeater. Toronto: New Hugtown Press, 1984.

Fong-Torres, Ben. "Kaypro Fights Back." *Microtimes*, February 1986, 28, 29, 32.

Frankl, Viktor. *From Death Camp to Existentialism*. (Later retitled: *Man's Search for Meaning*.) Boston: Beacon, 1963.
———. *Psychotherapy and Existentialism*. New York: Washington Square Press, 1967.

Friedan, Betty. *The Feminine Mystique*. New York: W. W. Norton, 1974.

Fromm, Erich. *Escape from Freedom*. New York: Farrar, 1941.

_____. *Man for Himself.* New York: Rinehart, 1947.

_____. *The Sane Society.* New York: Rinehart, 1955.

_____. *Current Biography, 1967,* p. 129.

Gard, Robert E. *University Madison U.S.A.* Madison, Wis.: Wisconsin House, 1970.

Gillenson, Lewis G. "Brandeis, A Young University in a Hurry." *Saturday Review,* March 17, 1962, 82–83, 100–103.

Golden, Harry. *Travels through Jewish America.* Garden City, N.Y.: Doubleday, 1973.

Goldfarb, William. "David M. Levy 1892–1977." *American Journal of Psychiatry* 134, no. 8 (August 1977): 934.

_____. *Changing Configurations in the Social Organization of a Blackfoot Tribe During the Reserve Period.* Monographs of the American Ethnological Society. Seattle, Wa.: University of Washington Press, 1945.

Goldstein, Kurt. *The Organism.* New York: American Book Company, 1939.

_____. *Language and Language Disturbance.* New York: Grune and Stratton, 1948.

_____. *Human Nature.* Cambridge, Mass.: Harvard University Press, 1951.

_____. *The Human Organism.* Cambridge, Mass.: Harvard University Press, 1951.

_____. "The So-Called Drives." In Clark Moustakas, *The Self.* New York: Harper & Row, 1956.

Goldstein, Kurt, and Scheerer, Martin. *Abstract and Concrete Behavior: An Experimental Study with Special Tests.* Evanston, Ill.: Northwestern University and the American Psychological Association, 1964.

Golemiewski, Robert T., and Blumberg, Arthur, eds. *Sensitivity Training and the Laboratory Approach,* 2d edition. Itasca, Ill.: Peacock Publishers, 1973.

Goodheart, Eugene. "The New York Review: A Close Look." *Dissent* (March 1970): 135–143.

Goodman, R. A. *On the Operationality of the Maslow Need Hierarchy.* Los Angeles: University of California at Los Angeles, Graduate School of Business, Division of Research, 1985.

Grinnell, George Bird. *Blackfoot Lodge Tales.* Lincoln, Neb.: University of Nebraska Press, 1962.

Grof, Stanislav. *Beyond the Brain.* Albany, N.Y.: State University of New York Press, 1985.

Gross, Lawrence. "Abraham H. Maslow: The Mystery of Health." Unpublished ms. Philadelphia: University of Pennsylvania, Department of Communications, 1964.

Grossman, Richard. *The Other Medicines.* Garden City, N.Y.: Doubleday, 1985.

_____. "Some Reflections on Abraham Maslow." Paper read at the twenty-fifth anniversary conference, Association of Humanistic Psychology, and Division 32, American Psychological Association, San Francisco, March 8, 1985.

Hahn, Emily. *On the Side of the Apes.* New York: Crowell, 1971.

Hampden-Turner, Charles. "Comment on 'Maslow's Other Child.' " *Journal of Humanistic Psychology* 17, no. 2 (Spring 1977): 25–31.

Hanfmann, Eugenia; Jones, Richard M.; Baker, Elliot; and Kovler, Leo. *Psychological Counseling in a Small College.* Cambridge, Mass.: Schenkman Publishing, 1963.

Hanks, Lucien M., and Hanks-Richardson, Jane. *Tribe under Trust: A Study of the Blackfoot Reserve of Alberta.* Toronto: University of Toronto Press, 1950.

Harlow, Harry. *Learning to Love.* New York: Aronson, 1974.

Hartley, Eugene L. "Gardner Murphy (1895–1979)." *American Psychologist* 35, no. 4 (April 1980): 383–385.

Hartman, Robert S. *The Structure of Value: Foundations of Scientific Axiology.* Carbondale, Ill.: Southern Illinois University Press, 1967.

Hartmann, George W. *Gestalt Psychology: A Survey of Facts and Principles.* New York: Ronald Press, 1935.

Hausdorff, Don. *Erich Fromm.* New York: Twayne, 1972.

Hayakawa, S. I. *Language in Thought and Action.* New York: Harcourt Brace Jovanovich, 1972.

Heilbut, Anthony. *Exiled in Paradise.* New York: Viking, 1983.

Heiman, Nanette, and Grant, Joan, eds. *Psychological Issues.* New York: International Universities Press, 1974.

Henle, Mary, ed. *Documents of Gestalt Psychology.* Berkeley, Calif.: University of California Press, 1961.

Herzberg, Frederick; Mausner, Bernard; and Synderman, Barbara. *The Motivation to Work.* New York: Wiley, 1959.

Hoffman, Abbie. *Soon to Be a Major Motion Picture.* New York: Berkley, 1982.

Hoffman, Edward. *The Way of Splendor: Jewish Mysticism and Modern Psychology.* Boulder, Colo.: Shambhala, 1981.

———. *The Heavenly Ladder: The Jewish Guide to Inner Growth.* San Francisco: Harper & Row, 1985.

Horney, Karen. *The Neurotic Personality of Our Time.* New York: W. W. Norton, 1937.

———. *New Ways in Psychoanalysis.* New York: W. W. Norton, 1939.

———. *Self-analysis.* New York: W. W. Norton, 1942.

———. *Neurosis and Human Growth.* New York: W. W. Norton, 1950.

Horowitz, Murray M. *Brooklyn College: The First Half-Century.* Brooklyn, N.Y.: Brooklyn College Press, 1981.

Hothersall, David. *History of Psychology.* New York: Random House, 1984.

Howard, Jane. *Margaret Mead: A Life.* New York: Simon & Schuster, 1984.

Howe, Irving. *The World of Our Fathers.* New York: Harcourt Brace Jovanovich, 1976.

———. *A Margin of Hope.* New York: Harcourt Brace Jovanovich, 1982.

Hull, Clark L. "Psychology of the Scientist: IV. Passages from the 'Idea Books' of Clark L. Hull." *Perceptual and Motor Skills* 15 (1962): 807–882.

Huxley, Aldous. *Brave New World.* New York: Harper & Row, 1946.

———. *Moksha.* Edited by Michael Horowitz and Cynthia Palmer. Los Angeles: Tarcher, 1982.

Ingraham, Mark H. "The University of Wisconsin, 1925–1950." In *University of Wisconsin,* edited by Allen G. Bogue and Robert Taylor. Madison, Wis.: University of Wisconsin Press, 1975.

James, William. *The Varieties of Religious Experience.* New York: Modern Library, 1936.

———. *Pragmatism and Other Essays.* New York: Washington Square Press, 1963.

Jay, Phyllis. "Field Studies." In *Behavior of Nonhuman Primates*, edited by Allan M. Schrier, Harry F. Harlow, and Fred Stollnitz. New York: Academic Press, 1965.

Joncich, Geraldine. *The Sane Positivist: A Biography of Edward L. Thorndike*. Middletown, Conn.: Wesleyan University Press, 1968.

Jones, Ernest. *The Life and Work of Sigmund Freud*. Edited and abridged in one volume by Lionel Trilling and Steven Marcus. New York: Basic Books, 1961.

Joseph, Samuel. *Jewish Immigration to the United States from 1881 to 1910*. New York: Arno, 1969.

Journal of Transpersonal Psychology 1, no. 1 (1969): statement of purpose.

Kardiner, Abram. *The Individual and His Society*. New York: Columbia University Press, 1939.

———. *Sex and Morality*. London: Routledge & Kegan Paul, 1955.

———. *My Analysis with Freud*. New York: W. W. Norton, 1977.

Kardiner, Abram, and Preble, Edward. *They Studied Man*. London: Secker and Warburg, 1962.

Kelman, Harold. *Advances in Psychoanalysis: Contributions to Karen Horney's Holistic Approach*. New York: W. W. Norton, 1964.

Kirschenbaum, Howard. *On Becoming Carl Rogers*. New York: Delacorte Press, 1979.

Knecht, G. Bruce. "Andrew Kay and Sons and Daughters and Father and Wife Are #4 in Computers." *Financial Enterprise*, Winter 1984/85, 3–5.

Koffka, Kurt. *Principles of Gestalt Psychology*. New York: Harcourt Brace, 1935.

Köhler, Wolfgang. *The Place of Value in a World of Facts*. New York: Liveright, 1966.

———. *The Task of Gestalt Psychology*. Princeton, N.J.: Princeton University Press, 1969.

———. "Max Wertheimer 1880–1943." *Psychological Review* 51 (1944): 143–146.

Kristol, Irving. *Reflections of a Neo-conservative*. New York: Basic Books, 1983.

Kuriloff, Arthur H. "An Experiment in Management—Putting Theory Y to the Test." *Personnel*, November/December 1963, 8–17.

Landesman, Alter F. *Brownsville*. New York: Bloch, 1971.

Landis, Bernard, and Tauber, Edward S. *In the Name of Life: Essays in Honor of Erich Fromm*. New York: Holt, Rinehart and Winston, 1971.

LaSale, Angela J. C. "Another Look at Maslow's Motivational Hierarchy." *Psychological Reports* 48 (1981): 938.

Laski, Margharita. *Ecstasy*. Bloomington, Ind.: Indiana University Press, 1962.

Leary, Timothy. *Flashbacks*. Los Angeles: Tarcher, 1983.

Leavitt, Harold. *Managerial Psychology*, 4th ed. Chicago: University of Chicago Press, 1978.

Leonard, George. "Abraham Maslow and the New Self." *Esquire*, December 1983, 326–335.

Levy, David M. *Maternal Overprotection*. New York: Columbia University Press, 1943.

Levy, David, and Munroe, Ruth. *The Happy Family*. New York: Knopf, 1947.

Likert, Rensis. *New Patterns of Management*. New York: McGraw-Hill, 1961.

McCullough, David W. *Brooklyn: A City of Neighborhoods and People.* New York: Dial, 1983.

McGregor, Douglas. *The Human Side of Enterprise.* New York: McGraw-Hill, 1960.

Mann, W. Edward, and Hoffman, Edward. *The Man Who Dreamed of Tomorrow: A Conceptual Biography of Wilhelm Reich.* Los Angeles: Tarcher, 1980.

Manuel, Frank. *Shapes of Philosophical History.* Stanford, Calif.: Stanford University Press, 1965.

Manuel, Frank, and Manuel, Fritzie. *Utopian Thought in the Western World.* Cambridge, Mass.: Belknap Press, 1979.

Marrow, Alfred J., ed. *The Failure of Success.* New York: American Management Association, 1972.

Matson, Floyd. *The Broken Image.* Garden City, N.Y.: George Braziller, 1964.

May, Rollo. *The Meaning of Anxiety.* New York: Ronald Press, 1950.

May, Rollo, ed. *Existential Psychology.* New York: Random House, 1969.

May, Rollo, ed. *Politics and Innocence: A Humanistic Debate.* Dallas: Saybrook, 1986.

Mead, Margaret. *Ruth Benedict.* New York: Columbia University Press, 1974.

————. "Ruth Fulton Benedict 1887–1948." *American Anthropologist* 51 (1949): 457–468.

Metzner, Ralph. *Opening to Inner Light.* Los Angeles: Tarcher, 1986.

Miller, Douglas T., and Nowak, Marion. *The Fifties.* Garden City, N.Y.: Doubleday, 1977.

Mintz, Alan L. "Encounter Groups and Other Panaceas." *Commentary,* July 1973, 42–49.

Mitchell, Arnold. *The Nine American Lifestyles.* New York: Macmillan, 1983.

Modell, Judith Schacter. *Ruth Benedict: Patterns of a Life.* Philadelphia: University of Pennsylvania Press, 1983.

Morant, Ricardo. "Eugenia Hanfmann: Memorial Minute." Unpublished paper. Waltham, Mass.: Brandeis University, Department of Psychology, September 16, 1983.

————. "In Memoriam to Harry Rand." Unpublished paper. Waltham, Mass.: Brandeis University, Department of Psychology, undated.

Munroe, Ruth L. *Schools of Psychoanalytic Thought.* New York: Holt, Rinehart and Winston, 1955.

Murchison, Carl, ed. *Psychologies of 1925.* Worcester, Mass.: Clark University Press, 1927.

"No-Assembly-Line Plan Gets Nothing But Results." *Steel,* May 25, 1964, 90–91.

Oates, Joyce Carol. "The Potential of Normality." *Saturday Review,* August 26, 1972, 53–55.

Obendorf, Clarence P. *A History of Psychoanalysis in America.* New York: Harper & Row, 1953.

Peters, Tom, and Austin, Nancy. *A Passion for Excellence.* New York: Random House, 1985.

Polanyi, Michael. *Science, Faith, and Society.* Chicago: University of Chicago Press, 1964.

Pomeroy, Wardell B. *Dr. Kinsey and the Institute for Sex Research.* New York: Harper & Row, 1972.

Rand, Ayn. *The Fountainhead.* New York: New American Library, 1943.

Riesman, David. *Individualism Reconsidered.* Glencoe, Ill.: Free Press, 1954.

Roazen, Paul. *Freud and His Followers.* New York: Meridian, 1976.

Roback, A. A. *History of American Psychology.* New York: Library Publishers, 1952.

Roberts, Thomas B. "Maslow's Human Motivation Needs Hierarchy: A Bibliography." *Research in Education,* 1973, ERIC document ED 069-591.

Rogers, Carl R. *Counseling and Psychotherapy.* Boston: Houghton Mifflin, 1942.

Royce, Earl. *Corporate Responsibility Planning Service: Personnel Management and Development, Program Profile.* Menlo Park, Calif.: Saga Corporation, June 11, 1976.

Rubins, Jack L. *Karen Horney: Gentle Rebel of Psychoanalysis.* New York: Dial Press, 1978.

Rudy, S. Willis. *The College of the City of New York: A History.* New York: City College Press, 1949.

Rutkoff, Peter M., and Scott, William B. *New School: A History of the New School for Social Research.* New York: Free Press, 1986.

Sachar, Abram L. *A Host at Last.* Boston: Little, Brown, 1976.

Saga Fact Book. Menlo Park, Calif.: Saga Corporation, September 1983.

Sanders, Ronald. *The Downtown Jews.* New York: Harper & Row, 1969.

Schein, Edgar H., and Bennis, Warren G. *Personal and Organizational Change through Group Methods.* New York: Wiley, 1965.

Schulberg, Budd. *What Makes Sammy Run?* New York: Random House, 1941.

Schwartz, Howard S. "Maslow and the Hierarchical Enactment of Organizational Reality." *Human Relations* 36, no. 10 (1983): 933–956.

Scroth, Raymond A. *The Eagle and Brooklyn.* Westport, Conn.: Greenwood, 1973.

Sears, Robert R. "Harry Frederick Harlow." *American Psychologist* 37, no. 11 (November 1982): 1280–1281.

Seidler, Murray B. *Norman Thomas.* Syracuse, N.Y.: Syracuse University Press, 1967.

Sheldon, William H. *The Varieties of Temperament.* New York: Harper & Row, 1942.

Simmel, Marianne L., ed. *The Reach of Mind: Essays in Memory of Kurt Goldstein.* New York: Springer, 1968.

Skinner, B. F. *Walden Two.* New York: Macmillan, 1948.

Smith, Brewster. "On Self-actualization: A Transambivalent Examination of a Focal Theme in Maslow's Psychology." *Journal of Humanistic Psychology* 13, no. 2 (Spring 1973): 17–33.

Sorokin, Pitirim A. *A Long Journey.* New Haven, Conn.: College and University Press, 1963.

Stagner, Ross. "Reminiscences about the Founding of SPSSI." *Journal of Social Issues* 42, no. 1 (Spring 1986): 35–42.

Storr, Anthony. "Book Review." *Encounter* 41 (November 1973): 85–92.

Sumner, William Graham. *Folkways.* New York: Ginn and Company, 1940.

Sutich, Anthony. "The Growth-experience and the Growth-centered Attitude." *Journal of Psychology* 28 (1949): 293–301.

Sykes, Gerald. *The Hidden Remnant.* New York: Harper & Brothers, 1962.

Tannenbaum, Robert; Wechler, Irving R.; and Massarik, Fred. *Leadership and Organization.* New York: McGraw-Hill, 1961.

Tannenbaum, Robert; Margulies, Newton; and Massarik, Fred. *Human Systems Development.* San Francisco: Jossey-Bass, 1985.

Tanzer, Deborah. *Why Natural Childbirth?* New York: Schocken, 1976.

Tolman, Edward C. *Drives Toward War.* New York: D. Appleton-Century, 1942.

Toman, Walter. *Family Constellation.* New York: Springer, 1976.

Vivas, Eliseo. *Two Roads to Ignorance.* Carbondale, Ill.: Southern Illinois University Press, 1979.

Walsh, Roger, and Shapiro, Deane H. *Beyond Health and Normality.* New York: Van Nostrand, Reinhold, 1983.

Watson, David Lindsay. *Scientists Are Human.* New York: Arno Press, 1975.

Watson, John B. "Experimental Studies on the Growth of the Emotions." In *Psychologies of 1925,* edited by Carl Murchison. Worcester, Mass.: Clark University Press, 1927.

———. "Recent Changes on How We Lose and Change Our Emotional Equipment." In *Psychologies of 1925,* edited by Carl Murchison. Worcester, Mass.: Clark University Press, 1927.

———. "What the Nursery Has to Say About Instincts." In *Psychologies of 1925,* edited by Carl Murchison. Worcester, Mass.: Clark University Press, 1927.

Watson, Robert I. *The Great Psychologists.* Philadelphia: Lippincott, 1978.

Way, Lewis. *Adler's Place in Psychology.* New York: Collier, 1962.

Weisskopf, Walter. *The Psychology of Economics.* Chicago: University of Chicago Press, 1955.

Wendland, Leonard V. "Book Review: Motivation and Personality." *Personalist* 37 (1956): 185.

Wertheimer, Max. *Productive Thinking.* Chicago: University of Chicago Press, 1982.

"Where Being Nice to Workers Didn't Work." *Business Week,* January 20, 1973, 99–100.

Wilson, Colin. *The Stature of Man.* Boston: Houghton Mifflin, 1959.

———. *The Outsider.* London: Arthur Barker, 1964.

———. *Introduction to the New Existentialism.* Boston: Houghton Mifflin, 1967.

Wilson, James Q., and Herrnstein, Richard J. *Crime and Human Nature.* New York: Simon & Schuster, 1985.

Wilson, Sloan. *The Man in the Grey Flannel Suit.* New York: Simon & Schuster, 1955.

Wolff, Michael F. "Riding the Biggest Wave." *Spectrum,* December 1984, 66–71.

Wolff, Werner. *The Expression of Personality.* New York: Harper & Brothers, 1943.

———. *Diagrams of the Unconscious: Handwriting and Personality in Measurement, Experiment, and Analysis.* New York: Grune and Stratton, 1948.

Yankelovich, Daniel. *New Rules.* New York: Random House, 1981.

Zuckerman, Solly. *From Apes to Warlords.* New York: Harper & Row, 1978.

———. *The Social Life of Monkeys and Apes,* 2d ed. London: Routledge & Kegan Paul, 1981.

Notes

Bertha Maslow has brought to my attention that her husband always signed his name professionally as Abraham H. Maslow. For purposes of readability, I have taken the liberty of dropping his middle initial throughout this book.

The reader should be aware that Maslow's published journals were slightly edited for various reasons. In particular, negative references to living individuals were expurgated.

Notes refer to books and articles listed in the Bibliography and to the following sources.

Abbreviations

AI	Author's interview.
J1	Lowry, Richard (editor). *The Journals of A. H. Maslow, volume 1.*
J2	Lowry, Richard (editor). *The Journals of A. H. Maslow, volume 2.*
LA	Unpublished letter to author.
MA	Unpublished letter or paper, Maslow collection, History of American Psychology Archives, University of Akron.
MD	Abraham Maslow's diary, Bertha Maslow's possession.

Chapter One: A Brooklyn Boyhood

1. "I was a terribly unhappy"   MA, Dorothy Lee seminar, October 1960, 6. "A Conversation with the President of the American Psychological Association," *Psychology Today*, July 1968, 36.   **2.** "I tested these various" MA, Lee seminar, op. cit., 10–11.   **2.** "To me, as"   MA, Lawrence Gross, "Abraham H. Maslow: The Mystery of Health," October 1963, 80.   **3.** "When I was a boy"   Film, *On Being Abraham Maslow*, 1969.   **3.** "I used to get up"   Ibid.   **3.** "When I finished"   J1, 232.   **4.** "I wanted to be"   MA, Lee seminar, op. cit., 8.   **4.** "horrible bitch" Colin Wilson, *New Pathways in Psychology*, 117.   **4.** "that smart Jew" AI, Bertha Maslow, 1987.   **4.** "I was just"   Wilson, op. cit., 118.   **4.** "My earliest recollection"   MD, 1932, unpaged.   **5.** "a freak with two heads"   J1, 372.   **5.** "I was a very ugly child"   MA, Gross, op. cit., 80.   **6.** "Isn't Abe the"   AI, Ann Kaplan, 1986.   **6.** "to spare others the sight"   J2, 835.   **6.** "My childhood and boyhood"   MD, 1932, unpaged.   **8.** "schizophrenogenic"   MA, Gross, op. cit., 82.   **9.** "What I had reacted to"   J2, 958.   **10.** "It wasn't until"   MA, Lee seminar, op. cit., 11.   **11.** "I was taught by rote"   Ibid., 16.   **11.** "You see!" Ibid. AI, Bertha Maslow, 1986.

Major interview sources were Ann Kaplan, Frank Manuel, Bertha Maslow, Harold Maslow, Will Maslow, and Ricardo Morant.

Chapter Two: Struggles of the Mind

12. "Humanistic concerns were"   Willard Frick, *Humanistic Psychology*, 19.   **12.** "I remember as a youngster"   MA, Gross, op. cit., 91.   **12.** "It taught me all"   David McCullough, *Brooklyn: A City of Neighborhoods and People*, 223.   **13.** "The Gold Dust Twins"   AI, Will Maslow, 1983.   **13.** "In general, I tried"   MD, 1932, unpaged.   **14.** "I feel lousy"   MD, April 22, 1924.   **15.** "I remember, I think"   MD, January 31, 1932.   **17.** "It was just inconceivable"   MA, transcribed tape to Colin Wilson, 1969.   **17.** "I signed up"   Maslow, *Farther Reaches of Human Nature*, 237.   **19.** "I am a student"   MD, 1925, unpaged.   **20.** "All my begging"   MA, tape to Wilson, op. cit.   **20.** "A man formulates"   MD, July 31, 1926.   **20.** *"Music, let it be known"*   MD, undated, unpaged.   **21.** "Nature presents to us"   Ibid.   **22.** "How stupid at bottom"   Ibid.   **23.** "seemed to deal only"   Wilson, op. cit., 119.   **24.** "Well, then, what"   MA, tape to Wilson, op. cit.   **24.** "I wanted to flee"   Ibid.   **25.** "It was very beautiful"   Ibid.   **25.** "In the entire time"   Ibid.   **26.** "Why does everyone"   AI, Will Maslow, 1983.   **26.** "awful and bloodless"   J1, 277.   **26.** "The right to"   David Hothersall, *History of Psychology*, 102.   **28.** "I am reminded"   Maslow, *Farther Reaches*, 235.   **29.** "For the love of Pete"   MA, Lee seminar, op. cit., 11.   **29.** "I was accepted"   Wilson, op. cit., 121.   **29.** "a Mount Everest"   "A Conversation with the President of the American Psychological Association," op. cit., 57.   **29.** "This is exactly"   Maslow, unpublished journal note, 1962.   **30.** "In the course of"   William Graham Sumner, *Folkways*, 254.   **31.** "Every civilized society"   Ibid., 50.   **31.** "I had a great feeling"   J1, 580.   **33.** "The thing that really"   J1, 277.   **33.** "In high excitement"   J1, 164.   **34.** "Civilization has"   John B.

Watson, in Clark Murchison (editor), *Psychologies of 1925*, 38.
34. "Give me a dozen" Ibid., 10.   **34.** "I was confident" "A Conversation with the President of the American Psychological Association," op. cit., 37.

Major interview sources were Ann Kaplan, Bertha Maslow, Harold Maslow, and Will Maslow.

Chapter Three: The Making of a Psychologist

35. "I wanted to be" MA, Gross, op. cit., 92.   **36.** "I took hot water" J2, 1240.   **36.** "I was looking for" MA, tape to Wilson, op. cit. **36.** "What did I think" Ibid.   **38.** "He fed us" Ibid.   **38.** "There was dinner" Ibid.   **38.** "[my] blessed graduate" Ibid.   **39.** "I drank dago" J2, 899.   **39.** "All my professors" J1, 278.   **40.** "It may sound peculiar" Ibid.   **40.** "the last despairing" MA, course paper, 1929.   **40.** "Our earth" MA, course paper. Oct. 23, 1928.   **42.** "psychology differs" MA, "Psychology as a Science," 1931, 10.   **42.** "About 1932" MA, "More Personal Notes," June 4, 1970, 1.   **43.** "Psychoanalysis acts" MA, "The Necessity of a Social Philosophy of Mental Hygiene and Psychoanalysis," 1932, 1.   **43.** "In our society" Ibid., 3. **45.** "did a great job" LA, Richard W. Husband, 1986.   **45.** "[Maslow] made" MA, Harry F. Harlow, "Reminiscences of Maslow," 1972, 2. **46.** "Well, you know" AI, Lucien Hanks, 1986.   **46.** "I have decided" MD, 1930, unpaged.   **47.** "They are all so cautious" Ibid.

Major interview sources were Lucien Hanks, Bertha Maslow, Emmanuel Piore, B. F. Skinner, Ross Stagner, and Eliseo Vivas.

Chapter Four: Monkey Man

49. "My primate research" J2, 851.   **49.** "My work with monkeys" Maslow, *Farther Reaches*, 16.   **49.** "Abe [Maslow] never" MA, Harlow, op. cit., 5.   **50.** "Hello, do you know" Ibid., 1.   **50.** "We tore it down" Emily Hahn, *On the Side of the Apes*, 74.   **51.** "the nicest and sweetest" Ibid.   **51.** "The fact is that" Maslow, *Farther Reaches*, 16. **53.** "The emphasis here" MD, January 5, 1932, unpaged.   **53.** "They all remind me" Ibid.   **54.** "My plans for the future" MA, letter to Robert Yerkes, February 11, 1932.   **54.** "To be quite frank" Ibid. **55.** "I have just received" MA, letter to Maslow, February 22, 1932. **55.** "Since you have so" MA, letter to Maslow, March 10, 1932. **55.** "If my application for" MA, letter to Yerkes, March 14, 1932. **56.** "As we ascend" Maslow, "Appetites and Hungers in Animal Motivation," *Journal of Comparative Psychology* 20 (1935), 82.   **56.** "It is possible" Ibid., 76.   **57.** "The reason I" J2, 800.   **58.** "the object of which" MA, description of doctoral thesis, 1933, 1.   **58.** "I consider one" Ibid., 2.   **58.** "I was told" Ibid., 3.   **59.** "I paid all expenses" LA, Richard W. Husband, 1986.   **59.** "The film opened" Ibid. **60.** "The screwing" Wilson, op. cit., 139.   **61.** "sexual behavior is" Maslow, "The Role of Dominance in the Social and Sexual Behavior of Infrahuman Primates: III. A Theory of Sexual Behavior of Infra-human Primates," *Journal of Genetic Psychology* 48 (1936), 321.   **62.** "To say that" MA,

Harlow, op. cit., 4.   **63.** "a royal road to knowledge"   Maslow, *Farther Reaches*, 116.   **63.** "There was a university rule"   Ibid.   **65.** "Violently disinterested year"   J1, 231.   **66.** "I was in the medical school" MA, "The Taboo of Tenderness: The Disease of Valuelessness," 1965, 8.

Major interview sources were Lucien Hanks, Bertha Maslow, and Ross Stagner.

Chapter Five: Explorer of Sex and Dominance

69. "I thought that"   "A Conversation with the President of the American Psychological Association," op. cit., 54.   **69.** "We had no"   MD, April 23, 1935, unpaged.   **70.** "For the first"   Ibid.   **70.** "A. H. Maslow" *Milwaukee Sentinel*, May 9, 1935, 1.   **71.** "How different things"   MD, July 31, 1935, unpaged.   **71.** "They gave me"   MA, Gross, op. cit., 93. **71.** "the nature and"   Edward L. Thorndike, *Human Nature in the Social Order*, 3.   **72.** "to determine the"   MA, tape to Wilson, op. cit. **72.** "I feel a"   MA, "A Statement on the Instinct Problem," August 1935, 1.   **72.** "If a certain"   Ibid., 2.   **73.** "Human nature is"   Ibid. **73.** "This is not"   Ibid., 4.   **73.** "This viewpoint differs"   Ibid. **74.** "I was [already]"   *On Being Abraham Maslow* (film), 1969.   **74.** "I dislike your"   MA, tape to Wilson, op. cit.   **74.** "I went off"   Film, "On Being Abraham Maslow," 1969.   **74.** "Do you know"   AI, Max Lerner, 1987.   **75.** "Your application for"   MA, letter from National Research Council, November 11, 1935.   **75.** "I thought that"   "A Conversation with the President of the American Psychological Association," op. cit., 54. **77.** "I was still"   Wilson, op. cit., 127.   **78.** "Do you ever"   MA, "Interview for Women," 1935.   **78.** "What kinds of"   Ibid., 2.   **78.** "for the good"   AI, Lucien Hanks, 1986.   **78.** "Do you often"   Maslow, "Test for Dominance-feeling (Self-esteem) in College Women," *Journal of Social Psychology* 12 (1940), 267–268.   **79.** "This experiment was" Maslow, "The Influence of Familiarization on Preferences," *Journal of Experimental Psychology* 21 (1937), 162.   **79.** "He urged me"   Geraldine Joncich, *The Sane Positivist*, 480.   **80.** "the solution of"   Abraham Maslow and Walter Grether, "An Experimental Study of Insight in Monkeys," *Journal of Comparative Psychology* 24 (1937), 127.   **81.** "The very definite"   Maslow, "Dominance-feeling, Behavior, and Status," *Psychological Review* 44 (1937), 418.   **81.** "It is interesting"   Ibid., 428. **83.** "practically all the"   Maslow, "Self-esteem (Dominance-feeling) and Sexuality in Women," *Journal of Social Psychology* 16 (1942), 282. **83.** "will always have"   Ibid., 267.   **83.** "sex [becomes] a"   Ibid., 291. **84.** "One day, it"   "A Conversation with the President of the American Psychological Association," op. cit., 54.   **85.** "I think that"   Joncich, op. cit., 540.

Major interview sources were Walter Grether, Lucien Hanks, Bertha Maslow, and Ross Stagner.

Chapter Six: At the Center of the Psychological Universe

86. "[Returning] to New York"   MA, Gross, op. cit., 86.   **87.** "The center of"   Frank Goble, *The Third Force*, 12.   **87.** "I never met Freud" Ibid.   **94.** "There seem to be"   Max Wertheimer, "Some Problems in

the Theory of Ethics," in Mary Henle, *Documents of Gestalt Psychology,* 40.
94. "Are there not"   Max Wertheimer, "A Story of Three Days," in Henle,
62.   **96.** "Wertheimer was probably"   J1, 293.   **99.** "I am a schizophrenic"   Jack L. Rubins, *Karen Horney, Gentle Rebel of Psychoanalysis,*
249.   **105.** "lie and a swindle"   Maslow, "Was Adler a Disciple of Freud?
A Note." *Journal of Individual Psychology* 18 (1962), 125.   **105.** "Well,
are you for me"   J2, 745.

Major interview sources were Heinz Ansbacher, Lewis Coser, Lucien Hanks,
and Bertha Maslow.

Chapter Seven: Idylls with the Blackfoot Indians

111. "As things stood"   Maslow, *Farther Reaches,* 192.   **111.** "The first
and foremost"   Maslow, *Motivation and Personality,* 144.   **113.** "These
years of"   Margaret Mead, "Ruth Fulton Benedict," *American Anthropologist* 51 (1949), 460.   **113.** "The anthropologist can teach"   Maslow,
"Personality and Patterns of Culture," in R. Stagner (editor), *Psychology of
Personality,* 409, 418.   **114.** "The biologist is able"   Ibid., 419.
115. "I did the Blackfoot fieldwork"   J1, 331.   **117.** "Some of the
chiefs"   AI, Lucien Hanks, 1986.   **118.** "That wasn't the way"   AI,
Jane Richardson, 1986.   **118.** "because she was"   Ibid.   **119.** "I
came into the reservation"   Maslow, *Farther Reaches,* 218.   **120.** "This
is interesting"   AI, Lucien Hanks, 1986.   **120.** "People would come"
Maslow, *Farther Reaches,* 197.   **121.** "When I asked"   Ibid., 196.
121. "In this ceremony"   Ibid., 195.   **122.** "The test was ridiculously"
MA, Maslow and Honigmann, "Northern Blackfoot Culture and Personality," 1945, 38.   **123.** "How do you regard"   Ibid.   **123.** "How do you
react"   Ibid.   **123.** "How do you feel"   Ibid.   **123.** "it gave no
index"   Ibid., 37.   **123.** "I realized that"   MA, Report to the National
Research Council, 1938, 2.   **123.** "that about eighty to ninety"   Ibid.
123. "in a fairly clear light"   Maslow and Honigmann, op. cit., 38.
124. "an insecure person"   Ibid.   **124.** "In the most solemn"   Ibid.,
24.   **124.** "When he appeared"   Ibid.   **125.** "The Blackfoot Indians"
Maslow, *Farther Reaches,* 221.   **126.** "[There] was a little boy"   Ibid.
127. "Every person has"   Maslow and Honigmann, op. cit., 15–16.
128. "It would seem that"   MA, Report to the National Research Council,
1938, 1.   **128.** "I missed her awfully"   J2, 1121.

Major interview sources were Lucien Hanks, Jane Richardson, and Bertha
Maslow.

Chapter Eight: Revelations at Brooklyn College

129. "In my career"   Maslow, *The Psychology of Science,* 7.   **129.** "In
the 1930s"   Maslow, *Farther Reaches,* 3.   **132.** "the Frank Sinatra"
George Leonard, "Abraham Maslow and the New Self," *Esquire,* December
1983, 331.   **134.** "Write down that"   AI, Al Green, 1983.   **135.** "The
first time you"   AI, Pearl Green, 1983.   **135.** "I have the feeling that"
MA, "Technique of Changing a Society in the Direction of Security," 1939,

10.   135. "The removal of economic"   Ibid., 11.   136. "He always told us"   AI, Al Green, 1983.   137. "It [now seems] more important" MA, "The Psychology of the Northern Blackfoot Indian," 1938, 3. 138. "Becoming a father"   "A Conversation with the President of the American Psychological Association," op. cit., 57. Maslow, *Farther Reaches*, 163.   142. "Most of my experience"   MA, "Psychotherapy Today," July 12, 1941, 10.   143. "lifting the lid"   Ibid., 8.   143. "If somebody comes"   MA, "Supplementary Therapies," March 28, 1942, 1.   145. "I suggested that she"   Maslow, "Cognition of the Particular and the Generic," *Psychological Review* 55 (1948), 24.   146. "Ours is a money" MA, "Technique of Changing a Society in the Direction of Security," 1939, 12.   146. "Our family is organized"   Ibid., 13.   147. "And this one" Gardner Murphy, "Memories of Abe," unpublished, undated, 7. Possession of Lois Murphy.   147. "I have no doubt"   MA, "Journal Notes on Intimacy, Friendship, etc.," April 29, 1968, 2.   148. "The manager was lousy"   J2, 1255.   148. "One day just after"   "A Conversation with the President of the American Psychological Association," op. cit., 54.

Major interview sources were Al Green, Pearl Green, Ann Kaplan, David Katz, Bertha Maslow, David Raab, and Robert Rothstein.

Chapter Nine: Glimmerings of Self-actualization

150. "My investigations"   Maslow, *Farther Reaches*, 40.   151. "I have no doubt"   MA, untitled, February 13, 1942, 1.   152. "People, even in different"   Maslow, "A Theory of Human Motivation," *Psychological Review* 50 (1943), 389.   152. "I went about it"   "A Conversation with the President of the American Psychological Association," op. cit., 55. 152. "They were puzzling"   Maslow, in Frick, op. cit., 21.   152. "what kind of"   J1, 412.   153. "science in its"   Maslow and Mittelmann, *Principles of Abnormal Psychology*, 44.   154. "It is quite true"   Maslow, "A Theory of Human Motivation," op. cit., 375.   154. "These [altruistic] people may be"   Ibid., 387.   155. "We may still"   Ibid., 382. 156. "Finally, those two"   Frick, op. cit., 21.   156. "peace, contentment"   MA, unpublished course notes, 1943.   156. "We believe that" Thomas Evans Coulton, *A City College in Action*, 109.   158. "Many characteristics of"   Maslow, "The Authoritarian Character Structure," *Journal of Social Psychology* 18 (1943), 402.   159. "in which [each] man's"   Ibid., 403.   159. "We can easily see this"   Ibid.   159. "If the world is"   Ibid.   160. "They have ordinarily"   MA, "Memorandum: Personality and Communists," undated, 1.   160. "It would seem, therefore"   MA, untitled, undated.   161. "That's what I call"   AI, David Raab, 1987.   162. "Abe, you like teaching"   AI, Harold Maslow, 1982.   163. "I consider it"   MA, "Nature of the Scientist," December 1943, 1–3.   164. "Most of the people"   MA, "Note on the Ability to be Passive," May 19, 1944, 1.   164. "This book is oriented"   MA, "Note on the Introduction," May 19, 1944, 1.   167. "It was really something" LA, Robert Rothstein, 1983.   168. "Kinsey, in his"   MA, letter to Amram Schienfeld, April 29, 1970.   170. "After fussing along"   Richard Lowry, *A. H. Maslow, An Intellectual Portrait*, 81.   171. "Is it *possible*" Ibid., 82.   171. "Saw X today"   Ibid., 87.   172. "Upon examining

all" Ibid., 88.   **173.** "Certainly, a visitor" Ibid., 90.   **173.** "The notion I am" Ibid., 91.   **175.** "As soon as I feel" Ibid.

Major interview sources were Daniel Katz, Bertha Maslow, David Raab, and Seymour Wapner.

Chapter Ten: California Interlude

176. "Supposing I'd stayed" J2, 1206.   **176.** "If you deliberately" Maslow, *Farther Reaches*, 35.   **177.** "There was one thing" MA, Lee seminar, op. cit., 12.   **179.** "If you want to succeed" LA, Nevitt Sanford, 1987.   **180.** "semipermeable membrane" J1, 173, J2, 729. **181.** "People who have enough" Maslow, " 'Higher' and 'Lower' Needs," *Journal of Psychology* 25 (1948), 435–436.   **183.** "The physiological needs" Maslow, "Some Theoretical Consequences of Basic Need-gratification," *Journal of Personality* 16 (1948), 402.

Major interview sources were Daniel Katz, Bertha Maslow, Harold Maslow, Will Maslow, David Raab, and Nevitt Sanford.

Chapter Eleven: Back to Brooklyn and Onward

185. "If we want" Maslow, *Farther Reaches*, 7.   **186.** "The psychology of 1949" MA, unpublished transcription, remarks at Cornell University, Department of Human Development and Family Studies, 1949, 1. **187.** "full use and exploitation" Maslow, "Self-actualizing People: A Study of Psychological Health," in Maslow, *Motivation and Personality*, 161–162. **188.** "In this sense" Ibid., 186.   **188.** "can devote [themselves]" Ibid., 192.   **188.** "I consider the problem" Ibid., 160.   **189.** "the most important" MA, unpublished course notes, pathological psychology, July 17, 1950.   **190.** "Very little is known" MA, "The Aesthetic Needs," January 10, 1950, 1.   **191.** "Most important for" Donald MacKinnon and Abraham Maslow, "Personality," in H. Helson, *Theoretical Foundations of Personality*, 646.   **192.** "they settled down" Maslow, "Resistance to Acculturation," *Journal of Social Issues* 7 (1951), 28.   **192.** "My impression is" Ibid.   **192.** "If this turns out" Ibid., 29.   **193.** "since only few people" Ibid.   **195.** "We want to be certain" "University with a Mission," *Time*, November 28, 1949, 60.   **195.** "For years, six hundred" *Saturday Review*, June 18, 1949, 4.   **196.** "As I grow older" AI, David Raab, 1986.   **196.** "Why not just go" AI, Bertha Maslow, 1986. **197.** "I've never heard" Ibid.

Major interview sources were Saul Cohen, Charles Hession, Max Lerner, Frank Manuel, Bertha Maslow, Rollo May, David Raab, Carl Rogers, Abram L. Sachar, and Seymour Wapner.

Chapter Twelve: Pioneering at Brandeis

199. "Until I became" J1, 514.   **199.** "The pioneer, the creator" Maslow, *Farther Reaches*, 4.   **200.** "We had about" Gillenson, "Lewis M. Brandeis: A Young University in a Hurry," *Saturday Review*, March 17, 1962, 101.   **202.** "My attitude toward all" J2, 843.   **204.** "The science of" Maslow, *Motivation and Personality*, 354. **205.** "Brotherhood and" Ibid., 373. **205.** "We spend a" Ibid., 371. **205.** "What have you been" AI, Max Lerner, 1987. **207.** "I must warn you" Maslow, "Deficiency Motivation and Growth Motivation," in M. R. Jones (editor), *Nebraska Symposium on Motivation*, 1955, 1. **208.** "who are predominantly" Ibid., 14. **208.** "at its core" Ibid., 3. **208.** "fulfilling of yearnings" Ibid., 14. **208.** "Do we see" Ibid., 25. **211.** "He had a" AI, Frank Manuel, 1986. **212.** "I have no real" MA, Gross, op. cit., 89. **213.** "Where's the party?" AI, Frank Manuel, 1986. **213.** "At present" MA, letter to Maslow, February 1, 1955. **214.** "Sachar would [ask]" Irving Howe, *A Margin of Hope*, 184. **215.** "How has Freud" MA, undated, 1. **215.** "The more we learn" MA, *Worcester Daily Telegram*, undated. **215.** "Cultural differences" Ibid. **216.** "The question is" Ibid.

Major interview sources were Saul Cohen, Lewis Coser, James Klee, Max Lerner, Frank Manuel, Bertha Maslow, Norbert Mintz, Ricardo Morant, and Abram L. Sachar.

Chapter Thirteen: Disappointments and New Dreams

217. "We fear our highest" Maslow, *Farther Reaches*, 34. **217.** "Obviously the most" Maslow, *Farther Reaches*, 294. **217.** "How many of you" AI, Norbert Mintz, 1987. **219.** "Most of all" Abbie Hoffman, *Soon to Be a Major Motion Picture*, 26. **219.** "I think of" LA, Lois Lindenauer, 1983. **220.** "I'm wondering" LA, Lois Lajic, 1986. **222.** "If you want" AI, Norbert Mintz, 1987. **226.** "Self-actualizing people" Maslow, "Cognition of Being in the Peak-experiences," *Journal of Genetic Psychology* 94 (1959), 43. **226.** "If self-actualizing" Ibid., 64. **226.** "as to remove" Ibid., 65. **226.** "are of course" Ibid. **229.** "1. A careful study of all" MA, "Tentative Plan of Long- and Short-Range Research of the Research Society for Creative Altruism," undated, 1–2. **230.** "to enrich the" Ibid., 1. **230.** "Finally, I may say" MA, "Memorandum on Institute Personnel," March 28, 1956, 2. **231.** "Things are still diddling" MA, letter to Robert Hartman, February 11, 1957. **232.** "Man is ultimately" Maslow, *New Knowledge in Human Values*, 130. **233.** "[partially] hereditary-determined" Ibid., 132. **233.** "Children . . . need, want" MA, "Notes on Limits, Controls, and the Safety Needs," November 19, 1957, 1. **233.** "contempt and disgust" Ibid., 2. **233.** "the big tasks" MA, "Problems Inherent In Self-actualization," January 1, 1957, 1. **234.** "essentially alone . . . [and] can" Ibid., 2. **234.** "I have been grappling" MA, letter to Diane O'Brien, October 9, 1956, 1. **234.** "this actualization [also]" Ibid. **234.** "our conceptions of" Ibid. **235.** "If only women" Ibid. **235.** "Granted that males" MA, untitled, July 7, 1957, 1. **236.** "Both males *and* females" Ibid., 1. **236.** "how childish and" MA, untitled, July 23, 1957, 2. **236.** "how . . . cultures have" Ibid. **237.** "that really strong" J2, 1033. **238.** "In the early stages" Maslow, *Farther Reaches*, 90. **238.** "I have no doubt" Ibid., 91.

Major interview sources were Steven Andreas, Joel Aronoff, Ann Kaplan, James Klee, Bertha Maslow, Norbert Mintz, Ricardo Morant, Ulrich Neisser, Abram L. Sachar, and Walter Weisskopf.

Chapter Fourteen: Slow Rhythms of Mexico

239. "I love working"   J1, 118.   **239.** "[On my] Mexican vacation"
J1, 232.   **241.** "One day, a traveling"   AI, Rogelio Diaz-Guerrero, 1986.
243. "So far, I have"   MA, "Self-actualization Critique via Homonomy,"
January 1, 1959, 1.   **243.** "If a man is"   Ibid., 4.   **245.** "1. All humans,
including"   Maslow, *Farther Reaches*, 363.   **248.** "the problems of"
Maslow, letter to John Weir, March 7, 1959, 5. Possession of Robert Tannenbaum.   **248.** "This is a"   Ibid., 6.   **248.** "Every intellectual"   Ibid.
249. "The sad thought"   Ibid.   **249.** "Practically none of"   Ibid., 26.
249. "It looks as if"   Ibid., 27.   **250.** "These old socialists"   Ibid., 23.
251. "Let's wait until"   MA, letter to Maslow, March 25, 1959.
251. "like a long-lost friend"   MA, letter to Maslow, April 13, 1959.
251. "As soon as you return"   Ibid.   **251.** "I didn't really know"   Ibid.
252. "The prevalent worldwide"   Pitirim Sorokin, *A Long Journey*, 292.
252. "We are in"   MA, "Inter-disciplinary Conference on Values—
Santa Barbara," June 20–21, 1959, 2.   **253.** "there is no"   Ibid., 8.
254. "an additional push toward"   Maslow, in Rollo May (editor), *Existential Psychology*, 56.   **254.** "No theory of psychology"   Ibid.

Major interview sources were Rogelio Diaz-Guerrero, Lawrence Gross, Ann
Kaplan, James Klee, Frank Manuel, Bertha Maslow, Rollo May, Abram L.
Sachar, and Walter Weisskopf.

Chapter Fifteen: Enlightened Managers, Mystics, and Entrepreneurs

255. "If we lose"   Maslow, *Religions, Values, and Peak-experiences*, 113.
255. "What conditions"   Maslow, *Farther Reaches*, 227.   **255.** "What's
not worth"   Maslow, *The Psychology of Science*, 14.   **256.** "Now, as I
do"   J1, 34.   **256.** "misunderstanding of"   Maslow, "Critique of Self-
actualization. I. Some Dangers of Being-cognition," *Journal of Individual
Psychology* 15 (1959), 24.   **257.** "who wins enlightenment"   Ibid., 27.
258. "Instead of cultural"   Maslow, "Eupsychia—the Good Society," *Journal of Humanistic Psychology* 1 (1961), 5.   **258.** "Throughout history"
Ibid.   **260.** "Abe, why not read"   MA, "Dialogue on Communication,"
1967, 2.   **260.** "taking a bath"   Ibid.   **261.** "enlarge the jurisdiction"
Maslow, "Are Our Publications and Conventions Suitable for the Personal
Sciences?" *American Psychologist* 16 (1961), 318.   **261.** "How the hell"
J1, 81.   **261.** "Some of my students"   MA, "Some Frontier Problems in
Psychological Health," 2.   **262.** "If a Martian"   Ibid., 14.   **262.** "It's
interesting that"   Ibid.   **262.** "Our spiritual height"   Ibid., 6–7.
263. "I guess one big"   J1, 93.   **264.** "Why are the B-values"   J1, 111.
266. "It's too easy"   AI, Timothy Leary, 1986.   **266.** "Every age but
ours"   Maslow, *Toward a Psychology of Being*, 5.   **267.** "The first time"
MA, "The Taboo of Tenderness: The Disease of Valuelessness," 1965, 34.
271. "under really bad"   Maslow, *Eupsychian Management*, 184.
272. "What do you want?"   AI, Bertha Maslow, 1986.   **272.** "A couple
dozen"   J1, 271.   **273.** "What do you have"   AI, Henry Geiger, 1986.
273. "They're being taken"   J1, 188.   **274.** "Professor Maslow told"
Betty Friedan, *The Feminine Mystique*, 326.   **275.** "In recent weeks"
Letter to Maslow, April 16, 1963. Possession of Robert Tannenbaum.
276. "I want to tell"   Walter Truett Anderson, *The Upstart Spring*, 112.

276. "The very beginning" Maslow, *Religions, Values, and Peak-experiences*, 19. 277. "Some perceptive liberals" Ibid., 43. 277. "The power of" Ibid., 75. 278. "[I wish to talk about]" MA, "The Taboo of Tenderness: The Disease of Valuelessness," 1965, 1. 279. "Innocence can be" Ibid., 11. 280. "If you are" Ibid., 12. 280. "the defenses against maturity" Ibid., 23. 280. "[The basic] value-question" Ibid., 26. 281. "I've been keeping" J1, 493. 282. "The Third Force is" Ibid., 524. 282. "Is it ethical" Ibid., 529. 283. "Very remarkable" Ibid., 543. 286. "The old-style" Maslow, *Eupsychian Management*, 262.

Major interview sources were Joel Aronoff, Warren Bennis, James Bugental, Betty Friedan, Henry Geiger, Thomas Greening, Lawrence Gross, Richard Grossman, Andrew Kay, James Klee, Timothy Leary, Richard Lowry, Bertha Maslow, Rollo May, Ricardo Morant, Michael Murphy, Ulrich Neisser, Carl Rogers, Abram L. Sachar, Robert Tannenbaum, Arthur Warmoth, Gunther Weil, and Leonard Zion.

Chapter Sixteen: Uneasy Hero of the Counterculture

287. "In recent years" Maslow, *Religions, Values, and Peak-experiences*, 8. 289. "These happenings" Ibid., 113. 290. "Take 'duty' " Walter Truett Anderson, *The Upstart Spring*, 135. 291. "This begins to look" Ibid., 137. 291. "Good individuals can" MA, untitled transcript, January 1966, 2. 291. "I have worked" Ibid., 3. 291. "A work party means" Ibid. 292. "I must urge you" Ibid., 4. 292. "I'm not a square" Ibid., 28. 292. "You know this" Ibid., 24. 292. "We've got brains" Ibid., 5. 293. "I have the feeling" Ibid., 15. 294. "Ellen's political" J2, 733. 295. "This book is not" Maslow, *The Psychology of Science*, Gateway edition, 1966, 1. 296. "I have got more" Ibid., 149. 296. "a quietly revolutionary" Ibid., back cover. 296. "I suppose I am" MA, letter to Maslow, March 11, 1965. 298. "If you deliberately" Maslow, *Farther Reaches*, 35. 298. "I was very shocked" AI, Carl Rogers, 1986. 299. "I've become a" J2, 895. 300. "how it is possible" MA, Maslow, July 10, 1967. 300. "There's [now] a whole" J2, 895. 300. "Not only does" Maslow, *Farther Reaches*, 310. 302. "thundered like an" J2, 828. 302. "It still hovers" J2, 827. 302. "The United States is" J2, 852. 304. "Why did you go?" J2, 861. 304. "could be of" J2, 865. 304. "I'm going to assume" J2, 869–870. 304. "But these duties" J2, 871. 305. "The old test" J2, 1009. 305. "Abe, slow down" AI, Ricardo Morant, 1986. 306. "interested in helping" MA, "Eupsychian Network," February 1968, 1. 306. "If I ever write" J2, 911. 306. "My whole psychology" J2, 885. 307. "the breakup of the" MA, "Journal Notes on Intimacy, Friendship, etc." April 29, 1968, 1. 308. "this feeling of" J2, 1045. 308. "I couldn't get anyplace" Maslow, undated letter to Ellen Maslow. In her possession. 308. "As psychologists, we are" MA, May 10, 1968. 309. "Since [my] heart attack" J2, 921. 309. "If I live long enough" J2, 922. 310. "the ultimate in amusing" J2, 1060. 312. "better people, better groups" J2, 1077. 312. "I think if the world" Maslow, undated letter to Ellen Maslow. In her possession. 312. "In my department" J2, 1072. 313. "Abe is a big-

mouth" AI, Neil Kauffman, 1987.   313. "Abe is copping out" Ibid.
313. "I think of the" J2, 935.   314. "I'm too old" AI, Ann Kaplan,
1986.   314. "I want more and more" J2, 933.

Major interview sources were Warren Bennis, James Bugental, Saul Cohen,
Thomas Greening, Gerald Haigh, Ann Kaplan, Neil Kauffman, George Leonard, Richard Lowry, Frank Manuel, Bertha Maslow, Rollo May, Ricardo
Morant, Michael Murphy, Carl Rogers, B. F. Skinner, Robert Tannenbaum,
and Deborah Tanzer.

Chapter Seventeen: California Rescue: The "Postmortem" Life

315. "I like to be"   "A Conversation with the President of the American
Psychological Association," op. cit., 56.   315. "I have a very strong"
Maslow, *Farther Reaches*, 168.   316. "Abe, what was that" AI, Bertha
Maslow, 1986.   317. "When you get older" AI, Neil Kauffman, 1987.
318. "Dr. Maslow will" Esalen Catalogue, 1968–69.   319. "Who are
you?" Maslow, "Humanistic Education vs. Professional Education," *New
Directions in Teaching* 2 (1970), 22.   322. "because of the" MA, "Dr.
Maslow Accepts Laughlin Foundation Grant," March 4, 1969, 1–2.
322. "A new image of man" Ibid.   324. "Only that which" MA,
"Levels of Newspapering," undated, 1–2.   324. "I feel strongly" MA,
"Politics 3," undated, 1.   325. "My attitude toward" "Editorial," *Psychology Today*, August 1970, 16.   327. "I'm a sidewalk boy" MA, "Remarks of Dr. Abraham Maslow at the End of the FSD's Meeting with Sherm
Moore," November 1969, 1–2.   328. "who are, unfortunately" "International Study Project," in *Abraham H. Maslow: A Memorial Volume*, 39.
328. "Esalen should not" MA, "Esalen Critique," March 20, 1970, 1.
329. "I think we can" Maslow, "Humanistic Education vs. Professional
Education," op. cit., 17, 19.   331. "make believe that" J2, 1278.
331. "can sometimes wind up" Maslow, *Religions, Values, and Peak-experiences*, ix–x.   333. "change our image" J2, 1280.   333. "A good
marriage" J2, 1284.   334. "His great heart" Robert Tannenbaum
and Warren Schmidt, unpublished memo, June 10, 1970, 1. Possession of
Robert Tannenbaum.   334. "I have never met" Allen Mather, unpublished note, 1970. Possession of Robert Tannenbaum.   334. "There was
something" T. H. Hartman, unpublished note, 1970. Possession of Robert
Tannenbaum.   334. "It felt good" Allen Mather, unpublished note,
1970. Possession of Robert Tannenbaum.

Major interview sources were Warren Bennis, James Bugental, William
Crockett, James Fadiman, Henry Geiger, Thomas Greening, Richard Gross-
man, Willis Harman, T. George Harris, Ann Kaplan, Bertha Maslow, Rollo
May, Ricardo Morant, James and Marylyn Morrell, Michael Murphy, Carl
Rogers, Earl C. Royce, Robert Tannenbaum, and Walter Weisskopf.

Index